AUBREY TAYLOR
BAD HONEY

Copyright © 2024 by Aubrey Taylor

All rights reserved. No part of this publication may be reproduced, stored or transmitted in any form or by any means, electronic, mechanical, photocopying, recording, scanning, or otherwise without written permission from the publisher. It is illegal to copy this book, post it to a website, or distribute it by any other means without permission.

For permission requests, contact Aubrey Taylor, Aubreytaylorauthor@gmail.com

This novel is entirely a work of fiction. The names, characters and incidents portrayed in it are the work of the author's imagination. Any resemblance to actual persons, living or dead, events or localities is entirely coincidental.

Aubrey Taylor asserts the moral right to be identified as the author of this work.

Aubrey Taylor has no responsibility for the persistence or accuracy of URLs for external or third-party Internet Websites referred to in this publication and does not guarantee that any content on such Websites is, or will remain, accurate or appropriate.

Designations used by companies to distinguish their products are often claimed as trademarks. All brand names and product names used in this book and on its cover are trade names, service marks, trademarks and registered trademarks of their respective owners. The publishers and the book are not associated with any product or vendor mentioned in this book. None of the companies referenced within the book have endorsed the book.

Book Cover by Aurora McGaughey

Editing and Proof Reading by Jessica Norton

Illustrations by Aubrey Taylor

First Edition 2024

To Momma,
Whose love of sports romance knows no bounds.

"But if you loved a thing, the work was never done"
—— Nikolai Lantsov (**Leigh Bardugo)**

CONTENT WARNINGS

This book contains themes of the following:
Anxiety
Panic Attacks
Drug Abuse (addiction)
Alcohol Abuse
Physical Abuse (from a parent/sibling)
Emotional Abuse (from a parent/sibling)
Loss of family
Car accident
Physical Scarring (face and body)
Suicidal attempt/thoughts (with intentional drug overdose)

Take breaks, get some water, snuggle your loved ones and pets.
Be kind to yourself, being a human being is tough.

OFFICIAL PLAYLIST

Don't Take the Money - Bleachers
Amen - Amber Run
Shake the Frost - Tyler Childers
Anti-Hero (ft. Bleachers) – Taylor Swift
Dial Drunk - Noah Kahan
King - SAINT PHNX
S.O.S (Sawed Off Shotgun) - The Glorious Sons
Long Story Short - Taylor Swift
CVS - Winnetka Bowling League
Terrified - Vincent Lima
In A Perfect World (with Julia Michaels) Acoustic - Dean Lewis
I love you, I'm Trying - Grandson
My Blood - The Glorious Sons
Mirrorball - Taylor Swift
In My Room - Chance Peña
No Ordinary - Labrinth

GLOSSARY

Positions:

Pitcher
Catcher
First base
Second Base
Short Stop
Third Base
Left Field
Center Field
Right Field

Terms :

Ahead in the count: A term that signifies whether the batter or pitcher possesses the advantage in an at-bat. If a pitcher has thrown more strikes than balls to a batter in an at-bat, the pitcher is ahead in the count; conversely, if the pitcher has thrown more balls than strikes, the batter is ahead.

Airmail: Slang for a fielder's errant throw that sails high over the player to whom he intended to throw the ball.

Alley: Also "gap" or "power alley", the space between the left fielder and the centerfielder, or the right fielder and center fielder.

Arsonist : An ineffective relief pitcher. Usually a pitcher who comes into the game with no one on base but proceeds to give up several runs. Opposite of fireman.

At Bat: A completed plate appearance by a batter which results in a base hit or a non-sacrifice out.

Automatic Double: A batted ball in fair territory which bounces out of play (e.g. into the seats) entitles the batter and all runners on base to advance two bases but no further. This term is used by some commentators in lieu of ground rule double.

Backstop: The fence behind homeplate, designed to protect spectators from wild pitches or foul balls.

Bad Hop: A ball that bounces in front of an infielder in an unexpected way, often as a result of imperfections in the playing surface or the spin on the ball.

Bag : A base.

Ball: A pitch that misses the strike zone and is not swung at by the batter.

Base Hit: The act of safely reaching first base after batting the ball into fair territory.

Batter's Box : the area within which the batter stands when hitting. The batter must be in the box for the pitcher to pitch.

Bullpen: The area used by pitchers and catchers to warm up before taking the mound when play has already begun.

Captain Hook : A manager who often takes a pitcher out of the game at the first sign of trouble.

Change Up: A changeup or a change is a pitch meant to look like a fastball - but with less velocity - short for a change of pace.

Clean-up Hitter: The fourth batter in the lineup, usually a power hitter. The strategy is to get some runners on base for the cleanup hitter to drive home. In theory, if the first three batters of the game were to load the bases, the No. 4 hitter would ideally "clean up" the bases with a grand slam.

Cut Off: A defensive tactic where a fielder moves into a position between the outfielder who has fielded the batted ball and the base where a play can be made. This fielder is said to "cut off" the throw or to be the "cut-off man".

Dead ball: The ball becomes "dead" (i.e., the game's action is stopped) after a foul ball and in cases of fan or player interference, umpire interference with a catcher, and several other specific situations.

Diamond: The layout of the four bases in the infield. It's actually a square 90 feet (27 m) on each side, but from the stands it resembles a parallelogram or "diamond".

Dirt-Nap: To trip or fall in the outfield or on the base paths. A blown save may also be referred to as a dirt-nap.

Dug out: The dugout is where a team's bench is located. With the exception of relief pitchers in the bullpen, active players who are not on the field watch the play from the dugout. A dugout is the area being slightly depressed below field level, as is common in professional baseball. There is typically a boundary, often painted yellow, defining the edges of the dugout,

Eject: A player or coach who is disqualified from the game by an umpire for unsportsmanlike conduct.

Fireman: A team's top relief pitcher who is often brought in to end an offensive rally and "put out the fire".

Fly ball: A ball hit high in the air.

Foul ball: A batted ball that settles into foul territory.

Gap: The space between outfielders. Also alley. A ball hit in the gap is sometimes called a flapper or a gapper.

A Gap Hitter: Hits with power up the alleys and tends to get a lot of doubles. A doubles hitter.

Glove: A baseball glove or mitt is a large padded leather glove that players on the defensive team wear to assist them in catching and fielding. Different positions require different shapes and sizes of gloves.

Grand Slam : Home run hit with the bases loaded.

Ground Ball: A hit that bounces in the infield. Also grounder. A bunt is not considered a ground ball.

Ground Rule Double: Under standard ground rules, there are conditions under which a batter is awarded second base automatically. If a ball hit in fair territory bounces over a wall or fence (or gets caught in the ivy at Wrigley Field) without being touched by a fielder, it will likely be declared a double. If a ball hit into fair territory is touched by a fan, the batter is awarded an extra base.

Hack: To swing awkwardly at the ball.

Hammer: To hit the ball hard, typically for extra bases.

Home: Home plate. For a runner to reach home safely is to score a run. Getting a runner who is on base home is the goal of any batter.

Home Run: A home run (or homer) is a base hit in which the batter is able to circle all the bases, ending at home plate and scoring a run himself.

Home Stand: A series of home games.

Inning: An inning consists of two halves. In each half, one team bats until three outs are made. A full inning consists of six outs, three for each team; and a regulation game consists of nine innings. The first half-inning is called the top half of the inning; the second half-inning, the bottom half. The visiting team is on offense during the top half of the inning, the home team is on offense during the bottom half.

Lead: When a baserunner steps off a base before a pitch is thrown in order to reduce the distance to the next base he takes a lead.

Line Drive: Also known as a liner, a line drive is a batted ball that is hit hard in the air and has a low arc.

Lineup: The batting order, which also lists each player's defensive position.

Meatball: An easy pitch to hit—down the middle of the plate.

Mound: The pitcher's mound is a raised section in the middle of the diamond where the pitcher stands when throwing the pitch.

MVP: Abbreviation for Most Valuable Player.

Opposite Field Hit: A hit to the "opposite" side of the field from the direction of a player's natural swing

Outfielder: An outfielder is a player whose position is either left field, center field, or right field.

Overthrow: When a fielder throws the ball so high that it sails over the head and out of reach of his target.

Paint: To throw pitches at the edges of the strike zone.

Picket Fence: A series of 1's on the scoreboard, resembling a picket fence.

Pickoff: A quick throw from the pitcher (or sometimes the catcher) to a fielder covering a base when the ball has not been hit into play.

Pinch Runner / Hitter: A substitute batter, brought in during a critical situation ("a pinch"). / A substitute baserunner, brought in during a critical situation ("a pinch").

Pitch: A baseball delivered by the pitcher from the pitcher's mound to the batter as defined by the Official Rules of Baseball

Pivot Man: Generally refers to the second baseman. A second baseman often has to turn or pivot on one foot in order to complete a double play. A short-stop also sometimes pivots to complete such a play.

Play: Any small sequence of events during a game, never lasting long enough to contain more than one pitch, during which at least one offensive player could advance, or score a run, or tag up, etc., or could be put out.

Poke: A hit. Referring to an extra-base hit or home run.

Pop: A batter with "pop" has exceptional bat speed and power.

Pop up: a batted ball that is hit very high and stays in the infield. Called a pop-foul when it falls or is caught in foul territory.

Power Hitter: A powerful batter who hits many home runs and extra base hits, but who may not have a high batting average, due to an "all or nothing" hitting approach.

Rain Delay: Rain delay refers to situations when a game starts late due to rain or is temporarily suspended due to rain.

RBI: An RBI or "run batted in" is a run scored as a result of a hit; a bases-filled walk or hit-by-pitch or awarding of first base due to interference; a sacrifice; or a single-out fielder's choice (not a double play).

Regulation Game: A standard baseball game lasts nine innings, although some leagues (such as high school baseball) use seven-inning games.

Relief Pitcher: A relief pitcher or reliever is a pitcher brought in the game as a substitute for (i.e., "to relieve") another pitcher.

Rifle: A very strong arm. A cannon, a bazooka, a gun. Also used as a verb, "He rifled the ball home to catch the runner."

Road Game: A game played away from a baseball club's home stadium.

Road Trip: A series of road games or away games occurs on a road trip, a term derived from the days when teams indeed traveled from one town to another by roadway or railroad.

Rookie: Conventionally, rookie is a term for athletes in their first year of play in their sport.

Run: A player who advances around all the bases to score is credited with a run; the team with the most runs wins the game.

Runners in Scoring Position: Runners on 2nd or 3rd base are said to be in scoring position, i.e., a typical base hit should allow them to reach home.

Series: A set of games between two teams. During the regular season, teams typically play 3- or 4-game series against one another, with all the games in each series played in the same park.

Shift: Where all infielders and/or outfielders position themselves clockwise or counter-clockwise from their usual position. This is to anticipate a batted ball from a batter who tends to hit to one side of the field.

Short Hop: A ball that bounces immediately in front of an infielder. If the batter is a fast runner, an infielder may intentionally "short hop the ball" (take the ball on the short hop) to hasten his throw to first base.

Slide: When a runner drops to the ground when running toward a base to avoid a tag.

Stolen Base (Steal): In baseball, a stolen base (or "steal") occurs when a baserunner successfully advances to the next base while the pitcher is delivering the ball to home plate.

Streak: A series of consecutive wins (a winning streak) or losses (a losing streak).

Strike: When a batter swings at a pitch, but fails to hit it, when a batter does not swing at a pitch that is thrown within the strike zone, when the ball is hit foul and the strike count is less than 2 (a batter cannot strike out on a foul ball, however he can fly out), when a ball is bunted foul, regardless of the strike count, when the ball touches the batter as he swings at it, when the ball touches the batter in the strike zone, or when the ball is a foul tip.

Sweep: To win all the games in a series between two teams

Switch Hitter: A switch hitter can hit from either side of the plate

Tag: A tag out. A runner is out if, while in jeopardy, a fielder touches him with a live ball or the hand or glove holding a live ball.

Three Up, Three Down: To face just three batters in an inning. Having a "three up, three down inning" is the goal of any pitcher.

Walk-Off: A home team immediately wins the game when they score a run to take the lead in the bottom of the last inning.

Wheelhouse: A hitter's power zone. Usually a pitch waist-high and over the heart of the plate.

Yips - everything is a little bit off and you can't pinpoint the issue but you're playing the worst ball of your life. You're booting casual ground balls, your throws are just a little bit off and you're popping up everything. You try to change your mechanics and it won't help. Career killer.

Contents

1. KING   1
2. MIELE   12
3. KING   19
4. MIELE   25
5. MIELE   33
6. KING   43
7. MIELE   51
8. KING   59
9. MIELE   66
10. KING   73
11. MIELE   80
12. MIELE   88
13. MIELE   94
14. KING   100
15. MIELE   110
16. KING   120

17.	MIELE	126
18.	KING	135
19.	MIELE	146
20.	KING	153
21.	MIELE	161
22.	KING	168
23.	MIELE	177
24.	KING	188
25.	MIELE	194
26.	MIELE	205
27.	KING	212
28.	MIELE	219
29.	MIELE	231
30.	KING	237
31.	MIELE	242
32.	MIELE	250
33.	MIELE	257
34.	MIELE	265
35.	KING	272
36.	MIELE	285
37.	MIELE	292
38.	KING	299
39.	KING	304

40.	MIELE	312
41.	MIELE	320
42.	KING	327
43.	MIELE	332
44.	GAME ONE	338
45.	GAME TWO	340
46.	MIELE	342
47.	MIELE	349
48.	KING	358
49.	EPILOGUE	363
	EXCLUSIVE CHAPTER	368
	Chapter	383
	Acknowledgements	384
	Also By Aubrey Taylor	386

KING

MID-FEBRUARY

"*Number eleven, King is primed and more than ready to see through the end of his college career. Taking over the pitcher's mound and a five-year national title from his brother Nicholas, at age twenty-two, he was a late starter with the promise of upholding the family legacy. Now, three years later, twenty-five, he finds himself at the tail end of a failing run, desperate for a championship.*"

Nothing was worse than the nonsense that rolled through the radio and into my car on game days, yet I always found myself sitting there, listening to it like it was gospel. There was never anything I could do to stop myself from flicking the radio on and listening to them tear me to shreds while thousands of other listeners all over campus agreed with them.

I rolled my hands over the steering wheel and tried pulling all my tight muscles loose as I stared at the stadium. A massive building of concrete and navy blue coated steel that hung over my head like a reminder I wasn't good enough to be there.

Home of the Harbor University Hornets.

Until the year I transitioned from backup to starting pitcher, the Hornets had been the best and only winning team that Harbor had to offer. But I had dragged both cleats through lousy karma on my way to the pitcher's mound because we hadn't seen a championship since I had taken over for my brother.

All the drive had been sucked from the team, and we were left with nothing but a group of players that didn't care how many runs or outs we had. Their worries were more extensive than the score, and I wished desperately that I felt the same way, but every game was a step closer to fulfilling a dream that I wasn't even sure was mine most days, but it was the only dream I knew.

A knuckle rapped against the window of my Mustang. Silas hovered just outside the driver's side door for me as I collected my bag and threw it over my shoulder. I took one last deep breath before exiting and slamming the door abruptly, causing him to flinch.

"You're late," he barked at me, blinking his serious blue eyes in my direction as he scratched a line into his scruffy, patchy, unkempt beard.

"You look ridiculous with a mustache." I shrugged, taking a peek at the time on my wristwatch. Silas groaned loudly, following me in his team-issued Hornet polo and navy blue cap. "What? I thought we were pointing out the obvious," I tossed him a tight smile over my shoulder as we approached the players' entrance.

He leaned around me, swiped the black box to unlock it, and filed into the tunnel before me. "Arlo," he turned, pushing his hand against my chest to stop our movement toward the locker room. "He's here," Silas' tone turned to ice.

"He's supposed to be, he's a coach." I shook my head and tried to scoot by him.

"Not Nicholas," the mention of my brother caused the nauseous feeling in my stomach to roll over. "Your dad."

Now, I might actually vomit.

"Of course he is." I rolled my eyes, trying to disguise the absolute fear that vibrated through my body at the idea of my father, Arthur King, sitting and watching my every move during the season opener.

It was bad enough when he called after matches to remind me of everything I had done wrong; now, he would be here to stare disapprovingly as I took the mound. I wanted to say it would only make me more determined to prove him wrong, to pitch that perfect game, but I couldn't guarantee anything, not with how spring camp had gone or the exhibition matches.

I was a mess, and the entire league knew it.

"Coach offered him a seat in the box, but he refused."

BAD HONEY

"Of course he did. He can't see my mistakes from the box." I shrugged deep inside of my suit and rolled my shoulders back. "Thank you."

For warning me.

"Don't let him get to you," Silas nudged me, "keep your focus on the pitches and Cael."

I shot him a look. "What happened?"

"Nothing," he tried to act like deflecting the subject would magically make the issue dissolve, and maybe I would forget about the concerned tone in his voice. It took less than fifteen seconds for him to break.

"He got into it with Coach on the way in. I'd use the *baby gloves*." He said. It was a term used for Cael Cody when something was blowing up. A term used regularly nowadays.

"Any other fucking surprises I should be expecting?" I asked.

"Logan is back from injury and pitching today," Silas choked out before jogging down the hallway in the other direction.

Joshua Logan played four seasons for the Lorette Longhorns with a disgustingly accurate arm and the ability to get under my skin like a thousand tiny bugs. I hoped he would be gone for the first two weeks of the season, giving me enough time to adjust and possibly win a few games before facing him. It felt like the universe was doing this out of spite.

Making my way back to the locker room through the long gray concrete tunnels underlying the massive stadium, I kept my head down to the interviewers lurking in the corners. A few of them called out to me, but between my prowling father, Cael's snowballing issues, and Logan, I wasn't in the mood to play nice and give smiles. The vultures would have to wait.

The locker room was chaotic. A massive circular room framed with sturdy beige wood lockers for each player. Our numbers were painted in large navy blue font against the back of each one, and our jerseys hung pressed inside before each game. It smelled of sweat, grime, and grown men. The atmosphere was loud, rambunctious, and overwhelming most of the time, but it was the only place I ever felt at home. I pushed past a few of the guys, and when the shoving crowd of half-dressed baseball players opened, I found Cael with his head between his knees and his long arms wrapped around himself.

"What happened, Kitten?" I kicked his foot, tipping him to the left and knocking him off balance. He turned a set of exhausted, bloodshot blue eyes on me and gave me a weak smirk. "If you didn't drink so hard before games, he wouldn't go in on you so hard."

"You and I both know that's not true, King," Cael leaned his head back, rolling his hands over the short-cropped bleach blond hair he was sporting lately, and closed his eyes. "If it's not my drinking or the drugs, it's always something else. Nothing is ever good enough for him."

"Don't be good enough for him," I said, meaning it as long as it didn't apply to my relationship with my father. "Be good enough for you. That's all that matters." These are words I wish I had taken more seriously.

I nudged his shoulder, pushing him over so I could sit next to him and slide into my cleats. "Have you seen Nick yet?"

"No, thank god," Cael laughed, and the sound eased the tension we were both reeling from.

"There he is."

The devil's ears were burning.

Nick paraded into the locker room like he had never left it, with his hair slicked back around the nape of his neck and his brown eyes on high alert. He always had to be the main focus. It was the narcissist in him. He stalked toward me, arms out wide already in his coaching jersey, and wrapped me into a fake, pillowy hug that we knew meant nothing.

"Dad's watching," he gripped the back of my neck, pushing our foreheads together, "time to prove your worth."

I pushed on his shoulders, shoving him back. "Just do your job, and I'll do mine."

Nicholas King, middle brother, playboy, retired pitcher, and massive asshole. It was his first season coaching for the Hornets. Coach Cody hired him after his failed season with the *Astros*. Much to my disdain, he accepted the position, and now not only would I have to

BAD HONEY

fight even harder for the title, but I would have to do it with Nick biting at my ankles every game.

Silas leaned against the wall, observing us, and he wasn't the only one. As most players shucked out of their dress clothes and into their uniforms, they watched our interaction. Cael kept his eyes trained on Nick.

"Nick," Silas called to him, watching the tension build between us, tentatively waiting for it to explode and hoping to avoid the blast, "Coach was looking for you," he said.

It took an intense moment of Nick staring me down before he forced that desirable fake smile on his face. But I saw through it that he was putting on a show like the clown he was.

"See you on the field," Nick slapped a hand to my face.

"Keep the bench warm for me," I mocked, pushing his hand away.

When Nick rounded the corner, I finally let out the breath I had been holding and turned to grip the edges of my locker. My knuckles turned white from the grip as my muscles strained tightly beneath my skin. Cael slid down into his locker beside me and cocked his stupid face under my arm so he could meet my gaze.

"Want me to slash his tires?" He asked with a half-baked smile that I couldn't help but laugh at. I shooed his bold blue eyes and dumb grin away from my sight with a swat from my hand and turned to sink into my own locker.

"He'd know it was you," I shook my head.

"Good," Cael stripped clumsily from his sweater and exchanged it for his home game uniform. "Maybe then he'd get his hands dirty and fight me instead of leaving bruises on you that no one looks for," Cael poked a finger into my sore rib cage, making me wince before shoving him away.

"Don't," I rolled out the pain and waited until everyone was busy to strip from my dress shirt and into my jersey.

The bruise Nick had given me was growing; it had started small at the base of my ribs but had spread across the bottom. But showing it to Silas meant having a conversation I refused to have.

The Shores had treated the Kings like family for years, ever since Grandpa Shore took my father under his wing and turned him into an All-Star pitcher for the Pittsburgh Pirates. My family was in debt to them.

The Shores created The Kings.

Nick and I had been running around with Silas for as long as I could remember. We even lived with the Shores while my father was living in Pittsburgh. They were the stupid kind of rich where money was just a number, and it was a number that I couldn't count to.

Silas was the same age as Nick, but he never got along with him or any of my other brothers, for that matter. The two eldest, Lucas and Sawyer, were long gone, leaving Rhode Island the second they could get out. I spoke to Lucas occasionally, but Sawyer was in the wind, and I didn't blame him. Silas was the only person that didn't take my shit, and ninety percent of the time, it pissed me off, but there wasn't much I could do about it. Without Silas, I was alone, and I knew that his tough love was just that, *love*.

"If you're gonna keep secrets from Silas, at least make them interesting," Cael whined.

It wasn't about secrets. It was about keeping it in the family. If Nick needed someone to take it out on, I would rather it be me than some girl or the other guys. I had seen the way Dad dealt with his anger before Mom died and then after she was taken from us. Nick had taken it all. At least until he was playing, then Dad turned on me. He couldn't injure his all-star son, but now Nick wasn't an all-star. He was washed up and angry.

"If you're gonna run your mouth, do it, but at least sit six feet away from me so I can't knock your teeth out," I growled and did the buttons up on my home uniform. White jerseys with the thin yellow pinstripe and navy Hornets font across the chest were snug around the shoulders and tucked into our navy blue pants.

Cael shook his jersey out, the large black nineteen on the back shaking as he tucked all the pieces into his ball pants. "Are you coming to Delta tonight?"

"Can we just get through this game?" I groaned, tucking in my shirt and doing up my belt. Although the mention of Delta had given me a good idea, "I'll make you a deal," I said as I walked over to the center of the room, trying to get their attention. "Listen up," I barked, making

BAD HONEY

all the players turn their focus on me. "You win this game tonight against the Longhorns. I'll *supply beer for Delta*."

The room erupted, but I wasn't finished. I needed them ready and focused. "Shut up," I yelled, the muscles in my neck straining, "You have to win, which means you have to play and you have to play hard. Don't go out there to prove something to Coach, the scouts, or the papers," my eyes drifted to Cael. "Go out and prove something to yourself. We are going to the World Series Finals this year and won't stop fighting until we get there. Two steps at a time."

"Yes, Cap!" Cael was the first to respond, filling his chest with air and making himself loud as he slapped two fingers to his chest on *my life*.

The small gesture was a handshake the team had started doing years ago. It was a pinky promise, a silent *I'm fine*, a hello, a goodbye. It was our oath to one another when words became too hard, and the world became too heavy.

And this game was a stack of bricks atop my chest.

The season's first game paved the way for the rest, all the way to the playoffs. In the first year I became Captain, we made it through to finals and were taken out by the Lorettes. In the last two years, we didn't even come close. I haven't been able to pinpoint the problem exactly. A muddled point between winning and the moment when we had stopped playing like a winning team, but I was convinced it was me. I had to have been the problem.

The rest of the guys followed suit, tapping two fingers over their hearts as they filed out of the locker room and into the massive concrete tunnel that led to the field. I could hear the immense roars from the crowd, so resounding that when I laid my hand on the wall, I could feel the vibrations rolling down to my fingertips. It was calming and welcoming.

I belonged here.

I closed my eyes and took a moment to center myself before joining the other guys as they waited for the team to be announced.

"And welcome back your Harbor University Men's Baseball Team," the announcer's voice rang over the stadium, *"The Hornets!"*

"Your first baseman, number twenty-nine, Dean Tucker!"

"Your dad is in the left stands, row nine." Silas patted my back as he slipped into the dugout before Cael was called to the field.

I appreciated the heads up. Knowing where he was sitting would save me time and energy searching for him. I could focus on the ball, the batters, the sand beneath my cleats. I inhaled as deeply as I could before the stadium lulled to a whisper in anticipation of my name being called.

"Put your hands together for your Harbor Hornets starting Pitcher and Captain, Arrrrrrrrrrlo King!"

The crowd erupted again, and I plastered on a massive smile that hurt my cheeks and made me feel like an idiot as I threw my hands in the air and ran out onto the field. The sun had started to set, and the sky had turned a dark purple behind the bright stadium lights that bore down on me. The second the air hit my face and the thrum of the crowd filled my chest, I felt at home.

I jogged to where the umpire stood with the Captain of the Lorettes. Logan's arms crossed over his chest, and a hat pushed down over his eyes.

"Arlo," he nodded.

"Logan," I said, my tone clipped.

"Keep the game clean, boys," the umpire warned.

Both of us extended stiff hands. Logan's trembled as we shook them. Stifling the smile on my face, I offered a quick 'good luck' before wandering back to our benches.

"Tucker," I called Dean, a sturdy kid with shaggy blonde hair and puppy dog eyes who was playing his second season with the team. "Logan's still weak," I leaned in, "his swings are going to be sloppy, which means they're coming to first base. Keep your glove up and your eyes open."

Dean nodded, eyes flickering from me to the Lorrettes' bench, where Logan stood staring at us. "Don't let him intimidate you." Cael walked up behind Dean, his fingers pinching into the first baseman's traps. "He moans like a girl in bed."

"Cael," I scolded, shaking my head, but Dean laughed, seemingly shaking loose of the nerves that had suddenly gripped him. "You can do it."

BAD HONEY

"Aye, aye." He tapped two fingers to his chest.

We brought in two runs, which wasn't bad considering everyone was hitting like it was their first time holding a bat. It was like the entire team had an eternal case of the *yips*. Everyone was riled up and ready for a fight by the time we took the field. I slipped my hand into my glove, wiggling my fingers in the leather and stretching out my hand.

"Arlo," Nick jogged beside me before I took the field. "Don't fuck this up," he said, "you get one game to impress him, and if you don't, he won't be back."

"You think I care if he comes to these games?" I snapped, pulling out of his hold on my jersey. "I wish he didn't."

Nick didn't say anything, all the muscles in his throat tightening as he swallowed whatever fight he had. "Good talk, Ar," he groaned, pulling away and returning to the dugout.

I took the mound, digging my feet into the clay and sand.

My eyes locked with my father's before I rolled the ball between my fingers to find the laces.

"*This isn't your game anymore,*" I told my father in nothing but a whisper, drowned out by the crowd's screams, before turning my eyes back to the batter waiting for me. The crowd lulled for a brief moment. Just long enough for me to collect myself before I arched back and pitched the season's first ball.

Cheers roared as the Ump called the strike.

I could feel the confidence roving through my exhausted, nervous limbs; before long, I felt like myself. Untouchable and ready for a win. I steadied myself again, digging my foot back as the wind kissed my warm cheeks and the crowd fell to murmurs.

Another strike.

"One more!" Coach Cody called from the dugout, his long, dirty blonde hair tucked under his dark blue Hornets baseball hat.

One more was easy. I studied the batter's stance, adjusting my own before throwing the third strike. After two hard outs, the Coach of the Lorettes sent Logan out for a last-ditch effort to start their run count. The Captain kicked up the dust and flirted with the girls behind on deck. He swung his bat around, stretching out his shoulders, and the moment he stepped into the box, his boyish charm faded into a deathly stare that seemed to burn through me.

I made a quick shoulder check to see that the outfield had all shifted in anticipation of Logan. Cael was making pretty eyes at some girl in the stands, "hey," I snapped at him to pay attention before throwing the first pitch.

I held my breath as Logan swung.

"Strike!"

I exhaled and took the ball to the glove from Jensen, the bat catcher, who crouched at home plate. I watched carefully as Logan took three long inhales, shifted his back foot, and repeated. *Thread the needle.* My brother's words crept into the back of my thoughts, and for once, I listened, throwing mid-inhale and catching Logan off guard with a slippery fastball.

"Strike two!"

"You need a minute?" I called out to Logan, who only shot me a dirty look as he readjusted himself for the third time. "Hey, it happens to the best of us, bud," I continued the jabs, and the Ump gave me a look to cut it out, but it didn't matter; I had already gotten into his head. The damage was done.

I threw the final pitch and listened to the loud slap of the ball hitting the back of Jensen's glove. "Strike three!" The Ump hollered, and the crowd went insane around us, drowning out the disgruntled comments from Logan.

"What was that?" I asked.

"I said you're a fucking clown!" Logan threw the bat to his dugout and charged toward the pitcher's mound. He didn't match me in size, but the Ump skirted to get between us nonetheless. Saving Logan from a nasty bruise as I cocked my hand back to remind him physically who was the better Captain.

"You don't seem very entertained. I must not be very funny," I clipped, grabbing the brim of my hat and whipping it backward before stepping off the mound.

"Calm it down, boys, or you'll both be thrown out," the Ump warned.

BAD HONEY

"That's the end of your good luck," Logan quipped, returning to his dugout.

"When does luck become skill?" I barked.

"King! Go," the Ump pointed when I didn't move, my chest still puffed out, welcoming the pent-up frustration and looking for a fight.

My pitching remained so on par that Nick couldn't whisper a word of discontent even when Logan managed to snag a double and bring in two runs during the last inning.

"Your Harbor Hornets won the first game of the season six to two," the announcer boomed over the stadium. The canons reserved only for wins fired off into the night sky as the crowd lost their minds and the guys celebrated, but my eyes dragged up into the stadium to where my dad's seat was empty. Dread sat heavily on my chest, and a night that should have felt amazing was soured by his absence as much as it had been his presence.

Nick noticed the pause in celebration because when my eyes met his, there was a darkness there, but it was one we both carried, an understanding even when we wanted to tear each other apart. The common enemy would always be our father.

"Let's go get fucking wasted," Cael slapped me on the back, snapping me from the intense stare back into reality.

"Beer on me, boys!" I hollered as they all engulfed me in a team hug.

MIELE

The house was packed, and whoever had chosen the playlist for the evening was stuck living in the nineties. *No Scrubs* blasted over the speakers as I held onto Zoey, who weaved us through the dance floor of sweaty bodies and drunk frat boys. I barely noticed when she came to a halt, the crowd parting slightly to give way to the packed frat house kitchen. Half the cupboards were missing their doors, and the countertops looked like they were all made of different wood slabs.

The only person I recognized was Van, Zoey's boyfriend, who towered over most of the guys huddling around the makeshift island in the center of the eclectic kitchen. Van sauntered across, scooping a tiny Zoey into his arms and kissing her excitedly all over her face.

"Hi, Ella," He turned to look at me with a smile, his brown eyes hazy and soft from the booze but his smile vivid and white. "You guys look cute," he set Zoey back on the ground, hands still tangled together. He spun her around to take a proper look at her outfit. We both wore jean shorts and a T-shirt. There wasn't anything special about the outfits, but that was Van's superpower; he always made Zoey feel like she was the only girl in the room.

It felt like they had been together longer than Zoey and I had been friends. High school sweethearts, long-distance lovers, university ride or dies. It had been nearly thirteen years watching them be in love, and sometimes, it hurt a little more than others. And even though I was Zoey's first best friend, I couldn't keep the jealousy from sinking its grimy claws into my skin to remind me how alone I was now.

BAD HONEY

"As much as I love watching you two suck faces, I would love a drink," I laughed over the loud music, and Van nodded, strands of his dark brown shaggy mullet flying around his face. When I first met Van, he was scrawny, not a muscle on his six-five frame, but baseball camp had been good to him the last few years. He was fit now. Lean muscle corded his long limbs but made him look strong and balanced. Van wasn't a little kid anymore. None of us were.

"Sorry, El," Van laughed, throwing his arms over the two of us, "did you come to the game?" He asked, knowing the answer.

"No, she sulked in our room until I dragged her kicking and screaming out of there." Zoey cut me off, pushing Van away as she fixed her two braids and shook her head at me in disappointment.

"I just don't think this is a good idea," I shrugged. "I'm not ready for crowds like this and house parties..." *always had drugs*. I didn't have to say it out loud as the look that passed between the three of us spoke a thousand words. I didn't want to relapse. Drinking was never the problem; I could put the bottle down. It was the medicine cabinet that challenged my resolve.

"Zoey's right," Van leaned over and touched my shoulders to look me in the eye. He didn't need to bend over nearly as much to meet mine compared to Zoey's, but the eye contact was a sign that he meant whatever he would say next. "You need to talk to people other than her and me. It's not good for you to sit alone."

His brows furrowed as I rolled my eyes.

"If you're not going to find a new therapist, the least you could do is socialize so we know you aren't slipping into any dark corners." He tapped my temple with his finger and eased off of me.

"That's where I do my best reading," I tried to shake off the deep guilt that started to settle against my chest.

They had done so much for me. Dragged me from so many dark corners over the last year that I had started to lose count.

"No reading tonight," Zoey groaned, "drinks!" She proposed, and Van nodded, shooing her further into the kitchen. She settled against the counter between two boys I only recognized from photos.

One was of average build, with blonde hair and gorgeous blue eyes that twinkled under the horrible fluorescent lighting. He winked at me and whispered something to Zoey, which produced the fakest laugh from her I had ever heard. I wandered closer, taking the beer that Van extended to me and pressing it to my lips.

"Ella," he said, waving his hand before her, "meet Dean, first baseman." he pointed to the cheeky blonde who extended his hand to me. "And this is Jensen, bat catcher."

Jensen had darker eyes, dark brown hair, and a sneaky smile. "It's nice to meet you. Zoey talks about you a lot. We were starting to think you lived in Canada."

"Surprise," I shrugged. "I exist!"

"Sour patch! Where have you been hiding her?" Someone from behind us bumped around Van to kiss Zoey on the cheek, and despite the scowl on her adorable face, she leaned into the affection.

He was nearly as tall as Van with sheared bleached hair and the devil's smile. I drank him in, from his cropped gray shirt that showed off just a sliver of his tan stomach to his loose beach shorts and pristine white sneakers.

"California," I answered. "And I'm suddenly regretting showing my face."

"But it's such a pretty face," he batted his lashes at me.

"Does that usually work on the girls?" I narrowed my brown eyes at him.

"No, but it almost always gets the guys." He said in a flirty tone. "They have no standards," someone scoffed from the side of the room, "but then again neither do I."

"We know," Dean sighed.

"Hey, I can't help it if my preferences are anyone with a pretty smile." He shrugged. "I want it all." I had just met him, but there was a comfort in someone so honest and challenging. "Cael Cody," he held his hand to me, wrist covered in silver bracelets and one noticeably frayed, ugly threaded one that seemed so out of place.

"Interesting," I didn't give him my hand, but his blue eyes glimmered with curiosity as he retreated and crossed his arms over his chest. "You're the shortstop," I said, earning a surprised smile. "Zoey talks about you guys... a lot."

BAD HONEY

It wasn't just that, and the annoyed look I received from Zoey nearly made me laugh. Since I could remember, baseball has been my life. Fastpitch, women's teams, school, and club. Finally, when I graduated high school, I didn't even play a year of college ball before I blew out my knee. So, I did the only reasonable thing. Filled my time with college reports and absent-mindedly listened to the games on the radio in the library while studying.

"I'm starting to think it's just a *Zoey talks a lot* situation," Van teased, kissing her cheek as she fought him off playfully. "Where's King?"

"Sulking," Dean laughed and pointed to the corner of the living room.

I followed all their eyes to a player slumped down in an oversized leather chair with a scowl on his handsome face. He was different from the rest, with glowy skin even in the dim lighting of the house, heavy dark eyebrows, and dark chocolate brown almond-shaped eyes that almost appeared black. The hair on the back of my neck stood as his tongue ran over his bottom lip, and his gaze turned to me slowly, jaw tight, with his hands flexed around a beer.

There was no introduction needed for Arlo King. I knew those eyes well. He was on every Harbor Hornet's promotional signs and constantly on the front page of the university's newspaper. He was even Mr. January in the Hornets promotional calendar. None of those photos did him justice. He was bigger than he looked. His long legs extended out like tripping hazards to anyone dancing around him. He held a darkness to him that I couldn't put my finger on, but that seemed to itch at the skin of my bare arms.

"Why now?" Van asked, looking at Cael, who clearly said something to him without opening his mouth. Secrets floating between players that neither Zoey nor I were privy to. "Gotcha."

"You're in my advanced biology class," Dean snapped his fingers, changing the subject just as quickly. "I knew I recognized you."

"You're the kid that Professor Fisher always throws pens at for sleeping in class," I laughed with a nod; I should have recognized him, but I preferred to hide away from prying eyes in the back of class.

"You're the girl they call *Scarface*—" Jensen blurted, followed by a loud slap.

"Get!" Van barked, hauling him from the counter by the collar of his shirt and throwing him from the kitchen.

"Van," I went to protest, but catching my reflection in the window silenced me. It wasn't worth the fight. He wasn't wrong. The scar was horrible, a constant reason to avoid mirrors, and a friendly reminder that the guilt would follow me for the rest of my life.

It dug into the bridge of my nose, twisted and pale pink. Drawing a serpentine line through my skin that looked like a strike of lightning ending just below my right earlobe. I had scars all over my body, but the one on my face was by far the worst I had endured.

"Jensen's an asshole," Van shrugged unbothered as Zoey rubbed my arm in sympathy. No one here knew what happened or who I was, and I wanted to keep it that way for as long as I could.

"Hey Peachy," Cael leaned on his elbows over the island, "you wanna dance?"

I could see what he was doing. It was written all over his freckle-kissed face. *Distraction*.

"No, thank you," I said with a soft shake. A few blond curls fell from my ponytail, and I let them rest against my cheek, partially covering the scar.

"Can I get you a drink?" He asked, pushing buttons he didn't know existed. I waved my beer in his face as his smile turned to a defeated pout. "We can make out in the closet?" he offered.

"Cael," Zoey made a gagging sound that made me laugh.

"Beer pong!" Dean suggested, clapping his hands together and hopping off the counter.

"No!" Zoey hollered as the guys cheered, "Absolutely not. Don't you remember what happened last time?"

"Yeah, you lost and cried about it for a week!" Dean threw his arm over her shoulder and batted his long eyelashes at her. "You can pick your partner this time, although I don't think anyone here can beat me."

"I'm not falling for this again," Zoey tucked out of his grasp and backed away with a shake of her head. "Count me out."

BAD HONEY

"Coward," I said, earning a range of looks from the guys. "You're on."

"We play doubles. You need a partner willing to lose with you." A voice came from the doorway of the kitchen. "Nicholas King," he introduced himself with a crooked smile. Arlo's older brother. His hair was longer but the same color as his brothers, like black coffee. It was shiny and looked soft to the touch. He narrowed light brown eyes at me, waiting for me to introduce myself, but I had been caught up in how magnetic he was.

"Ella," I finally said, and I swear I heard a chorus of groans around me.

"I'll be your partner Ella."

My name rolled off his tongue like it was meant to be there, and he extended an upturned hand toward me, inviting me to take the chance. My heart was beating a little too fast in my chest, and I could feel a swarm of butterflies starting to erupt as I stepped forward, tipping the rest of my beer down my throat.

"If you don't mind losing," I teased.

"I already won," he took my hand and led me out into the backyard, which was just as busy as the inside of the house, if not more. There were low-hanging strings of lights that illuminated everything in a hazy glow and a giant bright blue pool that tinted everything in a shade of blue.

Zoey hooked her arm into mine and tugged me back, "are you sure this is a good idea?" She asked in a hushed tone.

"You wanted me out of my dorm," I cocked my head to the side in response, "here I am."

"Beer pong with these idiots was not what I meant," she said sternly.

"Just admit it. It's going to feel amazing when they lose."

They didn't know that Zoey and I had never lost at beer pong unless we meant to. It was a con our brothers had taught us in the early days of sneaking around behind our parents' backs to drink. Zoey had a record number of four older brothers. I think that's why she loved the baseball team so much. They reminded her of back home in California and made her less homesick here in Rhode Island. I only had Ethan, and he only had me. Until we didn't.

"You okay?" She shook me from the suffocating feeling that threatened to expose itself in front of everyone. I rubbed my thumb over the bottle in my hand to attach my anxiety to something tangible.

"Yeah, where's your faith? I can beat these assholes with my eyes closed." I nudge her to force the mood back into a happier place than where I dragged it to.

A scoff sounded from behind me as Arlo wandered out onto the lawn. The dark t-shirt he wore hugged every tight muscle on his body, from his round biceps to his carved chest and abdomen. He walked over to where Cael stood talking to everyone else and whispered something to him before Cael started howling with laughter.

"Peachy, you best be prepared to fight for it," he clapped his hands. "Arlo King just came out of retirement."

KING

"For me?" She smiled at me, sunshine incarnate flashing me in the face, and a thousand tiny knots tightened within my chest.

"For my legacy," I said, crushing the butterflies that came to life and the overwhelming need to tell her how gorgeous she was.

Tiny pieces of blonde hair fell around her face from the pony she had it in, covering the scar that harshly cut her delicate features in half. Her smile fell but didn't fade completely, leaving the slightest upturn to the left side, making my fingers tingle.

"Well, that was pretentious," she quipped with a tight laugh.

I pried my eyes away from her lips as Cael started to talk.

"Let me explain," he put both hands on the table, rocking it a bit beneath his weight, "For one year, Nick and Arlo battled relentlessly back and forth. Party after party, it was brutal."

"You're making it sound like it was World War Three." She said, grabbing her hip and scowling at Cael.

"It was," three different people all chimed in simultaneously, causing her to shake her head at them. I wanted to know how soft her hair was and what it smelled like. How it would feel tangled in my fingers. *What the fuck was wrong with me?*

"How does the story end?" She asked.

"I beat him the night he graduated," I interrupted.

"The night I left for spring camp with the *Astros*, actually." Nick corrected me, clearly upset that I was selling him short in front of his new challenge. I hated how close he was standing to her, his chest up against her back, his hand on her shoulder. "I was distracted and drunk. He cheated."

"I don't cheat," I said. "You're *always* distracted and drunk."

Nick rolled his eyes behind her back, and as she turned, he flashed a smile and gave her a wink as his fingers danced across her bare shoulder. Case in point. "House rules?" Nick asked, and I nodded. "Nice to know nothing changes around here."

It was a shot, but it didn't land because nothing else but *her* mattered.

It's not long before the rest of the celebrations move outside to watch the game. The baseball team created a tight circle to keep everyone away from us. Cael had set up the red solo cups in triangles on either end of the table while Nick continued to flirt with Blondie. The closer he got to her lips, the more itchy I became, flexing my hands at my side to keep them from balling up and hitting something.

"You sure this is a good idea?" Cael turned to me, tapping a knuckle to mine. "You seem a little *tense*, sugartits."

"Don't call me that," I groaned, "I'm fine. I just want to shut him up."

"I mean, he wasn't running his mouth until you—"

Cael's sentence died on the tip of his tongue with one look from me, brows furrowed, and lips pressed into a thin line.

"Just don't lose because you're distracted. That would be unfortunate." If there was one thing Cael Cody did without fail, it was read me like a book.

"Inside voice, Kitten," I pushed him away from me with both hands and looked over at her again, *distracted*. I didn't get distracted.

I kicked at the grass with my dress shoes. Most of the guys had gone home after the game, but I had stayed, waiting for my father in the parking lot in my loosely unbuttoned shirt and dress pants, but he never came. So I grabbed a t-shirt from my trunk, picked up enough beer to fill the backseat, and drove to Delta, where the rest of the team waited for me. I had spent the first half of the party beating myself up for even waiting for my father to show up, to talk to me, even to yell. A stupid notion, but some small abandoned little boy inside me craved his feedback on the game. Good or bad.

Idiot.

"Ladies first," Cael tossed toward her, and much to my surprise, she caught it without fumbling the small piece of white plastic.

Nick leaned in, whispering something in her ear, his eyes locked on mine as a broad smile unfolded on her face again. Heat spread across my chest, an involuntary response from every dirty thought I was having about that mouth. I inhaled as deeply as I could. I was screwed. I was just a bird in a cage, willingly wanting my wings clipped by her.

Correction, *horny idiot.*

Her big brown doe eyes flickered to where Zoey Novak stood, her small frame molding to Van Mitchell's giant one in the crowd. A silent conversation passed between them, with Novak rolling her eyes and Blondie shrugging her shoulders. I smirked, knowing exactly what was happening when she let go of the ball, and it flew wide of the table by nearly a meter.

We were being conned by a bat bunny.

I leaned into Cael, bumping my shoulder into his and knocking him slightly off balance as the crowd waited for Nick to take his shot. "She's bluffing," I whispered, and his brows kissed in confusion for a split second, eyes darting to Blondie and back again before they relaxed and his classic mischievous bright smile returned.

Nick sunk a clean shot, spraying beer from the glass's top onto the sticky table. Cael popped the dirty ball into his mouth, earning more than a few disgusted groans before he drank back the cup it had landed in.

"You're going to get thrush," I scowled, taking the ball from him.

"If I'm going to catch anything from your brother, it won't be thrush," Cael teased, tossing the ball back and sinking it into the furthest row of cups.

Nick handed her the ball, dripping with beer, and consumed what was in the cup as he waited for me to shoot. The ball bounced off the table and veered wide off the front cup, clanking off the rim to the grass beneath.

"I don't know what I expected from the guy who gave up two runs today."

My jaw tightened as I ground my teeth together to keep from saying something I shouldn't, but I was caught off guard by the look in her eyes from his comment. It wasn't disgust or anger, but something lingered there, a familiar feeling that had been dragged to the surface unwillingly.

"I've pitched worse," I shrugged, trying to keep him at arm's length. "Take your shot, Nick."

His shot arched and, just like before, sunk deep into a cup, Cael snatching it up again before I could carry half the load. She watched me carefully, dark eyes tracing over my chest to the cups on the table. I cocked my head to the side, waiting to see if she would crack and play the game, but she smiled at me and threw the ball short.

Cael laughed wildly, rolling his hands over his hair, "Peachy, you were so confident. What happened?" he teased, and she shrugged. "Tricky," he clicked his teeth together and threw his ball back, earning a massive cheer as the ball bounced and sank. "That's two!"

"It's okay. We'll come back from it," Nick assured her as he tucked a piece of hair behind her ear. Her eyes tightened, creating little stress lines; she *didn't like to be touched like that.* I noted that, tucking it away and keeping it safe. Nick chucked his ball, missing the table and swearing under his breath.

"Butterfingers," Cael practically giggled.

"Are all of your insults of a juvenile nature, Cody?" Nick shook his head and waited for her to throw hers.

"About as juvenile as your last three girlfriends Nicholas," Cael spat, and I watched as Nick's cocky smile turned to a scowl.

Dean and Van howled with laughter, nearly toppling Zoey to the ground between them. In a moment of distraction and out of the corner of my eye, I watched the ball bounce across the table and land in the front cup.

"That's two," she wiggled two slender olive-toned fingers at me. "Drink up, Cap," she smiled while mocking me.

"We're still ahead, Blondie," I reminded her.

"I believe we're even now. Math must not be your strong suit." There was that soft, tantalizing smirk again.

BAD HONEY

From that point on, she wasted no time hiding her skills as she sank more balls than all of us combined, and as Cael threw our last ditch effort to regain a cup, she watched the bounce and flicked the ball from its target. Well, within the rules and brought a prideful smile to my face.

"Drink up, boys," Nick beamed proudly before turning to his partner and whispering to her again, producing a smile and nod. He took her hand and led her inside, leaving me standing surrounded by drunk idiots and a curious Cael.

"What the hell was that?" He asked, "You knew she was good. Why the hell did you throw the bounce?"

"I wanted to see if she'd stop it," I answered, not taking my eyes off her as she climbed the steps back into the frat house.

"Congratulations, you lost the game *and* the girl to your brother." Cael groaned, throwing his hands in the air and wandering off through the crowd to find something else to do.

I might have lost the game but wouldn't lose the girl.

I pushed through the crowd, ignoring Van calling to me as I bounded up the stairs and through the side hallway around to the living room. He had taken her to dance, and every jealous bone in my body lit on fire when I saw his hands touching her.

She looped her arm backward around his neck, grinding herself against him as he buried his face in her hair and gripped her stomach with one of his hands. Nausea rolled through me, and I wanted to blame it on something I ate, but I was running on three beers, two vodka shots, and a stomach empty of anything with nutritional value.

"I know that look," Silas' voice snapped me from my trance, leaning against the wall with his hands folded over his chest.

"Aren't you a little old to be at a house party?" I snapped.

I didn't care for what he was insinuating. She was just some bat bunny. A beautiful blonde bunny with almond brown eyes and full pink lips that I wanted— I shook free again, feeling the heat on my neck rise the longer I thought about her.

"Nick is here. I came to make sure you two played nice." He scowled at me like I had insulted him. "Who's the girl?"

"I don't know," I bit down on my tongue. "Novak's friend, I think. Never seen her before."

"She looks like she's having fun with Nick. Is that the wisest thing to let happen?" Silas pushed off the wall to stand next to me. Barely an inch shorter, I looked at him, meeting his heavy steel-blue gaze, "You remember what happened to the last bunny."

Nicholas' taste in women had never been socially acceptable. The blonde with him now was probably the oldest girl he had ever gone after. The last few relationships he had engaged in had all ended in screaming, negative press, and Nick swearing off anyone under twenty-two.

It never lasted.

"Your mistake coming into this conversation was thinking I cared what Nick fucked in his spare time," I rolled my eyes and started to walk away, both from Silas and the disgusting dancing playing out in front of me.

Silas hooked his fingers around my arm, "Except you do care this time. Why?"

"I don't."

"You do. I've seen that look twice in our lives." Silas' grip held, "One when you won the championship in high school with a perfect pitched game, and the second time was when Marissa Nelson gave you that hand-job in the closet junior year."

I groaned loudly, "There was no look."

"Arlo, do you understand how much of an insufferable asshole you are?" Silas asked, "Because it's exhausting."

"Then go take a nap, Grandpa," I shrugged from his grasp and went back through the house to the other side of the living room, where I could watch Nick in peace.

Silas wasn't wrong; my brother was a horrible person, and everything he touched seemed to wither and die. But that didn't mean I was about to step in between him and some random bunny just because she was pretty.

MIELE

His hands were everywhere all at once. The music thrummed through me, and for the first time in a long time, I wasn't drowning in the guilt of my past. For once, I was given the freedom to just be a university student, drinking the night away. I guess Zoey had been correct after all. I did need to leave my room more often.

It had become increasingly hard to find the will to do anything lately; my bed was comfy, my books were there, and the outside world was a constant reminder of what I had done, the irreparable damage I had caused. It loomed over me like a storm cloud, ready to rain whenever it pleased.

I wanted to forget the accident that had maimed me for life, tore my family away, and created a version of myself that I didn't recognize, but... suffering was punishment for what I did, a crime I couldn't run from no matter how much I tried.

Tonight, it all felt different. I felt alive and uncaged. With what little alcohol was in my system, my cheeks were flushed, and my chest was warm. It reminded me of the good old days when frat parties were the only thing on my mind. My grades were terrible, but my record in drinking games was flawless, and my tolerance for booze was even better. Tonight had been fun and carefree, and I felt weightless with the music pushing through my veins.

Nick was cute and tall, and his biceps were massive. He was a horrible dancer, but so was everyone at this party. I wanted to thank him for being my beer pong partner on no information other than my confidence and smile. Maybe I would still get the chance. It had been a while since…well. And from the feeling of him brushing up against my ass, he was more than ready.

Nick brushed his lips against my sweaty jaw and whispered something I couldn't hear over the music that thrummed over the crowd in the living room. What he had to say anyway didn't matter. Nothing could be better than the freedom that dancing and drinking seemed to create.

A façade strong enough to block out the noise.

Until the levee broke.

Like metal scraping against metal, a loud crash rang out through the house from the kitchen and snapped me from my daydream like an overused rubber band. *Snap*. I couldn't breathe when I opened my eyes. *Snap*. The images of my brother flooded my senses and projected around me on the dancefloor like a ghost. *Snap*. I rubbed my hand against my chest, pulling from Nick's suddenly suffocating grasp, and pushed my way toward the front door, gasping for a breath of fresh air.

I heard a voice call to me, but it echoed through me in my brother's voice. Ethan called out to me. Begging me to help him. Stepping down the stairs and moving toward the haphazardly parked cars on the front lawn. I clawed at my chest, the phantom pain of the seat belt cutting through my skin, searing like it was still there, holding me in place, unable to help my family.

Times like these, panic attacks as bad as this one, were the reason I never left my room, and just like I expected, the universe was there to remind me. I leaned against a random car, trying to catch my breath and talk myself through it, convincing myself that the blood dripping down my face into my mouth wasn't real. The copper taste that coated my tongue was just a memory and a distant nightmare that I couldn't forget.

Before I could even stop it from happening, the vomit rose in my chest, and I turned to puke in the grass beside the car. My stomach heaved, trying to expel the coiled, anxious feeling from my body, unaware that it couldn't. I vomited up the contents of my stomach and rolled back against the door of the car to catch my breath and clean my face off.

"You okay?" A tall, older-looking man in a navy long-sleeve and a backward hat held a water bottle out in my direction. "," he offered, catching the uncertainty on my face. "I'm the team doctor." He added when I didn't reach out. It was meant to be a bridge, a statement that said *I'm not a creep*.

"Thank you," I said, swallowing the stinging sour taste lingering at the back of my throat. "Too much to drink, I guess."

He stared at me momentarily, trying to figure out if he should dig for an honest answer or leave it alone as he shoved his hands into his front pockets. "You're Novak's friend?" He asked.

"Ella, sorry, where are my manners?" I laughed awkwardly as I properly introduced myself.

"I get it. A weird guy follows a drunk girl out into the darkness away from a frat party. I didn't mean to make you uncomfortable." He took a wide step back from me. "Do you study law, too?"

"No," I said with a soft smile. Zoey had always been insanely good at arguing, and while maybe I was too, she was the better of us. She wanted to help people, and I admired her for that. "Sports medicine."

"You just moved here, right?" He asked with a nod.

"Yeah, I transferred from Cal before the semester started."

"Why?" Silas asked.

I had prepared myself for the questions, but I felt the cords tighten around my throat as I thought of the *why*.

"I wanted to be closer to Zoey, and Harbor had the same program if not a better one."

"You transferred out of a top tier four-year program for Zoey, and *if?*" Silas leaned against the car. He knew more than he was letting on. A smirk formed on his face, and the street lights reflected at me in his gray-blue eyes. He stepped forward again, cocking his head to the side as he narrowed his eyes at me. "I knew I recognized you."

Panic sunk deep into my chest, "You're Estella Miele."

I tensed at the name I tried to leave in the past. It always seemed to find its way into the light to shame me. Everyone knew what Estella, what I had done, that version of me. The darkest part of me. It's why I purely went by Ella now, a small change that people usually didn't question. But now, the team doctor of the Harbor Hornets was standing before me, staring at me with recognition, and there wasn't a single place I could hide from that.

"Just Ella," I reiterated.

"Shore," he said. His tone led me to believe I should understand where he was going with it. "Silas Shore." He said, and everything clicked into place. "See, the Miele name isn't the only one that circulates in the NCAA circuit."

"Holy shit," the curse slipped from me before I could stop it, causing him to laugh as he pulled off his hat and ran his fingers through his hair nervously. "Like *The Shores*."

The Shore family was rich, *like old money rich*. They had their hands on almost every foundation and college baseball team I knew about. They funded the new stadium on campus and owned more than one across the country, and now I was standing in front of one with puke on my sneakers.

"That's a new reaction," he chuckled.

"Sorry, I just never thought I would ever meet a Shore."

"You can stop saying it like that now." He laughed. "If it helps, my father and grandfather are disappointed in me being a doctor." He shrugged.

It was hard to believe they could be anything but impressed with him. He didn't seem old enough to be a doctor, but everyone carried themselves differently, and who was I to judge? I had gone into the sports medicine field to follow my brother through his NFL career. The career that died on the side of a highway in the pouring rain. I swallowed tightly, pushing down the sound of shattering glass.

"You were an incredible fastpitch player," he added next, "it was heartbreaking," Silas shook his head, catching me off guard. "It's a shame about your knee. We studied those X-rays during my rotations. They were gnarly."

"You sound like every other doctor that told me surgery was useless." I gave him a pathetic smile. Doctors and medical professionals alike all looked at the X-rays and told me that I would never play again. I was nineteen.

I couldn't forget, not really. I just wanted to desperately. "I was an idiot. I knew it was torn and kept playing."

BAD HONEY

"Even so, you guys won. Was it worth it?" He asked, sounding genuinely curious.

It was my first year on the team. The University's fastpitch was utterly different from what I had ever played, and we were one game from qualifying for nationals. I hit third base hard, sliding forward and crashing into the fence behind it. I had walked off the intense burning sensation that built around my thigh and kneecap, but after two more innings, my entire leg gave out. I never played again. Doctor after doctor, hospital visits, and therapy. Nothing ever worked to retrain the muscle. It was dead weight after that. Deadweight and a bad memory.

"It was. They won nationals that year," I said with a sad smile.

"That's an achievement, yet it feels like you're hiding. Why?" Silas asked.

"Because of the look you're giving me right now," I said and watched him hide the sympathetic stare that had fallen on his face. I hated being looked at like I was pathetic.

"So you pivoted," Silas nodded like he was contemplating. "Studied sports medicine for what, so you could follow your brother through the NFL?"

The mention of Ethan stung, and I fought to control my emotions in the face of questions I hadn't planned on answering today. Another panic attack nipped at my heels.

"To help girls like me who were swept under the rug by a system designed to cater to male athletes," I answered with certainty. "Ethan blew out his knee in high school. I bet that wasn't in any paper you read up here," I nodded nervously, my throat sticky as I spoke. I looked down at my shoes, avoiding whatever concern or pity was in Silas' eyes. "The team supported him through everything and found the best surgeon. Within the offseason, he was back in near perfect condition, perfect time to start for Cal."

"Same injury?" Silas asked, and I confirmed. "I'm sorry that happened to you."

His apology caught me off guard. It was never about me. It had been Ethan *this*, Ethan *that*, all while I slowly suffocated myself with painkillers and booze.

"Don't be," I shook my head, pushing away the self-pity. "Fastpitch consumed my life. Without it, I got to see my brother grow up and spend more time with my parents." That was the truth: I was given the freedom to be a kid without spending time in batting cages and on the field. It only hurt when I was given a reality check on how different I would be treated my entire life. That's when the pain medications became something more. They numbed the realization that I was the invisible member of my family. I was no longer of interest because I wasn't what they had planned for me to be.

The drugs had welcomed me with open arms and made me feel wanted and alive.

I could tell on his face that he knew what happened to my family, but he didn't say a word, whether because he read what the news had said about me or he had heard it from somewhere else, less reliable, perhaps the whole truth. It didn't matter. He had let it die in the silence that hung between us.

"I stayed with my brother at Cal and started my degree." I shrugged. "It's not as flashy as being a record home run hitter with a Ph.D."

Silas had been good, *really* good. His career exploded, but he never followed it through, even though the majors projected him as a record-breaking rookie. He didn't even show up to the draft.

"Should have known you followed that." He nodded, "you probably know most of the guys."

I nodded in response.

"Cool, now that we're standing on equal ground, both newsworthy and all," he said, "I'm sorry about Ethan."

My breath seemed to catch in my throat at the mention of his name. No one ever said it around me anymore. Both Van and Zoey were so careful not to rattle the cage.

"Me too," I choked out.

The accident was a difficult conversation, the reality even more so.

"The program here is decent," he laughed, easing the conversation, "but it's not very hands-on." He ran his tongue along his teeth, looking back at the house where Zoey had appeared on the step, clearly looking around for me. "Ella, this may be forward and unorthodox, but I need an intern for the season, and, well, it's hard to convince people because it's not exactly glamorous."

"You want me to come work for you?" I cocked an eyebrow at him, "after one drunken conversation."

"You and I both know you aren't drunk," he said with a smirk, "you are a pretty good liar, though," he chuckled, shoving his hand back in his pocket. "Just think about it. It's exhausting, and juggling your final semester with that will be hard, but you know the team, and it'll look good on your resume. I'll be at the stadium tomorrow. Come see me with an answer."

"But—" I called out as he nodded to Zoey in passing.

He turned to look at me and tapped two fingers to his chest, leaving me even more confused than before as he bounded up the stairs out of earshot.

"What the hell was that?" She asked as I popped the cap on the water and drank some back, cooling my throat and my nerves.

"He just offered me a job." I shrugged, unsure really what it all meant.

"Silas Shore offered you a job?" Zoey blinked at me, turning toward where Silas was talking to Arlo in the front entrance of the frat house, their figures strong and coated in shadows as they both looked toward us.

"An internship, but yeah." I watched as Arlo shook his head, saying something to Silas, and then stomped away into the dancing crowd away from us. "I'm going to head back to Turner House. I'm exhausted," I say, pointing toward our dorm.

"Do you want—"

"No, you stay, have fun." I interrupt her with a tight hug.

The walk home was good. It gave me a chance to think about how stupid leaving my dorm was in the first place. It cleared my head and lifted the weight from my chest, leaving me exhausted and ready for my comforter. That was the last time I let Zoey convince me there were better places to be. There was nowhere better than my bed, where the monsters couldn't reach, and fictional men said sweet things to me in the dark.

I flicked on the lights to our shared dorm. Zoey's side was covered in pastels and stuffed animals, the fact that she was two years from the bar hidden beneath her teenage girl style. I wandered behind the door, shutting it tightly to reveal the calendar that hung, hidden on the wall, and flipped it open to August.

"I knew it," I tapped the image of Silas in a doctor's coat with nothing but a textbook covering his junk. The only thing missing was the awful mustache he now had, but the same pensive gray eyes stared up at me.

I laughed before kicking off my shoes and stripping, climbing into Pajamas first and tugging my hair into a ponytail before crawling under the blankets. I slid my laptop and half-finished copy of *Red, White, and Royal Blue* into my reach, setting the book aside to check my emails.

I had been going back and forth with Mr. Novak, Zoey's dad. He was trying to get my parent's estate settled. Because the testament passed almost everything to Ethan, it was proving to be a fight with the state of California to get my hands on it. The excuse of everyone dying in a car crash was invalid, and they needed to sort through some things. Meanwhile, I sat in my dorm, out of money and time.

The following email's big red flag was poorly timed and unwelcome, but I opened it. I had a week to pay my dorm fees, or— I would be evicted, out on the front lawn of Harbor. I closed my laptop, pulling out my phone quickly to text Van.

"Tell Silas I'll see him tomorrow."

I sunk into the comfort of my blanket, flipping open my book and praying that I could lose myself in it long enough to forget about every problem that followed me.

MIELE

M y hand shook around the binders I had gathered before leaving my dorm. I was still unpacking after weeks on campus, and Zoey was frustrated by the mess. Living out of cardboard made everything feel less permanent. I still hadn't gotten used to the morning chill of Rhode Island in March, but I loved the smell of it. Dewy grass, hazy clouds, and flowers licked with a light coating of frost made everything smell clean and new.

Just like I had hoped my life here would be.

"Hey," I looked over my shoulder to see one of the guys from the party jogging up the stairs toward the building behind me. His blonde curly hair was pressed messily under a black snapback, and he wore a t-shirt and jeans that hugged every massive muscle.

"Dean," he reminded me, and I nodded, unable to forget his charming smile. "You look like one of those kids lost in a department store," he quipped.

"I feel like one," I responded, looking down at my phone.

"Here," he held out one arm to me and took my binders as he slid closer to look over my shoulder at my schedule. "Oh, lucky you," he laughed, "Biomechanics, the Prof for that class, is a real piece of work."

"Great," I sighed, "just what I need."

I had been slowly starting my classes over the last few weeks to catch up on the course load. Dean was in most of my classes, making me curious about what he was studying, but that question could wait for now; we were late. Today was my last, *first* day. Most of the professors had been fantastic, only giving me what I could handle and letting me adjust before adding more. The last thing I needed was an asshole who thought I was a sympathy case for the university.

I had more than one confidential conversation with the campus dean about my situation, but it seemed like the professors had a meeting on my history before I started. I was being babied, and it wasn't a bad thing. It had given me time to collect myself and my thoughts. But I hated how they all looked at me. *The girl who killed her family.*

The whispers were there, and the nickname Scarface seemed to follow me around, but so far, I had run into no trouble from any students. Zoey and Van had kept their promise not to tell anyone about the accident that happened in California. The list was growing now that the team doctor knew who I was. It was going to become more challenging to hide everything. I just wanted a fresh start. I didn't want the stares and gossip that came with such a tragedy. I was slowly working on myself. Therapy helped a little, but I hadn't found a new one since moving to Rhode Island, and I could feel the nightmares starting to creep back in as my defenses against them weakened.

"Earth to Ella," Dean's voice snapped me from my daydream, and I saw him holding the front door to the science building open for me. "I'll walk you to class," he said with a smile, my binders still cradled in his arms.

"Thanks," I gave him a soft laugh, "I'm going to get one of those *Hello, I'm lost* stickers for my shirt."

"I'll buy you a pack in honor of that performance the other day at Delta. I've never seen Arlo so quiet."

I shifted beside Dean as he paved a path for us down the busy hallway into the concourse. "He doesn't like me very much," I said.

"King doesn't like anyone but Silas and Cael." He put a hand on the small of my back, guiding me to the left down a less crowded hallway into a section of the building with high ceilings and study cubbies against a long wall of windows. "It's just how he is."

I enjoyed how much the architecture of Harbor University involved nature. Through the windows was a closed-off courtyard of flowers and trees that was being tended by an older gentleman in the sun. Everything seemed to breathe in the nature on campus.

"Him and Nick don't get along?" I knew I was pushing my luck.

BAD HONEY

"There's a lot of history there that is better off left in the dirt," Dean shrugged, seemingly unbothered by the entire situation. He whipped his head toward me with a cheeky grin, "Besides, you're too good for either of them anyways."

"You're smooth," I laughed as he opened the classroom door for me.

"I do my best," He walked past the group of students chatting amongst themselves and plopped down in a chair up further in the risers. He patted the seat beside him, but my eyes were on who was sitting to his left.

Arlo watched me climb every step, his dark eyes trained on me as I sank into the seat beside Dean. He set my binders down on the extended desktop that ran the curve of the risers and pulled his own from his backpack.

"Arlo, you remember Ella?" Dean smiled.

"Unfortunately."

I chose not to respond, sinking into my books and pulling my laptop from my backpack. I only needed to pass three more courses, and I would have my sports medicine degree, and then I would be free of the campus. Free of the judgment, free of sports teams and assholes like Arlo King.

Before Dean could make the situation more awkward, the Professor entered the classroom, and everyone went quiet as he started his lesson. Halfway through, he called on me to answer a question from the readings, no doubt trying to catch me off guard and test my knowledge of the subject. When I answered without hesitation and with absolute certainty, he nodded, backing off and leaving me alone for the rest of the class.

Dean carried my books back down the steep riser to the main level, and as they brushed past the desk, Professor Tucker spoke again. "Don't forget your mother expects you for dinner on Sunday, Franklin."

Confused, I looked between Dean and Arlo, trying to figure out who he might be talking to, but I could see the resemblance much more clearly at this distance. Beneath the salt and pepper hair and well-trimmed beard was an older, wiser Dean with the same blue eyes and bright smile.

"Franklin?" I couldn't contain my laughter, and to my surprise, Arlo was laughing over my shoulder, but the moment I looked back at him, his bright smile faded back to a harsh scowl that made his face seem so hard.

"It was a pleasure to meet you, Ella." Professor Tucker held my hand, and I shook it politely. "I took a look at your transcripts. You're a bright girl, and I'm glad you could continue your studies. I'm sorry for your loss. We all are."

"Thank you," I said, trying to avoid a heavier conversation as my chest tightened.

"It's a shame losing so much at such a young age. You're very strong."

I tried to ground myself in the room, pushing my heels down into tiles beneath me and focusing on my breathing as the Professor made more muffled small talk that had been drowned out by the sound of screeching tires in the back of my mind. The panic attack was already itching beneath my skin. I needed out, and I needed out *now*.

"I need to go," I blurted, not meaning to sound rude, and pushed my way past Arlo into the busy hallway.

I did my best to stay upright as I shoved through all the bodies that pressed down on me as I weaved between them, trying to find a door that led outside. I felt more and more suffocated with each passing second. My lungs seemed to contract, and my breathing became more labored.

I could feel the tears burning lines down my face, and the scars on my hand seemed to throb. A searing heat ran from my ears and down the back of my throat, and I was instantly back there. Trapped in my car, pinned by metal, blood seeping down my face into my mouth. I licked my lip and could taste the copper that pooled there.

I spun, so dizzy and disorientated, yelping when a girl to my left laughed loudly and tossed her arms around her friend as another crashed into my right shoulder, sending me stumbling through the rush of students.

BAD HONEY

A hand grabbed my upper arm and spun me backward through the crowd just as my knees began to buckle, shoving me forward into a dark classroom and closing the door behind us.

"Breathe, Blondie."

Even with hazy vision and shortness of breath, I could see Arlo hovering over me as I fought to control my balance and stay standing.

Where the fuck had he come from?

My therapist had taught me that when the memories became too much, I needed to ground myself in reality, but that was easier said than done in a dark classroom. I looked around, tripping over the desk beside me and whispering, "One." I inhaled deeply and continued my search. My foot kicked my backpack at my feet, and I repeated, "Two," taking another deep breath.

I peered at the tiny rectangular windows that provided little light in the room and counted to three. Slowly, the sounds of shattering glass and twisting metal seemed to fade out, and the ringing in my ears became a dull roar.

I struggled to find anything else and could feel the darkness starting to creep in on the edges of my vision again. I had forgotten entirely the presence of Arlo until he reached out to me, "four," he said, turning his palm upright and curling his fingers into mine. He waited until I took another deep breath and slipped what felt like a rock or a marble into my palm, "five."

I rubbed the cool object between my fingers to reveal a solid gold wedding ring and pushed back everything that crept into my consciousness. He held out his hand for me to return it, and when I did, before I could even thank him for saving me during one of the worst panic attacks I had since moving, he was gone, the door to the classroom slamming behind him.

"What the fuck," I huffed out, my head lulling back as I stared at the ceiling.

Arlo was going to give me whiplash.

I collected myself with another long breath and gathered my backpack before ensuring the coast was clear. I exited the empty classroom, found the closet door to the outside, and let the fresh air wash over me for a moment.

The walk to the stadium provided some clarity. The panic attacks were only going to get worse if I didn't find some stable ground to stand on and, more importantly, a good therapist. I couldn't keep going like this, running in circles, waiting for the inevitable moment that someone or something triggered my trauma. It was unhealthy and unreasonable.

Walking up on the stadium, I realized I had underestimated the sheer size of it. Standing in the parking lot, I stared at the metal structure, the concrete pillars contrasting with the sharp blue metal beams. It was beautiful and daunting.

It had taken me nearly an hour to walk there from the class, my heels burning from wearing my tennis shoes, a mistake I wouldn't make twice as I pulled open the frosted glass doors to the main entrance. Silas had emailed me explaining where to meet him in the medical wing, which at the time had seemed ridiculous to me that the building had a whole wing for the medical team. Still, now, seeing how seriously Harbor took baseball, I understand.

Playing fast pitch for Cal during freshman year before I tore my ACL and having it kill my career, I tried to avoid situations like the one I stood in. I had avoided the stadium since moving to Harbor, but baseball seemed to follow me like a bad joke, no matter how hard I tried. The hallway smelled clean, like citrus and concrete, but the smell of clay, sand, and freshly cut grass seeped through the walls. My body demanded I go home, but my heart ached to create distance.

"Ella?" Silas appeared from my left carrying two boxes in his arms with a smile. I had forgotten for a moment how handsome he was, *how gorgeous they all were*. With his light brown wavy hair and shaggy beard, he stared at me for a second, waiting for a response.

"Yeah, sorry, the last time we met, I was a little..."

"Sober?" he shrugged, laughing about the lie, "follow me."

"Can I?" I offered to take a box, but he just shook his head and adjusted them before leading me down a more extended hallway toward the west side of the building.

He turned and used his back to push open two large blue doors, and the brutally clean hospital smell hit my nose.

BAD HONEY

I paused, taking a look around the massive square room. There were four elevated beds on the east wall, all with their stations and monitors. The north side of the room was set up for physio and strength training, with massive stretching blocks and machines.

"It's pretty impressive." Silas slid the boxes onto one of the long marble counters and crossed his arms as he looked around the room. It was one of the most advanced medical centers I had ever visited.

"Not even Cal looked like this—" I huffed out a shocked breath, completely speechless.

"My family owns the building, remember?" He laughed, "If their son was going to work as a lowly doctor, he would do it in the best facility." He mocked a voice I could only assume was his father's.

"So?" He cocked an eyebrow at me. "What do you think?"

"Does it pay?" I asked, knowing that was dumb to lead with, but it was all that mattered now.

"Better than any stuffy internship you'd get off campus." He said. Silas smiled, knowing it had gotten me.

"Are you staying in a dorm?" He asked, walking past me to a desk in the corner covered with stacks of paper.

"Yeah, Turner Hall."

"As staff, you get a room at Dansby House," he pulled a cream folder from the bottom of one of the piles and sent paper flying everywhere.

"Dansby?" I had never heard of that campus dorm, and it wasn't on any maps I had been staring at for a week, trying to find my way around.

"The Nest," he corrected himself with a sigh, "sorry sometimes I forget those idiots call it that."

That I had heard of, Zoey talked about it all the time.

I laughed, for real and for the first time in a while. "How much is the rent?" I asked, worried.

"No rent," he laughed. "Stupid rich, remember? *Only the best for the Harbor Hornets!*" he mocked again in his best old white man voice.

"Is that supposed to be your dad?" I shook my head.

"Grandpa, but close enough."

He grabbed a pile from his desk in the corner of the room, walking it over to me as he propped it open. "These are just basic forms. Can you return them to me before the game on Thursday?"

"You want me to start Thursday?" I couldn't even remember the day, but Thursday felt fast.

"No, I want you in here tomorrow," Silas laughed, "I'll run you through the physiotherapy schedule for some of the guys, and you can meet the rest of the staff before Thursday. I need the papers before the game because there are a few waivers about staff injuries."

"Staff injuries?"

"The reason we lost the last intern is because Van punched him while we were resetting his shoulder."

"Van? Big teddy bear, never hurt a fly, *Van Mitchell*?" I laughed.

"He'd hurt an intern over a fly." Silas, let me take the folder. "I'll show you around and introduce you to Coach."

"Coach Cody?" I asked, suddenly a lot more nervous than before.

"Are you blushing?" Silas laughed wildly, throwing his head back and clutching at his chest.

"Come on," I giggled, "you've seen the Harbor Hornet's calendar, right? Mr. March?"

Zoey had left March up long into July. Coach Cody proudly displayed, drenched tastefully in a blue sports drink, draped across a set of seats in the stadium, wearing nothing but boxers and a Hornet's home jersey that clung to every muscle on his body.

"You have a bit of drool," Silas smirked, pointing to the corner of my mouth before I swatted his hand away playfully, "maybe if you ask nicely, he'll sign a copy of it for you."

"You think?" I teased, chasing after him as he exited the wing toward the left.

"Personally, I think Mr. August is far superior." He looked back at me.

"We haven't gotten that far," I winked, "But Mr. January! I'm surprised you guys got that grouch to do that."

January was a fan favorite, Arlo King, in tight baseball pants that hung low on his hips, pulling back to throw a pitch. Every muscle in his body was taut and lengthened as the team around him threw buckets of water in his direction. It dripped down his body, and the image was burned into my brain.

"Zoey tried to leave January until Van found out." I laughed.

"Poor Mr. February shafted for *Oscar the Grouch*." Silas huffed out another long laugh as he opened the door to the administration offices.

The coaching offices were carpeted in dark blue and painted much nicer than the tunnels. They were also much more busy. Loud laughter bustled through, and the sound of people speaking on the phones echoed around me to the point of being overwhelming.

"I think I prefer the medical wing," I commented.

"You and me both," he laughed, opening the door to a large corner office.

"Ryan," Silas walked through a smaller, empty office into what could only be described as the pits of cluttered hell. Towers of boxes and paper consumed every inch of the space.

"Clean your office," he grunted as he ran into the arm of a chair with a muffled grunt. "This is our new intern."

"She's *a girl*," I heard him say in a funny Texas accent before I saw him. *Good start.*

"Yes," Silas rolled his eyes, "a girl that knows twice as much as the last three male interns, be nice."

Coach Cody stood from behind the boxes, and I stifled the gasp that tried to escape. The difference in person was shocking. *Seriously, what was in the water at Harbor?* He shook out a head of dirty blond long hair and flashed a soft, friendly smile at me that reached his big green eyes. "I'm Ryan Cody," *Mr. March*, I swooned as he leaned over, holding out his hand to me over a stack of boxes.

"Ella Miele," I offered my hand in a polite shake.

"Sorry about the *girl* comment," he swallowed his pride. "Not that you aren't capable, it's just a little surprising."

"It's okay, I can handle Mitchell's right hook. I'm the one who taught him how to throw it." I smiled at him and took my hand back. Ryan eyed me for a moment, weighing my response.

"She'll be fine," Silas promised. "She's going to come in tomorrow to meet some of the other staff—"

As Silas ran over the plan with Coach Cody, my eyes focused on his only photo in the office. On the wall, hanging just above his computer on the desk was a small wooden frame; enclosed was a photo of Ryan, a beautiful woman, and what I can only assume was their son. My brows furrowed, and I almost laughed when I realized it was a photo of Cael Cody. It took me an embarrassingly long time to put it together. He was younger and more boyish than the man I had met at the party, but I could see the smile that both Ryan and Cael shared. Father and son.

Silas guided me from the building to the main entrance after showing me around the locker rooms and the dugout. "When was the last time you were in a stadium?" He asked, the sun beating down on us as we stepped into the daylight.

"A while," I confessed.

"Ear plugs, at least for the first couple of games. I don't need you deaf." He said.

"Alright," I nodded, backing away. Silas turned to go back inside, but I stopped him, "This morning..." I stopped, unsure I should be asking the question, but Arlo and Silas seemed closer than anyone else. "Arlo helped me with something."

"Arlo helped you?" It came out of his lips as a surprise.

"Yeah," I shook off the feeling of utter shock as Silas came closer to listen. "He had a wedding ring, dainty, gold band?" I described the ring that I couldn't stop thinking about to him. The cool metal had burned a memory into my skin that I couldn't forget. "I didn't know he was married."

"He's not." Silas's face dropped, and I recognized the look of grief as it flickered across his pretty blue eyes. "Just show up, do your job, and stay away from him."

"That's it?" I licked my lip, "you all make him out to be the big bad wolf."

"Arlo *wants* to be the big bad wolf."

I didn't argue the topic further, but the ring would stay tucked in my thoughts until I found the reason for it. I wasn't even sure why Arlo King had piqued my interest the way he had. Arlo bothered me on a deeper level that felt personal. He didn't scare me. He confused me, and it felt like a distraction, at least for now.

KING

The stadium was chaotic after another hard win the night after the season opener. The Hornets had officially started the season better than we had in three years. Reporters flooded the player's entrance, making it impossible to get by without answering an onslaught of ridiculous questions. I just wanted to sneak by with my head down. I didn't need a big scene or praise. We were playing good, and we would continue to do so. I had to believe that.

"King!" Van called from the side door as I smoothed out my dress pants beside my Mustang. I closed the door as quietly as I could, jogging to where he stood in the frame. "They're fucking vultures today," his brown eyes flooded over the huddle of recorder tapes and clicking cameras.

He shut the door tightly behind us and followed me down the hallway toward where Coach Cody stood, his arms crossed, talking to Silas.

"We gotta get the tunnel up," Van said as we approached. He shifted in his dark green dress shirt and shoved his hands into his pockets. "Dean got smoked in the face with a recorder on the way in, and they're just getting worse."

"I'll get someone on it," Coach waved us off and returned to his serious conversation with Silas.

I hovered briefly, hoping to catch a tidbit of what they were discussing, but Coach shook his head and shooed me away.

"What do you think that's about?" Van asked, shuffling beside me. We barely fit through the locker room door side by side, and Van had to shuffle sideways.

The moment we entered, I knew exactly what that conversation had been about. Cael looked like he had been run over by a truck.

I dropped my bag and made my way to him, "what the fuck?" I grabbed his chin and angled his bruised face toward me.

His blue eyes looked so sad and bright against the deep hues of purple and red. "You should see the other guy," he teased, and I tightened my grip, unamused.

"Was it that dealer? The one from before?"

"Just a fight." His tongue rolled out over his busted lip. He yanked his face from my grip and pushed up from where he was sitting in his locker to strip from his shirt. His torso was in worse shape than his face.

"You can't play like that!" I smacked the side of the locker with a wide swing, making more than one player flinch from the sound.

"I'll be fine," he looked at me, his eyes glassy and heartbroken. The worst part of our friendship came to light time and time again when he chose drugs over everything. He pulled each arm into his jersey and buttoned it with shaky fingers.

"You're sitting," I barked. It didn't matter that I held no weight over Coach. Cael Cody wasn't stepping onto the field tonight, not in that shape.

"You can't fucking do that, and you know it," he growled at me, acting tough.

"This is my team, Cody," I tried to control my voice, keeping it low so only he could hear me when I said it, "and if you're not going to look out for yourself as a player, I will. If you go out there and play hurt, it will only make it worse, and then what?" I shoved him back with a firm hand, my fingers wrapping around the back of his neck when he tried to pull his face away. "You go out and buy more drugs to numb the pain. No. Fuck that."

"You aren't my fucking dad!" He pushed me with all his strength, but I didn't budge.

"No, I'm not! He's too fucking exhausted to care about you anymore," I let him go roughly and turned my back on him, wrapping my hands around my locker with a long, frustrated huff of air. "You aren't playing today, Cael; there are consequences to your actions." I rolled my head in his direction, staring at him directly so he understood how serious I was.

Cael threw his hand against the back of his locker and stepped toward me, "Fuck you, Arlo. You're just like him, you know. You bully everyone into doing what you want."

"Get out of my face before you say something you don't mean," I snapped at him, and by the grace of god, the motherfucking idiot listened.

Coach and Silas arrived just in time for Cael to shove past them from the locker room and down the hallway. "What the hell?" Silas huffed, looking around for answers.

"He's not playing today," I said.

"King," Coach grumbled.

"The call had to be made. I made it. We can win without him." I shrugged off my dress shirt and started to change silently, not bothering with the conversation anymore, when the door opened behind Coach.

"Boys, listen up," his voice boomed over us, drawing our attention to who came in with him. I turned slowly, buttoning up my jersey with my eyes on my fingers. "This is Ella, your new medical assistant."

My eyes snapped up to see her, blonde hair falling over her shoulders, soft brown eyes watching everyone in the room as she was uncomfortably displayed. The Hornet's uniform hugged every full curve of her body. My heart was racing faster than ever on game day, all because of her.

A few guys cheered and clapped for her, glad to have the new addition. She leaned in, whispering something to Silas, who nodded solemnly before she excused herself and exited the room.

"Anything you need from Silas, you can ask Ella," Coach explained. "Without Cael, Dougie, you'll play short today. Let's keep up this fire, you guys. You've been playing with your hearts and your heads lately. Don't stop."

Everyone tapped their chests and hollered in unison. The atmosphere went from strangled to relaxed within seconds. My mind wandered to Cael. I knew better than to yell at him, but it came out before

I could rethink my decision to do so. I huffed, tying up my laces and leading the team from the locker room.

"You did the right thing," Silas slapped me on the shoulder, his body angled in front of where Ella sat on the ground next to Cael, helping him ice his face. At least he hadn't gone far.

"It doesn't feel like it," I groaned, rubbing my hand against my chest in a rough circle to ease the ache that vibrated through me.

"The youngest King has a heart, after all," Silas joked, but it only made me feel worse. "Do you know what happened? Cael refuses to tell Coach anything," he said, shifting his tone.

"He's getting drugs from those dirty sellers across the bridge again," I sighed, "I'll handle it."

I watched as Ella scrunched her nose at him with a soft smile as he nodded. Whatever she was saying to him seemed to ease the tension in his shoulders. I knew the feeling but hated it as the jealousy washed through me, for him to be so close to her, talking about secret things. I felt my feet shift beneath me, threatening to move toward them, but I stopped, pressing my hand to the wall and letting the hum of the crowd above wrestle with those negative thoughts instead.

Cael looked at me over her shoulder, his blue eyes ice cold as I turned the corner toward the field. I knew it would be a while before he forgave me for this, but it wasn't the first time I had dealt with that guilt. Cael Cody was trouble, like a hurricane without a warning. The two of us had quickly bonded upon my arrival at the Nest. Cael was two years behind me, but with his father, Ryan Cody, being the head coach of the Hornets, he was a legacy of sorts in his own right.

Their family was just as tight-knit as the Shores' and Kings. Riona Cody was the team therapist, Coach's older sister, and why he had been offered the job. They had come to Rhode Island when Cael was seventeen, and shortly after, his mother Lorraine died of cancer, leaving Cael and Coach on their own. Lorraine had been a mother to all of us. She had come into the Nest with open arms and a heart of gold that seemed to ease our worries. Lorraine taught all of us what we knew about taking care of ourselves. She taught us how to work the washing machine, remove the stains from our sheets, and prevent us from shrinking our clothes. She taught us how to cook and created

BAD HONEY

the dinner schedule in the Nest. No one went hungry, got cold, and felt invisible with Lorraine Cody around. That was until she died.

That's when I stepped in. I knew the pain of losing a mother. I didn't know everything about what happened when the Codys moved to Rhode Island, but I had learned enough from Silas to realize it had been explosive. Cael didn't want to be here; Coach had to be here. Lorraine had been the buffer between the two, the only person patient enough to care for them both as they waged war on each other. But when she got sick, Cael spiraled, and Coach didn't know how to help him.

I did my best to help Cael adjust in the Nest without having his mom around to care for him but all the boys. She had been a mom to everyone. It was never enough to keep Coach and him from going in on each other.

The worst fights happened three summers ago on the front lawn when Cael didn't attend their Sunday dinner. Punches were thrown and egos bruised, but Cael... seemed to never recover from his dad yelling, *"It should have been you."*

Three years later; they barely interacted anymore. I was convinced that he carried those words around. Cael minded his own business as shortstop, drinking himself stupid and fucking anything that moved to feel less numb. Coach barricaded himself in his office beneath the stadium, surrounding himself with concrete so nothing could hurt him. He slept on the old couch in his office, barely leaving the campus.

The Cody's had fallen apart without Lorraine.

Cael turned to harder drugs, usually getting into trouble wherever he went. The worst of all the scenarios was his stealing. The sellers came looking and trashed the Nest while we were all asleep, and when I went to ask Cael about it, he was gone. It took us two weeks to find him, and he was a state over; hiding in a hotel room like that would solve the problem. That had been the first time I threw him into rehab. And it worked for a long time. But he always slipped. Tripping over his own need to self-destruct. I was afraid we were hitting a wall again.

A small hand tapped my shoulder, pulling me from the thoughts, and I looked down to see Ella standing beside me.

"Can I help you, Blondie?" I asked her when she didn't say anything, clearly working up the courage to speak.

"You don't have to listen to me, but I need you to hear this," she said quietly. "You are all he has left. Try to honor that."

My chest constricted like she had dropped an anvil on it.

What the hell did she know?

Before I could respond, I was being shoved from the tunnel and out into the screams of thousands of people who counted on me to make this the best season yet. I stopped short of the dugout, staring back at her as she crossed the field with Silas beside her, and ground my teeth together.

She was crossing lines, assuming too much with so little information.

It was a catalyst for what came next.

The game was over before it even started, everyone was too distracted. They all knew the dangers that Cael carried on his shoulders, and no one wanted to deal with the shit we had before. Dougie was horrible at shortstop. His movements were sloppy, and he couldn't read my mind like Cael usually did.

Nick spent most of the game flirting with Ella. Her soft laughter echoing through the dugout was driving me fucking mad as I tried to focus on bringing the game back in our favor. But when I watched his hand trail down her lower back I lost all composure and pitched three runs, serving them on a silver platter for the opposing team. I swore under my breath, pissed off to no end, as the announcer called the game nine-four for the other team.

"Arlo," Ella called to me in the crowded tunnel. Her blonde hair swung around her face, covering the scar that cut into her skin. It was the most interesting part of her, and she hid it. I hated it.

"Mind your business," I snapped, shoving away the urge to move her hair from her face.

"No," she shook her head. "Whatever you said to him fucked him up. He's trying to hold it together, but his only support system is cracking." She looked me over with anger laced behind her glossy brown eyes. "Addicts need love. They need to know—" she stopped. "You know what, never mind."

BAD HONEY

"You think you know me? You think you know Cael?" I snarled under my breath, "*You don't*." I walked away from her, leaving the field with shaking hands and collecting my bag from the locker room before any of the guys returned.

There was something to be said about how brave she had been to call me out. Not many people would dare but she had walked herself up to me and told me exactly what she was thinking, the severity in her tone matching the fire in her chocolate brown eyes. I forced down the hot feelings of desire that trickled up through me and prayed my anger wasn't simply masking something much worse. When I finally composed my misplaced anger, I drove back past the university and pushed my car up the hill to the Hornet's Nest. When the house came into view, I felt a little more at ease; it was the place I wasn't forced to wear a mask.

Surrounded by a massive iron gate and a circle of heavy oak trees, it sat prettily on a manicured lawn with trimmed hedges and a four-car garage. A legacy house, known by campus as Dansby House but known as the Hornet's Nest by the team and students, was one of the oldest frat houses still standing on campus. A two-story Victorian-era home with dark green siding and clean, well-cared-for, white shutters. At first glance, it was never taken for a frat house.

The property was owned by the Shore family and Silas's parents, and everything was maintained by a handful of caretakers barely seen around the house. The second floor was all dorm rooms. Most guys shared it with two other teammates. Silas lived in the basement, which had been converted into a separate apartment for him long before we played for the Hornets.

I parked the car in the garage and closed it behind me, taking two stairs at a time into the house. The inside was immaculate, with original dark mahogany wooden architecture and deep, rich wallpapers. I ignored the gnawing feeling that built in my chest over Cael. Ella's advice swirled in the back of my mind as I made my way to my room on the main floor. The Captain of the team got his own. It's the same room my father and my brothers had slept in.

Kicking the door shut behind me, I locked it, threw my keys into the bowl on the dresser beside me, and kicked my shoes into the open closet off to my left. Stripping from the sweaty shirt I had thrown on, I nearly tripped over the gear I forgot to wash that weekend. I pulled the heavy black curtains that covered the two massive windows in my room closed and lay back on my bed with images of blonde hair and frustratingly beautiful brown eyes taunting me.

MIELE

The longest week of study groups and balancing sessions with Silas to learn about the routines had exhausted me. It felt like I was a clown on display at the circus most days as I stumbled into class half awake, chugging coffee and catching up with my notes, but it was worth it. Getting to spend that time with team members allowed me to learn about how they operate as a unit. I was starting to catch the little changes in their body language, and figuring out when they were hiding injuries was crucial. Even more so, I was getting better at predicting Cael's blowups.

"So why are you so worked up?" I followed Cael up the path to the stadium.

I had fiddled with my hair for too long, only to leave it down. Lately, with all the work around the stadium and classes, more people have started paying attention to me. It made the scar on my face itch like it was opening all over again. Somedays, I woke up feeling like the glass was still embedded there, in my skin, and all I could do was wait, frozen in place, for it to slide deeper into me. Somedays I wish it had just finished the job.

I hid it with makeup or my hair. At least Cael didn't care; his eyes never traced the harsh, jagged line that crossed my face. Either he didn't notice or was too respectful to talk about it.

"This game is massive," he held open the door for me, pushing his sunglasses over his bleach-blonde hair as we entered the dark tunnel. "Boston State kicks our asses every year. Most of the time, we'd be better off forfeiting to them rather than suffering the embarrassment."

"But you guys have been winning," I said. It had been two weeks since my first game as an intern, and despite the first game being a wash, they had won every single one since. They were on a twelve-game win streak.

Arlo had been pitching like a god.

"Nothing is guaranteed," Cael shrugged, looking uncomfortable in his fitted brown suit and teal dress shirt. Coach didn't allow them to show up to games dressed casually. They showed up dressed to win, or they didn't show up at all.

"The problem isn't our willingness or drive to win," he hummed, "this team gets under Arlo's skin, and if he's even a little off, it's going to be hard to hold onto this high we have going."

Arlo had eventually come to Cael, and as far as I knew, he had been forgiven for his shitty attitude. But it still felt tight between them in a way it hadn't in my time with the Hornets. They had gone from teasing, laughing, wrestling, and fighting to a strained silence like Arlo was walking on eggshells around him, which didn't sit well with me. Cael needed Arlo, even if the guy could be a grade-A asshole. The night after he was thrown out of the game, we walked for hours just talking about everything. He was surprisingly honest about his life, everything that had happened to him, and everything he'd brought on himself.

That conversation had opened both of us up to a mutual friendship that had been working for the past two weeks. Cael hadn't touched a drug since that night, and I didn't feel so isolated. My panic attacks had started to dull inside my chest, giving me a moment to breathe and enjoy college life for once.

And then there was Nicholas. He was sweet, funny, and attentive. He was being patient with me, and there was a softness to him that I hadn't expected to find. He had taken me out to a few of the restaurants in town and introduced me to a few of his connections during long-winded, whiskey fuel bar rants. All the while, I would have been just as happy in my bed with a book, the longing to be alone constantly tugged at the back of my mind, even when I was distracted with Nick.

"Is there anything that doesn't get under Arlo's skin?" I laughed. Cael thought about it without a valid response and then joined me laughing, "That's what I thought."

BAD HONEY

But our laughter died under the crushing weight of tension as we rounded the corner to find Arlo shoving Nick against a brick wall.

"Fuck you," he spat as Nick fought to push him back and mumbled something I couldn't hear. "Open your mouth again, I dare you." He cocked his hand back to throw what looked like a nasty punch.

"Hey!" Cael jogged toward them, shoving them apart and pinning Arlo against the opposite wall.

"Keep that shit to yourself," Arlo snarled.

"It's just banter between brothers. Grow up." Nick snapped back, straightening out his shirt and hair with his hands.

"What the fuck is going on?" Cael asked, towering over Nick as he fought to keep a hold on Arlo from the other side. I looked around as the tension grew between them, hoping someone else would arrive to help because Cael's grip was faltering, and Arlo looked like he might kill Nick.

"It's not the time," I shouted, trying to diffuse the situation. "You should be getting ready," I said to Cael first and then Arlo.

"You heard Blondie," Arlo mocked my show of authority. But when he looked at me, his dark eyes narrowing on my face, his gaze showed no animosity. We stayed locked like that for a moment longer before he shoved Cael off and stormed down the hallway away from us.

Nick straightened out his polo and brushed a hand through his hair before turning to look at me.

"He's just riled up. Our dad is here today to watch the game. Lots of pressure," he brushed a thumb across my cheek and gave me a wink.

Cael watched with a tight expression, his blue eyes flickering back and forth between us.

"Maybe I'll introduce you after," he smiled at me.

"To *the* Arthur King?" I laughed, "I would love that."

"I'll see you later. I need to go get the guys ready." He kissed my cheek. "Your ass looks amazing in those jeans," he yelled from the end of the hallway, causing heat to lick at my nape.

When Nick finally disappeared around the corner, I turned to Cael with my hands on my hips, "What?"

"Nothing, Peachy," he answered, but he wasn't telling me something, and I could see it all over his face, "get ready for a long game."

"What is your problem with Nick? You've been making a stink face when I talk about him all week." I shrugged. I just wanted the truth.

"My problem isn't with Nick," he looked at me with a sad expression, "it's how he makes Arlo feel."

I stopped, and despite feeling off balance like someone had set the world on its side, I understood Cael and Arlo's connection for a short moment. They had been drawn and stuck together like two magnets. They were each other's family in the darkest moments, and I had somehow shoved myself into that unknowingly and without hesitation.

The locker room was a dead zone; no one even spoke. They were so nervous about Boston State. It was eerie, leaving a harsh, cold feeling on my spine. I could see how tense everyone was going into this game; the silence was deafening as they flooded into the dugout. Usually echoing with hollering and excitement, they were quiet as mice and focused on the game ahead. I gripped tightly to my clipboard as they kept to themselves and avoided stepping on Arlo's toes, but not Cael's. He was there poking the bear as much as he could, and Arlo let him because underneath that hardened shell, he craved normalcy, and Cael was the only one brave enough to give it to him during such a high-stakes game.

The crowd could feel how restless everyone was and was rowdier than usual as the first pitch was thrown and the game started. The other team came to play, not budging an inch on the field as the guys struggled to keep up. Pitch after pitch, Arlo was distracted, his head in the stands and the ball slippery between his fingers.

I scanned the crowd, looking for *him*.

"You won't find him," Silas said from beside me. "He left during the third inning."

"Why?" I asked, meeting his steel blue eyes.

"Arthur King doesn't watch anything but perfectly pitched games. He was gone after Arlo let in three runs in the second."

I looked back to the pitcher mound, where Arlo rolled his shoulders back with his head hung low, whispering something to himself.

"That's cruel," I sighed, catching a dirty look from Nick that flashed gone just as quickly as it had surfaced.

"It's just them," Silas huffed, "they're a bunch of frosty dickheads who believe tough love is the only way to love."

"That has to be exhausting," I said, rolling the fabric of my ID tag between my fingers.

"It's been a boys' club since—" Silas stopped, swallowing the words he was about to say. "It's just all they know."

That stung me in a way that I didn't understand. I wasn't sad because I couldn't relate to what Arlo and Nick felt, that anger toward their father, toward each other. I was heartbroken for him that something he loved so deeply had turned into nothing more than a stain.

"So why bother coming?" I asked.

"Because Arthur King cannot leave a good thing alone."

Arlo's voice broke them apart as he stomped into the dugout, cradling his hand and dodging the players who pushed past him to warm up. He threw his glove against the wall and flexed his hand, barely able to uncurl his fingers as his face scrunched up into a ball.

"What did you do?" Silas' grey eyes raked over Arlo in concern, reaching out to him only for him to wave Silas off.

"It's just a strain," he argued, but I could tell Silas was worried, so I grabbed the medical bag, sliding it on the ground beside him. I knelt beside Arlo's legs, putting my palm up to him to show me his hand.

He wouldn't look at me, flinching away from my touch as I tried to look at his fingers. "They could be broken." I snapped my own at him and gave him my palm again. "Let me see."

Again nothing.

Fine, a different approach.

"Don't be an asshole," I said.

Arlo looked up at me with harsh, dark brown eyes.

"Of course you respond to that," I groaned, and Silas stifled a laugh from behind us.

We sat there for a long moment, locked in a stare that neither of us wanted to break because it would mean defeat. When he finally placed his hand in mine, I could feel his body relax, the muscles that had been pulled so tightly uncurled.

I ran my hand along his fingers, inspecting the soft reddish purple bruises starting to form along the base of his ring and middle finger.

"Were they sore before today?" I asked, looking up to catch him still staring at me.

His hands engulfed mine, soft in touch, yet bruises and calluses covered his golden skin from playing ball. Such a stark contrast to my small, scarred hands that seemed so pale cradling his.

He shook his head gently without words and blinked slowly as I attempted to fold the fingers in on themselves again. A sharp breath of air left his lips when it got too sore.

"I'm going to tape them," I said quietly, "do you think you can pitch one more inning?" I asked.

He only nodded again.

"The silent treatment is getting old," I said as I wrapped the fingers together. "I said what I meant because that friendship is more important than your stubborn, brutish stupidity. I don't know him as well as you do, but—" I swallow the urge to tell him I know Cael's struggles. "I don't take it back. You needed to hear it."

A tiny throaty growl left him at the mention of his treatment toward Cael.

"Done," I said. It would be difficult to pitch like that, but with what little information I knew of Arlo as a person and not a pitcher or a player. He would play even if I hadn't taped them. Even if I told him, he couldn't.

He stood, not bothering to wait until I let go of his hand to move away from me. I shouldn't have expected anything more from him, but he turned back to look at me briefly, his eyes lighter in color, "thank you."

His lips pressed into a thin line as his head bopped slightly, and he tapped his two sore fingers with a wince to his chest, his mask slipping only for a moment before returning to the hardened expression he typically carried.

"Good job," Silas leaned into my shoulder, "that might have been a smile."

I laughed. Even though it wasn't anything near a smile, the congratulations sentiment remained the same. Chipping away at Arlo's armor would take time, but I could see the hurt beneath, and for a split second, I thought maybe we shared a similar pain. Of course, I couldn't be sure, but I wanted to find out.

Ever since my panic attack in class, I couldn't go more than ten minutes without having him intrude on my thoughts. The ring, the urgency, the look in his eyes. Like he might actually be worried about me. But he hadn't spoken more than a sentence to me since then, and I was starting to think that maybe the fleeting moment of kindness was nothing more than that.

Fleeting.

After one more hard inning, they lost to Boston State. Everyone but Arlo shared their thoughts on the game, flooding from the stadium past the reporters to their cars.

"Do you want a ride to Turner Hall?" Dean asked, passing me as he made his way to his truck. I shook my head. "You sure? It's almost an hour back there."

Walking, yes, it would take Dean less than ten minutes to climb the hill to Dansby House.

"I'm okay, the fresh air is nice."

I had been in a car a total of four times since the accident, and every time, I could feel my heartbeat in my ears and throat. I only got in them when I had to. It was the most significant trigger I had next to thunderstorms. I waved him off and started my descent back to campus from the stadium, the sounds of honking horns and celebrating from Boston state visitors filling the air as I walked.

I kept close to the side of the road as cars raced past into town, and eventually, the traffic began to die down, leaving only the sound of the wind and my feet on the pavement echoing around me. I tugged my hair into a ponytail, stopping only to pull my hoodie from my bag and slip it over my shoulders to break the chill that had set in.

"What are you doing out here?" Arlo's voice broke over the rumbling of an engine as he pulled tight to the side of the road.

"Walking back to my dorm." I hoisted my bag back over my shoulder and started walking again as he swore under his breath something about being *'absolutely useless.'*

"Why didn't Mitchell drive you? It's dark out." He pulled his Mustang up beside me.

"He went out with Zoey," I lied.

"You and Zoey live together, do you not?" Arlo snapped, revving the engine. "He could have dropped you off first."

"If you want to *talk*, Arlo, we can do that, but I'm not going to yell at you over the sound of a car on the side of the road," I scowled at him.

"Then stop walking away from me," he argued back, his brows kissing together in frustration. "Get in the car."

"Absolutely not!" I laughed, adjusting my bag and continuing my walk. "I've walked home every day since I started at the stadium. I don't need a ride. Go home, Arlo," I waved goodbye to him.

"Just get in the car, Blondie," he groaned, shifting down a gear to continue his steady pace beside me as I walked.

I turned, and he slammed on the brakes. As I leaned into the window, the smell of clean car leather, sandalwood, and cinnamon filled my nose, "An hour ago, you wouldn't even look at me, and now you want to give me a ride home. No, fucking *no*."

His eyes trailed over my face, tracing the shape of my scar. *Stop*, I wanted to say, but I looked away from his eyes, ignoring how his stare made me feel.

"You don't have to read into someone being polite," he licked his bottom lip, and I felt my body urge toward what it might feel like. *Shit*.

"You aren't being polite," I swallowed tightly, "you're being manipulative."

"Dear—" he scrunched up his face, stopping himself from saying something off the cuff that he shouldn't. "You know what? Never mind." He revved his engine again, threatening to peel off with me still hanging onto the door.

"Have a good night, Arlo," I waved my fingers at him and watched as he tore from the side of the road back down the hill.

KING

I slammed the hood to the fastback and turned to Silas, "She's driving me insane," I said, flexing my sore fingers.

Silas looked at them closer, determining it was just a light sprain. I was pushing my body too hard without a second thought of how it might react under the pressure. Losing to Boston hurt. We could have easily won that game, but I couldn't get what Nick had said out of my thoughts. And pitching with my brother's illicit thoughts on Ella echoing through my consciousness had proved a lot harder than it should have been.

"I see how you look at her tight little ass," he whispered behind me.

I had wanted nothing more than to fucking punch him.

"You should see what it looks like when she's on all fours," he pushed.

Counting to ten wouldn't have helped. I needed his head through the concrete wall.

He licked his bottom lip, stepping in front of me and blocking my way to the locker room, "I'm going to take her to meet Dad. Make things serious."

That was the final straw, thinking of her in that house with them alone. That fucking mausoleum to our mother. I shuddered at the thought and snapped at Nicholas just as he wanted me to.

Losing my temper was the last thing the team needed, especially if it was wasted on him. Even if he deserved it. It was more frustrating that Ella was affecting me in such a way that it was affecting my gameplay, and even worse, she had no idea she was doing it.

"That was very animated of you, Arlo." Silas raised his brow, cleaning his hands-free of motorcycle grease as he stood behind his bike. "You're doing a bang-up job of making her hate you."

"Good," I spat, unsure if that was even what I wanted. "I don't know what I want, Silas. I—"

"Are you flustered?"

"No, yes!" I had no clue.

I ran my hands through my hair and leaned against the tool bench behind me in the garage. The heat seeped through the brick and into my skin, making me sweat like I had just run a few miles. My sleeveless sweatshirt hung loosely off my chest, only sticking to the wet patch between my shoulder blades.

"It's your fault," I said.

"How?" He scrunched his face at me and waited for a reasonable answer.

"You hired her, and now she's around all the time."

"You sound like a lovesick thirteen-year-old boy," Silas howled, spinning his hat backward on his head. "Why don't you just try to talk to her?"

The evident approach would require me to keep my foot out of my mouth for an extended period. "And say what, Si?" The laughter that bubbled from me was tight and nervous. "I'm sorry I'm an ass, please stop dating my brother, I think you're really *fucking* pretty."

He stared at me for a moment with a goofy smirk, the ends of his unkempt mustache curling in every direction. "Yes." After staring at me for nearly a minute, he said it like it was obvious. "Exactly that."

"This is why you're single." I threw a rag at him, trying to remain composed, but with every second that ticked by, all I could think about was how small her hand was in mine at the game. How every nerve fired off in my body like it was the fourth of July.

"I'm fine," Silas scoffed, and I knew he was. He never had trouble with women. One look from those pale blue eyes, and they were on their knees asking *him* to marry them. "You're the one that hasn't had a date since... Oh wow. Erin Normandy," he laughed, "that was junior year!"

"I've been distracted," I confessed. "Now, even more so."

BAD HONEY

"She told me," Silas' tone dropped an octave, "that you helped her the other day. She asked about the ring. I didn't know you still carried that thing around."

"Mom gave it to me." *Why wouldn't I?*

"I don't know. Most people like to put treasured trinkets away in safe places," Silas added.

"It's safe with me," I said.

Silas never really understood, which was why Cael and I had clicked so quickly. Losing a parent was hard. Losing your mother was like having the most critical parts of you taken away. My mother had been the only light in my life for so long that when she died, I had forgotten what that darkness looked like. I was only thirteen when she was killed. When the lights went out for good. I fell asleep to the lullaby of flashing red and blue lights across my bedroom wall for a long time. The memories of that night burned into the back of my mind. It felt surreal.

I could feel it in my pocket, the gold ring burning a hole in my skin.

"What did she say?"

I hadn't planned on helping her, but when I realized she was having a panic attack, I couldn't leave her to suffer. She barely knew her way around on a good day, and seeing her like that, confused and in pain. I followed her until I could catch her, not expecting or preparing for how she looked. Breathless and heartbroken, guilty and scared. It rattled me to the core. It reminded me of a time when I felt out of control. When the panic attacks had the reins on my life, nothing seemed to help sans the tiny metal ring in my pocket.

"Whatever you did impacted her enough to ask me what your problem is, so what is it?"

"She had a panic attack," I shrugged.

"Like a full-on bonafide one? Or a hissy fit kind?" Silas had never sounded less like a doctor.

"She ran out of Professor Tucker's class after he gave her condolences about—"

Silas sighed, waving his hand out. "You don't have to, I know."

"You know what?"

"It's not my business, Arlo, but it's good you told me about the panic attack. Maybe I can help her." Silas chewed on his lip. "You should ask her to be your date for the fundraiser."

"Nice deflection," I grumbled. "And no, I should not."

"You can solve the problem plaguing you," Silas said, "and maybe she'll be better for it. Nick isn't the most gentle of lovers."

"The description you're looking for is an *abusive dick*," I rolled my eyes.

Nick had a track record, and it wasn't a clean one. It was riddled with underage girls and explosive endings. But I couldn't just walk up to her and say that.

"So what? I crawl on my hands and knees to her to tell her that my brother is a fucking royal asshole? That makes me sound like a jealous idiot, which I'm not sure is much better."

Silas shrugged, "you are a jealous idiot."

"Do you have any reasonable advice for me?"

"Ease off your brother, he's dealing with the same shit you are, and maybe if he sees that you lost interest in Ella, he'll back off that."

"You think he's doing it because it's driving me insane?" I asked.

"It doesn't help that you flirted with her in front of a party of people while she was hanging off of him," Silas cocked an eyebrow at me.

"You know Nick," he continued, "everything he does is for attention in some form. He could be using her as a pawn to ruin your season."

"I know I barely know her, and I know that this sounds insane, but I hate that he put her in the middle of this, that I let him put her in the middle. I would rather him—" *Beat the shit out of me regularly.* "I'm not going to give him the satisfaction of ruining this season over some girl."

"If either of us believed she was just some girl, I'd bet on that horse, but Ar," he sighed.

"But she's not just some girl." I huffed, admitting the truth was more complicated than mulling over it in secret, even if it was just to Silas.

"She's moving in here next week," he said. "Her dorm funding got cut, and staff have rooms anyways, but it means Dean is gonna have to bunk with someone for a while."

"He's not going to like that," I said.

"Doesn't matter," Silas shrugged, "you're the captain, that's your problem."

"That room is disgusting. Dean is—"

"A man slut," he howled, walking toward me and clapping me on the shoulder. "Show her that she belongs here. It's a small start and won't attract Nick's attention."

"Yeah, alright, but I'm not asking her to the fundraiser!" I laughed.

Silas raised his hands, "technically, she gets a ticket anyways, but it was worth a shot to push the idea."

"Keep your ideas to yourself next time."

I marched through the house and down past my room to Dean's, preparing for the fight of my life. I knocked once and kicked the door open to find Cael shirtless, wrapped up in Dean, and reading a book.

"Mm," I nodded, "I need you back in Mitchell's room."

Dean sat up, knocking Cael from his lap, "No! He smells like sex and gym equipment all the time."

I cocked my head at him, and Cael's laugh turned into a strangled whimper. "Ella is moving in at the end of the week and needs her own room."

Dean closed his mouth, cutting off what he would say, and changed his mind, "Yeah, alright." He groaned, "But I'm only doing this for her! And it wouldn't kill you to ask nicely sometimes." His face scrunched as he sat in the bed, leaving Cael to fall back against it.

"Are you two a—" I waved my finger between them.

They had dated for a while the season before, but I always thought that Cael was too much of a wild child for Dean. "No," Cael answered first, "his bed is just comfier than mine."

"Sure," I laughed.

"Thank you, Tucker," I said, tapping my fingers to my heart, and even though it came out painfully slow, I had meant it. "And fuck, bleach this room before she gets here and open a fucking window."

Dean scoffed, returning the tap. "You were almost completely nice to me for a moment. Did that hurt you?"

"It gave me heartburn," I tossed him a laugh.

"Good."

"Hey," Cael called to me as I turned to leave the room. "What's the deal with you and Ella anyways?" His blue eyes looked so exhausted, highlighting the bags under his eyes.

"There's no deal," I leaned against the door frame.

Dean looked at Cael as they laughed, "That was as believable as Cael telling Coach that he's straight when everyone knows the pole swings both ways."

"Shut up, Tucker, you aren't straight either," Cael slapped him across the back of the head as he sat up straight in bed and tucked his legs up against his chest.

"Shut up," He furrowed his brows at Cael in confusion, who looked back at him like Dean was the dumbest human he had ever met before, sighing loudly.

"Do you like her?" He asked me.

"She's nice enough, I guess," I shrugged him off, hating every moment of the awkward conversation.

"So the pet name, tense dugout conversations, and following her home after games is just... what? Friendly banter?" Cael leaned to his side with a cocky look on his face.

"Banter," I corrected, "Not sure *'friends'* is something Blondie wants to be."

"Have you asked her?"

"Have *you*?" I slumped against the door further, planting my feet and narrowing my eyes at him. The tone of the conversation had shifted so drastically, "What are you digging for Cody? And how the hell do you know I followed her home *once*, by the way? It was one time."

"It was *four* times last week. You drive the loudest car on the team. It's hard to ignore the fastback in the Turner Hall parking lot," Cael eyed me, "I've been with her for three of those, and she told me about yesterday. I'm just surprised it took you so long to offer her a drive."

"Well, aren't you two, buddy, buddy?"

BAD HONEY

"Simmer down, chief," Cael rolled his eyes as he rocked onto his knees and pressed his chest to Dean's shoulder. "No need to shut down on me. All I'm saying is that she's a really nice person, and she—" he swallowed tightly, looking away from me and pressing his face to the back of Dean's head to hide his expression.

"Spit it out, Cael," I barked, frustrated, sweaty, and needing a shower.

"I've gotten attached. I like having her around, so if you're going to be an asshole... rethink that strategy. For *me*... please." Dean's hand crept around, linking into Cael's as support, and I realized that he wasn't being an ass. He was protecting her *from me*. No better than Nick.

"Ok, Kitten, I'm trying, aren't I, by standing here." I raised an eyebrow at him, "it's a start."

Cael nodded sheepishly in response, still acting very cagey about the situation. "Help Tucker move his shit, and if Mitchell is a dick about it, tell him the same thing I told you."

"For Ella."

For Ella.

MIELE

"That one is heavy," I pointed to the box that Cael lifted without so much as a grunt. He laughed and climbed up the stairs to the Nest. The house was enormous and looked like it was pulled from every old scary movie I had ever watched.

At least seven of the ten massive boxes I had brought from storage were books. I wouldn't apologize for that, but the look on Van and Cael's faces when they realized they had to carry them was priceless. I had given them a list. All the boxes were labeled. They just needed to grab the correct numbers, and the plan had worked out nicely.

"They're all heavy, Peachy," Cael stifled a groan and shifted the box as I followed behind him with an arm full of clothes. "You're in here," he pushed the door open to a room just off the kitchen. "The house is three levels. Most players are upstairs, and all the staff rooms are on the main floor, but you're the first staff member that's lived here in a long time."

"It's perfect," I said, wandering into the room. It was a little smaller than the double dorm I had been sharing with Zoey, but it had a bigger window. One that looked out to the dense tree line and hill that surrounded the Nest. There was a double bed and two bookshelves, all wiped down. "You'd never know a boy was living here," I laughed.

"God don't rub it in, Dean's been sulking all week having to move back in with Van." Cael set the box down on the floor. "Silas lives in the basement apartment, and Ar—" he stopped himself.

"Arlo?" I waited.

"Is in the room over from you."

"He doesn't like me very much," I laughed.

BAD HONEY

"Don't count him out just yet," Cael looked over at me. "He's a pit bull."

"Vicious?"

"Nah," Cael shook his head, "But the assumption helps the explanation. He acts tough, really mean, snarly, and shit, but that's not him, not really. He's a big baby with a big heart."

"Arlo King, the big baby? Can I quote you on that?" I smiled.

"It would be worth the beatdown I'd receive to see you call him that," Cael whistled, "he needs a good kick to his ego every once in a while."

"So, who else is on this floor then?" I asked, trying to sway my thoughts from Arlo as his brown eyes crept into the back of my mind, burning bright through the darkness.

"No one, it's just Arlo."

"There's only two staff bunks in the entire house? It's massive." I cocked an eyebrow at him and slumped down onto the bed, bringing the clothes down with me. "There must be at least ten rooms."

He swallowed tightly and rolled his eyes at me.

"There's one more room off the main living room, but we use it as storage because the guys think it's haunted." Cael tugged at the collar of his lavender hoodie and pulled it over his shoulders, chucking it on the bed next to me. Underneath was the shabbiest-looking hornet's t-shirt held together by hopes and dreams.

"Haunted? Like ghosts haunted?"

"Jensen says during his rookie season, he saw a woman in there, and Dean swears that things move around on their own, but he just can never find anything. It's a mess in there, and they're idiots." A tight chuckle fell from him. "Is that a Hornet's calendar?" He gasped, changing the subject when he noticed it lying across the stack of boxes behind the door. "Oh my god!"

"You tell anyone I have that, I'll kill you."

"Oh, I'm telling everyone!" He howled and clutched his chest. "Who's your favorite?" He looked at me but shook his head and hands, "No, you know what, don't tell me, I'm fragile. I can't know if I lost to January again."

Cael was Mr. June, a nearly full frontal of him completely naked with nothing but a bat covering his junk. I gave him a soft smile, not wanting to tell him that his dad was my favorite or perhaps not wanting to deal with the fallout that it would cause.

"Yours is absolutely my favorite, very subtle."

"I knew it," he said proudly before inhaling deeply, preparing himself to say something. He moved toward the hallway, patting the door frame with his hand. The rings on his fingers clinked together as he looked back at me. "Peachy," he said, licking his bottom lip.

"Yes?"

"Are you ever gonna tell me why you're so sad all the time?" He studied my expression with bold blue eyes and waited in the silence that threatened to swallow me whole.

"Who says I'm sad?" I tried to joke, but the corners of my upturned lip shook with uncertainty.

"You don't have to say it," he turned back, stepping into the room again. "My momma used to say this thing about how misery loved company, and I never really understood that saying 'cause if you're miserable, why would you want company?" He flipped the hat he was wearing low on his forehead around.

"Cael, that's not—" he stopped me from finishing.

"I know," his Texan accent slipped the more nervous he became. "I get it now," his shoulders buckled lightly, "misery finds misery. I know you're sad all the time because I am too, and I just," he stopped again.

"Wanna know why?" I finished for him.

"Please," his brows lifted and knotted together as his voice dropped into whinny territory.

"You can't tell anyone."

"It's your story to share, Peach," he tapped his fingers to his chest.

"Why do you guys do that?" I asked and reached out to point at him.

"It's our version of a pinky promise," he smiled, looking down at his fingers as he crossed the room and sat at my feet. "Means, yes, no, maybe. I'll be there, I am here, I love you."

"So it can mean anything?" I asked, kicking his sneaker with mine as he rested his lanky arm over my bed.

"It means..." He paused and tilted his chin upward to find the right words, "Whatever is important at that moment. It's a promise to keep your story between us right now."

I thought about it for a long moment, the implications of telling him running through my mind before I finally decided that he had earned the right to know. He had shown me kindness and wasn't asking because he was curious about the story. He asked because he wanted to know how he could help.

"I got high on painkillers and killed my entire family."

Cael looked up at me, and all the color drained from his face. "Jesus Christ, Ella, that—" he said, caught off guard.

"It's not sadness, Cael, it's guilt." I sighed. "I—"

"Hey," he clicked his teeth together to get me to look at him again, "keep going."

"I was on painkillers for my knee at first, and then..."

"To be numb?" He nodded, clearly understanding the feeling well.

"We were going to a foundation event for my brother Ethan, and his car wouldn't start, so we took mine, and I insisted on driving, knowing I shouldn't have. My parents were in the back seat when the semi hit us, and I—" I stumbled through the story, "when I woke up, they were gone, and Ethan—" I swallowed tightly, the sound of shattering glass exploding in my ear, and suddenly I was right back there.

Tied down by my seat belt, it cut into my shoulder and chest like a wire. Blood dripped down my face, and I could feel the glass digging into my cheek and nose. I could hear my brother fighting to breathe in the passenger seat, barely about to turn my head, sobs wracking my body as I caught sight of his leg. The rain fell in sheets, crashing through the shattered windshield and creating a slick river of blood and dirt. Ethan's leg was crushed between the seat and the crumpled dash of my car. Bubbles of blood cascaded out over his lips, and his brown eyes were so dark.

"Peachy?"

I couldn't breathe.

Sliding to the floor, my vision cleared, and the room came into focus. My hands claw at my throat, just trying to breathe without an ounce of luck as Cael grasped my face, trying to bring me back to reality.

"It's a panic attack," he mumbled against my hair, "breathe with me," he whispered. "Easy."

A fire burned inside my chest, begging me to open my mouth and inhale, but my jaw was locked shut, and no matter how hard I tried, I couldn't get enough air through my nose. I was going to suffocate, trapped in my mind, dying beside my brother over and over again.

It felt like an eternity had passed without air when loud footsteps echoed around my head. It made me dizzy.

"What the hell?" Arlo's voice broke through the fog as he stormed into the bedroom and knelt before us on the floor, his eyes flickering back and forth. "What happened?"

"She's having a panic attack."

Everything they said felt so far away as their voice strung together, circling my consciousness as I fought to control what breathing I could. Cael's fingers rubbed methodical circles against my neck as Arlo struggled to pull something from his pocket.

The rain felt real, pouring down inside my memories and biting into my numb flesh, chewing and gnawing at me. It was a sick reminder that I was still alive.

He pried open my fingers, pressing the cool metal into the palm of my hand, and closed my fingers back around it gently. "Come on, breathe." He fell back on his heels, staring at the wall behind my head as I focused on how the ring felt against my skin. "Two steps at a time, come back to me."

I was okay.

I was alive.

I was not trapped.

I gasped for air, filling my lungs with it as I slowly returned to my body. Every muscle under my skin felt tense and exhausted from clenching. It had felt so real, and for so long, nothing had felt that horrible. I lifted my teary gaze from the floor to face Arlo. His eyes flickered with relief for a slow moment, making the world around me feel less alone, but as soon as it appeared, it was gone again.

BAD HONEY

"Where's your fight, Blondie?" His lip curled back over his teeth, "all bark and no bite."

I knew what he was doing, but I hated him for it because it was working. I could feel myself getting angry.

And if I was angry, I wasn't drowning.

I rolled the ring from my palm, holding it out to him.

"Keep it."

Out of the corner of my eye, I could see Cael's blue eyes drift down and back up in surprise at Arlo's gift.

"Helps you more anyways." He added. "Don't lose it."

His eyes watched me for another long moment, his jaw ticking tightly like he might want to say more, but he didn't. His fingers just flexed around his thighs as he fought to stay quiet.

I nodded, curling my fingers back around the metal over and over. Arlo pushed to his feet and left my new room. Cael sat frozen beside me, his hand resting gently against my neck. His fingers pulsed over the side of my throat.

"You alright, Peach? Your heart is beating real fast."

"Yeah, I'm okay," I swallowed as he pulled me closer to his chest. "I'm sorry."

"Don't be. It was scary, was all. I'm sorry, I shouldn't have asked."

"It feels good, Cael," I nudged my body into him, "it is scary and too real, but it feels good that you know."

"Are they—" He licked his bottom lip. "Always that violent?"

"Did I hurt you?" I pulled away, looking over him to make sure that I hadn't hit him or scratched him by accident.

"No," he shook his head, "no," he repeated, flashing a sympathetic smile. "It sounded like you couldn't breathe!"

"It always feels like I can't," I admit. "We were hit because I took a left thinking we could clear the highway before the semi, but my timing was off because of the rain and the—" I cocked my head to the side. "The impact alone killed my parents. Ethan was alive, but I couldn't do anything because I was trapped by my seatbelt."

I pulled my shirt collar over my shoulder to expose the nasty scar the fabric had left on my skin. Cael's eyes dropped to it, and then they looked back at my face, "And that?"

"Glass from the windshield," I looked away but could feel his eyes on me. "It was embedded. I was lucky to keep my sight."

"That's why you don't drive," he said gently.

"That's why." Being in a car was enough for me. Even the thought of getting behind the wheel made my fingers clench around the ring.

"How did you deal with your addiction?" He asked, and I knew the question was coming. He had been looking for comfort, for answers about how I had gotten to the place I was at now from where I was.

"Recovery sucked, three weeks in the hospital. Then Zo and Van came down, detox and therapy." I said.

"That's where he went," Cael nodded, "Mitchell told us he was going to visit Zoey's family."

"They're the only family I have left. Ethan died in the ambulance, and I woke up completely alone and in more pain than I could even explain to you." I nervously knotted my fingers together.

"You have me," his eyes softened, and he rapped two knuckles against my chest. "I can't promise to always be the most stable, but I can always be here for you when you're not either."

"Thank you, Cael."

"Now we're even," he winked as he shifted out from underneath me, "come on," he held out a hand, helping me up from the ground. "Let's get the rest of these boxes into the house. Stop for dinner, and then you can come to my meeting with me."

That was the brightest idea he had yet.

"Do you—" I stopped as he moved toward the door, rolling the ring between my fingers. "Know what this is about?"

"Not my story to tell, unfortunately," Cael clicked his tongue against his teeth. "You'll have to befriend the pit bull to find that out."

"Infuriating," I huffed but understood. "I'm not sure I wanna risk my fingers to feed that dog yet." I laughed.

Cael's unwillingness to tell me Arlo's secrets only meant I could truly trust him with mine, and that was more important than knowing who the ring belonged to and why Arlo was so willing to hand it over to me.

KING

Cael tied his shoes beside me on the bench. He had been stupidly quiet since the incident at the Nest, and despite me asking more than once, he wouldn't tell me what had triggered it in her. The commotion from her room as I entered the house through the back door was enough to have my heart racing but when I saw how small she looked, curled up on the floor, Cael completely unable to help her?

I panicked.

I should have left them to handle it. Cael would have pulled her out of it eventually, and then I wouldn't be caught in the middle of them, sick to death with feelings I didn't fucking ask to catch. Whatever happened to her to make her so cagey and scared must have been bad…

I rubbed my chest as the stinging feeling returned, along with the thoughts of Ella. Giving her my mother's wedding ring may have been a mistake, but the idea that it brought her back to the ground, steading her anxiety and helping her focus, brought me comfort. Especially in those moments that Cael *and myself* couldn't be around.

"I can't believe you woke me up two hours before practice just to practice more. You fucking sadist," he groaned in a husky, sleepy voice.

"You missed three last week. If you think being a liability will win your place at shortstop back, you're mistaken, Kitten."

"I'm going to piss in your shoes when you're not looking."

"Stop flirting with me, Cody," I nudged him with my shoulder as Silas paraded into the room in his shorts and t-shirt. He had dark sunglasses on and Hornet's baseball cap that covered his face.

"Hah!" Cael howled, "you're in trouble too?"

"Apparently," Silas chucked a shoe in my direction as he changed into his sneakers. "For what I don't know!"

"Fucking dramatic, the both of you." I pushed from my locker and grabbed Cael by the hood of his sweatshirt, "go warm up."

I pulled a sleeveless hoodie over my chest and brushed my hair beneath a hat before shooing Silas down the tunnel after Cael. The stadium was empty except for a few caretakers, and it was always nice to go out onto the field when everything was quiet. Cael was halfway around the outfield when we stepped out into the blaring sun shoulder to shoulder.

Silas looked at Cael, pushing himself forward into a second lap, "I know you aren't punishing him."

"He punishes himself enough," I stretch out my arms and roll my neck from side to side.

"So why then did you drag me out here?"

I looked up to the stands to find Ella's nose in a book and her ears covered with headphones. It wasn't unusual to see her like that. She always had one; if she wasn't working, she always wore her headphones.

"Why is she here?"

"She came in early to work with Todd on his knee," Silas answered checking his watch, "she has a meeting with Van in an hour."

"So she just lurks around?" I licked my teeth in frustration.

"The definition you are looking for in your thick skull is that she *works*. What the hell is up your ass?" Silas scoffed.

"He's freaked out. She had another one," Cael jogged to home plate where we stood, locked in a stare with me, unable to get the words out for Silas. But like the jerk he was, Cael had read my mind.

"Another panic attack. They're bad. I've never seen them like that." He looked up to the stands to check she wasn't paying attention to us.

"You alright?" I asked, noticing how his hands tangled together at the hem of his shirt.

"Yeah, it was just scary." Something like that in the past would be enough to trigger him. When his mom got sick, she had outbursts, violent ones, and usually, Cael was the only one around to help her when they happened. "But that's it isn't, that's why we're here... away from the Nest."

BAD HONEY

"Prying ears," Silas added, crossing his arms over his chest.

"I didn't do anything wrong helping her, and she's not my type, Arlo, you don't have to get jealous-"

"You know me better than that," I snapped at Cael, "this isn't about jealousy." *A small fraction of it might have been, but only because I wanted to be there for her and couldn't.* "Did she tell you anything? Why?"

A look passed between Silas and Cael, one that I hated, the one that meant I was being left out. "Arlo," Cael licked his bottom lip nervously, "it's—"

"Not your story," I groaned. "I get that, but I just wanna help. And why the hell do you know?" I chucked a handful of my rage in Silas' direction, the frustration rolling off my tongue.

"Cause I read the fucking news," he rolled his eyes.

"Grandpa," laughter erupted from Cael, only for the sound to die when he saw how serious I was. "You can't force her to tell you what's going on. She barely knows you."

"You're so accustomed to everyone meeting you wherever *you* are. Maybe this time you need to *meet her*," Silas suggested.

"Meet her?" I rolled my eyes.

"Mentally, emotionally. Walk out and meet her where she is, Arlo. Maybe she's not ready to come to you. It wouldn't hurt for you to try."

"And stop fucking following her home," Cael added.

"That might be helpful," Silas shook his head as an exasperated breath fell from his lips.

"You're a rat," I growled at the skinny little shit.

"You know who I'm not scared of? You!" He raised his hands and shimmied backward, mocking me.

"It's a wonder you're even alive today, Cael, with how badly I want to kill you regularly. I'm sure there are at least ten more people whose urges are worse than mine."

I swallow my pride and steady my shoulders, "I followed her home because she was walking alone in the dark."

"She doesn't drive," Cael shrugged, letting a small piece of information drop. "I don't mind walking her home. It feels nice after the games, and now I don't have to walk back to the Nest from Turner Hall after."

Silas nodded, quietly taking in our conversation.

I wanted to ask why she didn't drive, but I had a feeling neither would tell me. I rubbed out the tension in my neck with heavy pressure from my fingers, trying unsuccessfully to escape the images of Ella.

"She's coming with me to some meetings," Cael blurted out.

"Good," Silas said, "I'll see if Riona has any time to see her."

"The only Cody family member not rotten to the core," I mocked Cael. Riona was Coach's older sister and the team therapist. A damn good one too.

"Low blow," Cael rolled his eyes.

"I can go lower if you want," I motioned to his knees with laughter, finally feeling lighter, but anxious thoughts ate away at me. "So how do I-"

"He's like a goddamn lost puppy," Cael cackled, and I shoved him, watching him fall back against the pitch. Dust from the sand clouded around him as he rolled to his knees. Pushing up on them, he rubbed the sand from his bleach-blonde buzz cut and smiled at me. "Have you ever flirted with a girl romantically?"

I cocked an eyebrow at him, "No one is going to help you when I duct tape you to the back stopper. Tread carefully."

"It was an honest question. You can't even talk about flirting with her without turning three shades of red." He shook his head.

"Yes!"

Obviously, I had a string of girls. It quickly became apparent that being the Captain of the Hornets got me pretty much anything I wanted whenever I wanted it.

"No, I've seen you flirt," Silas interjects, wiggling a glove onto his hand and tossing one to Cael. "It usually consists of you being a fucking asshole." He threw the ball at me, the sound clapping loudly from impact.

Cael jogged out backward, holding out his mitt to me. "He's not wrong, your flirting style is, well... it's just you being rude."

"It works!" I threw the ball as hard as I could, the tension in my fingers screaming at me.

BAD HONEY

"It works on me. When am I going to get that kiss?" Cael joked, catching the ball in his glove with a groan.

"Never, Cody. Fuck off."

"It's not going to work on her. She sees right through my shit." Cael whipped the ball to Silas and pressed the glove to his chest. "And I'm good at flirting. It's proven so."

"It's true," Silas scowled at me and looked over at Cael, "but undeniably gross because he uses it like a supervillain power. He's damn good at convincing people he's worth their time. The kid has slept with half the Longhorn's baseball team."

"It's a talent," Cael boasted, long arms thrown into the air and a cocky smile on his face.

"It can't be that hard. Nick has her attention." I inhaled slowly, annoyed that he was even a variable.

"Nick is prince charming when it comes to women," Silas laughed.

"You're a street rat in comparison."

"I'm going to pretend you didn't just reference *Aladdin*."

"Let the genie out of the bottle, baby!" Cael yelled from the left infield.

"I regret every decision in my life that led me to this moment," I groaned, taking the ball hard to the glove.

"We know you can be charming," Silas shrugged, "the problem is you have to out-charm Nick."

The game that night went better than the last two we had played. Cael was back home in his spot over my right shoulder, and my fingers were less sore. We won nine to four, fighting back through the last inning to score five runs.

I did my best to give Ella her space, but the smell of her fruity shampoo engulfed me every time I stepped into the dugout. She barely looked at me, but my heart skipped a beat when she turned to talk to

Silas. The Hornet's polo she wore was slightly unbuttoned, and there, resting against another mean scar that cut deep into her olive skin, was the ring around a chain. *My ring.*

It was a tiny victory. It didn't even bother me as Nick wrapped her up from behind and pressed his lips to her neck. I had won, just for a moment. She giggled at whatever he said and turned so he could kiss her cheek.

"Do you ever wanna choke on your own vomit?" Cael appeared next to me, sticking his finger down his throat and making a horrible retching sound.

"Don't sneak up on people," I shoved him against the wall and turned away from the public makeout session about to happen.

"Sorry, I forgot you're getting old and jumpy," Cael bounced beside me as I wandered out to the parking lot.

"Do you want a ride?" I asked him, fishing the keys from my pocket.

"Nah," he leaned against the fastback, "I'm waiting for El."

I hated it. "Alright, you and Mitchell are on dinner tonight, don't fuck around. Come straight to the Nest."

"Yes, Dad." Cael saluted.

Ella walked out through the player's entrance with Nick in tow behind her, his fingers linked into hers lazily. She waved at Cael, saying bye to Nick, only for him to pull her back and ask her something. She nodded nervously, shrugging her shoulders before he kissed her again and let her go.

"Bring her with you," I snapped.

"She lives with us," Cael looked at me like I had three heads.

"Yeah, Cael, don't let Nick take her home."

"Oh," he laughed, "aye, aye!" He pounded his chest with two fingers before jogging over to where Ella stood waiting for him. Chucking his arm around her shoulder and pushing Nick back playfully. My brother's face dropped into a mean scowl as Cael dragged Ella off toward the Nest, clearly pissed off to be interrupted.

Nick walked toward where I watched them all from the side of my car. "You're letting your foot fall out of step when you pitch." He barked at me as he passed. "Tighten it up, or I will start subbing you out in the fourth for Reyes."

Nicholas King had a thousand tiny bugs under his skin and was showing just how uncomfortable he was with being undermined by Cael Cody.

"Yeah, alright," I laughed, loving the idea of him squirming all the way home. "Hey, Nick," I called out to him.

"What?" He snapped back at me.

"It's Mom's birthday next week," I said, trying to steady my shaking knee.

"I'm picking Lucas and Sawyer up to meet at Dad's that morning." He dismissed me.

"They're coming?" I must have sounded shocked because Nick finally looked at me.

"Of course they are."

He says as if they had come the year before or the one before that. Like I'm the idiot who missed out on something and not that they had abandoned us as fast as they could.

"Okay," I nodded, "I'll get them some tickets for the game that day."

"Don't bother, I already did."

These were the moments that I hated, the tiny shreds of resentment that hung between Nick and me and made our relationship so hard and strained. He talked to me like Dad would have spoken to us when we were kids.

I watched him climb into his car and leave the parking lot before I could say what I wanted. I wish he'd see I'm trying to be on his team. I hated the back and forth, the abuse, and the fighting. He should have been fighting Dad, not me.

MIELE

"Hey, come back," Nick tugged on my arm and drew me in close. "Would you want to go to the fundraiser with me?" He asked. "Like my date?"

I had already been given a ticket because I was a staff member, but I nodded anyway, "Of course."

"Perfect," he smiled at me, a small piece of his brown hair falling in his face as he leaned in for another kiss.

"Peachy!" Cael's arm flew around me, and he poked two sharp fingers into Nick's chest to separate the two of us. He smelled sweat, lavender, and gummy bears as he wiggled closer to me. He pressed his forehead against my temple, his scratchy blonde hair brushing against my face, and whispered, "We better start walking. I have to cook dinner tonight with Van, and if we don't hurry, he will make macaroni and hotdogs again."

He turned his head toward my ear, Nick's eyes darkening as his lips brushed against my ear. Cael was actively trying to piss him off, and I couldn't help but laugh a little at the interaction.

"*Please*, he let it cook too long last time, and it turned into oatmeal." He whispered, Nick unable to hear that what he said wasn't flirtatious but disgusting.

"Ew," a soft groan escaped my lips, "yah, alright." I patted his chest with the flat of my hand.

"Call me," I leaned over, brushing my fingers against Nick as he stared Cael up and down with an angry expression for interrupting us.

"I can drive you," he suggested.

"I got her. Don't worry, princess." Cael cut me off before I could answer politely.

His fingers flexed at his side, but he nodded, leaving us on the sidewalk. "You are a shit disturber," I mumbled as Nick wandered out of earshot.

"I'm serious. If we don't get home—"

"Yeah, yeah," I laughed, wrapping my hand around his waist. I tangled my fingers into his oversized shirt and let him shield me from the chill falling over the campus.

The trees grew taller the further we walked from the stadium, up against the side of the winding road that led to the Dansby House in all its glory. A soft glow came from it, and I could hear all the players softly echoing through the forest as they celebrated the hard win. Cael seemed to feel it, too. The overwhelming excitement filled his chest and made him stand a little taller. He had worked hard to stay clean this week, to take his spot back, and to prove to his dad and Arlo that he was serious about everything. He was trying, and to me, that's all that mattered.

Cael had been spending more time with Dean, and I wasn't sure if it was because I had been spending more time with Nick or because he was a safety blanket, but he seemed happy, happier than usual.

"So you and Tucker..." I whistled into the night.

"Old news, Peachy," he cooed, shifting his bag on his shoulder. "It's happened a couple of times. It's nothing serious."

"Just comfortable."

Cael nodded, "exactly."

I tucked my hands into the pockets of my jeans to keep my fingers warm, my heart racing from the smell of the rain in the air. Like he could sense it, Cael turned, "Up you go," he instructed, hoisting me onto his back for a ride.

His legs were twice as long as mine, and before long, we were nearly home.

"Does he know?" After about twenty minutes of comfortable silence, Cael asked with the Nest practically in view. "Nick. About everything."

"If he does, he's never said anything about it; why?"

"I don't know, I just..." he held back.

He stopped and let me slide down to the path, waiting until both my feet were on the ground to shift and adjust his shirt.

"You have no tact for conversation when you have to say something you think might hurt my feelings, Cael. Spit it out." I shoved his chest as he held out the iron gate that opened up to the back path to the house.

"Don't you wanna be with someone that understands that pain, instead of hiding from them to like... I don't know," he shrugged, locking the gate behind us, "please them."

"You think that's what it's like with Nick?" I asked, "Doing things to please him?"

"It looks like it most of the time."

"It's easy," I said, walking up the back steps of the Nest to the massive sheltered wooden porch that surrounded the back. "Comfortable," I looked at him with both eyebrows raised.

"Easy doesn't make it right," Cael shrugged. "Listen, Peach, I am in no position to give people advice. I'm a fucking mess."

"An honest mess," I corrected, and his lips curled into a tight smirk.

"You're too good to me," he rubbed a hand across his neck, "Nick is never going to be the person you need. He'll be who you want and crave sometimes but never what you need."

"Might as well tell me what I need while you're at it, Cael," I laughed, following him through the back door.

"You can start with someone you don't need to cover up for," he said, flicking a piece of blonde curl away from my face. I had been wearing more makeup to dull the red scar that split my features in two. It was easier than having him stare. Which Nick did, and often.

"Girls wear makeup," I tossed my bag on the chair as Cael tugged open the bottom of the freezer and grabbed a tub of ice cream from within. He slid it across the marble countertop toward me and fished two spoons out so we could eat. "Aren't you supposed to be making dinner?"

"Dessert first, Peachy, always."

"Focus," I snapped my fingers.

"You know what you need," he said, so sure of himself.

BAD HONEY

And I hated conceding to the shithead, but something deep down told me he was right. I was using Nick as a buffer. An excuse to keep myself hidden from the world. I wouldn't have to tell if he didn't ask, which he never did. Maybe that's just what I needed right now, and that was okay, at least for now.

"And the both of us know that you aren't going to find it barking up Nicholas King's tree."

"Who's barking?" Zoey's voice appeared from the kitchen archway as she and Van wandered inside. "Hi, babe," she scrunched her nose up at me. "Good game today." She swiped the spoon from Cael's hand and sat beside me on a stool to eat ice cream.

"Thank you," he nudged his body against hers as Van went digging through the cabinets, "Do not," he barked as Van shook the box of macaroni.

"What then?" Van threw the box down and pouted with his chin on Zoey's shoulder. She reached over and gave him a scoop of ice cream.

A massive thunder boom rumbled through the house, causing my entire body to tense as the lightning crashed moments later. "That storm is gonna be nasty," Dean wandered into the kitchen mouth first, brains second, and Cael shot him a *'shut the fuck up'* look.

Thunder rolled through the walls again, and all I could do was take calculated, long, deep breaths that did nothing to quell the sharp pain building in my chest.

"I'm going to go shower," I said, reaching out with a spoon of ice cream for Cael. He trapped the metal between his lips, and the lightning outside reflected at me from the kitchen window in his eyes. I let go of the spoon and turned my tail to get my things from my room, taking my bag.

I stopped in my door frame, not far from the kitchen. I heard Cael ask Zoey a series of questions that were met with mumbled responses and then, finally, silence as I closed my door. Instead of showering, I tugged a clean sweater from my closet, pulled it over my head, and moved straight to my bed. The comfort I craved was in the form of a weighted blanket and a good book. The rain started shortly after I tugged the comforter to my chin and buried my face in my pillow.

I forgot how scary the trigger point was between perfectly fine and falling apart.

Laughter echoed from the kitchen as the anticipation of my meltdown built below the hollowed-out space beneath my ribcage. It burned so brightly it stung at my heart and turned my blood to ice. I wanted to get up, move back to the kitchen, and feel loved and wanted, surrounded by friends, but it was a sentiment my foolish heart did not deserve.

The door to my room eventually creaked open, and I could tell just from the soft steps that Zoey had come to check on me.

"Hey, grumpy," she cooed, crawling across the bed and wrapping her arms around my middle. "If you wanted to cuddle, you could have just asked. The thunderstorm is a bit much."

I laughed against my pillow and snuggled down into her arms.

"I missed you, is all," I responded eventually, "it's weird not being roommates."

"It is weird," she said, "but now I get a two for one. I see you and Van all the time."

Thunder rolled loudly outside, scaring me and causing all my muscles to seize up against her hug.

"It'll pass," she sighed, "they all do. Storms are temporary."

"Unfortunately, the nightmares are not," I groaned and tightly shut my eyes.

Thunder boomed again, and I curled my knees to my stomach, wrapping my arms around my body. I pulled on the chain around my neck, popping the ring free from my sweater, and rolled it between my fingers. I had put it on the necklace to keep myself from losing it after having it in my pocket for a few days. I hated to admit how much it helped, but as I brushed my fingers back and forth over the metal, I felt my heart rate slow back down.

"One day," Zoey whispered over the rumble, "the nightmares will turn to nothing but memories, and you'll be glad they weren't."

"On days like today, it feels selfish to miss him."

I felt her squeeze a little tighter. Zoey never disagreed with me. She missed him too, and I know being there for me was exhausting. She hadn't decided to do so lightly. Our families had been so close growing up that her brothers were my brothers and vice versa. She had always been slightly jealous that I had a twin until she realized I wore his hand-me-downs as he grew out of them. Then, suddenly, she was over the idea. I sigh and grip her closer to my back and our friendship.

I'm so thankful for her.

Thankful that she was strong enough to heal and escape from her grief. It'd helped that she had Van. He never let her slip away, even when the storm became too much.

"I'm alright. You should go eat." I tapped the back of her hand. "I'm just going to go to sleep."

"Are you sure I don't mind staying here in the cave? Maybe if we wait long enough, Van will bust through the door like one of the boys from your books and bring us pizza." She teased.

"He could pull it off," I quietly laughed. "I'll gift him a billowing white tunic for Christmas."

"Like the one Mr. Darcy wears?" Zoey popped up and rested her chin on my shoulder.

I hummed and patted her head. Her addiction to period dramas was oddly adorable.

"Go eat. Thank you for coming to check on me."

It helped. I felt more at ease and possibly could fall asleep if I tried hard enough when she left. Zoey kissed my cheek and slipped from the bed, dipping from the room. When the thunder rumbled again, it rattled against the glass, reminding me how fragile it could be. Lightning shattered through my flimsy resolve, echoing off my bedroom walls.

The wind wailed at me from beyond the windows, begging me to open them wide and let the rain flood my room.

A long while passed, and the storm did not relent, but I could not seem to force myself from the safe confines of my bed, no matter how hard I tried. I just wished I could fall asleep.

"Ella?" a voice came from behind me that was muffled by the sound of rain relentlessly hitting the window.

Van, perhaps. Zoey sent him in as reinforcements so she didn't overwhelm me. Footsteps rolled over the old wooden floors in rhythmic creaks, followed by something being set on my set table.

"You should eat."

It was Arlo.

I unfurled my legs, rolling away from the wall to look at him over my blankets. "Are you okay?"

"Yeah," I mumbled, "just don't like storms. Thank you."

I nod toward the small plate of food.

He paused momentarily, a furrow of frustration and maybe concern forming as stress lines on his forehead. His tongue darted over his bottom lip, "where are your headphones?"

I scrunched my face together as another roar came from the clouds above, doing my best to keep my control.

"You wear them around the stadium. Where are they?" He asked, but I was still confused. Everything happening was so out of character. His brown eyes searched around my room.

"Blondie," he snapped, but it wasn't meant to be angry; he was just trying to get me to listen. Igniting the fire, I seemed to lose when the panic attacks started.

"My bag," I whispered, forcing my eyes shut just after the room erupted in light and cast a thousand beautiful, harsh lines across his hardened jaw.

I heard him rustle around momentarily before the bed dipped, and he sat before me. "Here," he held them up, using one hand to tuck my hair behind my ears before he slipped them down and held them tight. "Turn on your music." He whispered, sliding from the bed only when he was sure I was listening to his instructions. He scooped a blanket from the end of my bed as I fumbled to open my phone with numb fingers.

His muscles flexed tightly as he pushed to his toes and wrapped one end of the heavy blanket around the curtain rod. That time, when the lightning came, it was dull, muted, and distant, and I had not heard the thunder that came before. Thunderstorm proof. He paused, looking over my bookshelf, his eyes scanning the shelves of romance novels I had collected over the years before pulling one out with his finger and tucking it under his arm. He gave me a weak smile, the darkness hiding which one he had chosen as he wandered back in my direction. Grabbing my pizza from the table beside my bed, he slid it onto my lap,

BAD HONEY

pointing at it sternly before he disappeared, closing the door behind him.

MIELE

Arlo stood on the pitcher's mound, his hand methodically taping the ball. He and Jensen had developed some sort of lazy man's morse code, and it was always a treat to watch them work together to stump batters. He dug the toe of his black cleat into the clay and looked back over his shoulder to ensure that Cael was primed for the runner trying to steal third. Van clicked at Todd in the outfield, the two in sync with their bodies sunk low, ready for anything, as Arlo let the ball rotate from his fingers.

That was my favorite part of the game. The entire team in unison.

Faster than I could blink, the sweet sound of Jensen's glove slapping closed rang through the air, and the crowd erupted over the sound of the ump calling them out. My eyes stayed trained on where Arlo stood, his chest pumping rapidly at first, but then I watched as he slowed it down to match his stride and thought before throwing the pitch.

But the game wasn't finished. They had two more hard innings to play, and the opposing team's pitcher had been shutting them down all night. The score was still frozen at zero for both teams. They needed a run, just one to offset the pitcher's confidence. If they could rattle him, they could rattle the entire infield.

My heart was racing beneath my shirt as they took to their batting order, one after another, discussing how to slip through with even a few soft grounders. They would have a fighting chance if they could push a double to get someone on base.

Arlo swung the bat in a full circle, stretching out the sore muscles he undoubtedly suffered from after pitching another complete game. Nick never subbed him out, and whether or not that was because Arlo was just that good or because Nick wanted to push him until he hurt himself, I wasn't sure, but I didn't like it.

"Is your shoulder okay?" I leaned forward over the cushioned bar of the dugout to look at him warming up. "Arlo," I snapped to get his attention as he purposely ignored me.

"It's fine, Blondie," a guttural groan dripped from his lips as he rotated the shoulder back and forward.

"It looks sore," I added, forcing him to look at me. There were still aspects of my position that I disagreed with. The unspoken rule that the player decided when they've had enough was one of them.

"I said it's fine," he stared at me until the ump called for him. His dark eyes fixated not on my face but on the chain that peaked out from beneath my uniform.

"He's going to hurt himself," I turned to Silas, who was standing, arms crossed with his bottom lip tightly between his teeth.

We all heard the sound that tore from Arlo as he took his first swing. It wasn't loud, but it wasn't a sound he had ever made in a game to date. It was low, whiny, and sounded how a hundred bee stings would feel. Burning.

Silas pinched the bridge of his nose, turning away from the batting mound and facing the wall, but I couldn't look away. I ground my teeth tightly together. The feeling of them scraping against each other blocked out the sickening twist forming in the pit of my stomach. Arlo dug his foot into the ground, centering himself as the pitcher pulled back for another throw. A heavy crack rang out through the stadium. Both the ball and Arlo were moving. He rounded first with quick, light steps that made him look like he was flying but slid clumsily over second.

"Move your ass, King!" Coach hollered, moving forward like he might be able to run the bases for Arlo if he yelled loud enough.

But it worked. Arlo pushed off his back leg, propelling himself forward fast enough to sneak onto the third base before the rover brought the ball in for the out. The other team crumbled before our eyes. The pitcher was screaming orders repeatedly as the coaches yelled different plays and warnings.

Dean was up next, a powerhouse hitter. All he needed to do was drop the ball in the outfield and drop it hard. It was about giving Arlo time to get home; if the outfield caught the ball, Dean would be out, and the hit would be for nothing.

The stadium dulled to nothing more than static noise as Dean stepped to the plate. My heart was in my throat, my eyes flickering back and forth between home and third. Arlo was ready. Everyone was. Nick moved to stand beside me, his hand brushing back a piece of hair that had fallen out of place. I shivered at his touch but didn't move away.

The morning after the storm, I attempted to thank Arlo for his kindness, only to find his room empty. Cael said he liked to run in the morning, but it felt like he was avoiding me. Especially after he skipped breakfast and went straight to classes, all except Professor Tuckers. I sat beside Dean the entire class, waiting for him to stumble in late, but he never came. This routine persisted for three days. I only saw him at practice, but he consistently hid behind walls of "I have things to do" and "later."

He didn't want to talk, and even though I had done nothing wrong, it felt like I had.

Dean swung, and the ball slapped against the glove of the bat catchers.

Strike one.

He readied himself again, remembering to breathe as his fingers choked up around the bat's handle. Nick's cologne overwhelmed my senses, and I shook free of his touch, sliding closer to Van on my left side as Dean swung again.

Strike two.

"Fuck," Van swore beside me. "We need these points."

"He can do it," Cael shouted, "give him a minute."

I turned to look at him behind us, and he gave me a soft nod, tucking his chin down into the collar of his uniform. His bright blue eyes observed as Dean readied for the pitcher. His knee shook with nerves like it always did, but everyone held their breath as the pitch soared through the air. Dean proved everyone wrong by pushing the ball further than he had all season.

BAD HONEY

The crowd boomed as the ball smacked in the outfield seats, a campus kid catching it in his mitt as the stadium went wild. *A home run.*

Arlo waited at home for Dean, scooping him up in both arms and slapping him on the back in congratulations. Dean found his footing, and Arlo grabbed his face with both hands, yelling something intangible before jogging back to the dugout, where they were met with more slaps and cheers.

"See, Blondie," Arlo whispered as Cael grabbed him for a rough hug and a high five. "Just fine."

I shook my head at him but couldn't help but smile. They had done it, brought in two runs, and now had the lead. Arlo slumped against the bench, out of breath, and before I knew it, I slid down next to him, digging my fingers into the tightly corded muscle. Tucked against his body on the bench, I placed each hand on either side of his shoulder and began to crawl my fingers against the hardened knots that formed along his shoulder and neck.

"Not fine," I whispered as his face scrunched up in pain from my touch. "Why have you been avoiding me," I asked, still working out the knots as Van took to home plate.

"I haven't. I saw you yesterday and today." He answered with his face turned away from me.

"I'm practically sitting in your lap, and you won't look at me," I said, regretting it the moment I did because when he turned his face, we were too close together.

His lips hovered mere inches from mine, and I could feel every hot breath of air he exhaled as he fought to hold his composure together. He was indeed doing a better job than I at it.

"Happy now?" He asked, a sweet tangle of sweat and sand rising between us. His eyes flickered to my lips and then back up as I cleared my throat.

"I just wanted to thank you for the other night," I said quietly. Even though some of them knew, I didn't want the entire team to learn how unstable their new intern was. "What book did you take?"

His jaw ticked tightly, and he looked back at Van to watch him miss his first swing. "*The Notebook,*" he mumbled. "I've seen the movie, figured the book might be better."

"It is."

He looked back at me, a small smile itching at the corners of his mouth. "Are you liking it?" I asked, and he growled as I found a particularly deep knot.

Nick was watching us out of the corner of his eye from where he stood with Coach Cody, but he didn't seem to care. Perhaps it was just because I was doing my job, or it appeared that way at least, but the fact that he wasn't affected by our proximity... *bothered me.*

"I finished it," he said.

"You finished it in three days?"

"I finished it that night, and I was right. It's better than the movie." He wiggled from my grasp, "That's better, thank you."

"You're welcome," I smiled back at him softly, taking the chance to look at him. His cheekbones were sharp and pulled back the soft golden skin of his face to make everything look like an ice sculpture just as it started to warm. Beads of sweat, sun-kissed freckles, and the slightest hint of scars that I wouldn't have ever noticed if I hadn't been as close as I was. He had a thin cover of facial hair over his top lip and under his bottom that became sparse across his jaw.

I knew I was staring at them; his lips. But I couldn't help it. My eyes traced over the soft cupid's bow of the top one and along the delicate plump of the bottom. His mouth parted like he might say something but closed it just as quickly. He unlatched my leg from around him and slid off the bench. I watched as he walked back to where Coach stood, crossing their arms in unison as Van swung and missed again.

"Oh, Peachy," Cael slumped down on the bench and let his head rest against the dugout wall with his eyes on me.

"Don't start," I flinched at his sudden arrival. Knocked out of the daydream that flooded my body with heat.

Playful laughter tumbled from Cael as I looked over at Arlo again, ignoring the teasing from the 'chaos' kid beside me. "I was wrong about you not needing a King." His head lolled to where I was staring.

BAD HONEY

"Maybe it's not Nick," he whispered, leaning into me, "maybe you just have the wrong brother."

MIELE

MAY

The party following the game was at Delta, the same house we had visited the first time I met the team nearly three months ago. Now that the days were warming up, they had opened the pool, and everyone was meeting there to take advantage of the weather. I had tried to get out of it on the walk back to the Nest with Cael and Zoey, but neither was budging on the subject.

"Are you sure?" Zoey looked over my outfit with a scowl.

I had slid into a shirt and shorts, trying to avoid the topic of my scars by not wearing a bikini, but Zoey instantly took notice. I nodded, brushing her off. It was for the best. I could enjoy myself with them hidden.

"You look pretty, Peach." Cael nudged my side as we walked up the path toward Delta. Zoey floated inside at the sound of Van's boisterous yelling, momentarily leaving Cael and me alone on the front steps.

"You gonna be okay in here?" I asked him quietly, my eyes catching him, picking at his fingernails.

He exhaled a shaky breath and shrugged his shoulders, the fabric of his blue striped shirt pulling over the expanse of his chest. The brim of his hat was pulled down over his eyes, but I could tell he was worried. Being surrounded by drugs and drinking wasn't easy for anyone, especially not for him.

"Don't judge me harshly if I'm not?" Tipping his chin up to look me in the eye, I understood. He had already decided to come here tonight. He was going to break. He wanted to, perhaps even needed to, and all I could do was help pick up the pieces later.

BAD HONEY

I scrunched up my nose, highlighting all the twisted white scars tangled together like rope across my face, "I'm in no position, remember?" I said.

"I meant it. You look pretty." He smiled, his eyes tracing the scar.

Before we left the Nest, I had taken my makeup off; my skin had just felt so heavy and dirty. I was risking ridicule from drunk assholes, but if Cael wasn't afraid, neither was I.

"So do you," I teased, looping my arm into his and letting him lead me into the house.

Delta was full. Even more so than the first time. Bodies were crammed in every space they could find, grinding and drinking to the beat of the music. Cael licked his bottom lip. His height gave him a unique advantage. He towered over the crowd, his eyes scanning for anyone he knew before he shrugged in defeat.

"Everyone must be in the back," he told me over the blaring music.

We wandered through the house, his arm laid across my shoulders, and he kept me tucked in close as we fought against the packed hallways out into the backyard, where most of the team lounged drunkenly around and in the pool. A blue haze fell over everything, and Cael veered off to find us a drink, leaving me alone.

I wasn't a hopeless little kid, but I couldn't help but feel nervous. Van and Zoey were nowhere to be seen, and Dean was flirting with a group of girls at the pool's shallow end. I could feel his eyes on me before I even found him. Arlo stared at me, sitting at the center of the deep end with his legs hanging into the pool. He wore a dark shirt rolled to the elbows and left unbuttoned to show the rugged ridges of his chest and abdomen. His hair was wet, tiny pieces falling against his forehead, drawing attention to his big, sad brown eyes.

I wasn't sure Arlo and I would ever be friends, but at least he wasn't giving me a death stare, and perhaps today was the first step in something that felt like friendship, even if he was too stubborn to admit it happening. That's when Nick and all the other things Cael mentioned about him slipped into my mind. Why was I so damn fixated on making it work with Arlo? I wanted to tell myself it was for Cael that I was doing all of this so that his support system was a cohesive unit, but that made zero sense. I had just come into the picture. I was here for Cael in a way that Arlo couldn't understand, but I wasn't just going to replace what they had. Years of bonding over trauma they shared, secrets I would probably never know.

Secrets that, with every passing moment of our eyes locked together from across the pool, I wanted more and more to know. I wanted to hear him tell me about them. I swallowed tightly, trying to shove away that feeling of longing. It brought guilt that I didn't feel like processing at a house party.

I closed my eyes, trying to center myself before deciding I would go find Cael, and when I opened my eyes, Arlo was gone. The water around where his feet had been dunked rippled softly outward.

I sighed, turning to find Cael only to slam into some drunk idiot, their mouth wide open, and their beer spilled down the front of my shirt.

"Oh shit!" He said loudly, "I am so sorry," throwing the cup to the grass and trying to wipe the beer down. His grubby hands fondle me, and I push them away.

"It's fine," I said, holding my hands up so he'll stop trying to help.

Switching from apologetic to predatory in the blink of an eye. A crooked smirk formed on his face, "I can help you out of your shirt. Looks sticky," he said as his fingers reached the hem.

"No, thank you," I shoved his hand away.

"Oh, come on, I'm sure whatever is underneath is way better." His beady little brown eyes raked down my body as he advanced into my personal space.

"I said no," I stepped back, giving him a weak smile.

Again, the tone shifted, and his eyes narrowed when he realized he wasn't going to get what he wanted, "shit, I know you!" He said.

"No, you don't," I tried to walk around him, but he grabbed my arm, his fingers digging into my skin and holding me in place. "Let me go," I tried to yank away from him, but he was too strong.

"I do," he snapped. Stepping in closer, he shoved a leg between mine and pushed a piece of my hair out of my face. "Scarface." He whispered, "I should have known it was you," he laughed. His whiskey-tainted breath was hot on my neck as I turned my face away from him.

"Are you hiding more scars?" He laughed, his fingers digging at the skin on my arm as his other hand pulled at my shirt collar.

"Back up," I tried to shove him.

"Awe, come on, just show me one nasty scar," he leaned in, his eyes trailing lower to where he held open the collar of my shirt with one finger.

"Hey, Mike." That was all I heard before he was being manhandled away from me. Arlo's broad back slid between me and the creep like a brick wall. "Do your fucking ears work?" He pushed him backward, causing Mike to stumble over a group of girls sitting at the pool's edge. "Answer me," Arlo snapped.

"Yeah, man," Mike straightened himself out, "how about you stay out of it!"

Arlo tossed his head back in laughter, shaking out the amusement with a few last huffs, "You harass a hornet. You harass the whole Nest. Remember that."

"Oh, who's she's fucking to get that status, you, your brother, both of y—"

His words died on the skin of Arlo's knuckles as the sickening crunch of teeth tangled with a low whine replaced whatever sick thing he would say next.

"Arlo!" I said, pulling on his shoulder to yank him away from where Mike held his hand to a bleeding mouth. "Enough," I barked as he tugged from my hold and went to throw another punch.

"Get the hell out of here!" I heard him say as I started to walk through the crowd to the side of the house. I was going home.

I shouldn't have come out anyway. I should have stayed in bed with my books and ignored the pleas of Cael and Zoey. Both of them had left me to the wolves. All the warmth was sucked from the air, and the breeze nipped at my neck and arms, causing goosebumps to form on my skin.

It wasn't long before I heard him calling after me, yelling my name like I couldn't hear him calling me when I was just ignoring him. I didn't need him to fight my battles. I needed him to stay away from me so that I could figure out what I wanted.

"Go back to the party, asshole," I hollered back to him. I could walk myself home. I needed out of these suffocating clothes and a shower to wipe away the feeling of assault from my skin.

"Hey," he called again, but I didn't care. I just kept walking. "You're acting like a child!"

"Excuse me," I spun to face him as he stormed behind me. "You just punched a guy!"

"He wasn't listening to you," Arlo snapped.

"So what? I was handling it!" I rolled my shoulders, pinning them back as he approached me.

His jaw ticked as he turned his face away from mine, "It didn't look like you were handling anything. I was just trying to help, Blondie."

"That stupid fucking name," I sneered, rolling my eyes. "You come into my room, you invade my space, then you don't talk to me for a week, and now you think I need protection? I don't know what you want, and I don't need your help, Arlo. Stop trying to fucking save me!"

I pulled the ring from my shirt where it hung, tucked neatly between my breasts, and threw it at him. "Just leave me the fuck alone. Please?"

"I wasn't just going to stand by and let some fucking drunk asshole assault you," he barely flinched, raising his hand to catch the ring before it soared past his head. He snarled, "Don't throw shit at me."

"Don't fucking act like you know me," I retorted, walking toward him. I shoved him back with both hands.

I expected him to lash out, to get angry, but his shoulders collapsed, and he tilted his head to the side, "why do you let them talk to you like that?" He asked.

The question stung, nipping at the ends of my frayed nerves and causing my heart to sink further into my chest, "The same reason you let Nick talk to you the way he does. It's easier to let them than to keep fighting against something that will never change."

"These scars," I take a long, deep breath of air, "they aren't going to disappear. They're who I am now, and with that comes men who think their opinions on them should be heard. You punching one drunk jerk doesn't stop that. It makes them more inclined to pick on me when no

BAD HONEY

one is looking. So next time you decide to handle a situation like some fucked up white knight, think about the repercussions."

I backed away from him, looking disappointed and angry, bathed in the moonlight, his bruised hand wrapped tightly around the chain that swung lazily with the ring.

KING

Ella was rifling through her backpack, mindlessly talking to Cael in the kitchen when I walked through to the garage. They both fell silent, and I didn't blame them. I was yet again in the dog house. I was starting to think I might need to get comfortable. It was just that seeing her pushed around by Mike at the party snapped something inside of me. When I got home that night, she was fast asleep in her bed, her book left open in her hand. I gently set it aside, tucking the chain of the ring inside to mark her place. It didn't belong to me anymore. It became hers the moment she touched it. It made me feel like shit when she got angry enough to rifle it at me, finally exploding. She hadn't spoken to me since.

Cael only stopped by my room the day after to scold me as we went to the bus for the two away games we were traveling for. Once we arrived home, Ella kept to herself, sitting in the hammock out back most nights reading and avoiding me, leading us to this very awkward run-in. I hadn't expected anyone to be home as I snuck away to my dad's, mostly wanting to avoid Cael and Silas and their offers to accompany me. I needed to do this alone.

Sunday's at the Nest were quiet. Most players went home for dinner, and those who didn't have family in town tagged along. It was unusual that Cael was still here. After all, Coach was the one who had implemented the Sunday dinner rule. We used to eat dinner here almost three times a week. Lorraine had called it family bonding, but after she died, that fell apart. Everyone took turns making dinner, but we rarely ate together anymore.

BAD HONEY

"Why are you still here?" I dared to stop in the archway of the kitchen.

"I'm going to a meeting." He shrugged, "I'll go see Dad after."

I nodded, avoiding looking too long at Ella. Her blonde hair was tucked into a ponytail, and she was wearing a dark green sweatshirt two sizes too big for her frame. She looked beautiful. As she knelt to kick her bag into the closet, the chain peeked out from beneath the collar of her sweatshirt, and I had to keep myself from smiling at the sight of it.

"Text me if you need a ride," I said, backing out of the situation as swiftly as my sneakers would take me.

I opened the fastback trunk, pulled on a black hoodie, and brushed my hair beneath a hat before taking it down the hill and off campus, stopping to grab a flower bundle.

The second I crossed the bridge, the pit in my stomach seemed to churn and remind me how horrible of an idea this was. At least the year before, Silas had gone with me, somewhat protecting me from my father's verbal and physical abuse. Not that I couldn't defend myself, but the moment I stepped into that house, it was like I was a little kid again. No bigger than nine, fighting monsters in the dark that turned out to be nothing more than my mean, whiskey-drunk father.

My other brothers would be there, making it worse. At least with Silas, I had backup outside the tense relationship Nick and I shared. He made a good buffer. My brothers didn't care to get between us, and I didn't blame them.

The house looked the same. A tiny upgrade from the trailer we lived in the majority of our lives. Dad had bought the house when he went pro. A matchbook two-story house that smelled like mold and dust since my mother died. The saddest feature was that the bushes she had planted out front had all died from neglect. Funny how I related so much to a rose bush.

I slammed the car door, taking the bundle of flowers I bought into my hand as I walked around the side of the house out to the uncut grass of the backyard, past the rusted chain link fence, into the field behind my childhood home. The oak tree still stood, proud and strong, nestled among the long grass under a big blue sky.

"Hi, Mom," I huffed.

I always felt weird talking to myself, but I knew that if she could, she would be listening, and I would be damned before I let her be alone on her birthday. "Daisies this year," I raised the flowers weakly before setting them against the tree.

Mom wasn't buried here. Her ashes were in an urn on the mantel, but given the choice, she would have been. I ran my fingers over the messy carving in the bark. Her name was chipped away into the tree by me and Nick when we were just miserable, grieving teenagers. I remember when Nick treated me like a brother after Lucas and Sawyer left us to fend for ourselves. But like all good things, our father had poisoned our relationship as time passed. Without our mother around, Arthur did whatever the fuck he wanted, and usually, that meant we were met with violence.

"We're on a sixteen-game win streak. We might do it this year. Championships." I sighed, rubbing my chest above my heart, where it stung like someone had stuck a pin in me. "You never cared about wins," I laughed as the tree rustled above like maybe she was listening to me. Perhaps her worry over the state of our family matched my own. "We'll be okay, Mom. Happy birthday," I ground my teeth together. That's all I had for her. Anything else, and I'd lose my shit talking to a tree. Touching the bark one last time before I entered the house.

Nick was already three beers deep when I pushed the back door open, evidenced by the collection of empties on the kitchen table. Usually, I would make a nasty comment about the absence of tact on such an important day, but I knew how sad Nick was. Our mother loved us both as hard as she could, but she loved Nick so much more. I wasn't even sure how he had survived her death. Leaving our issues at the door, I chose a gentler approach. I rubbed the back of Nick's head gently as a hello, his hand brushing me away as I walked through the disgusting house.

Piles of cardboard boxes teetered in staggered, dangerous towers, all filled to their capacity with play tapes and old baseball games. Dust covered every inch of the house and filled my nose, making me sneeze.

BAD HONEY

"1988 World Series," I said from behind him, watching the old game flicker across the TV. It was like my father to be stuck in the past, watching reruns of the old World Series to make himself feel better.

"Just in time for Gibson to hit the walk-off home run," Dad grunted.

"Have you ever thought about how much pain he was in?" I asked, watching the old outfielder hobble around the bases on two injured legs.

"Pain doesn't matter when the whole world is watching, Arlo."

I couldn't stifle the laugh that tumbled from my lips.

"What's funny, boy?"

"Nothing, Dad," I clipped. "Where's Luc and Sawyer?"

"They didn't come."

"Why?" I asked, knowing I probably wouldn't get a straight answer out of him. They did this often. It wasn't shocking, just disappointing.

"Lucas said he was busy, and Sawyer didn't pick up the phone."

There was a reason for Nick's mood.

"What's for dinner?" I asked next.

"Whatever you make, I guess," Dad shrugged, not tearing his eyes from the TV.

I should have expected that, burying my frustration deep down, I wandered back to my brother through the hoarded path of boxes and magazines.

"He forgot," Nick mumbled, finally looking up from the tattered label he had been picking off the bottle, "that it was Mom's birthday, he forgot."

"That explains it. I'm sorry Luc and Sawyer bailed," I tugged open the fridge to find nothing but rotten takeout and beer before trying the equally empty and revolting cupboards. "Have you eaten?"

He answered by popping another beer and drinking half before putting it down. I stared at him for a long moment, wondering if he even contemplated that with every beer, he turned more and more into our father. I was jealous that Nick had gotten our mother's eyes, soft and warm, welcoming in all the ways a mother's should be. A stark contrast to my eyes which were dark, endless, and empty like our father's, and it pissed me off.

Instead of starting another pointless fight that would end in bruises and black eyes, I flicked my phone from my pocket, ordering two pizzas that would hopefully be enough to soak up the alcohol consumption between the two of them. By the time it showed up, Nick was down six beers, and our father had ripped the seal on a new bottle of whiskey. We all sat in the living room watching another game that we had seen a thousand times while our father berated us for not being as good as the greats. Utterly detached from what it was like now, the greats then wouldn't even be able to compete with the skill funneling through the NCAA these days.

I watched as Nick's phone rang on the couch between us, Ella's name popping up on the caller ID. I sighed as Nick ignored the call but caught my annoyed face.

"She's real pretty," he said with beer on his breath. Whatever sadness he had been feeling over the day pushed aside to torture me. "Makes pretty sounds, too," Nick added when I didn't respond. It was the only play he had, repeating horrible things about her to try to get under my skin. He wanted me to flip out in front of Dad. It was all a ploy to be able to show his dominance over me.

"I'm sure she does," I quipped, "probably the same as Jill, Jane and Josie." I rolled my eyes, "how do you keep them all apart to even know?"

I was doing my best not to lose my cool, but with every remark against Ella's reputation and things Nick should have kept between them, it was slipping from my grasp.

"Trust me, once you hear the sounds Ella makes, you don't forget them." Nick sipped his beer as my hand tensed around the arm of the tattered sofa.

"Can you please just shut up for once?" I snapped, unable to control myself.

"What do you care? She's just some bitch," Nick laughed, leaning closer across the sofa. "You can get your own girlfriend, have whoever you want."

BAD HONEY

I fought every urge that coursed through my body, every single one of them screaming at me to hit Nick, to start the fight and end it. To make sure he never spoke about Ella that way again. But that was stupid. Ella wouldn't even look at me, and why would I fight my brother over some girl? I knew the answers to my questions, but that stubborn, relentlessly angry part refused to acknowledge them.

"I was supposed to bring her over to meet Dad," Nick continued to press.

Ella would never step foot in this house.

"Yeah, show her how the Kings really live; she'll love that," I growled. "And then later, you can knock her up. You can put the nursery between Dad's collection of cobwebs and Mom's moth-infested closet. I'm sure any girl would be lucky enough to start a family in this fucking graveyard."

Something cracked in Nick's resolve as his fist pounded into my face. Coming across the couch without warning, the two of us tumbled to the floor in a mess of fists and grunts. My knee collided with Nick's stomach, knocking the wind out of him. I'm stronger than him, but I was never as good at wrestling. My arms were too long for my own good. His elbow connected with my face, getting the upper hand. Straddling my hips, he caught my jaw with his open hand and shoved my face into the musty carpet.

"When will you understand," Nick grunted, trying to catch his breath, "you are nothing." He spat in my face. "Say it, Arlo," he demanded, "tell me how worthless you are."

"Fuck you, Nick."

The carpet burned against the cut on my cheek as he ground my face deeper. My eyes trained in the distance on Dad's feet, doing my best to disassociate from the clawing feeling that ripped apart the delicate layers of defense I had built. "Say it or I'll break your fucking hand." He was pissed.

Deep down somewhere, I knew that if he did, Nick would regret it, but it didn't mean he wouldn't break my hand just to prove the point.

"I'm worthless," I grumbled, trying not to believe it as the words tumbled from my lips. We had been in this position a thousand times since Mom died. "I'm nothing."

"Good boy," he clipped in my ear, letting me up from beneath him and rubbing the cut on his knuckle free of the streak of blood. "Go the fuck back to the Nest. And stay away from my girlfriend." He snapped. "Fucking waste of space."

I licked the trickle of blood off my split lip as I readjusted my hat and collected my phone, not bothering to say goodbye to Dad, who hadn't moved from his chair throughout the entire fight. I slammed the back door shut as hard as possible, hearing it bounce off the hinges as I walked back to the car. I turned to the mirror, checking my face to find an extended cut across my cheekbone that was irritated and dripping blood. I pressed my sleeve to it and cleaned it the best I could before peeling out of the shitty neighborhood back to where I felt like I could breathe.

I parked the car in the garage and beelined for the kitchen. I could feel my face swelling with every step I took through the empty manor. *Silas was going to lose his fucking mind over this.*

I stopped in my tracks, seeing Ella curled up on the counter, her fingers aimlessly digging into a bag of snap peas, focusing on the book in her hand. I felt myself *smiling* as her brows scrunched up and her nose wiggled in protest at something in the story. I tried to be quiet, pinning back my shoulders and walking on the balls of my feet as I walked into the kitchen for ice, but her eyes looked over the edge of her book, and her posture changed.

She turned her eyes back down, but her voice surprised me as she asked, "What happened to your face?"

"Nothing, I didn't mean to interrupt." I said, "I thought you were supposed to take Cael to his meeting?" I asked, remembering their plans.

"I did," she looked at the clock that read nearly nine, "he's upstairs showering."

"Did he eat?" I asked with my hand on the freezer door. He was supposed to see Coach.

"I was waiting for him to return so we could make something," she explained.

"You haven't eaten?" I sounded worried without meaning to. "All of the guys are gone. No one is going to cook for you." I grumbled in a sad attempt to sound harsh, covering up the split-second concern for her.

Her eyebrow rose, and she shook the bag of peas at me, her eyes trained on my cheek. "I know the schedule, tough guy, and I can cook for myself; I just choose not to."

"That's not dinner." I rolled my eyes.

"And that's not *nothing*," she responded, carefully slipping from the counter. She pulled a clean rag from the drawer and soaked it in warm water before handing it to me. "Clean it, or it will get infected."

"You're bossy, Blondie," I groaned, leaning against the counter as I used the reflection in the kitchen window as a mirror. Ella moved around me, gathering ice from the freezer without a word. When I was finished, she handed me a bag. My eyes raked up her arm to her bare shoulders and across her chest, taking in the scar that cut into her skin and disappeared beneath her tank top.

"And you're an asshole. Guess that makes us even, Cap." She said forcibly, pressing the ice into the palm of my hand. She was so close to me that I could feel her breath on my neck.

"Thank you," I hissed softly as the frigid bag touched the sore split skin.

"It's just ice," she said, scooping her book from the counter and giving me a look that spoke volumes. *Don't be such a baby.*

"For looking after Cael," I added, reaching out to grab her arm as she made to leave. I inhaled that warm scent of her shampoo into my nose, trying to rid my memories of the musty whiskey stained there. My fingers brushed against her skin, and she looked down to where I had made contact. "Thank you."

"It wasn't for you," she said, but her gaze softened as she turned to look up at me.

"Let me make dinner for you," I said, looking over my shoulder to the stairs, "for Cael. Just go back to reading. I won't bug you anymore." I offered in the most genuine way I could.

I thought she might carry on to her room for a second, but she stopped, turned, and climbed back onto the counter where I had found her. I nodded, taking it as a yes as I stripped from my hoodie. I forgot that I had thrown on a dirty, stretched sleeveless shirt that exposed my rib cage and chest. I groaned, contemplating wearing the sweater.

Just make the pretty girl dinner, you idiot. I said to myself, tossing it over a stool before I started to collect the ingredients to make carbonara for them. Something that would fill Cael up, knowing he probably hadn't eaten all day. Sundays were hard. A day that used to belong to family dinners with his Mom had felt empty since her death. I'd make something that I knew for sure that he loved. I caught her watching over the brim of her book occasionally, her curious eyes trailing behind me, watching my technique. It warmed my chest, knowing that she was watching, and I fought to hide my smile.

"Who taught you to cook?"

Her voice startled me after so long in silence. I dumped the pasta into the boiling water, "Lorraine. Cael's Mom."

She nodded, seemingly satisfied with that answer.

"Why don't you drive?" I asked, cracking and separating the egg yolks into a bowl.

Her eyes flickered toward me, her jaw tensing from the question, and I knew I had hit a nerve somewhere within her. I hadn't meant to, but I needed to know everything about her. Not just the girl she showed people. I *needed* to know the girl with the scars.

"I don't have my license." She answered shortly.

"That's not what you told me," Cael stood in the doorway shirtless, wearing low-hanging gym shorts, drying his hair with an old towel. "You said *I don't drive anymore*, which is very different wording."

"You are so loud when you want to be," Ella laughed and threw a snap pea at Cael.

I stared at her, probably looking like an absolute idiot, but the sound of her laugh, up close and when I wasn't blinded by Nick's rage, was my new favorite sound. Her eyes caught mine, and the sound died out. *I'm sorry*, I wanted to say. *Sorry for stealing that sound from you.*

"I just don't like driving," she shrugged as Cael walked into the kitchen, sticking his nose into every pot and pan I had going. "I didn't know that was a crime." She defended herself.

Cael looked at me, widening those blue eyes and raising his eyebrows. I hated being out of the loop.

"It's not," I said, "just weird for a girl that grew up in California."

"Everything I need is on campus," she said as Cael wandered to stand beside her. She smiled at him and pointed out something on his arm, engaging him in a quiet conversation that I quickly became jealous of.

"Except for the good bookstores," I said, and for a moment, I thought she might scowl, but her smile remained as she looked me over curiously. It tickled warmly against my chest as she nodded softly.

"How'd you get this asshole to cook for you?" Cael asked her.

"I asked him nicely," Ella teased, not taking her eyes off me.

"You have to eat, Cael," I stayed stern, "you're too skinny as it is. One bad liner would snap half the brittle limbs in your body."

"He's not wrong," she shrugged when Cael looked to her for help.

"Hey!" Cael raised a hand in the air, swinging his towel around like a flag, "when did this turn into a tag team event?"

"Next week, you go to your dad's for dinner," I pointed at him, knowing he had found a Sunday meeting to avoid hard conversations with his dad.

"But then Ella will be alone." He said without skipping a beat.

"No, she won't," I looked from Cael back to Ella, tapping a finger to my chest. No malice or venom in my words, just a soft promise that I wouldn't let her be without Sunday dinner.

Ella's phone rang, interrupting our stare. She pulled it from her back pocket to answer it. I knew it was Nick from the tone in her voice, "of course."

She pressed the phone to her ear and excused herself from the kitchen as I handed a plate to Cael, who immediately set it down on the counter before him to grab my face between his long fingers. The metal rings pinched at my skin, and I shoved him off me.

"What did he do?" Cael asked, inspecting the cut.

"Tried to scare me," I grumbled, staring at the second plate meant for Ella.

"Did it work?"

"Just the opposite." I sighed, knowing she wasn't coming back to eat, and looked over at Cael, shoving food in his mouth with his eyes on the hallway where she disappeared.

MIELE

Zoey found me that afternoon, nose in four different textbooks, trying to finish my paper for Professor Tucker's class. My mind had been in a thousand other places, and usually leaving a paper until the last minute wasn't my style, but between work and not sleeping... It had quickly become so.

"Are you doing schoolwork right now?" She scoffed and closed the book on my fingers. "I've got two hours to make you look presentable for this fundraiser."

"One hour," Van corrected. He was carrying a duffle bag, no doubt full of makeup and hair products, a chair from the dining room, and a tray of drinks. "Here," he handed me a coffee and set the chair down, "you need to be ready, too. On time this year. I'm a starting position on the team. I can't be late."

The Harbor Hornet's annual fundraiser was being held tonight.

It made me nauseous to even think about it.

"Let's get this over with before I vomit," I laughed, but Zoey's face scrunched up in disapproval.

"In the chair," she snapped her fingers. She curled the ends of my hair as I brushed a coating of blush over my cheeks. I'd done a decent job of covering the remnants of my scar beneath the makeup, and it gave me the false confidence I needed to fit in with Nick and his friends.

"Is this fundraiser usually this fancy?" I asked.

Zoey had been going with Van for two years now. I stood once she was done with my hair and pulled the long dark green dress from its plastic, "he sent this over," I wiggled the strappy, satin dress at Zoey with my eyebrows in the air.

"I'm clearly dating the wrong Hornet," Zoey whined.

"I'm *literally* right here," Van groaned from the bed where he was flipping through a comic book.

"Be quiet," Zoey laughed, "Treat me like a princess tonight, and there are good things in it for you."

"What kind of good things?" Van dropped the book against his chest and rolled his head to look at us.

"Ew, stop," I waved the white flag of surrender before Zoey could describe anything. "I do not need to scrub that image from my brain."

"Van's eyes closed," Zoey warned as she helped me into the backless dress, resting the thin straps on my shoulders. Wearing a dress like this made me nervous with the way it beaconed the scars that twisted over my shoulder and chest.

"I don't think I can wear this," the words come out a strangled sob.

"You look beautiful," Zoey said in near tears as she pressed her cheek to my shoulder in the mirror, admiring me with big doe eyes.

"I don't know about this..." I pull at the dress's collar to cover the nasty, twisted skin.

"Stop," she pressed a hand to my chest. "No one is looking at your boobs."

"And if they are, I can kill them for you." Van groaned mindlessly.

"You might have to let him lift your skirts tonight. This is—" Zoey ran her hand down the dress with a playful smirk. "A really expensive dress."

"She doesn't have to do shit," Van sat up and gave me a sympathetic smile. He crossed the room in his blue knit sweater and jeans, hair messy from rolling around in my bed, "he says one wrong thing, does one thing that makes you feel uncomfortable tonight, find me."

"Thanks, Van," I scrunched up my nose as I battled the nerves that snowballed in my chest. I slipped on a pair of simple heels that the length of the dress covered before smoothing myself out.

"My pretty girls." He kissed our heads resting against mine as we looked at our reflections in the mirror. "You look amazing, El," he winked, "have fun tonight." A strange burst of confidence came with Zoey and Van hyping me up so hard.

"I have to get dressed. I'll be back in thirty, Zoey. Be ready, please; the players can't be late." He grabbed her face with both hands and kissed her hard. Zoey's tiny hands wrapped around his wrists and pushed up on her tiptoes against his lips. It didn't take her too long to get ready, and before I knew it, I was standing alone in the room, staring at myself.

I gave myself one last pep talk, staring at the ring hanging over my mirror. I was starting to become dependent on the little piece of metal, and I hated it. After finding it back in my room, I realized Arlo wasn't ready to stop fighting. It annoyed me, and perhaps it was a game to him, just like baseball, but a small piece of me craved his perseverance. I needed to replace it with a chip or a marble, something that wasn't attached to the thoughts and feelings that Arlo gave me. I decided against wearing it, steeled my nerves, pinned my shoulders back, and left the room.

A car was waiting to take me to the venue.

I hadn't thoroughly thought this through. My fingers shook at my side, unable to conceal my anxiety. I looked back up at the house, questioning whether or not I should go back in for the ring or just not go. The driver waited with the door open, and all I could do was get inside and close my eyes. I had been pushed twice today, the dress and now the drive. I wanted to cry, but it would ruin all the hard work Zoey had put into making me look so pretty. With one more shaky breath, I climbed into the car.

The drive there was shorter than expected, every second of it spent wishing I'd worn the damn ring so I'd at least have something to focus on. I was shocked to find out the event was on the stadium field. I was led through a door I'd never used by a security guard I had never seen before. I came out at the top of level one. I paused at the top of the stairs. The entrance was decorated eloquently with dark blue carpets and golden lights that cast a hazy glow over the entire field. Tables were set up in a circle pattern in the outfield, and the infield had a stage built atop the clay. I was surprised at how beautiful everything looked.

BAD HONEY

Nick was waiting at the bottom of the stairs, staring in awe as I descended. "Flawless," he extended his hand to me as I reached the bottom. "I have something for you."

As his eyes roved over my body, flinching at the scar, I tried to stand as rigid as I could, the world *flawless* worming under my skin as I watched him dig into the pocket of his gray three-piece suit and handed me a slim black box. I tugged the satin bow off the box, dropping it in his palm as I popped it open to expose the dainty silver chain and round pendant inside.

"It's St. Nicholas." He smiled at me and helped me put it around my neck. "Silver suits you better than that ugly gold thing you've been wearing." He said as he clicked the necklace into place.

I bit my tongue, a habit I found myself doing around Nick. His lips pressed warmly to the hollow between my neck and shoulder, his cleanly shaven face smooth against my skin.

The pendant felt heavy around my neck, even though it was lighter than the ring Nick had mistakenly replaced. *Guilty weight.* I wondered for a moment if Nick knew what I had been wearing all those days and if he had known where the ring had come from.

Nick wrapped his hand around my stomach, pulling me back against his hips. "Thank you for coming tonight," pulling my hair out of his way as he kissed the space behind my ear.

My focus should have been on his hands and kisses, but my eyes caught Arlo standing at the bar. I couldn't tell from the distance if he had seen me arrive, but I watched as he sipped on his whiskey and his eyes scanned the crowd.

Unsurprisingly, he looked more handsome than usual, with hair pushed back in dark brunette waves and wearing a tight black suit and pants. What stood out was the glistening, tawny color of his chest beneath. Layered against his bare chest was a stack of golden necklaces matching the ring layer on his hand. He shone like a beacon. He looked like a god.

"I want to introduce you to some people," Nick interrupted my thoughts and linked my hand to the crook of his arm.

I let him play host all night, parading me around the venue like he owned a little piece of me and had the right. Some of the folks I met were kind and interesting to speak to, and they were exactly how I expected. Others were horrible and rude.

Every single one of the players looked handsome in their dress clothes and carried themselves with prestige as they sweet-talked sponsors. In his lavender suit and white dress shirt, Cael had been cornered by a pack of old ladies who were trying to take chunks out of him. It was entertaining to watch as he begged silently for help from anyone who would make eye contact with him.

Silas found me in a quiet moment, leaning against the batting cage behind the stage with a whiskey and a tired scowl on my lips. I'd always hated fundraisers, and tonight, I was reminded why. Fake people with fake smiles and fake promises of loyalty. The moment you let them down in the public eye, they'd turn on you like a pack of rabid animals.

"You look pretty," Silas said, offering me a fresh glass. I set my empty one down on the stage beside me and took it from him. "Are you having fun?"

He shifted uncomfortably in his blue suit and tie, his hair stiffly pushed back with gel and his face cleanly shaven for the first time since we had met. "About as much as you," I laughed, picking out his insecurities from a mile away.

"This was always my dad's scene," he said.

"I met him," I raised an eyebrow at him, "interesting man."

"You can say it," Silas whispered as he leaned into my personal space with a smile.

"Oh, he's a massive dick." I laughed with Silas, letting go of some of the tension I had been holding onto. "I think he mentioned four times what a waste of a career in sports medicine was and how I had the face for commercial work." I pointed to the scar on my face, "I think he meant my boobs..."

"I am so sorry," Silas huffed, stifling his laughter and downing the rest of his drink. "So uh..." he played with the ice in the glass like it might make the question he was about to ask come out a little easier, "How is—" he looked around, nodding to where Nick was seemingly juggling a pack of cheerleaders turned high-class escorts for the night.

BAD HONEY

"Are you asking me about my personal life, Silas?" I asked, enjoying the sight of him squirming a little too much. "It's fine," I shrugged, "Nick is a gentleman."

Silas stopped playing with the ice and looked up at me with a new concern in his blue eyes that I had never seen before. "And you're doing ok?" He asked next, as if saying Nick was a good idea was out of character.

"I'm fine," I offered, swishing around the amber liquid.

"You say that word a lot, *it's fine, I'm fine*. Are you being honest? I'm your boss, Ella, but I'd like to be your friend. The past week at games and appointments, you've seemed a little out of it."

"With the new schedule, classes, and moving, I'm just settling in, that's all." I lied. Next Saturday was our birthday. Only I would be celebrating the year without Ethan. I had been holding my breath since the beginning of the month, and with every day passing by, I felt the overwhelming urge to scream and cry. My fingers tightened around my glass.

"Cael told me about the panic attacks," Silas sighed.

"That boy is loud at all the wrong times," I tossed back the second glass of whiskey, "that incident..."

"It's not the first?" Silas asked quietly.

"It will be the last. I've been good all week." I planted my feet. My hand distinctly went to the pendant around my neck, searching for the ring but finding cold, flat metal. It didn't have the same feeling and did nothing to quell the anxiety that stirred.

I had been doing everything I could to control my emotions while at the stadium. There were small moments of cracking, but I would find a quiet place to hide, count to five, and return to where I was needed. Being around the crowd and the game was more challenging than expected.

"You've been *hiding* it well all week. It has been anything but a *good* week." Silas' blue eyes seemed to see through me. "Grief and guilt are often talked about as separate feelings," he licked his tongue over his bottom lip, "but it's different when those two emotions are intertwined by our past transgressions. I know the feeling of wishing you could have done something different, changed something, anything."

I watched as he dug something from his back pocket, my mind on his words about grief and guilt being twisted around each other. No one had ever explained it to me like that. I just chose to feel guilty for grieving as well.

"I want you to go see Riona." He held out a card.

It was sleek and white and felt light in my hand. The writing on the back was gold. All it had was Riona Cody - *Therapist*, followed by a number. "Another Cody?"

"She's the best one, in my opinion, Cael's Aunt."

"Is that wise, seeing someone so close to everything else? Isn't that a conflict?"

"Only if you make it one," Silas responded, cocking his head to the side in frustration. "Are you going to make it a conflict, Ella?"

"Why?" I asked. I was nervous to talk to anyone who might be intertwined with the politics at Harbor, but I also desperately needed an anchor here. I hadn't been able to find a therapist that understood my situation.

"I'm looking out for everyone, but especially you. Riona can help you. Just trust her, and if you can't, trust me." He said with a wink before he flitted away into the crowd.

"That doesn't answer my question," I yelled after him, and he turned back to look at me with a smirk.

"I look out for you. You look out for them. It's a partnership." His eyes dragged to Arlo with his hands in his pockets and his jaw tight, talking to a group of old men.

Them. I ground my teeth and slipped the card into my phone case for safekeeping. I looked to where Nick had been, but he was gone. Wanting to go home, I started my search for him. I found Coach Cody at a table looking somber, and stood next to him, "have you seen Nick?" I patted him on the shoulder, getting his attention.

"I think he went into the dugout," he pointed toward the Hornet's dugout, returning to his food and drink.

I floated across the uneven temporary tiles set out as a dance floor toward the covered dugout. It had been raining, and the massive black tarps protected the wood and equipment inside without being a permanent fixture that had to be removed with tools. The caretakers could come out, rip the tarps down, and roll them up, and the dugouts were quickly ready for the game.

I could hear shuffling from behind the tarp as I got closer, recognizing Nick's stupid laugh as I reached to pull it back and go inside. I should have seen that coming the moment he had flirted with the waitress the last time we'd gone out, but part of me was looking for an excuse to remain unattached. He was kind and handsome enough, but he was vapid, which drove me nuts more often than not. But he was comfortable, easy, and distracted enough that he never dug deeper into who I was.

A large hand wrapped around my arm, tugging me back from the dugout stairs and the sound of laughter coming from within.

"Blondie, don't go in there," Arlo huffed, pulling me toward the doors that led to the locker room. Only when the doors shut behind us did he let go of me. "Control yourself, lunatic."

"Aye, aye Captain," I spat, giving him a phony salute.

I spun on my heel to go back to the dugout, but Arlo lifted me off the ground by my waist, carrying me down the hallway, kicking and screaming until we were safely inside the locker room.

"Why are you protecting your sleazy brother!" I pushed him off the second I was back on two feet.

"I'm not," he snipped, "you didn't need to see him dick-deep in some bat bunny. I don't need you losing your goddamn mind in front of all those important people. Acting like a crazy person doesn't help the team."

"Call me crazy one more fucking time, Arlo King, I dare you." I shoved him backward, my nails digging into the fabric of his suit jacket.

"Don't act crazy then."

I snarled at him, turning on my feet to leave. Walking home in what felt like half a dress and heels was the least of my worries.

"Enough," he shook his head at me, "if you go out there and cause a scene, do you think they'll take your side, feel bad for you? You're just some girl to them; he's fucking Nicholas King. It doesn't matter that he's fucking a cheerleader at a fundraiser. They'll pat him on the back, and you'll never get a job in this state because they'll blacklist you for being a *crazy* person."

"There's that word again," I rolled my eyes.

He stared at me, his eyes dropping to my throat where the silver chain hung. Hurt and confusion flickered over his angry features. His fingers reached out, and I found myself holding my breath. My heart beat rapidly against my chest as his finger brushed over the pendent, resting it in his palm. For a long moment, he studied it, his jaw ticking as he wrapped his hand around it and ripped it from my neck. The clasp snapping at my skin stung.

"Ow," I hissed.

I had been too angry to notice he was wearing the gold chain and ring amongst his stack of necklaces. Lifting it over his head, he placed it back around my neck, his thumb brushing over the spot left sore from his outburst. Arlo swallowed tightly, his fingers tracing down the chain, avoiding touching my scar, but his eyes followed it as he flipped the ring up and carefully tucked it into the collar of my dress. "Back where it belongs." He said as his dark gaze shifted lazily back to mine.

"You were in my room," I whispered as his fingers lingered against my chest, knuckles brushing my collarbone.

"You have no idea what you're doing to me." Closing his eyes, Arlo leaned in, his nose ghosting along my cheekbone as he inhaled deeply. I pressed my hand to his chest, my fingers digging into his bare skin as we stood silently for a long, tense moment. The heat that rose through me was overwhelming and addicting.

"This is infected," I scowled and ghosted my thumb over the cut on his cheek, but he ignored the observation.

"Ella," he exhaled finally, my name tumbling from shaky lips as he brushed my hair back off my shoulder. I felt his finger trace a line where the scar from the seat belt was until he was nose to nose with me finally, breathing the same breath. The pupils of his dark eyes were blown wide, and his jaw twitched as he fought to control himself.

The door to the locker room slammed wide open, throwing ourselves apart from the interruption. I suddenly felt cold and a million miles away from him.

BAD HONEY

"Ella, I need you," Silas stood breathless, his suit flung open and his hair out of place.
"What's wrong?"
"It's Cael."

KING

When I saw her arrive, the world seemed to grow fuzzy around the corners of my vision, and my heart stopped at the sight of her. Even as I tried to pretend like she was invisible.

The green dress she had chosen fit every curve of her body, the soft rounds of her breasts, and clung to the full shape of her hips. I wanted to push the satin fabric over them and find what was beneath with my fingertips.

She had covered the scar on her face, and I wasn't sure why, but it made me sad for her. A tinge of heartbreak flooded me, knowing that she chose to hide herself.

Ella's demeanor changed. She kicked off both heels, leaving them behind in a pile with her cell phone as she followed an urgent Silas toward the medical wing. She tossed her long blonde hair into a bun at the back of her head, rushing after him as fast as her little legs could. I grabbed her shoes and phone from the floor, a T-shirt, and a pair of sweatpants from my locker. I didn't care that they would be big on her. They would make her feel comfortable, and in my worry, I latched onto what I could control. Ella was beautiful, and it hadn't been the first time I had those thoughts, but it was the first time I was truly sure of them. Every time I looked at Ella, it was like experiencing the sensation of having the wind knocked out of me. I couldn't breathe around her, and I craved that feeling.

I wanted to kill my brother. Even the thought of her hurting because of him racked through me and made all my judgment hazy. I should have done a better job protecting her from him. Now, I had no choice but to stand by and hope she survived the torment that Nick had in store for her. Quickly, my worry for Cael engulfed every furious, hot-headed thought that spurred through my mind as I heard retching coming from the medical room. Everything was thrown around in the usually clean and organized room; medical supplies and bedding were scattered like someone had been searching for something.

Ella had slid herself beneath his massive, lanky body and was rubbing his head with a cold cloth, but it was doing nothing to wick away the sweat that dripped off him.

"What the hell?" I swore, setting down the clothing in my arms and wandering in to help Silas with whatever I could.

"Do you know what he took?" I asked, grabbing towels from the cabinet above me.

"No," Silas mumbled, looking for something in the drawer beneath the cabinets.

I looked back at him as Ella struggled to unbutton his dress shirt while she juggled him in her lap, but she whispered to him as she worked, brushing her hand over his head whenever he started to wiggle too much. Fighting the urge to sink into my dark spaces, I stripped from my dress jacket and hiked up my pants before kneeling on the floor to help her.

She continued to work at keeping Cael upright as I stripped the shirt from his overheated arms. Ella was practically in a trance as she ran her hands over his jaw and throat, whispering something to him that I couldn't make out. I was growing frustrated. I felt helpless as Cael thrashed around, crying and screaming. Ella's gaze flickered up to me, her big brown eyes watery and glittering back at me with so much fear.

"Peachy," Cael whispered, curling into her arms, his screaming dying on tired lips. I laid a hand on his arm, shocked at the temperature of his skin.

"Here," Silas handed me a cold, wet towel, and I helped him wrap Cael into it, "don't," he said as I made to pry his limp, sweaty body from Ella's arms. "Leave him," he said, "let his heart rate come down before you separate them."

"I've never seen him like this," I turned my head toward Silas, keeping my voice down. "What the hell is it?"

"Is he—" Ella cleared her throat, her trembling fingers still raking through his short, damp hair. "Is he on anti-depressants?"

Silas pushed up from his squatted position on the floor, marching to the filing cabinet to pull out Cael's folder. He flipped through it quickly, scanning each page with urgency. "Yeah," he nodded, "hard-core ones."

"Prozac?" Ella asked.

I studied her face as she closed her eyes, rested her chin against Cael, and put all the puzzle pieces together. I held my breath, the stinging warmth filling my chest as I fought to maintain my grasp on reality.

"Cael," she whispered, shifting him in her arms, "how many did you take?" She cupped his face so tenderly that I felt the touch on my skin from where I was positioned. "Cael," she repeated his name, and his eyes fluttered open heavily, watery and red.

She stared at him for a long moment before her eyes flickered up to me and Silas, nervous but confident in herself. She had done this before, seen it, or lived through it; I wasn't sure, but I knew the look of experience.

"Did you—" she licked her lips, "did you take more on purpose?"

Did you try to take your own life?

That's what she was asking him. I pushed off my knees, my chest so tight I couldn't breathe, as I swiped my jacket from the counter and fled the medical office. How had I not seen how bad Cael had become? How had I missed the signs that my own family, while not flesh and blood, was the closest thing I had to a little brother, and he had reached the edge of life and chosen something so permanent to deal with all the pain he had been feeling?

I slammed my hand into the flimsy storage room door, cracked the wood in the center, and slid down against the wall across from it. Silas found me with my head between my legs, unsure how long I had been sitting there. I felt him slide down next to me with a huff.

"Sorry," was all I could offer.

"Don't," Silas looked at me. He had been crying. I had only seen him cry twice, which always made his blue eyes' gray tones so vibrant. "That in there wasn't your fault, it wasn't my fault, it's not even Cael's fault."

BAD HONEY

I thought about arguing. I had a case that pointed in giant red flags toward my negligence, "we let him down," I whispered, rubbing my hands over the black fabric of my jacket. "Is he okay?"

"He's finally asleep. He didn't take enough to actually—" Silas paused, "hurt himself."

Silas looked at me with a scowl, grabbing my face to inspect the cut that festered on my cheek.

"Did he do that?"

"No, I hit my face on my dresser."

"Arlo," Silas groaned, rubbing the bridge of his nose. "When?"

"Last weekend," I hissed as he pressed a finger to it.

"It's infected, you fucking idiot," he scolded. "Wasn't that—"

"Mom's birthday."

"Where were Lucas and Sawyer?" He asked, knowing the answer the second the question left his lips.

"It doesn't matter," I shrugged. "My brothers wouldn't have stopped him even if they had bothered to show up for her."

"You should have called me. I would have come."

"I don't need protection, Silas, but thank you." *She wasn't your mom, and it wasn't your problem.* I almost left my lips, but Silas didn't ever deserve that venom, not over Mom, so I kept my mouth shut.

"What started it this time?"

"Ella," I laughed. Her name coming out of my mouth was just becoming a cruel joke.

He didn't say anything, whether because I didn't want to hear what he wanted to say or if he just couldn't find the right words. We sat silently, staring at the wall, trying to figure out where to go next.

"He tried to fucking kill himself, Si," I nearly sobbed, doing my best to swallow the tears that ripped through my chest, "how do we tell Coach?"

"We don't," Silas snapped, "what do you think he'll do if he finds out about this?"

"Send him to rehab, maybe get him some real help?"

"Taking away the two things that kid has left isn't going to help him," Silas seemed sure about it. "He needs baseball, his family, and meetings."

"Meetings aren't enough. He's been going to them with Ella. We aren't going to be enough," I shook my head.

"We have to be."

"Can I see him?" I asked after a long bout of silence. I was so angry at myself, at Cael, at my brother. It was bottled up so tightly that I feared what might happen if I let it all out.

"He's in the private room," Silas nodded, not moving when I climbed from the floor. "You could have punched the wall, you know," he shook his head, staring at the destroyed door.

"Concrete? Coach would kill me if I broke my hand," I said sadly, but it put a smile on Silas' tense expression. "You can afford to replace it, Doc."

The distance to the medical rooms felt longer than usual as I pressed through the door into the main space. I set my jacket down and quietly turned the knob of the private room, swinging the door open and closed behind me. I leaned against the door as it clicked shut, all the fight washing from my body, leaving me exhausted and heartbroken from what I saw.

I hadn't expected her to stay.

Ella was curled up, wearing the sweats and shirt I had found, eyes closed, her arms wrapped around a sleeping Cael who was twice her size but seemed so small curled into her chest. Ella's hair was messy and falling over her cheeks as she pressed her face deeper into the pillow. I slipped off my shoes to avoid waking them and crossed the room. As tired as I was, I couldn't help but revel in the peace that washed over me as I brushed a finger through the curl that covered her cheek, pushing it back behind her ear to expose her face. All her crying had washed away the makeup, and the scar she had tried so hard to hide from everyone was visible again.

"What happened that made you so wound up?" I whispered to myself.

I traced it, letting myself memorize how the twisted skin felt beneath my finger with my eyes closed. When I opened them, Ella was staring up at me. The lightness of her usually bright brown eyes was so dark and distant. The sight of her sent an explosion of unexplainable pain cascading down through me, filling every sore, tired muscle.

BAD HONEY

"Close your eyes," I said softly, and she listened to my surprise.

I rested against the dresser beside the cot, unable to force myself out of the room. I had just been unwillingly tied to Ella Miele and god, I hated it.

MIELE

Riona Cody looked precisely how I had expected her to. Long dark blonde hair that flowed in waves around her oval face and over her narrow shoulders. She stared at me with serious olive eyes that initially felt intimidating, but then she smiled, and it was like Cael was there with me.

Crammed into her bright white office and sat on her plush navy blue couch, my thoughts wandered to every dark corner of my mind. After everything that had happened to him, I knew that taking Silas' advice was serious. Witnessing Cael's downfall triggered a nasty, addictive monster that had been sleeping for nearly a year inside of me with the snap of a finger. This was the first time I had left the Nest in almost three days, spending ninety percent of my time curled up with Cael, reading books and keeping an eye on him. He refused the offer to find him a proper rehabilitation center, claiming that meetings and the Nest were enough to get him clean.

"It was an accident, Peach." He had woken through the night, whispering to me when he thought I was asleep. And if he had said those words in any other moment, I might not have believed him. But his confession wasn't for me. It had been for his conscience. He just needed to say it to someone he trusted more than himself.

And he seemed to be doing alright.

"You're nervous," she pointed to where I picked at the fabric couch beneath me.

This is the first time I've left your nephew since he tried to kill himself. I'm sick to my stomach. I'm terrified.

"Therapy isn't really my strong suit," I said instead.

BAD HONEY

"You made the appointment," Riona noted. "You showed up to it, that's a start."

"How much do you know?" I asked, watching her shift uncomfortably in her green blouse and pencil skirt. "Being the team therapist, I'm sure you have access to files, or at the very least, Silas pulled strings by telling you why I needed a last-minute appointment."

"I haven't spoken to Silas in weeks, and as for folders, the only folders I have access to are the ones in my filing cabinet. I'm not privy to the medical or campus folders; whatever you want me to know, it will be my first time hearing it."

I studied her for a long moment, considering my options. Spill my guts and tell her every tiny detail of my tragic past, or keep it to myself and carry on functioning at fifteen percent. I chewed on my lip and turned to look out the large window overlooking the stadium. Below, the guys ran drills, and I would have instead been down there, taking notes with Silas and helping with stretches.

"Ella," she sighed.

That was quick. It had only taken me fifteen minutes to piss her off.

"My birthday is this weekend," I said, licking my bottom lip nervously and meeting her gaze. "Our birthday, my brother Ethan. We were twins."

"Were?" Riona gets caught up on that for a moment, her brows pinching together.

"He died last year, just after our birthday."

"So this is your first birthday without Ethan?" She asked, and I nodded, the sound of him choking on his blood thrumming in the back of my mind as I fought to regain control of my thoughts.

"What are your plans?" She asked.

"Ignoring it," I laughed.

"Healthy," she shook her head, "Do you have any other family in Rhode Island you can spend the day with?"

"No."

They're all with Ethan.

"Friends?" She asked.

"Yeah, a few."

had been bugging me to go out for dinner and have a sleepover. I had blown her off a few times over the week but it would be nice to spend the day with her if she would still have me.

"Celebrate your birthday, Ella," Riona said. "Whether you do it with friends or alone, take a moment and celebrate."

"I don't have anything to celebrate," I bit down on my tongue.

"Yes, you do."

"What about this one?" Zoey held up a copy of *Twilight*.

"I have that. It's also like fifteen years old." I laughed, pushing the book away from my face and scouring the shelf before me. "Thank you," I said, "for today."

We had gone for lunch on Van's credit card and shopping, finally ending up at one of the small off-campus bookstores. She had even opted to walk instead of driving, which was kind of her after I blew her off all week.

"You're my best friend, El, and it's your birthday. This is exactly where I want to be."

I tucked a few books under my arm and continued to look around.

"Besides, Ethan would have killed me if I didn't make sure you got spoiled today," she added playfully, but the thought still wounded my tender heart.

"It feels wrong, you know," I said, "having fun without him."

"You aren't having fun without him. You're having fun for him." Zoey shook her head and nudged me with her elbow. "He would have hated seeing you sad on your birthday. It was his favorite day of the year."

"That's because it was mandatory to give him attention."

"I've never met a man that loved attention as much as Ethan," Zoey laughed, and I joined her, "Okay, wait, no, maybe Cael."

"Cael's need for attention is an excellent rival."

BAD HONEY

Ethan was the epitome of a sun shower. He was the warmth and the lightness, but the freshness and that specific freedom that comes with jumping in puddles under a rainbow. I closed my eyes, and he stood before me with mirrored smiles and big brown eyes. His blonde hair was long on top and blew in whatever invisible wind my mind created at the moment. I inhaled, looking away for a moment, and he was gone.

"I miss him a lot," Zoey sighed.

"Me too."

Once we were done shopping and I couldn't carry any more books, we made our way back up the hill to the Nest so I could drop off all my birthday gifts and grab my backpack to spend the night in the dorms with Zoey. It would be nice to curl up in our blankets, eat bad food and watch shitty romance movies that rotted our brains and raised all our romantic standards.

"Okay, Marry, Fuck, Kill," Zoey listed off some actors, "Tom Holland, Kevin Bacon, Miles Teller."

"Kill Miles," I answer instantly, "Fuck Kevin and marry Tom."

"You'd fuck Kevin Bacon before Miles Teller?"

"I'd fuck a lot of things before I'd let him near me." I laughed and opened the gate to the Nest. "I'm actually concerned about how often you bring him up during this game."

"I'd fuck Miles Teller," she shrugged.

"Yeah, I know, your standards started and ended with Van Mitchell." I teased.

"You are seriously messed up in the head, you know that?" Zoey skipped through the gate in her tennis shoes and turned to face me as I caught up.

"Alright, harder one," she cleared her throat and threw a chunk of brown hair over her shoulder as a mischievous grin formed. "Arlo King, Cael Cody, Dean Tucker."

"Absolutely not," I said, "I'm not playing with people we know!"

"Listen, little Miss, *changes the rules to suit her narrative*. Play the game."

"It was one time, and it's not my fault you didn't know the rules of Marco Polo!" In sixth grade, Zoey didn't speak to me for three weeks after I beat her. It was the longest time we had ever gone without talking.

"Play." She poked my shoulder, "the game."

"Fuck Cael," I said, instantly gagging, "duct tape Dean to the flag pole naked on campus."

Zoey snorted.

"Killing him seemed harsh," I smiled.

"Marry Arlo," she finished for me, a glint of curiosity in her eyes as her lips pressed together.

"Don't read into it," I rolled my eyes, "marrying Cael would be a death sentence."

"Excuse you!"

I looked up to the porch where he hung lazily like a cat, a ball cap pushed low over his eyes, watching us approach the back of the Nest. I had it in my right mind to tug on the long leg that hung over the railing and bring him crashing to the grass below.

"You heard me," I squared my shoulders to look up at him and smiled. "We'd kill each other in a week, and you know it."

"She makes valid points, Sour Patch," he flicked the brim of his hat up and smiled at Zoey. When he turned back to me, his fake offended expression softened as he whispered, "Happy birthday, Peachy."

He offered me a genuine smile, and every weight I carried that day was lifted from my chest. A sun shower on a day without clouds.

"Thought you two were having a sleepover?" He looked between us as we climbed the stairs. He slid from the railing and fixed the sleeves of his gray t-shirt before twisting his red hat backward and lifting the bag of books from my hand.

"We are. I just wanted to drop this stuff off," I link my hand to his outturned elbow and lean against him.

"Marry Arlo," he scoffed under his breath, looking down at me.

"Don't judge me," I scowled. "Besides, think of how much fun we could have duct-taping Dean to a flagpole."

"I think we should do that anyway," Zoey giggled as Cael opened the door for us.

"Naked," Cael added with a serious tone.

BAD HONEY

"That would hurt so—" I should have seen it coming, but when the lights surged on throughout the Nest, and every Hornet player sprung out from behind the walls and furniture, it made me smile.

"Happy Birthday Ella!" They hollered and cheered, setting off confetti blasters and canisters of silly string.

The banner above the kitchen archway leading into the stuffed and decorated dining room looked like it had been painted in the dark. The streamers they hung from the ceiling with the balloons were crooked and loose, but they had tried so hard I couldn't find a single reason to complain. My chest filled with warmth.

"I thought you said the Nest doesn't throw parties?" I said as Dean came forward to wrap me up in a tight hug.

"For strangers," he pulled away, leaving only his fingertips on my wrists, "you're a Hornet."

You're a Hornet. Tears pricked at the corners of my eyes.

I swallowed tightly as Riona's words came back to me, *'Do you have any family in Rhode Island?'* I had answered no, but that wasn't the truth. I had all the family I needed, and they showed up even though I asked them not to.

I couldn't stop the tears when they started.

"Hey," Cael stepped around me, blocking my body from the other players. "I can make them go away if it's too much." He tightened his body, sinking onto the balls of his feet and lowering himself so his shoulders were even with mine. He waited a moment before bringing his hands up and rubbing away tears that clung to my jaw with the pad of his thumb.

"No," I cleared the rest of my face with the back of my hand, "no, this is incredible. I'm just really happy."

I choked out the words and fumbled tight, but Cael just winked at me, tapping two fingers over his chest and turning to the players. "Well! Get the girl a goddamn drink!" He threw his hands in the air, and the other guys erupted again.

"You sure you're okay?" He asked again, quietly this time.

"*Peachy*," I scrunched my nose at him and clapped my hands around his face.

"Good, I have something for you," he wiggled his eyebrows and took me by the hand.

"Were you involved in these shenanigans?"

"Captain of them," Cael said in a matter-of-fact tone as he led us up the steps and away from the party toward his room. Over the last week, I had spent so much time there that it had become natural for me to slink and sit on the bed as he riffled through his drawers.

We had talked about so much, about his past, about mine. He was the first person since Zoey that I spoke to about everything. Talking about the accident had been agony, but it had helped him understand something he hadn't before about trauma and healing. It hurt, but if my pain could help him heal, I would suffer through.

I played with the corner of his pillowcase as he squatted in his jeans, still looking for something. "You lost it, didn't you?" I threw the pillow at his back, knocking him off balance hard enough for him to fall backward onto his ass in a fit of laughter.

"No, it's here, I swear," he chirped, the remnants of his Texas accent slipping out.

He went back to searching, and after a moment, he pulled a tiny velvet box from where it was tucked beneath unfolded clothes and textbooks. "Ha!" His massive, lanky body crawled across the floor before he straightened out and shoved himself between my knees. "Happy birthday, Peachy."

I had never really had a friend like Cael. Our relationship was built off a tragic understanding of addiction, and it connected us in a way that no one else could understand. It was silent but comforting, and I hadn't expected to find it waiting for me in the Nest, to find someone I could treat as a brother the way Cael allowed me to treat him.

It's like Ethan had gotten me a birthday gift from beyond the veil in the form of a six-three-man child. Even if Cael was a feral kitten soaked in gasoline, playing with a matchstick most days.

"What is it?" I asked, flipping the little box between my fingers.

"Don't get mad."

I tilted my head to the side, popping the box open to find a small, golden ring within the cushion. It was dainty and had a flat, sort of rectangle pendant as the focal point. My words caught in my throat, my finger rubbing over the engraving with tears in my eyes. "Ethan," I whispered, staring at the tiny 'E' engraved in the gold.

"Cael, this is—"

He stopped me, tugging the ring out and pushing it onto my thumb. "It's nothing. I know you don't like to talk about him often, but I figured..."

I'd never seen Cael so sheepish, especially not when a party was going on.

"It's perfect," I said, rolling the metal around on my thumb. "Thank you for thinking of me and *him*."

Cael leaned back onto his feet, his height keeping him at eye level even on his knees. I rolled my lip between my bottom teeth, scared to rejoin the party. My hand reached up around the necklace, fingers playing with the ring that hung there permanently. I wanted to do it for Zoey, Cael, and Van. But the tightness in my chest was returning, and the thought of facing a room full of people while battling an anxiety attack felt overwhelming.

"Peach?" His voice cut through the fog and settled against my chest like a weighted blanket. "What's wrong?"

Everything, "nothing."

"You sure?" His brow raised as his hand rubbed a lazy circle on my knee. "Van said you and Nick broke up. What happened?"

After the incident at the fundraiser, I was done. I wouldn't let him use me like that, especially not if I was merely a pawn to hurt Arlo. Which Cael, on multiple occasions, had hinted at. So, I ended things. He had taken it decently, more upset that I gave the necklace back with a broken clasp, complaining that he couldn't even return it in such a state.

"He's a man slut," I give him the same excuse I gave Zoe.

"Hey," Cael feigned insult, "there's nothing wrong with being a man slut."

"No, Kitten," I laughed, using Arlo's name for him as I pressed my hand to his face.

"So why, really? Don't lie this time," he blinked his big blue seafoam eyes at me with a soft, understanding smile.

"Nick wasn't what I needed."

His smile grew tenfold.

"No," I laughed, knowing what was turning in the gears behind those pretty, clever eyes. "Don't tell him, please," I said.

"Don't tell Arlo that you broke up with his brother because it's not what you needed…" Cael's smile was drunk on mischief as he climbed to his feet. "Sure, Peachy."

"I mean it," I warned, slapping my hands into his.

"Let's go get drunk," Cael nodded, letting go briefly to tap his fingers over his chest.

"Are you sure that's a good idea?" I let him pull me up from the bed into his side as he threw his arm over my shoulder.

"Light drinking, promise," he winked, pressing his fingers to his chest, "and no drugs today. I didn't take them."

"That's not a solution," I scolded.

"Let me have it, Ella," he said, using my name as a weapon. "Please."

"Be careful, we're going to a meeting tomorrow." I bargained.

"Yes, ma'am."

"God, don't call me that. I'm only two years older than you." I groaned as he led us back down the stairs back to the party.

KING

"Is she here?" I asked Silas, who was pulling more beer from the fridge in the garage.

"Yeah, you missed the surprise like the asshole you are," Silas set the box down on the bench.

When Cael had suggested the surprise party for Ella I had been against it at first, unsure whether it was because I was still holding on to the anger or out of selfish motive to have her alone on her birthday. But like Cael does he swayed me, arguing that she needed the party, she needed friends today and he wouldn't tell me why but I trusted the severe tone of his voice enough to go along with it.

After the fundraiser, I was stuck between continuing to push her buttons, meeting her where she stood, and leaving her to figure out exactly what she needed.

"King you got it bad," Silas laughed, "you should see the fucking look on your face from just thinking about her."

"Shut the fuck up," I groaned.

"What's that?" He pointed to the baby blue, wide-handled bicycle that I had leaned against the wall.

"Her present." I choked out, thinking he would laugh at me for it.

But he didn't. He stared at the bike, its brand-new wheels and white seat. Its clean, deep basket and matching white handles. I paid sixty bucks for it and painted it for Ella, the blue paint that wrecked my favorite jeans and still stained my fingernails. I have no idea what got into me but when I saw it for sale on the marketplace I couldn't stop thinking about her. Ella walked everywhere she went, I had never seen her in a car but walking wasn't efficient. Some mornings she left the house before five to hike down the hill to campus for class, a distance that would take ten minutes in a car but took her half an hour. Before I realized what I was doing I was shoving the bike into the back of Dean's truck and repairing it for her.

"Help me carry these inside," Silas pushed a box into my arms without a word about the bike and walked into the house.

"No jokes?" I said, following him.

"You deserve to be happy, Ar," was all he said. "If buying the Nest's newest orphan a bike makes you happy, I'm not going to crack a single joke at your expense."

I scowled at his back and followed him through the crowded house. Even with the invitation list small it still felt like there were more people in the house than there should have been. A group of players piled onto the massive sofas in the living room, hollering over a baseball game while Todd handed beers into outstretched hands. I adjusted the box in my arms and followed Silas through to the crowded kitchen. I was about to ask where Cael was when I found him lying across the island with Zoey pouring a waterfall of vodka into his mouth. I swallowed the urge to scold him, to say I told you so to Silas who looked back at me with the roll of his eyes. *We have to be.* The words resonated through me; we had to be enough, which meant I needed to pay closer attention to Cael.

As if the world wanted me distracted, Ella's soft laughter floated over the crowd like a chorus dragging my eyes to where she sat cross-legged in a pair of jean shorts and a daisy-covered tank top that showed all her scars without remorse. The gold necklace that contained my ring hung around her neck; selfishly, I was glad to see it. I had been in her room the night of the fundraiser. I'd climbed the stairs three times before knocking on her door only to find the room empty. Clothes strewn across her floor, the ring hanging on the mirror Zoey had picked out for her. I had convinced myself that it didn't match her outfit or that she was hiding it from Nick, proving how much the ring was starting to mean to her. And then the anger snapped in me when I saw the silver chain around her neck at the fundraiser, knowing that Nick had replaced it on purpose.

Like he was claiming her, marking his territory.

"You okay?" Van asked, cupping his hand around my shoulder.

"Yeah, it's just crowded."

He took that excuse, scooping the case of beer from me. He brought it over to Silas who was piling them into the fridge only to return. He handed me one from the fridge, opened and tapped his open bottle against mine.

"Thank you," he said quietly, "for keeping an eye on her."

"Don't thank me," I shook my head.

"I don't know if you've gotten the talk from Zo about Ella, but there are things you don't understand about her past, things that," he stopped, taking a swig of his beer and turning his face toward my ear as he lowered his voice. "She's lost everyone, Arlo, so if you're doing what I think you are, do not fuck this up." His words weren't a threat. Van wasn't the type, but I understood the protective tone of his voice. It was like she demanded it of people to guard her and keep her safe without asking.

"Relax Mitchell," I said, nudging his side. "She's too smart to forgive my attitude."

"Just be gentle, man. All she knows is grief."

I didn't take his words lightly, slipping them into my back pocket as a reminder to figure out why they all treated her with kid gloves. Ella moving from her spot caught my eye as she excused herself from the crowded kitchen into the back yard.

"Go," Van said before I even thought about following her. "Wish her a happy birthday, and don't be a dick, or I'll kick your ass."

"Shut the fuck up, Van." I shook my head, knowing full well he could. The fight would be interesting, and I'd get my fair share of shots in, but Van's size was an advantage I'd never beat.

I grabbed two fresh beers from the fridge between my fingers, bringing them outside to find her sitting on the deck with her feet hanging over the edge as she watched the stars in the sky.

She didn't turn around to see who had joined her but as I slipped down to sit next to her I felt her body tense like she hadn't expected it to be me.

"Happy birthday," I handed her the beer, watching her hesitate before she grabbed it.

"Thanks," she said tightly, turning back to the sky.

"How did you get that scar?" I thought but didn't ask; instead, I let the silence settle between us like it had done so many times before. *"What causes your panic attacks? Why are you so sad?"*

She turned to look at me again, and for a moment, between the slow blinks, I thought about how soft her lips were and how badly I wanted to kiss her. I inhaled deeply, rubbing the sharp pain in my chest away with the palm of my hand.

"You get them too," she said, "panic attacks."

"That's not what this is," I shook my head.

This wasn't panic.

"That's exactly what that is," Ella huffed, but it was soft and not the annoyed one she used to grant me. "Does your chest get tight like you can't breathe?" She asked, still staring at me. "Sometimes it hurts so bad it feels like someone is squeezing it between a vice grip and there's nothing you can do about it?"

It was agony.

"Having panic attacks doesn't make you less of a man," she added. "Just means you can't stare at me like I'm broken," she stared, her eyes glassy and reflecting the starry night sky at me, "not if you're broken too, Arlo. That's the pot calling the kettle black."

It was desire.

I wanted to laugh at her, to brush off the strangulated feeling around my throat that her words gave me but I couldn't because she was right. And I fucking hated it. Despite being put together on the outside, I wasn't whole. I was completely unsure if that was something I could be anymore, but when she looked at me, I thought I might have a chance just for a second.

It might be love.

"You say the most outlandish shit," I chewed the inside of my cheek as the burning in my chest rescinded.

"You just hate it because I'm right," she took a swig of beer, keeping an eye on me as she did.

It was absolutely and unapologetically love.

"You let that get infected." She pointed to the cut on my face.

BAD HONEY

"Both team doctors have been ignoring me all week," I teased, my whole body tensing beside her as she started to laugh.

"How do you expect to get any dates, pretty boy? With a scar like that?" She laughed louder, her body rocking into my shoulder.

I sucked in the cold night air through my clenched teeth, "got any tips?"

I didn't regret saying it, but I hated how she reacted. The tension between us seemed to explode and consume her laughter, silencing her and stealing away any of the progress we had made.

Before I could mend the hole I blew in our conversation, people started hollering from inside the house, demanding her attention. As she turned to look my eyes drank in every inch of her skin, including the scar I loved so much. *Idiot*. I sigh, causing her to look back at me.

"I know it's ugly."

It's not, I wanted to say.

Ella snapped as she caught me staring, "Thanks for reminding me. I should go see what that's about." She said pushing up from the porch, leaving her half-drunk beer behind in her place.

I ran my hands over my face and tried to roll out the tension in my shoulders as she walked away. I had no clue what the fuck was wrong with me lately. I couldn't seem to show her that I wasn't the asshole she thought I was. Whenever she tried to start a normal conversation, I found a way to sabotage it without even trying. I hadn't even gotten to tell her about the bike, not that she would even want it now.

I pulled out my phone, texting Silas.

> I need to get out of here and give Ella her bike. Don't tell her it's from me.

I sent the message, standing up and getting ready to leave when my phone vibrated in my hand.

> Come inside, Nick showed up.

Why the fuck would I care if Nick was there? If anything, that was a good enough reason to turn tail and leave the party. The last person I wanted to deal with was that drunk asshole and I certainly couldn't handle watching him molest Ella with his mouth anymore.

But something about Silas' message seemed off, strained, and short, so against my better judgment, I shoved my phone into my pocket and pulled open the back door to the kitchen.

Nick was drunk, more drunk than usual.

His hands were all over Ella, and just as expected, they coated my throat with a sticky film of vomit, but it wasn't like before. She wasn't enjoying it. She quietly pushed his hands away whenever they crept up her shirt or around her neck.

She looked uncomfortable.

He was persistent and it made me wanna cut his hands off for touching her when she didn't want it.

Ella was a big girl; she had told him so.

"Stop trying to save me."

I'd already put my foot in my mouth tonight, and I stood, hellbent on letting her figure it out. She could be with whoever she wanted, but it had to be on her terms, and whatever was happening before me was not. I stepped forward, itching to do something about it, but Silas shook his head across the kitchen. There was something else at play, some Silas understood, and from the looks of it, Van too, but Ella was oblivious to what was in Nick's other hand. A thick book was hidden behind his back as he whispered against her skin and she squirmed from his hold.

I resisted the urge that rumbled inside of my chest, the vicious want to throw him off of her, but she shoved her hands against his chest, slamming him into the wall behind him.

"I brought you a birthday present," Nick hollered, throwing the book on the counter loud enough to make Ella flinch.

Where the hell was Zoey?

"I thought you might like it," he said, pushing the book toward her hand. She looked down at it and all the color drained out of her face. "Now I know why you're attached to cokehead Cael Cody."

Cael was also missing, his tall frame noticeably absent from the crowd. I scanned around and only received a shrug from Silas. He was just as out of the loop as I was.

BAD HONEY

"You're just like him, aren't you?" Nick laughed in chorus with two of the assholes he had brought in with him. I stepped forward but one of them pushed me back with a heavy hand and a dirty look. "*Estella.*"

"Holy shit," Dean swore from my left, and that was the consensus from every player in the room. He did his best to break the barricade that Nick's friends had created but couldn't get through or even make room for me to try. *Fuck.*

"Painkiller popper Estella Miele kills her all-star twin and parents in a fiery blaze." Nick smiled proudly as his voice ran out over the kitchen.

The pain in Ella's eyes thrummed through me. I could feel the knife sinking deeper into her chest from across the room. Her whole body trembled as she stepped back from him with tears in her eyes, but Nick followed; stepping forward, he hovered over her.

My thoughts swirled trying to make sense of everything. I remember the NCAA news buzzing when the accident happened. They had been on the way to the draft when the female driver had been clipped by oncoming traffic.

Everyone in the car had died. She wasn't charged. They had called the whole thing an accident. But Ella's expression was wracked with guilt as the secret she tried so hard to keep under wraps was exposed. *All she knows is grief.* Van's words rang true.

"And you walked away scott-free except for these," his hand came up to touch her face, and that was enough.

I slammed into the body next to me, and chaos ensued. I pushed my way through his barricade of friends grabbing Nick by the collar as tightly as I could before dragging him out of the Nest backwards.

"That's it, Arlo, defend the little druggie whore," Nick laughed, stumbling into the grass as I tossed him away from me.

Everyone exited the kitchen behind us to watch the two of us argue. I hid a side of our relationship from the team, but he had crossed a line tonight. No one acts like that in the Nest, not even Nicholas King. This was my house.

"Makes sense," Nick righted himself and cleaned off his shirt, "you took Cody under your wing. What's one more drug addict lost cause?"

My fist connected with his face before I could stop myself, slamming against his cheek and nose without warning, and with so much anger behind it, I knocked him off his feet. "Get up," I barked, kicking his shoe. "You know why I let you kick the shit out of me Nick?" I grabbed him by the collar, yanking him to his feet only to shove him back hard against a tree. "Because it makes *you* feel better, it makes you feel bigger than Dad, and maybe that's what you need."

I stared at him, knowing that everyone was listening, my chest tight and my feelings out in the opening, "But you don't get to pick on everyone else, not in my house, not in the Nest. You keep that anger, that guilt, and pain for me. You take it out on *me*. Not them."

"Such a protector," he laughed but gagged at the same time forcing me to step back as he vomited in the grass at my feet. When he straightened out, wiping his mouth clean, he tried to take a cut at me, but I leaned back, and his punch fell short.

I shoved him back hard, "You're just like him." I said, "Mom would hate you." I could see the levee break behind his dark eyes as the pain flooded his chest. Overwhelmingly cold, it nipped and tugged at his veins and heart.

"Fuck you, Arlo," he snarled.

"Someone take this fucking idiot home," I spat, turning away from him.

I pushed through the house straight for , "where the hell is Zoey?" I asked, "Or Cael?" I yelled, turning to Dean who just shrugged at me.

A horrible feeling clawed at me.

"Everyone shut up."

If he had devised a plan to hurt Ella, he would have ensured the two people hovering over her would be out of his way. Nick had a thing for locking me in closets. He had never grown out of it.

As the noise in the house died, I listened, and before long, the sound of banging resonated from the garage door. I stormed toward it, unhooking the chair that someone had propped against the door, and unlocked it.

"Nick fucking locked us in there," Cael said, shoving past me like I had anything to do with it. Zoey slammed into Van's arms behind me, tears streaming from her face.

BAD HONEY

"Take her to your room," I said, "are you okay, Zoe?"

"No, your brother is a dick." She mumbled into Van's chest. "Where is Ella?"

"I'll find her. I'm sorry. I'll check on Cael." I nodded to Van, who effortlessly scooped Zoey into his arms and carried her toward the stairs.

I found Cael downing a shot of vodka, huddled in the corner of the kitchen. "Are you okay?" I ask as he swallows a second one.

"I'm fine, is Zoe?" He choked out as he wiped a dribble of vodka from his chin and turned his sad blue eyes up to look at me. "It's my fault; Nick said he had a present for Ella, and we just got so excited to see it that I didn't even- oh god, Ella."

"Did you know about her family?" I asked.

He nodded, "she told me after... what happened?"

"Nick told everyone."

Cael's face hardened, and anger flooded his emotions as he searched around the room.

"He's gone," I said.

I could feel the stares of every player on me. They knew our relationship was complicated and that it was rocky. But no one had ever seen us fight like that. I could not take back the things I had said. The rift was out in the open.

I had expected to feel sick to my stomach, having my image tarnished in such a way, but it wasn't the feeling of shame that hit me like a truck. It was *relief*.

"Go find Ella, I'm fine," Cael said, redirecting my attention.

"I'm the last person she wants right now," I said.

"It's not about what she wants, Arlo." *Meet her where she is.* "Don't be a pussy," Cael groaned.

"Drink some damn water," I snapped, grabbing a bottle for him and then one for her, brushing my hand over my neck before wandering back through the house. "Have you seen Ella?" I asked Silas as he passed.

"She's in her room," he said without hesitation. He had already gone to check on her. "Is your hand alright?"

I inhaled sharply, looking down. The adrenaline rush had utterly numbed the shredded knuckles on my pitching hand. I flexed it for him, trying to hide the pain from my face as the bones beneath the skin ground together uncomfortably.

"Is she okay?" I asked, avoiding his question, seeking only the answer he could give.

"I can't answer that," he shrugged, "Cael?"

"Fine, downing vodka shots."

"So acting normal then, I'll handle him," Silas groaned, "bring her that." He pointed to the water, "And be nice, Arlo."

"I'm trying." I snapped because it seemed like no matter how hard I tried to be nice to her everyone seemed to think that I was pissing her off on purpose. Or that I enjoyed her being frustrated and sad in my presence. In reality, I just wanted to hear her laugh again. What happened tonight would surely steal that sound from her permanently. *Fuck.*

I stopped at her door. The last time I was in here, she was not. But it smelled like her even from the other side of the door and I took a moment to center myself. Pressing my forehead to Ella's door I inhaled the smell of the original wood to steady my thoughts and the rapid beat of my heart.

Knocking once, I waited for her to open the door, but no motion came from the other side. I waited for another long moment before I spoke.

"Ella," the name caught in my throat, tumbling in a clumsy, suffocated cough. "I'm sorry," I whispered, barely loud enough for anyone to hear, let alone her, through a heavy wooden barrier.

I wasn't even sure what I was sorry for. My behavior, my attitude, my brother, my misstep in words that led to her leaving me on the deck? Would she have stayed under the stars with me if I hadn't admired her scar? Protected from Nicholas and from the hurt that the world continuously beat into her.

On the off chance that she didn't lock the door, I tried the knob, turning it in my hand and popping it open softly to find her curled up, still in her shorts and tank top above her comforter. "Ella?" I whispered not getting a response from her.

BAD HONEY

I made to leave. It had been idiotic even to come up here. I wasn't just some guy tonight; I had been part of the problem. I was setting the water bottle on the table when I heard the sob leave her lips, and it broke a fragile wall inside of my heart so quickly that I couldn't help but sink to my knees beside her bed.

"Blondie," I whispered, hoping she could see through her agony to at least snap at me for the nickname.

"I can't-" she said, tightening her arms around her legs.

I tried to remember how to help her, how I helped Cael in the past out of the panic attacks. Even in denial, I dug through my memories, the techniques, and the rules Riona gave me a hundred times.

Without words, half expecting a fight I slid onto the bed behind her, wrapping my arms around her center and tugging her body against mine until I had her cradled in my chest. I pressed my fingers through her hair.

"Ella," I said again, trying to get her lucid enough to take a deep breath. Another long minute of breathless cries that not only sounded painful but her entire body seemed to tense with every attempt made. When the only noise that fell from her was another suffocating sob I did the only thing that ever helped me. I balled my hand into a fist and rubbed it against her chest, in a circular motion that seemed to ease her tense muscles.

"I'm so sorry," I whispered as her sobs lulled to silence, and she finally fell asleep.

MIELE

I avoided every family meal for three days before Cael came to find me. Zoey in tow. I held up in my room, staring at my phone and trying to figure out if I could transfer. Again. Games were easy, the boys were winning, and no one pushed themselves too hard. I was barely needed in the dugout, and most of them had completed their physiotherapy.

Silas had tried more than once to get me to open up about what happened, but anytime I tried, the panic attack took over, and I found myself sitting under my desk, trying to ground my feelings into something tangible. Riona had emailed me, but I didn't have the courage to respond to her.

"Peachy, you gotta leave this room; it smells."

He hovered in the doorway, a pale blue sweater pulled down over his lanky frame and a soft smile on his face. I liked that he had shaved his head to remove the bleach. Rubbing my hands over the dark blonde fuzz that had grown back was calming. Zoey hovered behind him with a bag of snacks and a warm smile.

"That's rich coming from you," I said, chucking my phone to the side so he couldn't see what I was looking at. "I see you brought the cavalry."

Zoey laughed, setting the bag at the end of my bed and curling up against the pillows beside me. Her hair was braided in sections and tucked into the loose collar of her long-sleeved shirt.

I swallow the tight feeling in my chest as Cael flopped over on my bed, his head resting against my knee. He felt guilty for not being there when Nick exploded. I think they both did, but it hadn't been

BAD HONEY

their fault. It wasn't anyone's fault but my own. For getting close to someone without contemplating the consequences that might come from letting another person into my life that I knew very little about. And for what? To get laid? To feel better momentarily. It was stupid and foolish to think I could have happiness, even the fleeting kind.

"Have you been going to your meetings?" I asked him as Zoey combed my hair to braid it down. I just wanted to avoid discussing anything that might hit too close to home.

"Just got back from one," he lied.

I could see it all over his face that he had stopped going. The bags under his eyes were dark again, and he reeked of day-old booze.

"Have you talked to Arlo yet?" He countered, knowing full well that wasn't a subject I wanted to discuss with them or anyone for that matter.

The morning after my birthday, I had rolled over with a massive headache, and Arlo was asleep on my bedroom floor. I hadn't drunk enough to forget why he was there or when he arrived, but he looked softer when the world wasn't weighing on his shoulders. His typically heavy brow and signature scowl were smoothed over and peaceful. Instead of waking him, I just watched the slow rise and fall of his chest until he stirred, at which point I pretended to be asleep so I didn't have to explain. Talking felt too hard.

After all, that had to be why he was there, waiting to question me about every little secret I had been keeping. Fleeting memories of hands in my hair and his voice trying to soothe me flickered across my thoughts. But I had dismissed it as a dream. When Nick exposed the accident to everyone, I could feel Arlo's eyes watching me, judging me. He probably had been waiting for something like this to prove I didn't belong in his precious Nest.

So, I avoided him for three days as I tried to figure out where to go when the past finally caught up with me. If he was going to kick me out of the Nest, the least I could do was have a backup plan before he did so.

I had spent hours on the phone with Mr. Novak. We were trying to figure out how to access the fund my parents had left me, but there was no way to get into it.

The world was catching up to me, and without a cushion of money, there was no way I would survive whatever heinous plans it had for me.

"No," I said to Cael, leaning back against my headboard.

"You really should," Zoey said.

"Why, so he can kick me out? Say, I told you so?" I looked at her, and she scowled.

"He's not going to do either of those things," Cael said.

"How do you know? He might have a soft spot for you, but after everything." I swallowed tightly, "he doesn't owe me anything, Cael. I'm just a liability for the team, for the season."

"If you're a liability, what do you think I am?" He laughed, rolling back against the mattress. Zoey laughed as his hand curled around her calf and squeezed.

"Adorable, that's why he keeps you around." I laughed, but it was strained and nervous sounding. "Besides what Nick said—"

Zoey huffed beside me, "I've never wanted to hit someone more."

"Don't listen to a fucking thing that guy says," Cael sat up on his elbows to look at me.

"He's right. Arlo is just collecting addicts. He can't even stand to be around me, yet here I am. And why?" I shrugged.

"Because Arlo isn't collecting addicts, maybe if you talked to him, you'd find out why!" Cael argued.

"You aren't an action figure, Ella," Zoey added. "Also, we all see how he looks at you. It's not a secret he cares."

"It's nauseating and dreamy," Cael winked at me.

"I'm scared," I admitted, tangling my fingers into Zoey's.

"So is he. It's a fatal flaw that the two of you seem to share. The lack of courage to communicate is outstanding." Cael rolled his eyes as I kicked his elbow out from underneath him.

A confession of sorts nipped at the back of my mind, "I can't lose another family, as silly as it sounds."

Zoey tensed beside me, but her hand squeezed in mine.

"It's not," he inched toward me, shoving himself between us. Zoey snuggled in comfortably, and Cael looked at me with understanding in those big blue eyes. "I know exactly how you feel, and it's not silly. Talk to him, Peachy."

"I don't know if I have the guts," I sighed.

"It's the only thing that's gonna make you feel safe."

Later that day, after searching for an hour for a quiet space in the house that wasn't my room, I curled up in the hammock outside between the giant oak trees that shaded the property. Cael had fallen asleep in my bed, groaning only when I pulled away to find something to eat. I balanced the apple on my chest and popped open my book, letting the sunlight warm my toes and push out all the sad thoughts that seemed to want to drown me.

"What are you reading?" His voice was like getting hit by a car. Anxiety flooded my body, and I wasn't sure how to even speak, so I let my book drop to make eye contact with him.

God, why is he always sweaty? It dripped down his flexed biceps into the crooks of his crossed arms. His hair was pushed back under a backward hornet hat, and his shirt was cut low around where the sleeves would have been, showing off the toned muscle of his chest and stomach.

"Your favorite," I quipped, trying not to sound flustered as he moved closer, tilting his head to the side to read the cover.

I watched him tug something from his back pocket, "this wasn't bad. The guy was an asshole, though. He should have fought harder." He set a copy of *Pride and Prejudice* on my lap, causing me to sit up in surprise.

"Did you take another one from my room?"

"Well, I didn't buy it, Blondie," he laughed. He actually fucking laughed. "What?" he asked, fidgeting with his hat.

"Nothing, I just don't think I've ever heard you laugh," I said in shock.

"I laugh," Arlo shrugged. "I laugh all the time."

He stared at me for a long time, his brows knitting together the longer the silence stretched, "what did you want, Arlo?"

I waited for him to say it, to tell me that I needed to pack up and get out. That being in the house would be bad for the team and Cael. Bad for him. Just because I had been expecting it didn't make it hurt any less.

"Here," I said, pulling the necklace from its hiding place, ready to return the tiny shred of kindness he once showed me. "I'll get Van to move my boxes out. I can be gone by tomorrow."

He let me drop the ring into his palm, staring down at it like it was burning his skin. He closed his fist around it and said nothing in return.

"I have something for you," he shifted on his feet, and for a second, I swore he was nervous.

"For me?"

"Will you just... follow me and stop being difficult?" He groaned, extending a hand to help me out of the hammock. The bruises from where he had punched Nick seemed to be fading into a sickly yellowish green, but as my eyes flickered back up to his, I saw the hurt there. He was avoiding talking about things, too.

"I'm sorry," he said suddenly. "For the other night, I shouldn't have hit him."

"I'm not mad that you hit him. He deserved it. I'm sorry you had to." His face changed then into that softer boy, someone unafraid and unapologetic. Shielded from the horrors of his mind for a brief second, he processed what I had said.

"I—" he started, his plump lips parted before closing again. The lines around his dark almond eyes scrunched tightly as he looked away toward the sun that barred down on us.

"What did you want to show me?" I interrupted him before he could say anything else.

He shook from his thoughts nervously, rolling out his tense shoulders before he led me around the side of the house and into the garage. My bare feet crunched uncomfortably through the sharp gravel surrounding the driveway, finding relief when I brushed them off on the concrete slab. Arlo disappeared around a corner, returning with a wide-handled blue bike that made my chest tight with the best kind of excitement.

"That's mine?" I set the books and apple down on the tool bench, moving further into the garage. When Arlo stepped back to give me space as I inspected its pretty white details, my heart fluttered for him to return. The seat was soft, and the handles were new, but it looked like one of the bikes from an old movie, like one from *The Notebook*, and I couldn't believe he had found it for me.

"I figured since you don't drive," he said, the words laced with curiosity. He wanted to know what happened and not in a malicious way, or so it seemed. He wasn't pushing the conversation, and for that, I was thankful. I don't think I'd have the words to explain myself anyway.

"If this is an apology for ruining my birth—"

"I bought it before your birthday. I was going to give it to you. It's not an apology. It's a gift." He seemed to take a big breath after saying what he needed to, his dark eyes trained on me as I ran my hand over the baby blue metal handle.

"It's blue," I smiled.

"That's your favorite color, right?" He asked quietly like a little kid.

"Arlo," I looked up to find him still staring, a nervous look on his face.

"You don't like it," he said with a groan, his jaw tightening. I watched him hide that vulnerable part of him away before I could even stop it from happening.

"Stop that," I shook my head at him. "You can't just get mad at me before you even know what I'm going to say!"

"I wasn't getting mad," he rolled his eyes and crossed his arms again.

I raised my eyebrow at him in response, and he uncurled them, trying to act relaxed.

"Thank you for my bike," I said softly, leaning it up against the tool bench to move around it closer to him. I stared down at my hands, rubbing my palm with my thumb as I tried to calm the rapid beating of my heart. "I will understand if what you want and what's good for the

Nest is for me to leave. None of you signed up to be a halfway home for a scarred-up, addicted orphan. And I'm sober now, from drugs I have been since-"

"Ella, stop," Arlo's voice was so soft it didn't even echo on the garage walls. "I know I don't act like it, but I'm not... heartless."

"I never said that," I sighed.

"You didn't have to. The Nest has always been a safe place for players and staff, and I don't recall Silas removing your job title from the roster. So, if you want to stay on the internship with the team, you have a home here. With us."

I chewed on my lip, trying not to cry in front of him. I'd been doing that enough lately, and I hated that it had become a habit. Arlo waited patiently for me to compose myself before quietly lifting my hand, "And stop giving this back to me. I'm starting to take it personally."

He dropped the ring into my palm, "You clearly aren't done with it, and it helps you more than it helps me."

"We can be friends, you know." All I could think about was his hands around my waist in the locker room. His lips were so close to mine that night that they stole the air from my lungs. But I couldn't fall out of one relationship into the arms of Arlo King. "At least we can try," I said, rolling the ring into my hand and looking up at him. His brown eyes flickered over my features, always snagging on the scar across my face. The look in his eyes turned the knife and reminded me that I'll always be that girl no matter how well I hide her from the world.

"Like you and Cael?" He asked; the question laced with, *"Will you tell me what really happened?"*

"Yeah," I smiled, "friends."

"We have two away games coming up," he licked his bottom lip, "I know you don't like to come on the road trips but please don't take advantage of the empty Nest and disappear. The guys like you, and Cael needs you."

He looked at me for a long moment, words he wanted to add dying on his lips as he pressed them together in a line. Part of me couldn't help but think maybe he wanted to add himself to the list but was still searching for the courage to do so.

KING

I spent the entire time in Pittsburgh, worried that Ella would be gone when we got home. I had Cael call her as we rode the bus back to Harbor. "Put it on speaker," I poked him, receiving a disgruntled snarl from under his baseball hat.

It went to voicemail.

"Is that normal?" I asked.

Cael pushed the brim of his hat up so I could see his eyes, "you're the one being a fucking weirdo," he groaned. "She's not just going to leave Arlo."

"I fucked up, Cael and—"

"She forgave you, didn't she? For something that wasn't even your fault, you protected her from Nick."

"After she told me to stop doing that!" I slumped down in my chair and pulled the dark hood over my eyes to get some sleep, but every time I closed my eyes, I just saw her. Her delicate curls, sad brown eyes, her nose scrunched up tightly when Cael made a gross joke, or how the right side of her smile was lopsided.

I missed her.

"We barely spoke before this trip, and I thought maybe—"

"She'd talk to you about everything." He finished for me. "She will when she's ready, it's heavy shit, and it all makes her feel," he took a deep breath, "like a coward or something."

She wasn't a coward. She was far from one with everything I had learned about her. She was brave. I couldn't stop wanting to wrap her up like I had done the night of her birthday, a catalyst event in my life that I'm not even sure she remembers happening. I'd slipped out from under her once she was asleep and used my sweater as a pillow on the floor. I couldn't leave her. Her slow breathing was the only thing that seemed to quell the ache in my racing heart.

Her panic attacks were fucking terrifying.

"Look," Cael pinched me, showing me his phone.

> **Sorry, in class.**

She texted him back, and even though I was wrestling with my jealousy that Cael had her phone number, I was glad she had. It was another four hours home, and the lack of sleep nipped at my heels as the rain poured outside. I started making a list in my head of everything I knew I liked about Ella.

How much I missed her laugh when the silence became too loud.

Most of the guys went to Hilly's, a local diner off campus, for dinner, leaving the Nest quiet and unoccupied for me to shower in peace, but before I did, I couldn't help myself. I dropped my duffle bag at my door and took the ten steps to hers, knocking gently. The door was ajar, but she wasn't inside. Her bed was neatly made, and a stack of books was piled at the foot of it. Everything looked so untouched. I took inventory of her shelves and closet, not noticing any bags or boxes. But the anxiety of her absence gnawed at me.

I changed quickly from my sweaty bus clothes and pulled on a clean blue shirt with a pair of sweats. I made my way upstairs, hoping maybe if she wasn't in her room, she might have found comfort in Cael's, but she wasn't there either. Starting to worry, I texted Cael.

> **What time did her last class end today?**

> **She only had one.**

BAD HONEY

> She's not here.

> You aren't looking hard enough.

I shoved my phone into my pocket and jogged back down the stairs to the main level of the Nest. Nothing looked out of place or bothered. The caretaker would have come in to tidy things, but it felt weirdly undisturbed. She had been here all alone. There had to be some trail. Before continuing my search, I dug the book I had bought her from the gift shop in Pittsburgh and palmed it as I made my way into the kitchen. There were no dishes in the sink, but sitting on the countertop was an empty bag of snap peas that brought a fluttery feeling to my chest. She was here. Or at least she hadn't left.

"I know where you are," I swore under my breath for not thinking of it sooner and pulled off my socks to pad out over the damp grass to the hammock. The air had become frigid from the rain storms over the week, making everything a little colder than a usual afternoon. "Isn't that cold?" I asked her as I approached.

Her toes stuck out from under the blanket, and her hair was messy beneath her purple hoodie and beanie. "Do I look cold?" She said, not looking up from her book.

"Alright," I nodded. She looked cozy aside from her red cheeks and nose, "what are you reading?"

She lifted the book so I could see the cover before laying it shut at her side and finally looking up at me. The breath of air I inhaled at that moment felt like flying.

"I uh—" I stumbled over my words as my heart picked up to an ungodly pace at the sight of her lopsided smile. "I got you this," I handed her the copy of *Wuthering Heights*.

"I don't own this copy," she smiled, shifting in her hammock to sit up. She ran her hands along the floral-decorated hardcover.

"I know," I said, trying not to sound like I had spent hours staring at her shelves, figuring out what she had and didn't have. Noticing simply that her copy of *Wuthering Heights*, seemed to be worn down and falling apart. It was her favorite, besides her tattered copies of *The Hunger Games* and *The Princess Bride*.

"Thank you," her brows pinched together. "How were the games?"

"Good," I shifted onto my left leg. I knew I was staring but couldn't figure out how to look away from her. "We won, nine to three, seven to four, and then eleven to six," I recalled the series scores.

"I listened," she admitted, "and your hand?"

When she reached out, I held my breath and untucked my hand from my pocket to extend to her. It's not like we hadn't touched before, and in far more compromising ways, a ghosting of the massage she had given me in the dugout haunted me every night before bed. But this was different. She carefully slid from the hammock, bare feet in her pajama shorts and oversized sweater. She wrapped her delicate fingers around my hand and held it up to her face so she could closely inspect the knuckles and fingers.

"It's healing. Did Silas have you ice it?" She asked, her gaze flickering up to me through thick lashes.

"Yes," I answered tightly, trying to keep a straight face as she rechecked it, brushing the pad of her thumb delicately over my knuckles. It made the butterflies in my chest go crazy.

The wind blew her hood off, pushing her hair around her neck and cheeks. She groaned, shivering as the damp air nipped at her bare legs. "Have you eaten today?" I asked her, knowing she probably had only snacked on the snap peas and called that proper nutrition.

"If you answer yes and only ate peas, I'll know Blondie."

"Then my answer is no," she stifled a laugh, and I wish she hadn't.

"What are you hungry for?" I asked her, scooping her blanket from the hammock and handing her the two books. She lazily walked up the hill to the kitchen door and curled onto one of the stools at the island. "Here," I handed her the blanket and watched as she wrapped herself tightly in it, just trying to warm up.

"I thought Rhode Island was supposed to be warm in June."

"Sort of, I guess. It's temperamental," I couldn't help but laugh at her scowl and knitted brows. "Later in the month, sure. Right now, all you get is rain. How about chicken soup?" I asked, and she nodded happily.

BAD HONEY

I pulled two cans and a package of crackers from the cupboard, sliding them across the island as I opened them and dumped them into a pot on the stove. "Where is everyone?"

"They went to Hilly's for dinner."

"Why didn't you go?" She asked as she nibbled on a cracker.

I needed to come make sure you hadn't left me.

"You try being stuck on a bus with a sober Cael Cody for eight hours and then ask me that," I said instead.

"He didn't drink in Pittsburgh?" She dropped the blanket over her shoulder to her arms and set the cracker down, tucking her foot up onto the stool.

"I think," I stopped to look at her, "he blames himself for what happened at your party. He hasn't touched a drink since. At least not that I've seen, and he's been attached to my hip for a week thinking you're mad at him."

"Why would he think that?" Her mood shifted, anxiety and guilt flooding her features, replacing the happy stares she had mere moments before.

"Something you'll learn about Cael is that when something happens, outside of his control, mind you, and he's drinking, he'll claim responsibility. Coach raised him to believe that everything is his fault."

I watched her process my words, her eyes glazed over as she tried to formulate an answer. "That doesn't mean it was your fault," I added. *Nick ruined that night, not you or Cael.* I wanted to tell her, but I didn't think bringing him up would make it better.

Her mouth parted to say something as her brows pinched together, but she closed it again and looked away.

"Guilt is tricky," I scratched my temple and walked around the island to sit on a stool beside her. I titled my head, trying to catch her eyes in a feeble attempt to get her to look at me again. I wanted to be the one she opened up to. To be there for her in ways she unknowingly was for me. "My mom died when I was younger, " I said. It had been a long time since I said those words out loud to someone other than Silas or Cael. "My dad killed her," I swallowed tightly, "they got in a car accident and survived, but a week later, she suffered a brain hemorrhage and died in the backyard. There was nothing anyone could do to prevent it."

"I'm sorry," her voice was quiet, but she stared at me when I looked up from the marble counter. "I didn't know," she tucked two fingers out of her blanket, wrapping them around my pinky and ring finger with a gentle squeeze.

"Lucas was supposed to pick them up the day of the accident. It was her birthday. But Nick forgot me at practice to sneak off with one of his girlfriends, so Lucas came to get me, and Dad drove home plastered off cheap beer."

"But—"

I shook my head, "what I'm trying to say is that guilt is subjective, Ella. I feel guilty for that day. Lucas feels guilt, even Nick and Dad. You can feel guilty over a situation that's clearly not your fault. It was just circumstances piled up and tipped over."

She swallowed tightly, and her gaze dropped to the counter.

"I piled them, Arlo," she said, discussing the circumstances that led to the accident. "I tipped them over." Her voice cracked as her hand came up to grip her chest.

"Nick wasn't wrong." She seemed to retreat into a place where I couldn't reach her. "I was strung out that night. Took a left turn into oncoming traffic-"

"You don't have to tell me this," I offered.

I could feel the hurt that radiated from her, the fear trickling down out of her fingertips every time she inhaled through quivering lips. Hearing it from her was different than the vile way my brother outed her on her birthday. He had made it sound so ruthless like she had murdered them on purpose, but that wasn't it. She had made a mistake. One that any one of us would have given the situation. And anyone could see that she was trying.

"He wasn't wrong," she said again, "it was my fault, not my parents or Ethan's," she brushed her finger over the ring on her thumb, "it wasn't even the semi-driver's fault. I made a decision. I carry the guilt, the scars."

"Punishing yourself for what happened is cruel," I pursed my lips together.

BAD HONEY

I hadn't realized how close we had gotten, our bodies leaning into each other's warmth, hands still intertwined by two fingers. I swallowed tightly, my eyes flickering to her lips as hers did the same. The fire in my chest seemed to rage as she inhaled slowly, her eyes fixated as mine traced the delicate lines of her scar to the freckles above her cheekbone. I wasn't even sure what to say because I was consumed by the desire to find out how soft her lips were. "Ella," I breathed out as she braced herself with a hand against my thigh, my skin itching where she made contact, begging for more. Hissing sounds filled the air and caused her to flinch away from me suddenly. I turned to the stove, ripping away from her touch to find the soup boiling in foamy bubbles.

I dropped from the stool, unlinking our hands.

"Shit," I flicked off the heat.

I had almost just kissed her. I would have, too, if the soup hadn't boiled over and made a mess. I took a minute, busying myself with cleaning up to steady the way my heart raced in my chest. *"We can be friends, you know."* The words from the previous week in the garage played like a bad record in my head. She didn't want to be kissed, she needed a friend, and I had almost fucked it up. Again.

"So, the panic attacks?" I asked as I poured her a mug of soup and gently handed it to her with our fingers brushing together.

"Products of severe trauma, I'm told." She shrugged, and her nose scrunched up from the steam in the cup.

"That day with Professor Tucker?"

She nodded and blew on her soup to cool it down as I dunked a cracker inside my own.

"I used to think my only triggers were cars and rain, but—"

I looked outside, knowing that it had rained heavily this morning and she had been alone in this massive house with only the sound of thunder and her thoughts. I could only hope that she had sunk into her bed and pulled her headphones on like she had the time before, ignoring her trigger blissfully with her nose in a book.

"Actually, I uh—" she stopped, a tiny smirk forming on her lips, "I might have slept in your bed last night."

Jesus fucking Christ.

"Why?" I asked with a more composed reaction.

"I don't have curtains, and neither does Cael."

"You don't have to explain," I stopped her. She had gone into my room because of the black-out curtains. "If I'm not home, you can use it... the bed. When you need it." The words came out one at a time, like I had a stutter, but I couldn't control the flow as her smile grew.

"Thank you."

I cleared my throat, licking my bottom lip before I spoke again, "There's a family barbecue next Sunday."

"I can keep myself busy in my room. I have studying to do anyway." She interrupted me.

"Blondie," I hummed, "stop cutting me off."

She laughed and put her hands up in the air in surrender.

"I have a plus one, so I can bring a friend."

"I can't do that, it's a family thing." She shook her head, taking a sip of her soup.

"Are you staying at the Nest for good?" I asked her, and she nodded reluctantly. She had nowhere else to go, and a tiny piece of me hoped she had grown attached to the people within the old walls. "Then you're family, Ella," I said in a way that made her sit up straighter in her chair. "You're coming. Besides, I know this isn't about you not being family. It's about the drive."

"I'm not very good with cars, Arlo." She added. "This is a horrible idea."

"It'll be fine." Anything for her. That seemed to be the mantra now. It was no longer avoiding her, hating her, pushing her away. It was finding her, helping her, soothing her. I hated it and how out of control it made me feel.

MIELE

"Wake up, Blondie," Arlo's voice pulled me awake. "Get showered, I'll get breakfast."

A week ago, I had almost kissed Arlo King, and now he was standing over my bed in a tight black shirt with a sleepy grin on his face, his hair tucked messily under a backward hat.

"What time is it?" I asked, rolling over to grab my phone. "Three in the morning! What the hell, Arlo?"

"We have somewhere to be!" He shrugged, pulling back the blankets.

"The bus isn't leaving here until nine!" I tugged the blankets back to fight the chill from my open window.

"Yeah, but I want to show you something. Besides, the highways will be quiet if we leave now."

The highway. I had tried so many times to forget about the drive ahead of us, but every time I tried, it sunk back in and triggered a panic attack. I chewed on my lip and curled my toes up tightly to quell the thrum of worry.

"Ella." He demanded my attention again. But I couldn't hide the fear in my eyes when I finally looked up at him. "You don't have to come if this is too hard. We can stay here."

He watched me process what he said, unable to hide the confusion and frustration. "You have to go. You're the Captain."

"That's exactly why I don't have to do anything," he said, forcing a rigid smile on his face for me.

"This weekend is important; Cael has been talking about it non-stop," I said, like that was reason enough to push through. I avoided the idea that when Arlo wasn't around- *I felt homesick.*

"Cael will talk about anything if you give him the chance." He laughed.

I wrapped my hand around my chest, my fingers digging until I found the ring there. "I have been in a car exactly four times since," I said, shocking him with the omission. "Once in the ambulance, once on the way to the airport, once on the way to my dorm room at Harbor, and then once for the fundraiser."

"I googled it," I said after a beat of silence. "The drive to the cottage—"

"It's three hours." He finished.

"Three hours," I choked out.

He chewed on the information momentarily, working out what to say to me, and decided on, "I finished Twilight." He looked at my stack of books. "Do girls really like the whole monster fucking thing?"

I snorted, sniffling for a moment to clear the few tears that escaped me, "technically, there's no monster fucking in the first book. You finished that in...what? Two days? You must have enjoyed it."

Arlo scoffed, "Which book are you bringing with you?" He asked me. "I'll read it when you're finished."

"Arlo," I huffed.

"Pick one that will distract you. You don't get car sick, do you?" He asked, clearly worried about the leather in the fastback.

"No," I shook my head.

"We do this together, two steps at a time," Arlo held his hand to me. "I bought road trip snacks." He cocked his head to the side with a smile.

I stared at him for a moment longer, causing him to wiggle his fingers impatiently, "Oh come on, Blondie, it'll be fun."

"Okay, okay!" I slapped my hand into his and let him haul me from his bed, our bodies slamming together awkwardly. His hand wrapped around my waist and held me steady, pinning our hips in place. "Hi."

"Morning," he whispered.

Inhaling sharply, his hand tangled into the hem of my shirt. I could feel his grip tighten as he balanced himself against my body. He blinked slowly, his lips hovering and brows pressed together. I traced his sharp features, taking in the lines of his face. The scar on his right eyebrow, the tiny flecks of gold in his eyes, the way his lip twitched when he was fighting with his thoughts. I smiled and felt his entire body flex around me in a silent, unwilling reaction.

Arlo was losing control.

I pushed to my toes, pressing against his chest, and felt him tense, his whole body rigid as he held his breath watching me. For a mere moment, I think he might try again, that he might lean down and kiss me. His eyes flickered to my lips, and I could feel his heart racing under my hands against his chest.

His lips parted, "shower, you stink."

Arlo pulled away, grabbed my duffle bag off my dresser, and disappeared toward the kitchen. I growled at the empty door, releasing all the pent-up sexual frustration that seemed to flood me when he was around. I was a goddamn mess, and the last thing I needed to be focusing on was the way Arlo's lips looked when he was resisting.

I took an extra long shower to spite him, cleaning my hair and shaving my legs before slipping into tights and a baggy sweater I could hide inside. I braided my hair into two long sections before walking toward my door. I wasted nearly ten minutes staring at the doorknob, swallowing the nausea that rolled through me.

When I padded into the kitchen with my book of choice under my arm, Arlo poured coffee into a tall stainless steel cup and shoved muffins into a bag beside the sink. He turned to look at me briefly as I entered but pretended like he hadn't as he returned to his task. It was going to be a long car ride.

"Here," he handed me the cup. "Ready?"

It was a loaded question. I wasn't sure I would ever be, and maybe I could still sneak out of it by projectile vomiting all over the pristine interior of his car. "What did you pick?" He asked, brown eyes narrowing in on the book under my arm.

"*The Fault in Our Stars*, you'll like it, no monster fucking."

"Is it going to make you sad?" He asked as we walked toward the garage.

"Books are supposed to make you sad, Arlo," I shrugged.

His brows were knitted together when he looked over his shoulder at me, "Why wouldn't you pick books that make you happy?"

"It'll make me happy, too," he threw the bag of snacks into the back seat through his window and opened the passenger door for me. "Books are written to incite emotions in us, ones we may never get to experience on our own or perhaps to prepare us for them when we finally do. If you aren't feeling anything when you read them, you aren't picking ones for you."

"I'm picking them for you," he answered quickly.

"You shouldn't be," I tried not to smile at the gesture's sweetness. The thought that he sat down and read *Twilight* in two days for *me* quelled the anxiety that tickled at my heartstrings. "Pick books that make you feel something, Arlo, not so you can impress a girl."

The look on his face was priceless as I slipped into the passenger side of the fastback, his hands flexing at his sides as he wandered back around to his side. The music blared through the radio as the car rumbled to life, and before he pulled from the garage, he turned to me.

"Ready?" He asked.

No, I wanted to answer, but instead, I took a deep breath, threaded my fingers into the pockets of my hoodie, and nodded. It was still dark out as he pushed the car down off-campus. And as I attempted every trick to busy my mind, I found my fingers tracing across the stitches of the seat. I had never been in a car so gorgeous. The white interior of the *'69 fastback* smelled like cinnamon, sweat, and leather. The black dashboard was dustless, and he had swapped the old radio out for an electronic system that showed the GPS and tracklist that played through the pristine, crisp-sounding speakers.

"It was my mom's," he said, noticing me inspecting the manual crank windows. "It went into storage after she died, but I didn't have the heart to let it rust in some container. So I pulled it out, and Silas helped me bring her back to life."

Back to life.

BAD HONEY

Memories bubbled roughly up my throat. This car was his way of being close to his mom, and I had nothing of Ethan. Nothing like this, so tangible and physical.

"It's incredible," I whispered, noticing the only imperfection was a birth date etched into the console behind the steering wheel. The highway was, as expected, empty, but the darkness that loomed over it scared me to no end. Not seeing what was in front or behind us made my heart race. I kept one hand on the ring around my neck and both eyes on what road I could see in the headlights in front of the Mustang. I kicked off my shoes and tucked my knees to my chest as Arlo tapped away on the steering wheel and kept his eyes trained on the road.

"What did you wanna show me?" I asked after nearly an hour of pitch-black silence.

"You'll see. Can't ruin the surprise." He turned to me briefly, "You should eat."

I unclicked my belt and turned in my seat, grabbing the bag of snacks from the back to find muffins, apples, and three bags of snap peas all shoved inside. I looked over at Arlo, jaw tensed, and shoulders pinned back, always ready for a war. Yet, he was kind enough to pack enough snap peas to last me the weekend and read my favorite books. I dug out a muffin, "do you want one?"

"Uh," he flicked his tongue over his bottom lip. "I don't want crumbs everywhere. It's okay. I can eat when we get—"

"Here," I said, pulling a piece of the one I took from the bag, "open up," I laughed.

Arlo's head flickered from the road, mouth open as he slightly leaned toward my fingers, his lips wrapping around and teeth taking the muffin from me.

"Is that carrot?" He scowled and swallowed it down. "Who the hell looks at a package of muffins, sees chocolate chip, and *chooses* to eat carrot? You know what," he laughed, "don't answer that. You eat snap peas for dinner. You clearly have no taste."

I scoffed. "Arlo King likes chocolate chips?"

"Everyone likes chocolate chips!" He rolled his hands over the wheel, checking the road again before leaning over for more of my carrot muffin.

"No way, you just insulted me," I popped a piece into my mouth.

"*Please*?" He leaned closer, using the center console to steady himself. The corners of his mouth curled into a soft smile and the corners around his chocolate brown eyes tightened into tiny lines.

Like a rubber band, my resolve snapped. I leaned toward him and slid another chunk of muffin into his mouth. "Thank you," he said with the smallest of smiles.

The car rattled over something in the road and kickstarted the anxiety that I had been keeping at bay until then. The sound of shattering glass and screams flooded in and took over, engulfing the smooth highway and our laughter like a dark cloud.

"Ella?" Arlo said, looking down to where my hand had grabbed onto his and was now linked. His thumb brushed over the top of the ring that Cael had gifted me in long, delicate swipes. "It was just a bump." He said as I tore my hand away, tucking it back into my sweater.

His abandoned fingers flexed tightly before wrapping around the stick.

"We've only got an hour left. Try to sleep." His tone changed.

"I'm sorry," I rubbed my hands across my face, rubbing not only the stubborn sleep that stuck there away but staunching the urge to cry in front of him.

"Get some sleep, Blondie," he responded without turning from the road.

But I couldn't, no matter how hard I tried or how long I sat, curled against the door with my head against the window. Sleep never found me. When the highway turned to trees, and the road turned narrow, Arlo pulled us onto a rough gravel road nestled between massive trees and dense brush.

"Hey," he tapped me as the car's engine died, "come on," he climbed from the car without checking to see if I was awake and wandered toward the massive cabin. I slipped on my shoes, tucked into my sweater, and climbed from the car in awe of the building before me.

Sitting elevated, with a massive porch, was a two-story log cabin that screamed *Shore money*. It must have been more extensive than the Nest, with cushioned outdoor seating and two elegant French door entrances. One was on the deck, and one was below, surrounded by a simple patio and flowers. It was beautiful.

"That's not the surprise, Blondie," Arlo said from the side of the cabin, "quit gawking at that monstrosity Silas calls a cabin."

I followed him, sneakers crunching against the gravel until it turned to a sandy path. I could see how tense he was, each muscle in his back pulling beneath his tight black shirt.

"It's slippery," he stopped, turning with his hand out to me. *It's just a hand*, I thought to myself as he waited on me. The few times we had touched had been simple, friendship just like I'd suggested, but I looked back to the car nervously and spooked him.

"Fine, just be careful." He snapped.

I sighed, taking his warning, and dug my heels into the soft path as we descended toward the lake. There was a long pier that cut through the glassy water and a boat that I could see from the hilly path, and as the trees thinned out, I understood why Arlo wanted to come up here so early.

The sky was painted every shade of red, yellow, and orange, with deep pink and lavender streaks tangled between the fluffy clouds. I followed him onto the pier, expecting it to sway beneath our weight, but it was sturdy and strong under our steps.

He pulled off his hat, tipping his chin to the sky, shoulders tight, but as he inhaled slowly and closed his eyes, his body seemed to silently undo all the knots he had worked deep into his muscles. His shoulders dropped, and his neck went slack as he drank in the cool morning air. Little tuffs of his dark hair danced in the breeze, falling against his forehead, and his full lips parted as his body finally relaxed for the first time since I had known him. It was surprising that I hadn't honestly noticed how beautiful he was, but painted with the sunrise, he seemed to glow in a different light. It made my heart race uncomfortably in my chest, causing my fingers to tingle with the need to touch him.

"This was worth it," I whispered to him.

"Mmm," he hummed, turning his head to look at me. The sun caught in his brown eyes and lit them up with streaks of gold. "I told you."

KING

We sat silently on the dock for nearly an hour, bathing in the sun as the birds started to sing and the lake came alive. It wasn't until she mentioned the time that I realized I should show her where she could sleep and set her up before the chaos ensued.

I set her bag down on the kitchen counter, everything in the cabin was made to look homey and warm but it didn't hide the fact that the Shores had too much money. Grandpa Shore had commissioned this cabin for one reason: Harbor Hornets family weekend. Half the time, it sat empty unless the team decided on an impromptu getaway.

The enormous kitchen was made for groups of people moving around to cook meals. The tall double-wide fridge, hidden within the cupboards, would have been stocked with food the night before. The coolers in the loft with beer and the refrigerator in the lake shed are fully loaded for the day by the lake.

"This place is endless," she ran her hand against the back of the enormous L-shaped sectional in the main living room and tilted her chin to admire the high ceilings.

"Silas tells people he's going camping when he comes up here," I shook my head, "come on," I nodded toward the massive stairs that led up and over the kitchen into the loft above. She climbed them one at a time, looking down over the living space, the fireplace, and the dining room with a tight expression.

I didn't know much about her family, refusing to google the name for fear of finding something she wouldn't want me to know. But I did know that Ethan Miele was an all-star NCAA football player with a set career in the NFL before he died and that a lifestyle like that was not cheap for any parent. Ella didn't come from money as vast as the Shores', but she came from a decent amount. And still, the sheer size of the cabin had her eyes wide with every reveal.

The loft was created for the players, and all family rooms were in the basement of the home, away from the noise and chaos of the team for the weekend. The loft was a miniature nest. A large destroyed leather sectional and a few recliners sat in a circle near the banister that overlooked the living room, with a massive table in the center. To its left was a line of ugly blue coolers and a pool table that Dean was convinced had fleas when and Todd had hauled it up from the dump.

Its red top is frayed and stained from god only knows.

"The player bedrooms are back here," I walked her back to a hallway with six doors. Each room slept five players in the most uncomfortable bunk beds I had ever had the pleasure of sleeping in.

"Where do I sleep?" She asked.

Shit.

I opened the door to the room Cael, Dean, Van, and I had shared since joining the team and leaned against the door frame. She slid in, leaning on her shoulder to inspect the room, from the messy, tattered posters on the wall to the piles of records and books in the corner. This room was a catch-all for their personalities, ever-changing over the last three years.

"In here," I said without hesitation.

There was no way I was letting her sleep in the family quarters on the off chance that my family showed up. Besides, I was getting used to having her sleeping ten steps away. An entire floor between us was too much distance.

"Scary, I know," I licked my bottom lip, "selling point," I pointed to the beds against either wall, "you'll get to watch Cael and Van try to fit in youth bunk beds."

"You all share a room?" She looked over at me. The sun from the single window in the room washed over her in warm rays and highlighted her scar.

It framed all the best parts of her delicate face.

"You don't have to if you don't want to," I tried to play off my disappointment. "I just figured you'd want to be closer to Cael."

Her eyes drifted from mine, looking back into the room nervously. "Van spends most of his nights with Zoey in the family quarters, and Dean snores, but if you want, the bottom bunk is yours," I nodded to mine. I would sleep on top of her, my chest tightening at the thought of her tangled between my sheets.

"Are these yours?" She asked, finally stepping into the room toward the stack of books.

"No," I shook my head. "They're Dean's."

"Dean reads?" She laughed, and the world around me became unimportant.

"Not well," I teased just to keep the smile on her face. Despite never picking up a novel before meeting Ella, I had read nearly five books in the last two weeks. Lying in the darkness, thinking about her in the room over from mine. What was she doing? What was she thinking?

I hated them. Hate is a strong word. Because I loved the look on her face when I finished one, and even more so when I told her I liked one. *Twilight* had pushed it, though. I enjoyed the stories that involved a little less fantasy. I liked the ones that gave me ideas.

She turned one of the poetry books over in her hands before setting it back down and moving across the wall to stare at all the posters. "Not a word about the Baywatch posters," I said as her shoulder shook in a silent giggle, "those are relics."

Silas and I had grown up here during the summers. Most of the other guys only had the pleasure of the time they spent on the team. He and I had been coming here since we were fourteen and fifteen. Since the cabin was erected. Those posters were the only proof I had left of a normal childhood.

Through the beatings and berating, we always had this place.

Mrs. Shore would scoop Nick and me up during long, lonely away game weeks and bring us out here just to be kids. It was a haven.

"And the weird Asian Horror is Cael's. Maybe you can convince him to take them down." I nodded to a black-gray poster of a woman with a blurry screaming face.

"It's cute," She said without mockery. "It's honest. I actually wasn't sure if you had interests outside of baseball."

"Sure I do," I scoffed, my entire body tensing as she explored.

"Right," she laughed again, "Baseball and Baywatch."

"What did I say!" I smiled at her, and when she looked over her shoulder at me, I felt every locked door in my heart fly open.

"You said no teasing the posters," she raised her hands, "clearly I'm teasing you."

"I must have missed that distinction while you were mocking my childhood. How foolish of me." I shook my head.

"And the records?" She grazed the record player below the window sill, dropping to a squat in front of the crates that acted as a table. "Oh, these are Van Mitchell's. I've never seen a man so obsessed with the *Beach Boys.*"

Comfortable silence hung between us as she ran a hand against the bunk bed frame. I diverted my eyes as she looked at me, focusing on the poster of Kelly from *Saved by the Bell* that hung on the wall.

"Is this your mom?"

I looked back at her, focused on a tiny, tattered photo that I had pinned to the wall beside the lower bunk. Usually hidden by a pillow, she had moved it out of the way and ran her finger against it.

"Yeah," I managed to say, fighting with the immense sadness that hit me like a tidal wave.

"You look like her," she whispered, "you have her eyes."

No one ever said that to me, and hearing it for the first time seemed to break a wall within me. I pressed my tongue against the roof of my mouth to keep from crying, the feeling of really being seen overwhelming. I rubbed my fist against my chest, easing the ache that resided there as she stood, wandering back to the window to look out over the lake. I was grateful that she hadn't turned around. I didn't want her to see me like that. Falling apart over a death that happened so long ago. That's not who I was anymore, but sometimes the sadness slipped in.

"One condition," she finally spun around, braids spinning. "Cael and Dean are to remain a bible apart at all times."

Laughter erupted from me, engulfing the grief.

"I wouldn't worry about that. Dean's parents have no idea he's bisexual." I shrugged, "Professor Tucker is—"

"Old school?"

"Slightly homophobic," I shook my head.

"Does Coach know about Cael?" She asked, walking toward me.

We returned to the kitchen, and I grabbed a bottle of water from the fridge. Her eyes widened when I opened it. I lobbed it at her as she leaned over the counter.

"He does. Cael's never been one to hide who he is from anyone, not even his dad. That kid's gone through so much heartbreak over the years, and sometimes I think he might have his shit together more than any of us. He knows who he is and is that unapologetically, without hesitation or worry. He's just him, loud and honest. Sober or not."

"I think that says a lot about him," she smiled, "and you."

I stared at her momentarily and was trying to respond when the front door swung open. "We know you're here!" Cael's voice echoed through the empty cabin.

"Prepare yourself," I swallowed tightly as the footsteps boomed up the stairs. They were looking for us.

"For what?" She looks at me in surprise.

"You have about thirty seconds."

"Arlo!" Her brows pinched in worry.

"I'd take your sweater off." I smiled at her, trying not to laugh too hard at her confusion as the sound of players flooded the main floor.

"I'm not wearing a shirt, just my—" she was cut off by Cael and Dean sliding roughly into the kitchen, their shoulders fighting for dominance as they stalked toward us.

"Peachy!" Cael screamed in my ear as he pushed around the counter.

"I warned you," I groaned, dropping my hat to the counter and kicking off my shoes as I felt Van looming behind, "I fucking hate you guys," was the last thing I said as they scooped me up from the ground.

Cael threw Ella over his shoulder, kicking and screaming, her bare feet flailing in the air and her fists beating against his back as they carried us down to the lake. Every year, without fail, the first thing the team did was get in the lake. Captain first. It was one of the only times I let them get away with something as stupid as treating me like a sack of potatoes. Man-handling me, Van grunted under the weight as Dean slipped on a patch of mud.

BAD HONEY

"Fuck Tucker, carry your side!" He yipped.

Ella pushed her hands against Cael's back, angling her neck to look at me.

"I hate you!" She yelled.

Warmth filled my chest at the sight of her, trying not to laugh as Cael adjusted his hold on her. Her lips curled up on her face as Cael laughed her off and continued toward the lake.

"What kind of warning was that?" She mocked me, "I'd take your sweater off!"

"Cael, I swear to god!" She continued to scream, trying her best to wiggle from his grasp. "Put me down right now!"

They stopped on the pier, the team behind me kicking off their shoes and shirts. "Sorry, Peachy, rules are rules."

Her protests were silenced by the sound of splashing water.

The water was so fucking cold that my entire body burned as I pushed to the surface beside her and the rest of the team. She berated Cael, her head bobbing up and down as she fought the weight of her drenched sweater.

"Oh god!" Cael laughed, realizing quickly that she couldn't touch the bottom where he had thrown her, "come on," he turned so she could get on his back, her soaked sweater sleeve slapping roughly against his chest as he walked her back to the dock.

Zoey stood on the dock in a pair of jean shorts and a tank top, looking at the lake full of Hornets with a smile. "Did you know about this idiotic event?" Ella asked.

"It's tradition." Zoey handed her a towel. "You're a Hornet now."

She helped Ella strip from her sweater, leaving her standing in nothing but a tight black sports bra and the ring hanging around her neck. The scar on her chest was on full display. It was bigger than I had thought, cutting down between her breasts to the soft expanse of her stomach to her hip. The chilly morning air bit at her skin, hardening her nipples beneath the fabric, and even in the frozen lake, my dick reacted uncomfortably to the show.

I dunked beneath the surface, rubbing my face roughly between my hands and adjusting myself in my sweats before rejoining the land of the living to find Nick standing on the dock. The mood soured, and everyone was annoyed.

"You idiots still do this?" When Nick was Captain, he never got in the lake, refused, and warned anyone that put him in there would be sat for the next week of games. "Now you're going to get the cabin soaked, get out, we have shit to do before the families get here."

I should have known that he would have to come up. The head staff needed to be present for the weekend, and it was his job now as pitching coach to be there.

"Water's warm, Nicky boy. Why don't you come in?" Cael called to him with a smile.

"You fucking know better," he pointed at me. All the guise of the loving brother was gone since having his ass beaten on the front lawn of the Nest. "Out, now!" He ordered again, and some of the guys moved, but most stared at him.

"You aren't their captain anymore, Nick," I called to him.

"You're a child," he called back to me, "I should have let dad beat your fucking ass until you—"

His words were cut off by another splash as Ella shoved him roughly into the lake, fully dressed just like the rest of us. "New tradition," she smiled at him as he broke for air, "staff goes in the lake too."

"Fuc—" Cael pushed Nick's head back beneath the surface before he could say anything that would get him knocked out. The adrenaline was already pumping through my veins as he turned on Ella with his venom.

"Cody!" Nick choked out water as Cael pulled himself onto the deck, his clothing sticking to every inch of his tall, muscular body. "I'm gonna fucking kill you."

"I'd be scared if you ever got your hands dirty," he leaned back on the dock, not a care in the world, as he stripped from the soaked t-shirt and tossed it back toward Zoey and Ella.

Nick slapped the water with his hand, causing a scene before swimming away from the dock to the rocky shore and disappearing up the path to the house. Cael dropped his head back and shook the water from his hair, making Zoey squeal and retreat, but Ella just rubbed her fingers through it with a lazy smile, plopping down on the deck beside him in the sun.

"Shit," Cael went rigid as I lifted from the water to the dock on my knees. I pulled the wet fabric from my skin, letting the sun beat down on my back as my eyes followed his gaze to the top of the hill. "Arlo, don't," Cael called as I thrust to my feet and marched up the embankment.

It didn't matter. His protests were muted by the rage that filled my ears as I came to stand before Nick. "Why are you here?" I asked.

"I'm staff, dipshit," Nick dried his hair with a towel. "It's mandatory."

I stepped forward, feeling the eyes of everyone on me as I got in his face, "If you make this weekend uncomfortable, even a fraction of a second of it, for her. I will show you how much I have been holding back all these years."

"I'm sober now, Arlo," he puffed out his chest. "You think you're tough just because you beat up a drunk guy at a party?"

"You never learn," I shook my head, flexing my hands. "You're just like him."

That broke the rope that Nick kept taut within him, and he shoved me backward.

"Boys," Coach's voice boomed from the door below the deck as he stepped out into the sun, his hair brushed and face shaved for the first time in months he pressed himself between us. "Are you accosting players, Nick?"

"No sir," Nick swallowed tightly and tried not to roll his eyes at me.

"Good because I've warned you about that, and I wouldn't want you to have to leave early from family weekend."

"Just some brotherly love after he dumped me in the lake," Nick scowled. "Idiotic tradition."

"Captain goes in the lake," Coach dryly responded.

"Don't come in the house until you're dry," Nick told me.

"You look like a drowned rat, King," Coach looked up at him, "go shower."

"Round up the boys," Coach patted me on the shoulder, "you have an hour before I need prep work to start."

"Yes, sir," I nodded and walked back down the hill away from them. I could hear Coach ripping into him quietly and smiled to myself.

"Alright?" Ella looked at me.

She had pulled out her braids, and now her hair was falling loose around her face. Cael stood directly behind her, his skin dry from the sun but his jaw tight with worry.

"Alright," slipped from me, but I was distracted. Tempted to look up the hill, to check over my shoulder for my brother's stare, but Ella tilted her head to the side, the sun catching her brown eyes and lighting them up like amber. "Let's go dry off," I nodded, tapping two fingers to my chest to quell the anxiety that laced Cael's boyish features and composing myself.

MIELE

The sun felt good on my skin. It had been a considerable amount of time since I had felt comfortable enough to lay out in such a way. And even though my scars were out bathing in the sun, I didn't feel the need to cover myself with my arms or a towel. I stared at them in the bathroom mirror as I stripped from the clothes that had been soaked and smelled like the lake.

Not a single one of them had stared. No one had cared.

Coach let us be lazy for far longer than he should have. He and Silas prepared lunch without a word and brought it down to the docks. I couldn't tell if I was starving or if they were the best sandwiches I had ever eaten.

"These are incredible!" I washed it down with a bottle of water. "I didn't know you cooked."

"I don't know if sandwiches are cooking," Silas laughed, stripping his shirt and laying out in the sun with us on a chair nestled into the grass by the dock.

"Don't listen to him," Dean rolled his head over from where he and Cael seemed to form one giant mass of sun-kissed body parts. "Cael's mom taught us all to cook. It's the only reason we eat."

Arlo snapped his fingers, silencing Silas before he could protest again, and pointed toward Dean, "he's not right often. You should probably let him have that one."

A few hours later, the boys prepared dinner, fighting each other in the kitchen as parents, siblings, and old friends arrived for the party. The sun started to set over the cabin, and Zoey helped Van and Cael hang string lights around the back porch. Her version of helping was handing them fresh beers before theirs even ran empty. I was happy watching them all work together in tandem, smiling and laughing together. There was no stress or worry outside of the campus. They didn't care about the games or the win streak. School was an afterthought, something they would worry about on Monday. All their troubles seemed focused on which cocktails they should make their moms.

Every so often, Arlo would scan the room to find me. Three hours into prep, he found me snuggled beside Dean on the sofa, folding napkins over utensils. "Do you guys need more?" He asked awkwardly, shoving his hands into the pockets of his low-hanging shorts. He had forgone his shirt and pushed his hair under a backward hat.

It didn't matter how often I saw him like that, his lean muscular body, tanned and taut. I lost track of my sensible thoughts. He shifted on his feet, and every tense muscle moved in tune, his pelvic bones rolling with the motion and catching my eye as they trailed deeply below his waistband.

"I can grab them," Dean coughed before he pushed off the couch and disappeared before I got a say, instantly missing the buffer he provided between Arlo and me.

Arlo looked around, checking for watchful eyes before deciding where to sit. He looked at the empty spot beside me, his eyes seriously considering it before sliding the utensils away and settling on the coffee table across from me.

"I'm sorry that Nick is here," he apologized.

"He's staff, he was supposed to be here." I shrugged. It didn't bother me as much as it should have. I was grateful that Nick had exploded. I would have liked to hide away forever, to keep that dark side of my past hidden. If I had stayed in that place, alone and afraid, I wouldn't be sitting across from Arlo now, happy and relaxed for the first time in months.

"You've been actively trying to babysit my emotions from across the room all day, but if I'm being honest, this is the best day I've had in a long time, Arlo." I tapped the back of my hand on his knee and forced a wobbly smile to my lips. "Are you—"

"I'm fine," his words cut me off before I could finish.

BAD HONEY

"You're a horrible liar," I rolled a set of utensils together.

"Later maybe," Arlo swallowed tightly, "would you want to..."

His question was quieted by the front door swinging open, "here we go," Coach groaned as he walked by the back of the couch.

Arlo stood rigidly, his thoughts dying on the strained curves of his neck and shoulders. I turned to see why he had grown so tight, only to be met face-to-face with Arthur King. Legendary pitcher and, even more so, a legendary drunk. I had heard the rumors of him. Everyone did. He had left the majors for a reason, not because of the injury. That tear in his arm was minor, fixable with an off-season surgery that would have had him back in the game by spring camp. No, it was a cover for his drinking. The team had grown sick of him. He had gone from irreplaceable to a liability within his third season with the Pittsburgh Pirates.

"Dad," Arlo moved around me. Blocking me with his body, he stepped back half an inch, pressing his shoulder against my chest. Electric tension rolled down through him to his fingertips; wiggling at his side, I felt them brush against me. "Why are you here?"

He was shielding me, and even still, I'd never seen Arlo make himself small.

He wasn't the type. When faced with danger or stress, he made himself bigger, pinned back his shoulders, puffed out his chest, and stuck out his chin. But he seemed to curl down on himself, making his body smaller than Arthur, and it thrummed through me in the form of blind rage. *What had Arthur done to him?*

I pushed my hand into his without a second thought, tightening my grip in his palm as he tensed from the contact. He didn't look down or show it on his face, but he pushed everything he felt to me with a tight squeeze in return. Shielding the little boy within him in return with nothing more than a touch.

"It's family weekend," Arthur narrowed his eyes on me.

"You've never come before."

Out of the corner of my eye, I watched Silas approach from the kitchen, weary of the situation; he was close enough to interject but far enough away that Arlo wasn't suffocated from all angles.

"Arthur," Coach extended his hand to him in an unapologetic show of diffusion. "It's nice to see you."

"You as well, Ryan," Arthur said before returning his hazy gaze to where I stood. "We haven't had the pleasure."

He held his hand out to me with the clear expectation that I should also be afraid of him, but I pushed forward, Arlo tensing in my hand to stop me as I shook hands with my free one. "Ella Meile. Medical team."

"You're beautiful, Ella," Arthur said tightly as his head turned slightly to the side. The gears turned behind his bloodshot eyes, "are you not Nicholas' girlfriend?" His eyes trailed to where Arlo and I were linked together.

"No," I said without hesitation. "We broke up. Nick has some issues he needs to work out."

"And now?" his lips pursed, his eyes still attached to our hold. He wouldn't even look me in the eye, abandoning all semblance of respect.

"I'm enjoying my weekend."

"You look like a smart girl," he said, finally looking up, but his gaze turned to Arlo. "Maybe you can teach Arlo a thing or two before you move on to a new player."

"Maybe I could," I said with a fake smile. "I'll start by reminding Arlo that he's nothing like his dad." *Washed up, drunk, and cruel.*

"Please," Arthur's brows pinched as every man around me leaned closer. "Tell me how."

"Maybe some other time," Coach cleared his throat.

"No, let the girl speak. She has something to say."

I had so much to say. Because if Arlo, even terrified of his father, could still find it in him to be courageous enough to protect me, then I could at least try to return the sentiment. After all, that's what friends did.

"Your lack of respect is glaring, for not only me but everyone else trying to enjoy this weekend," I said as politely as possible.

Arthur laughed, a burst of mocking, loud laughter that filled the space with thick, uncuttable tension. "You have a mouth on you."

"Dad, please," Arlo swallowed.

BAD HONEY

The tension pulled tight until Arthur realized that I wouldn't back down to him. And then, finally, it snapped.

"Oh, be quiet, Arlo. We're just having a laugh." He flashed a tight, crooked smile at me.

No one said a word, but I could see Silas's jaw clenched at his tone. He clearly had been present for more than one blow-up between father and son. A worry dug deep into my consciousness as I realized Arlo had been searching his entire life for a way to escape his father. But being a legacy pitcher, doing what he loved and thrived at, meant he was forever stuck in Arthur King's shadow.

"Season seems to be going well." He changed the subject back to baseball, having successfully insulted my moral code. The stare toward Arlo was full of disdain. I had seen that look before when Arlo was staring at Nick. It was pure, unbridled hatred.

"Arlo's been supporting the team the whole way," Coach said, "he's been a major asset."

"I'm sure he has," Arthur cut him off disinterestedly.

"Have you been able to catch many games?" Silas sauntered closer without a sound and rested against the back of the couch. Another wall, this time one that protected Arlo.

"A few. Arlo needs to work on his splitter."

"That's your pitch, Dad," he said, "I've never been good at those."

"You can't be one-dimensional," his dad stepped forward, and Silas slid over on the back of the couch instinctively. "Fastballs," Arthur looked at Silas, "are easy to spot. You're playing lazy."

"Alright, Arthur," Coach slapped him on the shoulder, "let's get you some food and introduce you to Todd's mom. She is drunk and single."

Coach cast his green eyes over Arthur's shoulder at Arlo, a silent check-in with him as he distracted his father.

"Arlo, breathe," I squeezed his hand, and finally, something that sounded like a startled breath loosed from his closed lips. He tugged from my fingers and started toward the back door without another word, leaving me standing there with my hand open and my feelings momentarily hurt.

"I don't—" I turned to Silas.

"Give him a minute," he instructed, but something inside me warned me against waiting. Arlo didn't need the space they all seemed to give him in such moments. He needed a wall to beat his fist against. They were so accustomed to letting him deal with it alone from being pushed away so many times before.

"Ella," Silas warned.

I shook my head, "he wouldn't give one," I said and followed out the doors he disappeared through.

Walking past Cael on the porch, who looked surprised, "he's down there," he pointed out without so much as a conversation.

"His dad is here," I said from the top step.

Cael looked into the house, past a group of women to where Arthur stood listening to a conversation he had no interest in. "Be gentle with him, Peach." Cael flipped open a cooler, handing me two beers. "He may not want them, but you will."

I tried to laugh for him but formed nothing but a pitiful chuckle as I turned to descend the stairs. I followed the dimly lit path toward the dock, scooping up one of the blankets from the chairs on my way, and settled down next to Arlo.

"Not now, Blondie," he groaned and looked away from me.

"Take the beer Cap," Back to nicknames, two can play that game. "Don't be an asshole."

I tapped him on the chest with the cold bottle, waiting for him to take it, and eventually, after some persistence, he wrapped a hand around it. The sky was now deep purple, the sun swallowed by the thick line of trees surrounding the lake.

"He implied it, but you aren't a bat bunny," he said after what felt like hours of silence. "I'm sorry I didn't—" he licked his bottom lip. "You shouldn't have done that."

He meant standing up to his dad.

I curled into the blanket, facing him, and crossed my legs to rest flush with his thigh and back. His shoulder leaned carefully toward my chest like a string tugging on him. "I'm sorry," I said, causing him to look at me.

"Don't do that," he shook his head and looked back to the water, "don't look at me like that."

BAD HONEY

"Like what?"

"You feel sorry for me, and you shouldn't." His words came out a tight, twisted mess.

"I don't feel sorry for you," I scoffed.

It was the truth.

"I feel sorry for *him*," I said, "he sees you as a machine, something he can hit with a wrench if it's not working how he expects it to. But you aren't a machine, Arlo." As he listened, I watched him grind the stubborn gears in his heart and mind. "Arthur King can slap labels on whoever he wants. I can be a bat bunny if that's who he wants me to be. Cael can be the cokehead, and Silas can be the pretty boy. I see how he looks at them, too. He judges the people around you not because he's confident in his assumptions that we're all detrimental to your career but because he's scared and jealous of your support system."

"Ella," he whispered, cocking his head to the side and rolling all the anger out through his body.

"He chooses to ignore the man you are," I waited until he looked at me again before pressing two fingers to his chest above his heart. "You're the man who cares for Cael, even when he doesn't deserve it. You're the man who captains a baseball team better than I've ever seen anyone do. Arlo, you think you're mean and ruthless, but you can't even look at me like you hate me even when you're trying to."

He swallowed roughly, his Adam's apple bobbing in his throat as he reached forward and fixed the blanket as it slipped off my shoulder. He tucked it tightly against my chest, rubbing the scratchy fabric between his thumb and finger.

"Hell, you got me in a *car*," I laughed, "not even Zoey's been able to achieve that."

"I did do that," he finally mumbled, clearly fighting with unfamiliar emotions. "I should have stood up for you back there."

"You stand up for all of us, all the time," I rested my arm on my knee, two fingers still brushing against his heart as he leaned closer. "Besides, I can stand up for myself," I teased, "we covered that."

His finger brushed against the ring around my neck, slipping into it and holding it out under the rising moon. "It was mom's," he said, and I looked down at the gold band shining in the light that shone from the bulb above the lake shed.

Why would he give me something so special to him and trust me not to lose it even when we were not on the best of terms with one another? I couldn't form the words to ask. When I looked back up at him, he was staring at me, gauging my reaction to the information I had sought out repeatedly, only to be met with silence from everyone I had asked.

"She would hate who dad is now," he rolled his tongue over his teeth. "She would hate who we all are."

"I know it doesn't stand against the memory of your mom, but I don't hate who you are," I said, looking back down at the ring.

I could feel his eyes on me, processing what I had said.

"I have something for you," he said out of the blue as he pushed to his feet and extended his hands to me.

"Cael's right," I let him hoist me up from the dock, dropping the blanket around my feet. "You're a deflection artist," I rolled my eyes and shoved him backward with my hands.

"I was sad," he teased, walking behind me to the end of the dock. "I showed some emotion."

"For half a second," I shook my head, ready to scold him for real, when he tickled the palm of my hand with his fingers, slipping them down until they were gently tangled together. The touch was feathery, making my heart flutter like never before.

"Give me some credit," he whispered as he moved around me. "This way," he tugged on my arm carefully and took me down a path I hadn't noticed earlier that led away from the cabin and all its noise.

Along the quiet side of the property, where the trees parted across a high spot in the shore, was a hammock, strung carefully between two massive trunks was the hammock from the backyard of the Nest.

"Did you haul this up here?" I asked.

"It's the only place you're comfortable at home," he said, not looking back at me as he pulled me closer.

Home.

"We're here two days, Arlo," I scrunched my brows in confusion. I looked back up at the house, fully aware of the party happening, and then back to him waiting. The longing in his eyes spoke volumes as a smile spread across his face.

He shrugged in response as he tilted his head toward the hammock, "it's been a long day."

It had been...challenging, to say the least, and as I crawled into the hammock, toes first and heart full, I felt myself relax. The idea that Arlo had taken the time out of his own complicated day to set the damn hammock up swirled nervously around in my chest.

"Thank you," I said, snuggling down inside of it.

"Anything for you, Blondie," he tapped two fingers to his chest, and even though he didn't use my name, a different sentiment fell over us. A feeling that was undoubtedly best left undiscovered. He stood by watching me get comfortable, and when satisfied, he backed away from me with a proud smile. One I'd never seen before.

"Don't leave," I whispered, barely audible as fear overtook me. I had told him that we could be friends, and yet I sat, snuggling in the hammock, wishing and hoping that, for once, he would break the rules he worked so hard to follow. "I don't have a book," I said to cover my tracks.

Break the rules, Arlo. For me.

"You have the stars," he pointed to the sky, "you'll be okay."

"Please," I said. "Stay."

"That's not a good idea," he rubbed the back of his neck and looked back up at the cabin.

"It doesn't have to be a *good* idea," I smiled, "it can just be an idea."

"It won't hold both of us, Ella," He laughed, stepping back further.

"Sure it will." I held out my hand to him.

Arlo stared at my outstretched hand for a moment before he stepped forward and curled his fingers into mine, "slide over," he mumbled as he dipped into the hammock, settling down to the bottom. "Fuck," he swore as the hammock rocked and creaked beneath the weight.

Laughter tumbled between us as we navigated each other's bodies in such a small space. I shifted clumsily and rolled against him, gripping his sides as he steadied himself and relaxed. Propped up over him, his dark eyes watched me as every other sound around us seemed to fade into nothing but a dull roar. No sounds of laughing or music, just the shallow breaths passing between us as our lips gravitated toward one another.

"Ella," he whispered.

I wouldn't wait for his excuse or a list of reasons it was a bad idea. I pressed my mouth to him, dragging his bottom lip between mine and sinking against his touch. He pushed back. His tongue pulled against mine, deepening the kiss with a guttural moan that racked through my body, begging for more. But as quickly as the decision had been made to connect us, his body tensed. Momentarily confused, he pulled away, ripping a soft, complaining whimper from my mouth.

My heart thudded in my chest faster than it had ever beaten as he stared at me breathlessly with plump, kiss-bitten lips. I opened my mouth to say something or kiss him again. I wanted to prove to him how good it felt, to convince him how much we both wanted and needed it, but his nose brushed against mine and held me back from kissing him.

"If we do this," his voice dropped an octave as his hand pushed over my jaw and tangled into my hair. He inhaled so deeply his chest brushed against mine, "promise me you won't ever stop because I don't think I'll survive the fallout."

I had been so sure that he would protest against it, against me, that when he demanded the promise of me, I nearly cried. The ring dangled between us, brushing against his bare chest as he waited for me to say anything that might quell the worry he was experiencing. I shifted, properly straddling him with my thighs settled down against the sides of his stomach, and admired him in the moonlight that reflected off the lake.

I raked my hands over his chest, memorizing every hardened curve of his body before steadying myself against it and lifting my pinky to him. He stared at me for a long moment, dark eyes flickering over my face to the literal promise left waiting, hanging between us in the air. He chuckled then, a smile tickled at the corners of his mouth as he ran his hand over my thigh slowly before linking his pinky into mine and pulling our hands against his chest, over his heart.

BAD HONEY

"How long have you been waiting to do that?" I asked him as I leaned back into him.

Instead of answering me with more words, he looped a finger through the chain and tugged me down against his lips, the warmth of his kiss washing through me like a tidal wave. His hands raked around my back and tugged me tightly against his chest, trapping the heat between our bodies as his tongue slid back into my mouth. There was no worry about me stopping; I could spend eternity kissing Arlo King.

KING

B irds chirped loudly in the trees above me.

"Put your phone away," Zoey's voice whispered, followed by the sound of a camera shutter going off. "Cael," she hissed, and a loud groan filled the air.

"What do you two want?" I huffed, my arms tensing around a body that was not my own. I opened my eyes, the sun glaring down over me, nose buried into the crown of Ella's messy blonde hair. *Shit.*

"Just proof of the workplace canoodling," Cael waved his cell phone in the air as Zoey sheepishly hid behind his massive frame with reddened cheeks. "Morning, Peachy," he giggled as she stirred in my arms.

"Cael, I swear to god, if you don't fuck off right now—"

Ella squeezed my thigh to hush me, and all the blood in my body rushed between my legs as she worked to get comfortable again. I needed to get out of this situation, which needed to happen faster.

Surprisingly, I had never slept so well crammed into the hammock. Ella's legs tangled around mine, her chest pressed to my stomach and head on my chest. Who knows how long we might have laid there if our sleep hadn't been disturbed.

"Breakfast is ready," Zoey finally piped up. "We couldn't find you, and then Cael mentioned you had set up the hammock, so we came looking."

"After breakfast, we're choosing teams, and I have heavy bets placed on when you get picked this year, so get up." Cael kicked the bottom of the hammock, his foot digging into my ass.

BAD HONEY

A rabid growl vibrated from me, and a sleepy laugh filled the air as Ella turned her face into my chest, resting on her chin to look up at me through her heavy lashes.

Everything faded away.

I loved how she looked first thing in the morning.

Her lips curled into a lazy smile as she pushed up to take my bottom lip between hers. "Good morning," she scrunched her nose up, and all the lines of her scar wiggled like tiny bolts of lightning.

"Morning," I returned, letting her kiss me again despite the audience.

"*Morning,*" Cael moaned, rubbing his hands down over his arms in a mocking motion as he kissed the air.

"Cael?" Ella turned to look at him, pushing up from her position and untangling her legs from mine. "Run," she huffed, jumping up from the hammock and taking off after him.

There was no way she'd catch him, not with her five-nine frame against his six-three, but she sure tried. Laughter filled the air as she cornered him up against a grouping of trees he couldn't slide through and socked him playfully in the gut. Whatever he said to her next dampened the mood, but not in a sad way. They grew quiet, and Cael became more serious than I had ever seen him. Every so often, his eyes flickered up from her over to me.

Zoey disappeared into the house, leaving me alone long enough to adjust my shorts and roll from the hammock to the grass beneath. I pressed my forehead into the damp ground, centering my thoughts as I heard Ella's soft footsteps approach. I tilted my head to see her standing over me in last night's clothes, the sun pouring down around her, framing her like the angel she undoubtedly was.

"You alright?" She asked, kicking me gently in the shoulder.

"He's never going to let this go," I groaned, rolling onto my back as she settled into the grass beside me.

"Let him have it," she brushed a piece of my hair away from my face.

I tapped her knee with my finger, "you don't regret it or anything?"

"Arlo," Ella laughed as she leaned close to me and dropped her volume, "we made out like teenagers for nearly four hours last night in a hammock under the stars..."

"Okay, but Ella," I groaned, slightly embarrassed about my uncontrollable boyish desires, "do you regret it?"

"Not for a second."

The lack of hesitation tickled at all the strongholds in my heart.

"I'm not in the habit of breaking pinky promises," she said softly, her brows pinched together in worry. "Do you regret it?" She asked, brushing her hand into my palm.

I sat up, wanting to curl around her and pull her into my lap, but resisted the urge. Scared that doing so might be too much, too fast for her. I could feel her freaking out. It radiated off her like a live wire, growing hotter the longer it took me to answer. But how was I supposed to answer a question so simply? Of course, I didn't regret it. The memory of her lips would be forever burned into my brain. I could feel myself fall off the cliff with no way to stop from plummeting to the bottom.

"No," I shook my head, sliding closer to her, and cupped her face.

"The silence was deafening, Cap," she sighed, something cracking in the depths of her dark brown eyes. She was worried about the hesitation, but what she didn't know was that I could barely look at her without tripping over my thoughts. I needed a second to organize them, so I didn't blurt out. I *love you*. Which wasn't a lie, I think I knew a long time ago just how much but scaring her wasn't on my list of things to do today. No matter how badly I wanted to say those words, I wouldn't ruin the mood.

"And look too eager," I smiled, "do you even know me?"

Yeah, play it cool, idiot.

She smiled back at me, but it didn't reach her eyes, and I could tell how scared she was about this. I knew that the gossip would come down harder on her shoulders when everyone found out about what we were doing, whatever that may be. They would pick apart and analyze every aspect of our raw feelings and make assumptions about her motives. She had, after all, moved from one King brother to another in a matter of months. I couldn't protect her from the media, the campus news, or the fans. And the thought terrified me.

"Ella," I said, her face still resting in my hands, "we should probably keep this quiet at least until—"

"The season is over," she finished with a sad nod, pressing her cheek deeper into my hold. "And around Nick, I don't need him targeting you."

"I can handle Nick on my own," I said.

"This is our mess," her brows knit together tightly, "you don't do anything on your own anymore."

"Okay, settle down, tough guy," I laughed, leaning into her. I pressed my lips against hers, drinking in the lazy morning kiss, knowing it would be hours before I was granted another.

Ella broke the kiss and pushed to her feet, extending her arms to help me up from the ground. "What was Cael talking about?"

"Oh, Blondie," I threw my arm around her shoulder and nuzzled my lips against her temple. "You're in for a surprise."

Breakfast didn't take long. Everyone settled into the places around the massive dining table, the island, and on the couches, having small conversations. Nick avoided the table. Ella, Zoey and I gathered around with Van, Dean, and Cael. Van's father had made the trip into town and looked exactly like him: tall, broad with dark hair and dark eyes. A stark contrast to Dean's, whose mother and father were the perfect Scandinavian pair, with light hair and bright blue eyes. I could tell that Ella hated it. Every moment she spent forced into small talk with parents who weren't hers, asking questions about things only parents ask their children. One hand was on her fork, and the other was fiddling with my mother's ring. It was torture for her. I ran my hand beneath the table and squeezed her knee softly to stop her trembling.

Professor Tucker asked her a question as she pushed her scrambled eggs around her plate, unaware that everyone was staring at her. I gave her another squeeze.

"Sorry, I'm scatterbrained without coffee," she rubbed the ring between her fingers and clenched her jaw. "What did you ask?"

"How is your internship progressing? Having Silas Shore as a mentor must be wonderful," he repeated.

"It's been incredible." She spoke elegantly, her intelligence showing as she elevated the conversation with a soft smile. One that flawlessly hid the pain she carried beneath. "Before the program, I wasn't sure where I would go after university, but I'm starting to think that therapy is where I want to be."

"You'd work in a stadium like Mr. Shore?" Dean's mother asked.

I hadn't thought about what we would do when the season was over, how far away she might get from me. Sponsors, the majors, games, work, life. I swallowed the fear that threatened to rise in my throat and shoved a piece of bacon between my lips.

"A stadium gives off a special vibration, a rush of adrenaline that working with a team provides. It took a moment to figure it out, but I'm not sure I could live without that excitement."

The vibration is what I felt every single time I pressed my hand to the concrete tunnel. It was a feeling that not many people got to experience, but it seemed to quiet every anxious thought in my heart and head within seconds. I liked knowing that she felt it, too, that she understood it.

"Ella's a lifetime Hornet now," Silas said, settling down on the bench across from her with his food. "Here," he slid a mug of coffee toward her. "For your scatterbrain." He raised an eyebrow at her.

"Silas will have to give me a pay raise if he wants to tack *lifetime* onto my job title." She teased lightly, bringing the mug to her lips, "Thank you."

Dean's mother whispered something to him, causing Dean to roll his eyes before pushing from the table awkwardly with his plate and disappearing into the kitchen.

"Excuse me," I said, leaving Ella in Silas' care as I wandered to find Dean. His massive frame slumped over the kitchen sink. He ran the water hot enough for it to steam up as he stared out the window to the lake.

"What was that about," I turned, leaning my back on the sink and crossing my arms.

"Just mom, being a mom." He sighed after a long moment. "Ella's pretty. Is she single?" He mocked her high, polite accent.

"She's just curious, Dean," I nudged him, trying to skirt around the jealous pang that rebounded inside my chest at the thought of anyone near her but me. "Moms do that kind of shit. It's their job."

"You know better than anyone what she means," he set the plate down in the sink and turned off the water. "She doesn't care about that. She cares about continuing the Tucker legacy with grandkids."

"Doesn't your brother have like six?" I asked, trying not to laugh.

"Six girls," Dean looked over at me.

"*Fuck*," I groaned, and that's what broke him, laughter bubbling out of his lips as he braced himself over the sink with both hands. "You can have whatever you want, Dean," I said, certain now more than ever of my advice as my eyes found Ella's. "You just have to be brave enough to take it. And if that thing so happens to be Cael," I inhaled deeply, "the only person you have to worry about is me because if you break him, I'll kill you myself."

I gripped his shoulder, digging my fingers into his muscle enough to make him squirm, "But if it's that, and you're sure. Then stop worrying about your mom. Focus on your heart and baseball. That's all you need."

"You're an asshole King," he shook his head, but I could feel the sentiment behind his words. "Thank you," he didn't need me to be nice to him. He never had. That's what Van was for, Cael, even Silas on occasion. The only thing that Dean Tucker had ever needed from me was honesty.

I slapped that same hand over his heart and waited as he tapped two fingers to the face of it. "Good talk, Tuck," I laughed, patting him twice. "Go clear plates. We have a baseball game to play."

MIELE

The guys lined up in the grass beneath the porch as Zoey, and I settled on the stairs with cups of coffee in fuzzy socks and oversized sweaters. The morning air was chilly and nipped at my skin as I watched the players whisper to one another. Arlo had swapped his swim trunks for a pair of low-hanging black gym shorts and a ripped sleeveless band t-shirt that hung off his chest and exposed the hard lines of his ribcage. His hat turned backward over his messy hair. He winked at me before whispering something to Cael, standing next to him in a pink and purple tie-dye cropped shirt that framed his taut stomach and a pair of gray sweats. Cael nodded once before walking toward me.

"Did you bring your sneakers?" He leaned against the banister, adjusting the knot in the black bandana he had rolled up and used as a headband.

"Yeah, they're in the house," I shrugged.

"Go put them on. We're short a player."

"For what?"

"Just go put on shoes, please," Cael pouted, and my resolve melted away.

When I returned in shorts, a shirt, and sneakers, everyone else had disappeared, and Cael was waiting by a path leading down away from the cabin and the lake. "Where are we going?" I asked as he threw his arm around my shoulder and guided me through the trees.

"You're horrible at being surprised. Why this, where that?" He mocked, "Relax."

BAD HONEY

"I trust you as far as I could throw you, Cael Cody, and that's not very far."

"Hey," he leaned closer to me as we walked, "you kissed Arlo. Was it good? He won't let me kiss him. I've tried... more than once. I guess consent is important. I'll get him to give in eventually. Or is that coercion? Dubious consent?"

"Where did you even learn that term," I laughed.

"One day, I'm going to kiss your boyfriend Ella. I'm sorry, but I just have to know if it's good!" He rambled on.

"Oh my god, stop." I laughed wildly and tucked into his side with my reddened cheeks. "Yeah, it was really nice."

"I fucking knew it!" He celebrated, "he's good, isn't he?"

"Very."

"Ulterior motives aside," he stopped me just as the trees broke away from the path and the sun poured in. "Is that what you want?"

"I think it's what I needed," I poked him in the chest, "and that pisses me off cause I hate being wrong."

"I think I need to hear you say the full sentence, *Cael. You were right, I was wrong.*"

"Absolutely not," I shook my head.

"Oh, come on, Peachy," he begged. "I'll get that too. A kiss from Arlo King and a confirmation from you that I was right! Bucket list."

"Over my dead body," I shoved him back, and he shrugged, already bored.

He mumbled something about being picked last as we wandered into a massive cleared field.

"Holy shit," I swore, looking around. There was an enormous, well-kept baseball field on the property, surrounded by trees, guarded from the highway with bleachers and dugouts. "The Shore's have too much money."

Cael pulled me over to where all the players stood, "Ella's on the roster since we're down a player."

"No," I shook my head. I hadn't played an inning of baseball since the game that ruined my career. "I appreciate the excitement, but no."

I expected protests from them, but everyone stood quietly for a long moment, unsure whether or not pushing the subject was appropriate.

"You can just say you're a chicken," Arlo shrugged, the muscles in his shoulders already glistening from sweat in the sun. "Zoey has wine in the dugout. You can go sit with the *girls and parents*."

I tilted my head to the side, wanting to tell him that peer pressure wouldn't work when he opened his mouth again. "We can't all be winners."

Stepping forward into his space, our chests nearly pressed together, I felt him inhale sharply from the near contact. "If I remember correctly, you lost the first time we met."

"So give me a rematch, Blondie. It's the least you can do," the words rolled off his lips, and my body ignited, remembering all the places he promised to put them the night before.

"Ask me nicely," I whispered.

Arlo's jaw clenched as the muscles in his neck strained, and he cocked his head to the side with a soft nod, "Please."

A strangled howl of laughter tumbled from Dean beside us.

"Okay, fine," I agreed, terrified of how it might go but unable to back down from a challenge. Everyone erupted into cheers and created a circle around us.

"Who are the captains? You and—"

"No, on this field, I'm just a player. Zoe," Arlo called to her, and she climbed down from where she sat next to Silas, chatting.

Arlo flipped off his hat, hair messy in the wind, and held it out to her. She pulled a baggy paper from her jean shorts and filled the hat with the names. "We draw for the captains."

He moved the hat toward me, holding it just out of reach and forcing me to push to my tiptoes to reach inside. I stumbled a step, digging my fingers into his chest as my other hand wrapped around two slips of paper.

"Dean," I read and opened the second one. "Coach?" I must have sounded baffled because a few of the guys laughed.

"Fuck," Cael rolled his eyes, "there goes my bets."

"Coach plays?" My mouth dropped open.

"Coach plays," he appeared from behind Van carrying a crate of balls in a dark green sleeveless shirt, a pair of Hornet's gym shorts, and a backward hat. Mr. March did not disappoint, both arms an impressive display of muscle and an ode to how well he had aged.

"You're drooling," Arlo whispered from beside me, and I elbowed him in the stomach.

"Okay!" Coach clapped his hands with a shitty grin on his face. "Dean, you can pick first."

"Mitchell." He pointed in Van's direction.

"Jensen," Coach picked next.

"Ella," Dean said, and the players all hollered. "I've seen the reels. Come on." He waved me over, and Van threw his arm around my shoulders.

"Cael," Coach said surprisingly.

Arlo stood with arms crossed over his chest and a dirty look on his face as they slowly filled their teams with players, leaving him beside Todd. The last two players.

"Is this normal?" I whispered to Van, who just nodded.

"The guys like to knock him down a peg every year. He pretends it bothers him, but I don't think he cares. Dude is a big softy somewhere beneath all that grouchy exterior."

"Todd," Dean picked, leaving Arlo to coach and us on opposite teams.

"Come on, Cap." Coach called him over and patted him on the back.

Van massaged his fingers into my shoulders and leaned down over me, "you ready?" He asked in my ear.

It had been a very long time since I held a bat. Running wasn't the issue. Short-term hobby games didn't place the same amount of pressure as competitive games, but... "One inning at a time," he said.

Ethan used to say the same thing, and it never worked to quell the anxiety and stress I was feeling before games, and it wasn't going to work now. I huffed a breath and made my way toward the dugout where Dean and Zoey were huddled, creating the lineup for the game.

"Is this a yearly thing?" I asked as Van set out a few bats.

"Yeah," he smiled, shifting on his heels where he was squatting, inspecting the metal and wood ends. "Coach started it when he took the job a few years ago, and we've been doing it ever since. It's just for fun, but it always refreshes everyone for the second half of the season."

"Peach," Cael called to me, jogging over from the other dugout with a mitt beneath his arm, "here."

My eyes watered as I reached out for the tattered black leather glove. The white stitching pulled along the thumb, and the palm was worn down and grayed compared to the rest of the mit. "Where—" I barely formed the word.

"It was in one of the boxes in your storage unit. We found it when Van and I were moving boxes to the Nest. Thought you might need it today."

The glove that had won so many games and caused me so much turmoil. It was nostalgic and painful all at the same time. "I wasn't even sure I was coming this weekend, Cael," I swallowed the memories surrounding this glove, pushing them down away and locking them back up.

"I was sure," he smiled, backing away, "don't go easy on us just because *Princess* is on our team. You can make it up to him later." Arlo was warming up his shoulder, swinging a bat in wide circles with his head turned to the sky.

"Go away," I rolled my eyes, wiping the tears that had escaped my cheek.

"Ella, you're pitching," Dean said as I stepped into the dugout.

"No, I am not."

"You're the only one good enough last year. Van let in six runs!"

"That's not even that bad," I shrugged. I wasn't doing it.

"In the first inning!" Dean added, raising his hands in the air, and stepping toward me. "Do it for the kids!" He leaned down to get eye level with me and pushed his bottom lip out. "Most of us haven't been on the winning team in years. Coach always takes Cael and King! They're our best hitters."

"So why didn't you pick either of them!"

"Because Arlo has to go last! And I can't not pick my best friend!" Dean argued, looking at Van, who smiled like a little kid.

BAD HONEY

"Get him a friendship bracelet next time, you idiot! Leaving Cael to be snagged is your problem, not mine! This isn't going to work."

My heart was pounding in my chest.

"I chose you because you're better than him," Dean pointed to where Arlo watched us across the infield with a cocky grin on his face.

"Think of how good it'll feel to strike them out," Van propped himself against Dean with his arm and wiggled his eyebrows at me.

I sighed, wrapping my fingers around the ring, and counted internally to ten. I looked back at the boys, feeling insane as I said.

"Remember you wanted this," I sighed, letting the thrill of the game and the adrenaline fill me up.

Nothing would feel better. I pushed my hand into my glove, stretching my fingers out within the tight confines of the old leather, and smiled, slapping it against Dean's chest.

"Keep it tight. Don't worry about Arlo. Watch Cael and Coach. They're going to cause trouble in the infield for grounders. And Van," I turned to him, lowering my voice. "I want you at shortstop."

"I play—"

"I know where you play normally. You're as dense as you are tall. I want you at shortstop."

"Alright, alright, " he threw both hands in the air. "You're bossy."

"You wanted this monster," I pointed at him. "Arlo's going to drop everything he swings into the belt, put Dougie there to pick up the slack, but Dean, you stay first and watch the liners from Jensen and Burton."

The rest of our team huddled around to listen as I instructed them where to be and when. I had been watching the Hornets play baseball for months as an outsider. I knew exactly how each ticked, and now that the fire had been lit, I wouldn't lose.

As everyone settled down and Van went out to bat, I walked over to where Zoey stood, her fingers linked to the fence. "What?" I asked, noticing her giant smile.

"It's been a while since you glowed like this," Zoey looked at me. "I'm really proud of you."

"Pass me your hair tie," I said, ignoring her because I would cry if I stopped to digest her words. Women's fastball was very different from men's, and I knew most of the pitches. Throwing them was a completely different story. "Thank you," I use it to pull my hair back into a messy ponytail and exhale a hard breath. "I haven't played in like three years."

"You were the best pitcher I've ever seen. Maybe it's like riding a bike." She shrugged.

"It won't be, but if I don't at least try, I'll never hear the end of it."

Van cracked the ball as far as he could, sending it deep into the outfield, bouncing past where Todd sprinted past it and into the tree line beyond. Van's long legs quickly carried him around all three bases, and the team cheered for him as the next few guys took their chance.

Arlo garnered two outs before I stepped out onto the field. Cael stuck his fingers between his lips and whistled at me from his position behind Arlo as I rolled out my shoulders and adjusted the grip on the bat.

"You ready, Blondie?" Arlo smirked at me, tossing the ball and catching it again. I narrowed my eyes on the outfield as they all took four strides in, leaving the backfield completely unguarded.

"Throw the ball, cap," I quipped back, digging my feet into the dirt and inhaling one deep breath as the ball soared toward me. I curled my knee up, putting all my weight into the swing, and the bat connected with the ball effortlessly.

Every ounce of skill that had been shoved aside seemed to flood back through my veins and into my heart as the world shifted, and I started running. *Fuck that felt good.* I pushed to first base without noticing, my feet guiding the way while my heart and head pounded excitedly.

"Shit," Arlo swore as the ball dropped in the outfield far past where they had shifted.

"You're an asshole for having them shift closer," I screamed, entirely out of breath as I rounded second base, shoving Cael out of the way as he tried to cheat by wrapping me up in his long arms. I jumped with two feet, planting firmly on third narrowly as Coach caught the ball behind me.

"It's just the game, sweetheart," he called back with a shrug.

BAD HONEY

"Nice hit," Cael said, shaking his head and getting back into position. "You rattled him," he kicked a piece of clumped clay away from his feet.

Arlo looked over his shoulder at me, but I wasn't met with the horrifying, grouchy stare he usually carried. No, his brown eyes were filled with sunlight, and a stupid, massive grin was on his face.

"I think you broke my pitcher," Coach huffed from third base.

Dean brought me home shortly after, but we were quickly shut down before getting more than the two runs. I flexed my fingers around the ball, twisting it in my hand and trying to remember all the throws before embarrassing myself on the mound. Van stood over my right shoulder, uncomfortable at shortstop, but without Cael, there wasn't a single other person on the team capable of covering the spot.

Of course, Arlo was the first to bat, strutting out into the box with his bat swinging by his side.

"Do you remember how to work that?" He nodded to the ball in my hand.

I shook my head and looked back to the team, waving them in a couple of steps just to fuck with his head.

"Do you want pointers?" He asked as I turned back, "Cause pulling them in, playing mind games," he tapped a finger to his temple, "isn't going to work."

Women's fastpitch was thrown. Differently, there were no styles or different throws. There was only windmill. I watched Arlo closely, knowing he expected me to try a fast pitch, forgetting how easily I had conned him the first time we met. I drew my arm back, not giving him a second inhale. Swinging my arm around in a circle I watched his jaw tighten as the ball hurled toward him at an angle he would never hit.

The ball bounced wildly off the backstop, missing the batter's box.

"Okay—" Arlo scoffed, his frustration showing. "You can't throw windmills!"

"No rules on pitches, King. You know that!" Coach called from their dugout with a smile on his face. "Besides, that was entertaining."

He held up his hand to stop me from throwing another before he was ready, "god damn, that was fast. Try again," he groaned.

"Keep your eye on the ball, Cap," I bit my lip, hearing him scoff as I returned to the mound.

I took another second to steady my breathing and visualize the throw.

"It's harder than I make it look," Arlo flashed a smile at me. "Take your time."

I narrowed my eyes at his playful taunting and shook my head. The ball curved through the air straight past his bat and into the glove behind him before he could swing.

"Choke up on the bat, *sweetheart*," I caught the ball in my mitt, "and plant your feet."

Van howled from behind me, his laughter triggering a chorus around the field.

"Ella," Silas called from the bleachers, "don't give him a fucking inch!"

Everyone cheered in agreement, and I could see Arlo settling down to focus, all the playfulness leaving his body. "What?" I asked him, "Don't like being teased?"

"You aren't playing fair," He mocked me.

I cocked my head to the side, "have I ever?"

"Throw the ball, Blondie." He chirped when I didn't instantly release it.

And so I did, and again, he missed the ball by nearly half a second.

He huffed, twisting his hat around on his head and sinking it over his eyes as he rolled his shoulders back and stretched out his arms before regripping the bat.

I gave him a moment to prepare himself before throwing the last pitch. My arm fully warmed up. I threw the ball, and the glove behind him cracked loudly before he could even blink. Zoey screamed from the sidelines, high-fiving Silas as everyone clapped and cheered. Coach crossed his arms over his chest, stifling laughter as he leaned against the dugout fence. Cael buckled in laughter, rolling around in the sand and covering his shirt in dust without care.

"I'll make you pay for that," Arlo teased with a smile, kicking dust up with his boot before chucking the bat at the fence and walking into the dugout.

BAD HONEY

I felt Van approach from behind me, "You're the first person to strike him out like that in nearly two years. He's not going to go easy on you now."

"He wasn't before," I chuckled.

If there was one thing about Arlo, I knew for sure after watching him for so long. I knew when he was easing up, taking it slow, or giving someone a chance. And the pattern followed the next five innings he hadn't budged. Every pitch he threw was purposeful. Every swing he took mattered. The game was close, and everyone was having so much fun. I had even found myself laughing and smiling more than I had in a long time.

The sweat dripped down his temple and ran lines down his neck beneath his shirt as he shifted the ball in his hand, concentrating on nothing but me.

When the ball left his hand, I swung the bat and knocked the ball out of the infield past Cael, who pushed himself into the air in a sad attempt to glove it as it bounced down the line to the outfield.

I rounded second breathlessly, "We just need this run, Dean," Van called to him from third base. We were down one, with two outs.

"*You're their only hope, Obi-Wan.*" Cael mocked. His hands over his chest, pretending to swoon into the dirt beneath him. I laughed with him, softly knocking my sneaker's toe into his side. Sometimes, it was hard to tell the difference between sober Cael and drunk Cael.

Dean dared to wink in Cael's direction, the ball connecting with the bat before cutting through the air toward the back line. *An authentic home run swing.* Cael doubled over in laughter, throwing his mitt to the ground and turning his back to me, "Your ride, m' lady!"

I hopped up, wrapping my legs around his waist as he took third, jogging lazily as Van waited at third with open arms. The two hoisted me by a thigh each, resting on their shoulders. Everyone was cheering, but my focus wasn't on the crowd of rowdy players. My only focus was on Arlo. He smiled up at me, arms crossed over his chest, pride in those sun-kissed dark brown eyes.

"Alright, boys," Zoey yelled over the noise, "how about some ice cream floats before dinner?"

I waited until everyone was asleep to slip from my bed that night. Pausing to admire, Dean curled around Cael's back, snoring lightly, both too big for the bunk bed. They looked so peaceful there, untouched by the world outside that room, and I understood why Arlo liked the cabin so much. It was heaven. I looked over at the picture of him and his mom again, biting down on my lip to quell the pain that bubbled there. He was surrounded by everyone. The Hornets, his family, and still, at the best of times, he was still so alone.

I shook the feelings loose and climbed up to where Arlo was wide awake, staring at the rafters.

"Move over," I whispered and he lifted the blanket for me as I tucked tightly against his chest and closed my eyes.

"You were amazing today," he brushed his nose against my temple, his sleepy voice husky in my ear.

"Playing baseball in the forest is very *Twilight* of you," I teased.

"Shut up," he tried not to laugh too loudly.

I wrapped my arms around his middle, digging into his back and burying my nose to drink in his sandy, sweaty smell. "Get some sleep," he hugged me tighter, "we have a long drive tomorrow."

"If you wake me up at four am—"

"Not this time, Blondie. Close your eyes."

MIELE

"Is that everything?" Arlo stuffed the last duffle into the bottom of the bus before closing the compartment.

"Yeah," Silas nodded, "you guys will be okay?" He looked between us, and we nodded at the same time.

I was looking forward to having a quiet moment with him. I had expected him to wake me before the sun to hide our relationship, but I woke up engulfed by his warmth and the sun pouring into the room. Cael peered up at me from the bottom bunk with a stupid smile and scrunched nose. I pressed my finger to my lips to keep him quiet, and he tapped two to his chest to promise. *Not my story to tell.*

"We'll lock up and get on the road." Arlo's voice cut through the happy memories, returning me to the driveway. I leaned against the Mustang in my sweater and a pair of sweats, watching Silas remind Arlo of everything he needed to check before leaving.

Nick closed the car door, slamming it loud enough for us to turn and look at him as he wandered over.

"Great, here we go," Silas groaned.

"Dad wants to have dinner on Sunday," he looked directly at Arlo, ignoring my presence.

"Yeah, alright," Arlo said, licking his bottom lip.

"Ella," Nick turned to say something to me.

"Don't," every muscle in his body went tight beside me as his brother turned in my direction.

"Relax," Nick bit at him, "you've got a good arm. That pitch was impressive, you should have worked harder to get back."

The tension rolled off Arlo as I processed the compliment. At the time, working toward returning to baseball felt pointless. I'd been so numbed by the painkillers that all I wanted to do was get drunk and have fun for once. I didn't wanna work. I wanted to live.

"That's not me anymore. The game was fun, though," I offered him a tight smile. I hadn't even noticed them watching in the bleachers. Surprised that he hadn't played, too.

"I'll see you tomorrow," he said through a clenched jaw before sauntering back to his car. Arlo finally inhaled when the door slammed shut, and Nick peeled from the gravel driveway.

"What was that about?" Cael hung from the bus's entrance.

"Nothing," Arlo snapped, "get on the bus."

"Ar," Silas turned and lowered his voice.

"Do not go to that house."

I wasn't meant to hear it, but it came out loud and clear as Arlo pinned his shoulders back tightly. He had made a fool of his father in front of a room of people. Whatever Arthur King had in store for him, wasn't dinner.

Moments after Silas climbed onto the bus, it pulled from the driveway and left Arlo and me alone. I hooked my pinky into his and looked up at him, "You're not actually going to indulge them, are you?"

He didn't answer me, not with words at least, but he slipped out from my hold and wandered around to the passenger door, holding it open for me in silence. "Get in the car." He asked when I paused, looking up at him with my fingers on the frame. "Please," he added when I didn't budge.

I raised an eyebrow at him, challenging his silence.

"I have to," he finally said, "is that what you want to hear? I have to go there."

"Why?" I asked.

"Because if I don't, it makes everything ten times harder than it needs to be." He argued, fear flickering with anger, interchangeable emotions all tangled together behind a pair of dark eyes.

"It's already hard, Arlo," I noted, lifting my hand to play with the string on his hoodie.

BAD HONEY

He looked away from me into the tree line, and his jaw ticked in time with his frustrated thoughts. "If I don't go to him," he finally looked back, "then he comes to me and everyone suffers."

"The only person who suffered this weekend was you," I poked him.

"It's different here," he sighed, "there's no pressure to perform. This isn't a packed stadium waiting for a perfectly pitched game. He was sitting in the stands, all his expectations bearing on me. He's like a breathing, talking form of the *yips*. My game takes a hit when he comes to me, and if my game is off—"

"Then you lose," I nodded, understanding. "There's got to be another way."

"Until I graduate," he leaned close, allowing me to inhale him as he pressed his forehead to mine. "This is the only way."

He sat there for a moment, a smile creeping to his face, "this is still weird," he chuckled to no one other than the birds and breeze. "I didn't think after being such an asshole you'd ever let me near you."

"There was a lot of internal debate," I teased, taking my time and stealing a languid kiss from his lips. "And if you were wondering, you're still an asshole."

Throwing his head back, a throaty laugh tumbled from him as I climbed into the car. "At least we're on the same page," he closed the door.

He jogged back up to the cabin, checking all the doors before sliding into the driver's seat with a tiny smile. Such a difference from his usual scowl, a smirk reserved only for the quiet moments when no one was watching.

The engine roared to life, and just like the drive up here, Arlo turned to me before pulling out, "You ready?"

Never.

But today, a little more than the days before.

I nodded, and he pulled the fastback from the drive back down toward the highway. I tucked down into my sweater, pulled out a bag of peas, and opened my book to where I had stopped the day before. I had read *The Fault in Our Stars* too many times, but it comforted me when I needed a proper distraction. Which worked until the raindrops started to fall on the windshield and demanded my attention.

"Arlo," I swallowed tightly and pushed myself flush with the seat as if I could melt into it and forget about the rain that slowly grew heavier. The dark clouds had come out of nowhere, and almost as if he was racing through the storm, the car pushed harder against the concrete.

"It breaks ahead," he pointed with his hand before dropping it into my lap and tangling his fingers into mine. "Close your eyes."

Closing my eyes wouldn't work this time; the rain was too much in combination with the moving car. I could see every memory of the accident clawing out of the locked boxes within my mind. And even with Arlo's thumb rubbing across the back of my hand and the music covering the sound of the rain pelting the tin roof, I was brought back to that night. Screeching tires and breaking glass shattering around my senses like I was there. Ethan's garbled cries for help as I fought through my own blinding pain.

"El," his voice broke through my screams, "Ella!" he coughed out louder.

"I can't-" panic coursed through me as I tried to rip the seatbelt free of my torn flesh. It had embedded itself so tightly that it felt as though *the fibers of my skin were tangled with the fabric of the belt.* "Breathe," *I fought out as I pawed at the clip. The painkillers had worn off, and I could feel everything tenfold, screaming in pain as I clawed.*

"Ella!"

Fists pounded at the windows and roof so loudly that everything around me became some form of a sick, silent movie. "Ethan," *I stretched my fingers as far as they could go, desperate to get to him, but still too far.* "Hey," *I whined, "don't fall asleep!"*

"Ella!"

The engine died beneath me, forcing me to open my eyes. Arlo's hands were cupped around my face, and the car pulled off onto a side road. The rain beating down on the roof in sheets sounded like fists... "I'm sorry," I scrunched up into a tight ball and pulled away from him to the back corner of the seat.

BAD HONEY

I rubbed at my chest, the scar emitting a burning ghost sensation beneath my skin that throbbed painfully as I tried to regain my composure. I dug my fingers beneath my sweater to find my ring and brushed my fingers around it methodically until my breathing slowed.

He unclicked my seatbelt, tugging on my hand as he pushed his seat back and made room for my legs. "Come here," he held his arms out to me.

The rain didn't seem daunting as I settled my legs around him, balancing on my knees, and sank into his lap, finally relaxing. "Breathe, Ella," he said, pressing his hand to my chest, "it's just us here."

I wished that was true, but the ghost of Ethan lingered. I could feel his touch and hear his voice pushing through the safety blanket of the radio and Arlo's breathing. His fingers ran down my neck, tracing the lines of my shoulder as I inhaled slowly and exhaled even slower.

"Atta girl," he praised, "keep going."

I inhaled again, pressing my forehead to his as I exhaled.

Leaning into him, I pulled his bottom lip between mine and kissed him, slowly at first, before his hand wrapped into my hair, and everything became a fast, needy entanglement. His hand pressed against the flat of my back and lifted my hips against his as he rolled up into the kiss, deepening it and sliding his tongue into my mouth. I tugged against the collar of his sweater, my hands begging for more skin, and Arlo obliged, pulling away only to fumble with the hem in a messy attempt to strip.

We laughed as his hat went flying and his necklaces caught in the collar, helping him to rearrange everything before I sat back in his lap. The rain faded to nothing but a dull roar as I tickled my fingers delicately over the sloping curve of his hips, crawling them up the soft expanse of his stomach and rib cage to his pecs and shoulders. I pressed my lips to his neck beneath his jaw and nibbled on the smooth, warm skin, dragging a tight, rumbly growl from him.

"Ella," his grip tightened around my hips as he separated us. "Is this okay?" he paused.

I didn't want to tell him it was the perfect distraction because his fingertip imprints on my skin were so much more than that. So I just nodded. I was as sure as I could be with so many intense emotions coursing through me, and all I knew was that I wanted more.

He pulled me back down for another kiss, his tongue diving into my mouth as his fingers squeezed around my hips, sliding me down against him as far as he could get me. He groaned against my mouth as we connected roughly, and his hand slid up under my sweater against the curve of my spine, pulling me against his chest.

I wrapped my hands around his face, tugging his jaw up to me to deepen the kiss and get as much as I could. Nothing else existed, not the rain or the road. There was no shattering glass or carnage. It was just his hands, mouth, and rocking hips. A stronghold against the memories that threatened to destroy me.

His hands explored the territory beneath my sweater, rolling across my shoulder blades under my arms against the soft fabric of my sports bra to the curve of my ribcage and stomach. Fingers mapped out every inch of skin as he kissed the corner of my mouth, his smile against my skin setting free a thousand tiny butterflies.

"Arlo," I squirmed against him as his thumb brushed behind the elastic of my sweatpants.

He inhaled slowly, his nose brushing against my cheek as he steadied himself and pushed his hand deeper. He kissed a delicate line to the soft spot behind my ear and buried his face in my shoulder. One hand braced my arching back as the other worked deeper, pushing between my legs. His fingers rubbed gently at first, working tiny gasps from my lips as his teeth marked lines across my skin down to where the collar of my sweater met the hollow of my throat.

"Stay with me," he whispered, pressing his lips against the chain into my skin roughly as his fingers dipped deeper. I lifted off my knees, hovering above him to give him room as he took his time to completely undo every tense knot tied within me. He pressed another finger into me, his thumb rubbing circles against my clit. Every touch was meticulously timed with the noises I couldn't control. I could feel his smile grow against my warm skin with each breathless gasp and moan. He was so proud of himself.

"Quit gloating," I sank into his hand, riding through the tension, begging silently for the cord to snap. It had been a long time since someone had touched my skin the way Arlo was. Even with Nick, everything was hot and heavy but never taken too far, and it was always about him. Arlo was deliberate with his touch, every nip, pinch, and stroke purposely torturing the orgasm out of me.

"I can't help it. Every pretty little sound from you is a win," he moved his hand faster.

That was all it took, the pride in his voice, the shortness of his breath, the pressure building cracked the damn and flooded through me like fireworks. I clenched around him tightly, pleasure cascading up, engulfing every single one of my senses and leaving my vision spotty with stars.

He painted my jaw and face with tiny kisses as I came down, freeing his hand and wrapping around me tightly with both arms.

"Listen," he said quietly, brushing his nose against mine.

It had stopped raining.

KING

My fingers were fucking sore.

And for all the wrong reasons.

The crowd was quiet as we sat deadlocked against the Royals, nine to nine in the last inning, with only a few chances to turn the tide. I looked back at Cael, uniform covered in sand, hat abandoned for a rolled dark blue bandana to push back the sweat dripping from him, and a determined look on his ordinarily lighthearted face.

Nick had tried to talk me out of playing the last two. He even had Reyes warming up in the bullpen, but I had to finish this. The Royals were nasty, and they had no right to this win. We had fought too hard and come too far to lose a twenty-game win streak to a bottom-bracket team.

With a man on second, Cael crept the line between third, watching everything around him like a hawk. The sun had finally set on the stadium, giving us a slight reprieve from the intense heat wave that had hit campus days after we had returned from the cabin. I had been attempting, and failing spectacularly, to give Ella her space. I didn't want to force her hand into something so fast, mainly because I expected her to keep it a secret from the team.

But she looked so fucking pretty hung over the dugout banister, blonde hair falling in strands around her big brown eyes. Her brows pinched in concern as her focus flickered between the scoreboard, second base, and me.

"Hard and fast, baby," Tucker yipped from first, his massive frame crumpled in a ready stance.

BAD HONEY

Everything was riding on this last pitch.

I twisted, digging my left heel into the mound as my right extended backward in line with my pitching arm, and I released the ball as hard as I could. A perfect fastpitch that cracked so hard into the glove behind the batter that Jensen swore loudly, shaking out his palm.

"Strike three!"

The batter kicked the dirt, stomping off the field back to his dugout, dragging his teammate from second with him. Cael slapped my shoulder as we wandered back to our own.

"That was sexy," he laughed, hopping over the banister and into the dugout on both feet.

Ella high-fived everyone that came down the pipe, including me, but her touch lingered on my hand, her grip tightening around my wrist as she took notice of the purple bruising.

"Games almost done," I said flatly, holding it steady so that everyone else around us would hear me being mean but holding her gaze in a way that she understood that later she could take care of me.

Her jaw ticked, wanting to say something, but she released me, turning away with a clipped, "Ice it."

"The gooey eyes are gonna get you caught," Cael mumbled beside me as Van took the box with Dean on deck. "You have to keep it safe, and if you can't look at her like you hate her, I might suggest just not looking."

"Shithead," I pushed his head down with my palm and held my breath as Van swung. The crack that erupted from the bat was backed by a chorus of applause and whistles as I angled out of the dugout, watching the ball soar through the air, over the gloves of the outer fieldman, and into the rafters of the back seats.

"*That marks twenty-one wins under the feet of the Harbor Hornets!*" The announcer boomed over the crowd as the cannons shot off. Everyone flooded off the field after shaking hands, hooping, and hollering excitedly as our spirits remained in the sky.

"Arlo!" the press called, forcing me to turn and walk down the tunnel toward them. "What do you make of this win streak? It must feel good! A real ego boost for the team!" One man asked, shoving a mic in my face.

"It feels like pressure," I answered, "we're confident but not cocky."

"If you carry on like this, you'll shatter the record for win streaks, previously held by your older brother Lucas King," another recorder shoved toward me.

"What's your question," I tried not to snap.

"Is there any tension at home between you and your brothers, knowing that new records are being set at their expense?"

"Lucas and Sawyer left the baseball scene a long time ago," I said, "if you want to know how Nicholas feels, you can ask him yourself. I'm here to focus on bringing a national title home. Breaking records isn't even on my radar."

"It seems you have plenty to focus on lately." The statement was pointed.

"I go out there every game with my guys, and we play hard. That's all that matters."

"And what about a smile for Harbor University's single ladies?" Someone flashed a camera in my face. I clenched my fists at my side, stepping forward as I blinked the stars from my vision. "Or has the Hornet's most ineligible bachelor finally been locked down?"

I rolled my shoulders back, rage coursing through my bloodstream. "Why the hell are you all so interested in my personal life—"

"King," barked from my right, "showers!"

"Don't let them get in," he walked shoulder to shoulder with me. "All they want to do is find a crack in your armor, do not give it to them. Not a fucking inch." He looked at me when we stopped at the locker room door. "Do you understand me?"

He wasn't talking about me. For a split second, his concern fell for the unspoken relationships. Protecting Cael, protecting the team, and a growing concern for Ella.

"I understand, Coach," I buckled down the emotion and pushed into the locker room.

"Shut the fuck up!" I exploded through the door and barked, quieting the celebrations that were going on. The guys settled down, shirtless, pantless, sweaty, and exhausted but all focused. "Today was fucking hard, but you guys did that. You went out there, and you

BAD HONEY

left yourselves on that field. The fight isn't over. We've got some hard months left of this shit, and if you think one record-breaking win streak is gonna bring home that trophy, you're delusional."

They all nodded, some rubbing their hands over their faces and closing their eyes as they listened. "We work hard, stay focused, and don't let anyone into the Nest."

I tapped my hand over my chest and watched them all fall in line.

"I want you all here at six am tomorrow for a practice. We can't keep letting runs in like we did today." Groaning and whining filled the air. "Five a.m." I barked. "You think I'm fucking around."

"There's a party at Delta." Van was the only one brave enough to pipe up.

"Good, crawl your fucking hung-over asses from Delta, up that goddamn hill to the stadium at five am. I don't give a shit if you're still drunk tomorrow morning. You can run and vomit at the same time."

Some of the players sounded like they might vomit from the thought alone. Cael laughed, and I shot him a look that had him throwing his hands in the air.

"I've puked and ran sprints before, boys. It's not enjoyable."

"Fuck you're an asshole," Dean groaned, throwing his jersey into his locker.

"Good job today, Tuck," I slapped his face as I walked by to remind him how valuable he had become. "You too, Kitten." I slumped down next to Cael in a moment of silence. Observing them all as they celebrated and talked through the game's plays. It felt good to have them working together cohesively again.

When I finally got out of the stadium, showered and exhausted, Ella was waiting against the fastback. Her hair loose and tucked deep into a sweater, she flipped the pages of her book, oblivious to the world around her. I stopped on the curb to admire her for a moment, smiling for the first time in hours. And even exhausted, sore, and sick of standing, I could have watched her doing something so mundane like that.

"Blondie," I called to her, and she peered up at me through her lashes with a smile. "You waiting on someone?"

"Oh, you know," she closed her book with a heavy sigh, "he's handsome, dark, and mysterious. Has a bad attitude and is about two inches too short to be considered tall."

"Nick already left."

That warranted a scowl from her that slowly curled back into a smile.

"It was too easy," I walked toward her. "Besides, I'm six-two, that's plenty tall."

"Alright, alright," she nodded in defeat.

"Handsome, though? You think?" I wanted to kiss her so badly that even the little trickle of flower scent wafted from her skin drove me mad.

"Can I see, please," she held her hand to me.

I let my bag slip from my shoulder at our feet and held my hand palm up for her in the light of the parking lot lamp. Her nose scrunched up, and her brows kissed in concern.

"Arlo, this is getting worse," she hissed quietly, applying pressure on my fingers so they were painfully fully extended. "You need to let Silas look at these, I can't-"

"Silas will bench me," I tugged my hand away.

"Rightfully so!" She snapped and stepped in front of me as I bent down to retrieve my bag. "This isn't some minor injury anymore," she scolded me. "If you keep pitching on these fingers, you're going to rupture the pulley in your hand. That's nearly a month on the bench."

"So tape them, make it better."

"I'm not a doctor, Arlo!"

I shook my head, grabbed the bag from the ground, and threw it in the backseat before moving around the car to open the door for her.

"In the car!" I barked louder than I meant to.

She stood with her arms crossed over her chest, a scowl on her perfect face, and her hip popped out in protest. Where Cael could win an argument with his puppy dog eyes, Ella would burn a hole through me with her brown, angry ones.

"Don't be so damn stubborn," I groaned.

When the laughter started, I knew I was in trouble.

BAD HONEY

"Me, stubborn?" She laughed again. "That's cute."

"Ella," I pointed to the seat. The last thing we needed was a rogue camera capturing her screaming at me in the parking lot. "Get in the car. You can yell at me all the way to the Nest."

"Now you're talking my language," she shook her head and started for the passenger side.

And she held that promise. From the moment I turned the engine on, she distracted herself by talking shit. During the ten-minute drive up to the house, she listed all the horrible ways a flexor tendon can tear and pull. By the time we pulled the fastback into the garage, I was sick to my stomach with medical jargon and all the disgusting surgery images she kept pulling up on the internet.

"Okay!" I opened the door for her, claiming defeat as she cleared the door. "You win, I'll talk to Doc tomorrow."

"I'll text him so he knows to expect you."

She called my bluff, and rightfully so. I would have never gone to see him.

"Did you eat?" I changed the subject without skipping a beat. I threw my bag next to the washing machine as we walked through the house to the kitchen.

"I thought we were going to that party?" She turned and laid her bag on the island.

"You hear that?" I asked her as I came up behind her and wrapped my hands beneath her sweater. She pressed against me, tangling her fingers into mine, and shook her head. "It's a quiet Nest. You really wanna give that up for some loud party just to watch the guys strike out with girls and get wasted?"

"No," she giggled and turned in my arms. I grabbed her hips and lifted her to the island, hovering between her legs as I looked around at the empty kitchen.

"Means I can do this," I kissed her gently, holding her chin between my fingers and lingering longer than I should have. "And this," I kissed her jaw and neck. "And no one can say anything about it."

Cael cleared his throat from the archway.

Ella rested her head against my shoulder with a defeated laugh, "For someone so loud, you sure are sneaky."

"Sorry, Peachy," he smiled at her and patted me on the back before wandering toward the garage. "Just came to grab something. You two behave," he motioned from his eyes to us with his fingers.

When the garage door closed, I went back to kissing her everywhere and all at once. I hadn't been able to sneak even one all day and wouldn't waste a second. But her stomach grumbled in my arms, and my exhaustion was taking hold.

"I have to change the oil on the Mustang," I groaned.

"Right now?" She laughed, pushing her fingers through my hair. She tugged at the base on purpose and dragged an unavoidable rumble from my throat.

"It's a thing," I licked my bottom lip. "I use the time to unwind from the game—"

"I can help you unwind," she teased. Slipping from the counter, she pulled the hem of her sweater over her head and tossed it to the floor. The bra beneath cupped her breasts and pushed them up, teasing me.

"Please don't make an oil change porn joke. It will ruin how turned on I am right now." She took off through the house, stopping at the break between our doors, unsure where or what to pick.

"We haven't—" she turned to me.

We haven't talked about any of this, what it means, what we are. She was just as concerned and confused as I was. Choosing a room seemed like such a minor decision, but suddenly, it hung so heavily over our heads.

"Ella," I said, scooping her into my arms and against my chest before carrying her to her room, "we don't have to."

Nothing needed to be figured out or planned. It didn't need to be discussed.

It could just *be,* and that was enough.

MIELE

JUNE

"I want to take you on a date," Arlo slid out from under the Mustang in a dirty muscle shirt and a pair of jeans that hugged the thick curves of his thighs. "A real one, not whatever this is."

"I thought we were keeping things quiet until the season was over?" I looked up from my textbook. I had picked up two summer courses that I didn't need to graduate but would look incredible on my transcript. Arlo completed his sports management and sports communication degree with excellent scores. I would graduate at the end of the summer, but Arlo had taken to the stage with a smile, a tassel hanging in his eyes, and the guys cheering in the stands.

His dad hadn't bothered to show up.

"A degree doesn't win baseball games," Silas shrugged when I was foolish enough to ask where he was.

I should have known better. Arlo had gone to that house for dinner, alone and without Silas being able to stop him, and had come back with bruises that broke my heart. His collarbone had been purple for days, and he had pitched through the pain like it didn't exist.

But I knew it was there, and it made me sick to my stomach.

Seeing the bruises across Nick's knuckles, knowing he had caused Arlo's pain and showed it off like a badge of honor, was even worse.

It made sense, but it still ate away at me. Arlo didn't deserve that.

Zoey threw a massive graduation party for him at Delta, which ended with everyone in the pool fully dressed and Arlo sneaking kisses when their backs were turned. His wet hair, hopeful brown eyes, and big, beautiful smile were a memory I would never forget. I was grateful to have a front seat to the transition. I could see how much more relaxed he was when school finished. He could focus on the last goal he had.

The most important one.

He had cleared out one of the dirty recliners, liberating it from dusty boxes of car parts and spider webs before covering it in a blanket and dragging it out to a spot in a garage where we could talk while he worked. But it turned into weeks of just me sitting curled up with my summer coursework, writing essays on my laptop, and him silently working on the *fastback*. It was comfortable and easy.

They had continued to win their games, and even better, they were doing it with fewer runs left in each game. Coach pushed them hard, but Arlo kept his promise and let Silas rehab his hand before playing more games. Thankfully, Reyes was prepared, and the streak survived Arlo being benched.

I could tell it took a toll on him. He was grouchier than usual and had been taking it out on Cael with five a.m. runs. It was getting difficult to juggle their emotions. The more Arlo closed himself off, the wilder Cael became. He was slipping again and there were very few options at my disposal to do anything short of telling his father.

Which both Silas and Arlo stressed could not happen.

The Hornets had ended the regular season seated at the top of their division for the first time in six years. The pressure was mounting, and everyone was tense. Regionals were the next step before the team found themselves in the middle of Super Regionals.

Everyone needed to have their heads on straight, and Cael Cody was a stripped screw, just endlessly turning in the socket.

"There's this—" he went to bring my chin up so he could kiss me, but his hand was covered in grease, and he stopped with a scowl, "bookstore!" His voice rose in volume as he spotted his towel. "Off-campus. Really small, but it sells romance novels. I thought I could drive you."

"You wanna take me to a bookstore?" I set down the book I was reading and pulled my knees from under my blanket to sit up.

"If you'll let me?"

BAD HONEY

I still hadn't gotten used to how soft Arlo could be in private. With no one waiting for him to be an asshole, he turned into this sweet version of himself that blushed and used his manners. The first time that Cael heard him say please without prompt, he nearly choked to death. Lying in my bed studying for his finals, Arlo had come to see if I wanted dinner, not knowing that Cael was there with me.

Now, anytime Arlo ordered anything from Cael, it was met with a snarky "say please" response that had Arlo fuming.

"Like a real date," I chewed on my lip as he knelt before the recliner. "When?" I asked him.

"Are you busy now?" He ran his hands across my thighs, leaning in to kiss the inside of my knee.

"I'm in my pajamas," I laughed.

"So go change," he kissed again, higher, his lips trailing slowly as his fingers tickled the hem of my pajama shorts. "I need to shower, you've got," he looked at the old analog clock hanging over the door. "Twenty minutes," he said, "we have to be out of here before the guys get back from dinner, or Cael will wanna come."

I cupped his face and brought his gaze back to me, "such a romantic," I whispered and gravitated toward him, bringing our lips together slowly and softly. "I'll be right back."

Arlo was leaning against the fastback when I returned, waiting for me, looking like he had just walked out of a movie.

Holy shit.

His hair was combed back off his strong face. Still damp from his shower, he seemed to glow. He exchanged his dirty clothes for a clean black t-shirt that gripped every toned muscle in his abdomen, paired with a leather jacket I'd never seen him wear and his stack of necklaces. He looked up at me with a smirk, his eyes growing wide at the sight of me.

"Hi," I whispered, barely audible.

I wasn't nearly as well dressed as him, in jeans and a long-sleeved maroon shirt that felt fancy enough for a first date without overdoing it. His ring hung in plain sight against my chest.

"Consistently amazed but never surprised," he swallowed tightly. "Come on, Blondie, before the hooligans get home."

He kissed my cheek in passing and opened the passenger door for me, closing it once I was comfortably inside. The ride off campus was shorter than I expected. I had dug my heels into the rough carpet, taking it one turn at a time, when he pulled into a small parking lot at the edge of town.

Seeing him so excited seemed to warm all the cold parts of my heart and tickle at the butterflies that slept peacefully within me. The bookstore was just as he had described. The walls were lined with books from end to end, seemingly disappearing back into the darkest parts of the tiny store. There were couches and chairs scattered around, and an electric-looking woman with blue hair standing behind the counter making coffee for a customer.

"Told you," he whispered.

He pressed his chest to my back, his nose brushing against my neck as I drank in every aspect of the bookstore. It was incredible. I don't know how long I spent there, running my fingers along an impressive old and new romance collection. Indie and traditionally published.

"I think this might be heaven," I said at one point as Arlo quietly followed behind me, his eyes solely on me as I wandered around in awe.

"You haven't picked out a single one," he laughed at me as I circled.

"I don't know how I'm supposed to!"

I was overwhelmed in the best way.

He was about to say something else when his phone rang. He pulled it from his jeans with a scowl on his face. "I'll be right back."

Arlo left the store, standing outside by the Mustang, and while I should have been looking for a book to buy, I could only stare at him. I remembered the last time anyone other than Zoey had been so thoughtful. Every memory of my parents and Ethan was tied to baseball and football, fundraisers, practices, and therapy. There was no time to just enjoy ourselves or enjoy time together.

Arlo had taken his one chance at a date and spent it doing something that didn't necessarily make him happy. It worried me. Everyone he talked to seemed to pile more weight on his shoulders, and I was terrified for the moment he snapped. Tension boiled up inside him, bubbling and building until he eventually became out of control.

BAD HONEY

"What was that about?" I asked as he stalked back into the store.

"Nothing," he wrapped a hand around my head, kissing my temple. I knew from that motion that it was something, and he was hiding his worry. "You pick something?" He asked, turning his eyes to the shelves instead of me.

"Arlo," I tucked my hand into his. "Thank you for this."

"You're welcome, Blondie. You like it?" He said, focus still on the books and not what mattered.

"Arlo," I said again, tugging on his hand. "Thank you."

He finally looked at me, and I could see how stressed out he was from one glance.

"You wanna go get something to eat?" He asked, letting the tension he held hold through him and into me.

"Please," I smiled.

"There are lots of restaurants here—"

"Can you make that pasta, the one you made for Cael that time?" I asked him.

"You mean the time I made it for Cael *and* you."

I had walked away that night and didn't come back. Nick had called upset about something, drunk off his ass, and needed someone to calm him down. He had gone on to spew about how Arlo attacked him at their dad's and how he just wanted to celebrate their mom's birthday in peace, but Arlo could never leave anything alone.

That was the first time Nick had made it abundantly clear that he was a loose cannon.

"Cael brought me a plate," I laughed at the confession.

"Of course he did," Arlo sighed, "are you sure you want that? There's an incredible Italian restaurant. We can have something edible."

"For completely selfish reasons, I would like to go home, sit on the counter with my book, and watch you cook pasta for me." I smiled at him.

He wrapped his hand around my neck, pulling me onto my toes and kissing me in the romance aisle. "Mmm," he groaned, licking his bottom lip as he pulled away. "I can't argue with that," he squeezed his hand around mine and let him walk us from the store.

The drive back was spent worrying about the phone call he took, but I tried to shake that from my mind as I changed into my shorts and t-shirt in my room before padding back to the kitchen.

"Hey," I nudged Van, who hovered in the kitchen talking to Arlo about their new practice schedule. Arlo hadn't changed out of his jeans and tight shirt, a stark contrast to Van's hoodie and shorts.

"Hey you," he stopped mid-sentence. "Are we still on for that session tomorrow?"

"Yeah, I already told Coach you'd miss the first half." I slid up onto the counter as Arlo gave me a dirty look. "I don't run my therapy sessions through you."

He rolled his eyes, "Or you could schedule them around practices."

"I could," I shrugged. "But you and Coach decided to run two-a-days this week, and you're burning the guys out. They need the physio to combat the abuse you're putting them through, or you won't have a team for regionals."

Van's eyes flickered back and forth between us, "you guys bicker like an old married couple."

"Fuck off, Mitchell." Arlo groaned, hands wrapped around the kitchen sink as he rolled his shoulders back and tilted his head toward me. "Fine, but don't waste their time with conversation, quick sessions."

"You also aren't my boss." I quipped, watching my attitude drive him nuts and fed off of it.

"I'm going to go before the atomic bomb goes off," Van stuck his hands in the air and slowly backed out of the kitchen.

"You drive me nuts," Arlo mumbled under his breath tightly so only I could hear him.

I poked him in the rib with my toes, "good."

"You and Cael will be my death," he groaned and continued cooking.

The pasta was even more amazing warm, and I didn't even make it off the counter before my bowl was empty. He stood across the kitchen, watching me devour every bit of it, with a stupid smile as he ate his own. He dumped the dirty dishes into the sink and turned to check the hall for anyone before scooping me off the counter.

BAD HONEY

"Thanks for dinner," I wrapped both legs around his waist, his fingers raking over the curve of my ass. At this distance, I could count all the little imperfections on his face, each freckle, scar, and sunspot that helped make his handsome, scowly expressions. He carried me to his room, kicking the door closed behind us.

His room was so much cleaner than every other space in the house. The only light poured from his lamp on his bedside table, creating a hazy yellow glow over the both of us.

"Not so sassy when we're alone," he kissed me slowly, dragging his teeth against my bottom lip as his hands dipped beneath the fabric against my back.

"Correction," I groaned against him, propping my elbows on his shoulders and tucking my fingers into his hair. "I cannot be sassy while kissing you," I tugged his head back by the hair between my fingers, kissing him back harder that time.

"You can try," he teased, his tongue darting into my mouth as his hands wandered further.

"Wait a minute," I pulled back and rested in his arms, "it gets you off, doesn't it?"

Arlo smiled up at me like a man possessed before dipping his head down and kissing a delicate line against my exposed throat. Ideally, avoiding the situation in the best possible way.

"Answer me." The words fell from me in a strangled moan that came out far louder than I intended as his fingers dug into the curves of my shoulder blades.

His hips rolled upward, proving just how much he enjoyed it with a show of his impressive hardened length pressing against my ass. "I like it," he laughed, the sound that left his lips falling against my skin in ticklish vibrations.

I held my breath as he worked his fingers back down and gripped the hem of my shirt. He tugged it over my head and tossed it to his floor. "It's only fair," I looped a finger into the collar of his shirt, and he obliged, rolling it up and over his chest to join the pile he had created.

Arlo inhaled, his breath catching in his throat as his thumb brushed the edge of the scar on my shoulder. I raised my hand to push him away. His attention made me feel self-conscious under the soft lighting of the lamp, but he caught it, kissing my fingers and holding them away.

His dark eyes traced the line his finger made, down across my chest to where the scar dipped below the band of my bra and appeared out the other side in patchy pieces that curved into my rib cage.

"Turn out the light," I swallowed the nausea that licked at the back of my dry throat.

His response was a muffled no, as his fingers looped around, unhooking the clasp against my back. He gently slid the straps from my shoulders, finally letting go of my hand so the bra could fall loose away from my body. His whole body tensed beneath me, his fingers sinking into the muscles of my hips as he leaned in.

"Arlo," I whined, unable to catch my breath as he started tracing the scar with his lips, working slowly as if trying to memorize it as he went along.

"Shh," he whispered, pulling away for only a second.

I laced my fingers through his hair, tempted to pull him away, but my body slowly started to give in to his methodical, slow kisses. His mouth strayed, lips and teeth wrapping around my nipple, sucking and nipping as his hips rocked beneath me.

"Jeans," I huffed out. There was too much fabric between us. "Get them off," I dropped my hands between us, working hastily at his belt as he continued to suck at my neck. "Arlo," I snapped at him, pushing back on his chest.

A breathless "bossy" left his lips as he adjusted his grip and flipped me onto the bed.

Arlo yanked on the belt, shucking it from the loops as I worked at the button and impatiently folded his jeans down over his hips. He stood over me as I shuffled backward onto his bed, his intoxicating, sweaty, cinnamon cologne floating up from the sheets.

"Light stays on," he slapped my calf as I moved toward the lamp. "These," he tugged at the hem of my pants, pulling them over my hips. "Are in the way."

I wrapped my arms around my chest as he pushed my legs open with his knees. The bed sunk low as he crawled across, situating himself so he hovered above me. Carefully, he took each wrist and pinned them to either side of my head, his nails digging softly into my skin.

"Your scars aren't flaws," he brushed his nose against mine before kissing the tangled crease of scar that stained my cheek. "They're beauty marks," he kissed the bridge of my nose, "they're stories."

When he kissed me that time, the world seemed to melt away, leaving only the feeling of his body against mine and our hearts thudding in time with one another. His hands released my wrists and dipped between our bodies to free himself from his boxers. Words caught in my throat at the sight of him, the impressive length was far larger than I had expected, and a cocky smile formed on his lips.

"I love you speechless," he chuckled with three rugged pumps from his hand before returning to me. He pushed my legs apart with his hand, rolling it over my inner thighs and tickling a line down my center.

Ignoring his jest, I let my head fall back against the bed and drank in the way my body reacted to his hands all over me. "Don't stop now, Cap," I pushed my toes against his shoulder when he leaned back onto his knees to admire me. "My patience is not as strong as yours."

"Cap? In bed?" His head tilted to the side in response.

"Put that mouth to good use," I pushed again, but that time, his hand wrapped around my ankle, and his lips started a long-winded trail down my leg to my thigh. My body responded to his touch like it was starving, arching and whining into him every time he teased with his tongue.

I stifled the moan that threatened to fall as his tongue flickered down my clit, wasting no more time. His hands circled my thighs, hooking my knee over his shoulder as his hand came to lay flat on my stomach, holding me against the bed. His tongue slid down deeper, dragging a ragged moan from my lips.

His glossy dark eyes looked up at me as he settled against me, "fuck, you're so pretty," he groaned.

He worked at my clit as my fingers tangled into the sheets of his bed and the ends of his hair. Slipping a finger deep inside, my hips bucked against his face, but he pushed me back against the bed, holding me tightly as he added another. I couldn't control the sounds that left me as his long fingers grazed against every sensitive spot within me. The pressure was building and coiling tightly, but it wasn't enough.

"Arlo," I whined, "I need more."

He stopped, looking up at me from between my legs. The sight was enough for my core to throb once more.

"Fuck me," I clenched my legs against him.

"Ask nicely," he chuckled. His breath was warm against my core, and my cunt throbbed for him.

"*Please,*" I rolled my eyes, expecting him to fight more, but he folded like a cheap suit at the sound.

"I'd be a fool to deny you," he growled, lifting, rubbing his thumb against my clit lazily before slipping his fingers out.

Arlo's kisses became rushed as his hand tangled deeply into my hair, and his tongue rolled into my mouth. My hand found him between us, fingers barely able to wrap around him as I lined him up with my entrance and scooted down. His teeth found my bottom lip and bit down hard as I rolled the tip of his cock across my drenched cunt, stopping him as he thrust forward.

"You're a menace, Blondie."

"Ask nicely," I whined against his neck and reveled in how his entire body tensed from the touch.

"Let me fuck you," his teeth found my ear, his throat vibrating with a deep groan as they sunk in painfully to the skin, "*please.*"

I gasped and stifled the sound with a quick, "Atta boy," as he hooked my leg up with one of his hands and suddenly pushed himself inside. My body screamed from the intrusion, stretching around his length as he thrust deeper with slow, delicious precision.

Arlo licked a stripe down the column of my throat as he rolled his hips faster, each time pushing a little deeper until I could feel everything, and he settled down to the hilt.

"Not so mouthy now," he pushed down and tugged at the nape of my neck.

He wore a smug smile as he cradled my ass with his other hand. He pulled out sharply, striking back deeper with a new angle that hit a spot I didn't even know existed until my vision blacked out. He held the tempo, moving faster as his mouth found home against my sensitive, warm skin. My toes curled up into the sheets and against his skin as his hand snaked between us and started on my clit again. That was enough, the dam within me breaking from his very touch.

I moaned sharply with every sloppy thrust and sweaty, lusty kiss. I was driven to insanity beneath him. The pressure built so fast I couldn't form the words to warn him as my nails dug into his back. A soft moan dripped from him, Arlo's gaze intensifying from the pain I produced.

"I don't know how long I can last," he groaned, "seeing you like this."

"Don't you dare stop," I warned, holding him in place, my hands finding one of his taut ass cheeks. I rocked him harder against me, his skin slapping against mine as the thrusts increased in strength.

Hearing him moan only caused the pressure building to coil as tight as it could until I felt it snap deep within my stomach. "Fuck, Arlo," the whimper that left me was feral and rolled down over us as every sensation flooded my body like a tidal wave. He cut me off with a languid kiss and coaxed me through the rest of the wave, taking my bottom lip between his teeth as I rode it out.

My eyes rolled back as I clenched around his cock and pulled a dirty moan from his lips. My legs trembled as Arlo continued to thrust. Each one ripping a new sensation from me, pain and pleasure tangled together. The feeling was delicious. The bed rocked beneath us as my hips started to stutter, and Arlo sighed my name like he'd forgotten how to breathe. He finished hard and fast, seizing my mouth roughly as he moaned through his aftershocks, holding on so tightly that he'd leave hearty bruises come morning light.

He kissed a line across my sweaty skin, his mouth devouring whatever he could as our chests rose and fell rapidly in time with each other. "Don't let it go to your head," I fell against the bed, dragging him down with me. "But you're really good at that."

He peered up at me, hair matted to his forehead from the sweat, cheeks flushed, and eyes glossy with a cocky look on his face. "Give me ten minutes," he huffed, "I'm sure I can improve."

"Practice makes perfect," I yelped dramatically as he crawled up over me, and his mouth crashed down on mine with a lusty smile on his handsome face.

MIELE

> **Where are you?**

> Coming up the steps, chill out.

> I brought you candy, so you can't legally yell at me.

I set my phone on the table and looked around the empty library. Tutoring Cael had become a way for us to hang out during the week between practices, sessions, and games. It felt like we barely saw each other anymore in a setting that had nothing to do with baseball. Summer session had sucked me in and dragged me beneath a pile of schoolwork that I wasn't sure I'd ever climb out of, but Silas was right. The few courses I picked to buff my transcripts were excellent and exciting. It excited me to go from a classroom to the stadium. I hadn't felt like that in a long time.

It had been nearly two months since the cabin, and everything had changed. Games were more demanding, the boys were exhausted, and Arlo was meaner. Regionals were easy compared to Supers. The more stress that mounted, the more I watched Cael stumble to stay upright. I had suggested tutoring to keep an eye on him without it feeling like he was being babysat.

"Peachy!" He called from the entrance, turning to flirt with the librarian as she scolded him for yelling. Whatever he said to her seemed to work, a smile plastered on her face as he turned away from the desk with a stupid pout. He was wearing a dark hat pulled down over his fresh buzz cut and a gray t-shirt that was too short for his torso.

"So Janice, the librarian, is free on Tuesday. Where should I take her?" He slid into the chair beside me and leaned his back to toss her a wiggly finger wave.

"You're late," I scowled at him.

"Arlo ran us into the ground, and I drove over here too early so I could nap. *Huzzah*," he raised both hands in the air, "successful, but then I napped too long." He groaned on and on.

"I won't keep tutoring you if you're just wasting my time, Cael."

"Peachy," He sat up, sensing how serious I was. "I'm sorry," his bottom lip jutted out, and he stared at me with big blue eyes. "I'm just exhausted. This is important to me, though."

He brushed his knuckle against my hand and smiled, "I won't be late again. I'm sorry."

"It's alright," I sighed, knowing how hard he was working. "Are you okay though?" I asked, my eyes shifting to how fast his leg was shaking under the table.

"Yeah." His clipped answer worried me as he flipped open his binder and laptop. Cael, denial or not, was far from okay. "Do you have those notes?"

I pulled the ones he asked about from my bag and slipped them across the table to him. "Are you lying to me?" I asked, hanging on to the corner of them so he couldn't dive into his work and avoid the conversation.

"I don't know," he shrugged.

"What does that mean?"

"I'm slipping, maybe," he sighed. "Last couple parties, the drugs have just been there, at my disposal, and this morning," he stopped himself from saying anything more. "I didn't, but I wanted to."

"Have you called your sponsor?" I asked.

"Yeah, he just suggested more meetings, but lately, having people talk at me isn't fucking doing anything but making me more angry." His lips pressed together in a thin line.

BAD HONEY

"Okay," I shifted in my chair. "What's the stressor? Anytime I slipped in the past, it was because I felt crushed or hopeless. So talk to me and actually *talk*, no mewling about nonsense."

"It's Momma's birthday," he whispered with a hint of his Texan accent. All traces of goofy, light-hearted Cael disappeared behind a tight jaw and distant stare. "I'm just sad, I guess," he chewed on his lip, swallowing tightly as he looked toward me.

"Misery finds misery," I looped my fingers into his and scrunched my nose at him.

He laughed under his breath, nearly soundless as his chest shook from the motion. "When I was little," a half smile formed between where his teeth sunk into his bottom lip, "we would go into town and let Momma pick out whatever the hell she wanted from this weird little antique glass store. She loved it there. I hated it. I wasn't allowed to touch anything or run around."

His brows pinched together. "The lady that owned the place sounded like she had swallowed a bullfrog and hadn't seen the sun in a hundred years. I swear she was the boogeyman. But Momma loved that place, and Dad..."

Coach looked like he'd seen a ghost today and had been meaner than usual to the boys. It showed in their therapy sessions. Tight, sore muscles that took hours to work out with stretches. He'd been on edge, and I'd assumed it was the approaching threat of playoffs, but for nearly the last week, he'd been cruel to them, and everything was starting to make a little more sense.

"He didn't care as long as she was happy. When she died, she took whatever '*happy*' Dad had left, and it took me a long time to figure it out. But I realized he didn't know how to make his own because she always made it for him."

Cael had a way of making the most profound thoughts sound dumb, but for once, I understood exactly what he meant.

"Ethan was my '*happy*'."

Cael looked at me, sad and defeated. "I don't know how to make Dad happy," he said. "I don't know how to do that for him."

"It's not your responsibility."

"Arlo makes you happy, doesn't he?"

"I think it's different," I wiggled my nose. "The kind of '*happy*' I found with Ethan was sibling and forgiving. Even when I thought I had lost my '*happy,*' even when I was numbing myself for all the wrong reasons to find it again. Ethan was there. He was that special kind of '*happy*' you brought back to me."

He played lazily with the ring on my thumb, not looking up from the table.

"Cael," I continued when he didn't say anything. "I don't think you can replace the '*happy*' your mom gave your dad."

"So what, I just continue to let him down?"

"Have you actually talked to him about it?" I asked.

"Tried," Cael sighed and leaned over the table. He dropped his head into his crossed arms and huffed a long breath against the desktop. "She died in the Nest, you know," he said after a long time, his voice muffled against the table. "When she got sick, it was the only place that fit her hospital bed."

"The storage room," I nodded.

"Yeah," he said, resting his temple against his arm, remnants of tears in his eyes.

The day he had told me about it, I could feel something tense leaking from his thoughts, joking about ghosts and haunted houses. I'd been too caught up in my own shit to even ask about it.

"It was close to Silas in case she needed something, and my dad's house was too small, too far out of town. She had taken care of all of us, every Hornet player walking into the Nest. She made them feel like they were home, and now," tears returned and pricked at his sad blue eyes.

"There's a little bit of her in you," I brushed my hand out of his and wiped away the tears that ran down his cheeks. "You were the reason I felt at home at the Nest."

"You don't have to be nice just cause I'm crying," he leaned into my touch.

"Do you even know me? I said *a little bit*, don't get crazy. You're still ninety percent your stubborn, rude dad."

BAD HONEY

"I feel better, I think," he chuckled, "now show me how to do this," he swallowed his feelings, pulling his hat down over his eyes and diving back into his work.

I knocked on Coach Cody's door and waited for him to answer before sliding into his messy office. The small couch in the corner was covered with a blanket and pillows, and a duffle bag on the floor overflowing with dirty clothes.

"What can I do for you, Miele?" He asked without looking up from his desk.

I would deal with the aftermath, which would be Arlo and Silas's anger later.

"It's about Cael," I said, waiting as he slowly set his pen down and finally acknowledged me properly. He pointed to the chair, so I would sit, "I'm sure you're aware of his addictions?"

"Yes," he sighed, "what did he do now?"

I swallowed the urge to snap at him. I had been privy to these conversations between teachers and professionals more than once, and it was never a concerned tone. It was always disappointment that wafted from them.

"Nothing, sir." I shook my head, "he's been going to meetings and controlling his issues, but I'm afraid that the pressure of playoffs and school is weighing down on him."

"You think he can't handle it?" Coach shifted in his chair, disappointment turning into defense.

"Not exactly, sir," I sighed, "I'm confident that Cael believes he can."

"Belief doesn't cure drug addicts," he clicked his tongue.

"You can't cure an addict," I snipped without meaning to and took a moment to collect myself. "Cael needs you, sir. He needs to know that you see him trying."

"Every time I've seen Cael this week, he's been drunk. Did you know that?" Coach leaned on the arm of his chair, the dark circles making his green eyes even more vibrant. "He's come to every single practice smelling like vodka."

"But he's showing up," I said, "and it's not drugs."

"It's still a problem."

I could see it, the tangled, horrible feelings that swirled around behind those sad green eyes. He was fighting demons, too, but he wasn't strong enough to fight his and Cael's simultaneously. Suddenly, it was so obvious why Arlo had taken the weight. Cael needed someone sturdy, and Ryan Cody couldn't provide that.

"Alright," I picked at the ring on my thumb as I stood to leave the room.

"Ella," Coach said, "don't mistake my coldness toward Cael. He's my son, and I love him, but we have too many years of anger to return from so easily. Even if I offered my hand to him..."

"Maybe you should try," I sighed, patting the door frame. "I'm sorry about your wife. She sounded like an amazing woman."

I watched the color leave his knuckles as he clenched around his pen. "Good luck in Washington this weekend. I'll see you guys when you get back."

"Go Hornets," he mumbled as he went back to work.

KING

The library was the last place I wanted to be after a long flight home, but Ella hadn't been in her room when I arrived at the nest, and Zoey had pointed me in this direction. I found her sitting in the corner at a desk facing the large row of windows overlooking the Harbor courtyard. Her long curves never ceased to amaze me. She took my breath away, even dressed in a loose white t-shirt and jeans.

"Blondie," I pressed my cheek to hers, pressing my lips to the scar that drew me in impossibly so. "What are you doing?"

"I *was* studying," she leaned into my touch and sighed like she hadn't a moment to breathe since I left her.

"I need a new one," I pulled the last book she gave me out and set it on the table.

"What was wrong with this one?" She asked me.

"Nothing," I laughed, pulling out the chair beside her. "I finished it on the plane," I shrugged in my hoodie as she stared at me.

"You didn't like it, why?"

"Sure I did," I lied, but only because she scrunched up her nose in protest when I did. "The main character couldn't make up their mind about the guy. It was frustrating."

"It's human," Ella leaned her body toward mine, and I couldn't help but steal a kiss. I cupped her face in my hand, holding her in place as I swiped my tongue into her mouth. I lifted from my chair onto my feet, leaning into her because I needed her closer. "Arlo," she laughed, tangling her fingers into the collar of my hoodie, "we're in the library, and people are staring."

"Let them," I ran my lips against her jaw to her ear and kissed the skin there gently as she leaned into my touch.

"This isn't exactly subtle," she huffed, and she was right. Even one blurry camera photo would be enough to set the hounds on her.

"I missed you," I whispered, unsure how to act, how light I needed to tread with her. I was still so afraid to startle her back into her shell, but I couldn't have her leaving. I couldn't bear it.

She sighed, bumping her face against mine to get me to stop. "You can't undress me in the library."

I sat back in my chair, her fingers still knotted into the strings of my hoodie, and her eyes still locked on mine. "Undressing wasn't exactly on my mind," I wrapped my fingers into hers at my chest and stood up, tugging her gently behind me as I found a quiet aisle of books with no peering eyes.

I kissed her without hesitation, tangling my hands into her hair and stealing all the air from her lungs as she wrapped around me. With her arms around my neck, she pushed into the kiss with hungry desire and tangled her hand into my hair. Kissing her came easily. I welcomed getting lost in the time with my arms holding her close.

"I missed you too," she huffed, admitting it out loud.

"You admitting defeat is hot," I laughed.

"It's not defeat if you admit it first."

"I'm not stingy with my feelings," I kissed her again.

"Neither am I." She protested, melting into my touch.

"Don't make me pull out my phone," I warned. Getting her to text was like pulling teeth. Every message met with fewer words until I would eventually break and just call her to make sure she wasn't upset or lonely. Sometimes just to hear her voice.

"Just keep kissing me, King."

I nipped at her bottom lip and brushed my nose against hers so she'd stop and look at me for a second. What little of the sun was left in the sky painted the dark corners of the library in deep oranges, lighting up her big brown eyes like pyres as a smile spread on her face.

"You're beautiful," I pushed one hand into her hair, angling her chin to me again to steal a slower, less frantic kiss from her and then another, increasing in pace until we were moving in time with one another, matching each other's sloppy lusty pace.

Her fingers tucked into the band of my jeans, tugging my hips against hers, and ripped a throaty moan from her lips. Obliging out of my own selfish needs, I rolled against her and the shelves, causing everything to wobble and creek under us. She giggled nervously against my skin, and a shockwave of excitement rolled down to my toes.

"Seeing you like this, nervous," I kissed her again, "breathless. It's doing something to me. It's making my head spin." I pressed another messy kiss to her neck as she hung off me with one arm, her leg hooked tightly against my hip. "I can't wait to get you home, but I don't have the patience. Get on your knees," I tickled her ear with my breath, "right here for me in the library."

Ella stared up at me, her eyes half closed as her fingers silently worked at the button of my jeans. She sank to her knees as I angled myself in front of her. The feeling of getting caught was a rush of adrenaline that challenged my resolve not to fuck her against the bookshelves.

I cupped her chin between my fingers and forced her to look at me.

"That's my girl. Now show me how much you missed me."

Ella, for all her stubbornness, liked being told what to do. Double-checking our surroundings, she pulled on my zipper and roughly tugged my boxers down, freeing me from them. Already impossibly hard for her, from the first look after not seeing or touching her for days, I was uncomfortable in my jeans.

I ran my hand through her hair and over her jaw, brushing my thumb against her bottom lip as she prepared to take it. Her hand rubbed methodically down the length of my shaft in carefully timed pumps that had my entire body tensing beneath her touch.

She looked up at me, catching my gaze and running a hand under my sweater against my stomach before she slowly opened her mouth and licked a deliberate stripe up the length of my cock. Ella worked her lips over my head, tongue roving in circles. My hips twitched under her touch, eager for more. I curled over slightly, bracing myself on the shelf ahead of me. I wrapped my hand tighter into her hair. Her tongue worked up and down in little licks, and she brushed her teeth over the delicate skin as I fought to remain quiet.

Without warning, Ella brought her lips back to the tip of my cock and swallowed me down as deep as she could. Her watery gaze flickered to me, seeking approval I was happy to give as I tugged on her hair and smiled down at her.

"Good girl," I praised as she bobbed her head up and down, saliva pooling around her lips.

A throaty moan left her throat, rattling around my cock as her eyes closed in focus, pumping up and down on my shaft. A strangled laughter tangled with tight groans filled the air. She was the picture of debauchery, on her knees in the library with her mouth full.

I loved the way she looked with my cock in her mouth.

"Fuck," I hissed, hands raking through her hair. My fingers curled into her nape, tugging hard enough to rip a whimper from her as her teeth scraped faintly against my shaft. Not hard enough to hurt, but enough to warn me to play nice as long as my cock was between her lips. "Don't stop, Blondie." I breathed out.

Her hands moved to grab my ass, squeezing. She pulled me even closer, and I could feel myself rub against the back of her throat. A shiver ran up my spine, forcing me to throw my head back as Ella let go of a long, needy moan. She pulled back, swirling her tongue around my tip once more before swallowing my cock to the root.

"Ella," I gripped her hair and the shelf. The view of her bathed in the sunset, with messy hair, glossy eyes, and her lips wrapped around my cock was enough to push me over the edge. I pumped hard twice more before filling her with long thick ribbons that dripped down her lips as she retreated, releasing my throbbing cock from her mouth. "*Baby*," I praised, the word slipping out before I could stop myself, my thoughts sideways as I shoved myself roughly back into my boxers.

She laughed with a crooked smile as I helped her to her feet and tucked her into my chest with a thousand tiny kisses to her cheeks and the corners of her grin.

"Baby?"

"Cael can never know," I whispered with a smile and inhaled the breath I had been holding for ten minutes.

BAD HONEY

"You are never living that down," she spoke quietly, her fingers doing up my jeans as her tongue darted out over her bottom lip.

"Be quiet," I kissed her, gripping her chin. "*Please.*"

MIELE

"So?" Riona sat back in her chair, setting her notebook to the side, and waited.

"Four days," I swallowed my spit in a meek attempt to wash down the vomit from the hour before.

She nodded, urging me to speak freely.

I didn't want to be here, but I had broken down in the medical office, and Silas had walked in on me, huddled in the corner crying. If not for that intrusion, Cael would have never shoved me in his car and forced me over here to see his Aunt. I would rather be curled up in my bed away from the eyes of people who didn't understand. Riona may have been educated enough to process what happened to me, but she would never know how it felt.

"Four days until the anniversary of their death."

"Whose death, Ella?"

Say their names.

It was more complicated than it should have been. The sharp pain from their memories clawed at my ribcage, trying to escape. The guilt that wrapped around me like a blanket seemed to tighten and choke the air from my lungs. Coming here was hard. Riona had this way of digging up all the negative feelings I had worked so hard to shove away. All those feelings that satiated the guilt, the heartbreak, the loneliness, the grief. The ones that made me feel like it wasn't my fault. But it was.

Emotions could change, but facts could not.

The fact of the matter was I had killed my entire family because I had been too selfish to just feel sad about my injuries and my career ending.

BAD HONEY

Say their names.

When I didn't answer, her brows pinched together. That way, she looked so much like Cael. It seemed to have a calming effect on my anxiety and forced me to take a breath.

"My parents, my brother," I flexed my hands tightly, unable to resist the urge to untuck the ring under my shirt. I rubbed it intensely, letting the metal irritate the pad of my thumb, "four days from now marks one year since I killed them."

"How did you kill them?"

She asked that often, always to prove a point.

My first instinct was always to answer with murder, but she steeled her mossy green eyes on me, waiting for me to correct myself before even uttering the words out loud.

"It was an accident."

"Don't answer what you think I want to hear. Answer what you believe." She said.

"It was murder." I corrected myself.

"Did you plan it?" She asked, sitting forward in her chair and setting her book down.

"No," I shook my head and swallowed the bile rising in my throat. *I didn't want to be here, not now.*

"Do you regret it?" She asked me.

"Of course I do," I answered without hesitation.

"I want you to take the time this week to really sit in those feelings, to let yourself be sad and not feel guilty for it." She explained and offered me a soft smile. "Can you do that?"

"The sad part I can," I'm honest with her. "The guilt."

"Look at it like a monster under your bed," Riona offered, "if you keep the lights on, it can't hurt you."

Of course, she wasn't actually talking about the lights. She was talking about allowing people to help. She didn't want me to shut anyone else out during this time.

"You have a light in your room, right Ella?"

Arlo. Laughter bubbled up and out of me, "Yeah, I have a light."

"Good," she smiled, "let it help you fight the monsters."

"Hey, Blondie."

On any other day, I would be happy to see him. Especially how he looked as I walked from the campus toward the parking lot. Tan muscles glistened under the sun, necklaces hanging loose against his chest, and shorts hung low enough on his hips that I could see the hard outline of his hip bones. I could tell by how his chest rose and fell that he had been running after practice had ended. The man was a sadist.

"What's wrong?" He pushed off the Mustang, the smile on his face dropping as he walked toward me.

"Nothing," I forced the corner of my mouth into a tight smile and waved him off.

He seemed offended by that answer, but I didn't have the emotional capacity to deal with his reaction. If I didn't get back to the Nest and into my bed, I might have collapsed in the parking lot. As badly as I wanted to keep the light on, I couldn't. Not today.

Arlo being *Arlo*, he wasn't ready to let go of it that easily, his body sliding between me and the passenger side door.

"Please just take me home," I whined.

"What's wrong?" He asked again, slumping his body to the left to catch my eye line as I avoided looking directly at him. "Oh, come on, Ella, I'm here. Talk to me."

Talk to me. He made that seem so easy, but talking seemed so trivial even after everything. It wasn't about him. It never had been. I trusted him enough to tell him everything, but it was exhausting and never made me feel better afterward. Releasing the information didn't soothe the ache in my chest. It usually just made it worse.

"I'm just really tired, Arlo," I lied.

"Bullshit," he pushed.

And even though I knew exactly what he was doing, every alarm bell went off in my mind, "You know what's bullshit?"

"What?" He narrowed his eyes.

BAD HONEY

"You fucking pretending that you care about this on some deeper level than just one-upping, Nick." I didn't know where the comment had stemmed from. I was exhausted and overworked, and none of my emotions was regulated. Everything that dripped from him felt like pity at that moment, and it itched at every nerve in my body. "I'm sorry."

The expression changed on his face as the concern was pushed behind the wall of frustrated anger. Shame filled me. I felt better after snapping at him. It wasn't his fault I was feeling like this, and it wasn't his job to take care of me like this. He already had so much going on between baseball, his family, and Cael. He was stretched thin enough, and here I was stressing him out even more.

I couldn't do this. Lay my burdens at his feet with everyone else's. Not to him, not now.

"Arlo," I clenched my jaw, closing it just to stop any more of the nasty feelings from spilling out. "Just take me home, please."

"Take yourself home," he pulled back from me, tossing the keys to the fastback in the air.

"What?" I caught them before they hit the ground but panicked as he started climbing into the car's passenger side. "Arlo, that's not funny."

"You want to be independent, Blondie? You wanna pretend this," he waved between us over the car's roof, "is one-sided. Fine. If that helps you feel safe, I can do that."

The word *pretend* hung between us, so tense it might snap if I stepped back even an inch. He looked over at me, with brown eyes and heavy brows lingering in the shadow that my body cast across him from above.

"But if you want to push people away, you need to learn how to take care of yourself. Get in the car." He climbed into the passenger seat.

"I don't know how to drive stick," I snapped, holding the keys out to him through the open window.

"This is very obviously a teaching moment."

His tone was low, riding the line between cautious and harsh.

"Two steps at a time." He said, watching me, knowing he was walking the tightrope. "I'll be here the entire time, Ella. I'm not leaving you just because you get snappy with me. If I was that fragile Cael would be in a ditch somewhere."

My hands shook, the keys clanging against each other as I wandered around to the driver's side of the fastback on wobbly, unsure steps. I inhaled slowly, wrapping my hand around the handle of the car, hesitating for a moment before climbing into the driver's seat.

I hadn't sat on this side of a car since that night, and my entire body seized up as it hit the leather and realized where we were. Every muscle tightened, screaming in protest as I wrapped my hand around the wheel and shoved the key into the ignition. My foot on the clutch, a tiny whimper left my lips as the car rumbled to life and my hands wrapped around the steering wheel.

"This is cruel," I huffed.

"Consider us even then," Arlo snapped, upset about what I said.

I closed my eyes. A pathetic attempt to ground myself in reality.

My giggling filled the front seat as Ethan shuffled through a playlist of songs ranging from mainstream pop to some of the worst eighty's rock.

"That one," I yelled, pointing to the dash as he skipped past one I liked. "Go back!"

My head felt fuzzy, and my body felt weightless as I tapped against the steering wheel and let the music thrum through me. Every note felt like it was pushing through my bloodstream as Ethan and I sang.

He was full of more life than any person I've ever known. His short-cropped blonde hair pushed back off his face in carefully placed waves. Our matching brown eyes and goofy crooked smile, screaming at the top of our lungs.

My parents sat in the back, noses in their phones. Always there, but always working.

"Hey!" I yelled, turning the music up louder, "Don't you see the karaoke happening!"

My dad looked up at me through his glasses, brows pinched together in disapproval.

"Watch the road, Estella."

"Ella," Arlo's voice cut through the memory only to thrust me back into the real world, where my chest was wracked with uncontrollable sobbing. "Get it out," he encouraged with a hand over mine on the wheel.

I pulled back from the wheel, putting my hands in my lap and sinking as far back into the driver's seat as possible. My outburst hadn't been about Arlo. It never was; he was conveniently always there to take the blow. "I don't trust myself," I swallowed the hiccup and wiped the tears away from my cheeks with the back of my hand.

"I trust you."

I looked at him, angled in his seat, eyes watching without judgment. He was serious.

"You shouldn't."

A small smile tickled at the corner of his mouth as he reached out and brushed away a rogue tear that dripped from my jaw. "Baby, I'm not sure you get to decide for me."

"You weren't there, Arlo. You don't understand what I did." I looked at the steering wheel again and could somehow feel the glass explode against my skin, a thousand tiny stinging needles sinking into my flesh.

I deserved to feel it.

"Center pedal, brake all the way to the floor," he pointed with his finger, ignoring what I said. "Come on, Blondie, I know you can follow directions."

I growled at him, letting the anger displace the sadness for a split second.

He smiled with pride as he watched me shift into first gear.

"Let up on the clutch. She's going to roll," he warned softly, "just a little, but it's because this lot is on an angle." He looked out to the nearly empty parking lot.

"Arlo," I swallowed the bile that formed. I couldn't do this. It was too much pressure. Too much responsibility. What if I crashed his car and ruined what he had created for his mom? "This is—"

"Press the accelerator down while you let up on the clutch." He ignored my worry, proving how much he trusted me through deflection. "Feel through it. She'll tell you when you need to shift."

The fastback slowly started to gain speed, and my hand wrapped around the stick as I pulled around the parking lot. I felt Arlo slide his hand over the top of mine, "feel it." He whispered as the car silently at first and then loudly demanded second gear. "Feel everything," he instructed, not understanding how much there was to feel.

"Gentle, take us home," he whispered proudly as I pushed into third, and the Mustang flawlessly climbed up the hill toward the Nest. "That's my baby," he nodded and released my hand, sinking into the passenger seat.

A shiver ran up my spine, but it wasn't one of shame or guilt. It was my body reminding me that I was alive. I was here with the wind in my hair and a beautiful boy beside me. Living for Ethan, living for me.

The ten-minute drive back to the Nest felt like three hours as I finally slowed the car into the driveway and turned off the engine. With free hands, I turned, punching Arlo in the arm with a loud smack.

"Ow!" He rubbed his bicep with a dirty look on his face. "What the hell was that for?"

"For making me drive!" I snapped.

I could see on his face that he wanted to quip back that nobody had died and the car was in one piece, but the joke died on his lips.

"I meant it," he said instead. "I trust you."

"Still unsure what that means. I am sorry, though. I shouldn't have said what I said."

He chuckled, sliding back his seat like he had done that day in the rain, and motioned for me to come close. I climbed over the middle and into his lap without trouble, settling down in his arms as he tucked a chunk of hair behind my ear.

"I have spent the last two months tip-toeing around what *that* means," he said so quietly it barely made a sound. "Two months of holding back so that I didn't scare you into or out of a relationship you weren't ready for, Ella."

"Arlo," I sighed.

"For once, just listen," he shushed me with a soft kiss. "Do you remember the night we met?"

"The Delta party."

"It's always been *for you*."

BAD HONEY

It's for my legacy. I remembered the look on Arlo's face that night when he retorted without hesitation. But at the time, I wasn't smart enough or too unaware to look beneath the surface. To push past the hardened expression and mean banter.

He flipped the ring out from underneath my shirt and rolled it in his fingers. "I've always been here, Ella, in any way you'll let me. I've been here, waiting for you to be sure of what that means."

"What if I don't know?" I asked.

He brushed his finger over my chin as a sad smile formed on his lips, "I've more than proved I'm a patient man."

MIELE

I needed sleep. I couldn't go much longer without it.

"Are you going to be okay?" Zoey asked from beside me, hair braided back and baggy sweater over her tiny frame.

Zoey had spent the morning with me, fingers interlocked with mine as we sat out in the grass crying amongst the Dewey grass. Her thumb rubbed against mine, and I tried to face her without starting the tears again.

"Not today," I sigh.

"You can always stay home, in your bed. We can order Ethan's favorite for dinner."

"Ethan didn't have a favorite food. He just liked food." I squeezed her hand.

"I could eat. Order something from everywhere?" She offered a pathetic smile back. "Call Silas, tell him you need the day."

No days were left to countdown, no breathing techniques or tricks that could distract my mind.

It was the day I killed my family.

It was also the last game before the College World Series.

The team needed the win. The series was deadlocked.

I had woken up that morning, barely. With the intention of doing just that, hiding away until the day passed. But something had dragged me from bed. There was a horrible sinking feeling weighing against my chest, and for once, it wasn't guilt, but it felt just as horrific.

"They need me at the stadium."

BAD HONEY

"Now, you really do sound like old Ella." Zoey smiled, but the comment stung.

Old Ella buried herself in problems that weren't hers to forget the ones she did have. Estella Miele, the pill-popping monster that killed her family because she just wanted to numb the pain and the stress. Just for a moment. Maybe for today, I needed her. Estella would get up, go to work, and smile like nothing was wrong.

I pushed out of the grass, the sun well in the sky now. We had sat out there for hours. "That's enough crying for the day," I held my hand to her and swallowed all the emotions that threatened to escape in protest of my decision. "Van needs you today."

"Van understands," Zoey hummed, but her smile fell.

"Too often," I smiled at her. "And usually when he shouldn't."

She nodded, sad in her own way about today but willing to do what I asked just because I asked it.

The stadium was buzzing. I had never felt it so alive or heard it so loud. The tunnel was packed with bodies. I kept my head down, minding my business, and ensured I had everything in my bag.

Cael pushed past me roughly, snaking through the tight-shouldered crowd of players and staff. "Hey!" I grabbed him by the back of the jersey, "what the hell?"

"Fuck off," he tensed up, shoulders squared as he turned to spit at me until he realized who had grabbed him. "Sorry, Peach," the breath he took flooded through his body and helped him release the tension he was holding.

"What the hell is going on?" I asked, sliding my bag over my shoulder and pulling him off the main tunnel into a room. I closed the door behind us and poked him in the chest, "You were fired up enough to knock me on my ass two seconds ago. Spit it out, tough guy."

"Tucker's..." he swallowed the words he was trying to say and took another strangled breath in. "Tucker's mom saw us."

"The homophobic woman from the cabin?" I tilted my head to the side. "I thought you were handling that with baby gloves?"

"I don't *own* baby gloves, Ella!"

Cael was panicking like I had never seen him do before. Sweat dripped down his neck into the collar of his uniform as he turned his hat backward and paced around the tiny room I had pulled us into.

"I'm like a fucking freight train without a conductor on my best days! The baby gloves get used on me! Not by me!" Cael fell limp against the desk behind him.

"He always does this," he ground his teeth together. "Wants the comfort, wants the connection, wants the sex," he licked his lip. "But he gets scared."

"People are allowed to get scared," I tried not to lean on the bias that I was going through the same thing with Arlo.

I enjoyed the comfort, craved the connection, and dreamed wildly about the sex in the quiet hours of the night, but he wanted more, needed more from me. And I wasn't sure he was ready for that burden or if I was prepared to let go of it. I rolled my hand over the ring inside my uniform and tried to ignore my problems simply by focusing on Cael's.

"Sure, yeah," he shook his head and mumbled something else, "but," he ran his hands over his face erratically. "I *need* him."

"Are you high?" I stepped toward him, reaching for his face to look into his eyes, but he angled his shoulder away from me and spun back off the table to create space between us.

He threw his hands in the air, "just a little."

"It's never just a little," I chewed on the inside of my cheek and extended my palm to him. "Give me it."

"I don't have—" he started but saw the look on my face and dug it free of his ball pants.

"So what, you got in an argument, got high thinking you would talk to him at the stadium? Fuck Cael," I tried to steady my thoughts. Today had already been challenging enough with the tiny plastic baggy of pills rolling between my fingers. Every ounce of my resolve was being tested.

He ran his hands down the front of his pants and curled over on his thighs, "I—" he mumbled. "I needed him," he looked at me through thick lashes.

"You have me, you have Arlo, you have *yourself*."

"No," he straightened out and walked toward me. His tall frame was terrifying in this state as he backed me against the wall with a rough thud. "I had you, I had Arlo. Now you have each other, and I'm alone."

"I'm here!" I resisted the urge to push him away from me. "I've been here, at school, the library, the Nest, and meetings! With you, even when I'm falling apart, I'm here with you," I lowered my voice and pressed my hand to his racing heart. "I'm here," I said again.

"Misery loves misery."

I gave him a moment.

The words spun around in his crowded mind at top speed. He inhaled sharply, and for a moment, I thought he might just walk away, the longest moment of my life, but when the cord snapped, Cael fell into my arms. Sobbing uncontrollably, his dead weight was enough to sink us both to our knees in a crumpled ball on the floor. I pressed his head to my chest, threw his hat to the side, and softly ran my fingers through his hair as he cried.

Cael could seem so big and brave when he wanted, but in moments of vulnerability, he was so small, like his whole body could fit in my arms.

The door creaked open, and Arlo stuck his head in quietly, his eyes trailing down to the baggy on the ground beside my leg with a scowl. I wasn't sure if the look was disappointment or anger, but I shook my head at him, *not now*. And he nodded, closing the door behind him.

"Cody," he tugged at his ball pants, squatting beside us, and replaced my hand in Cael's hair with his own, tugging gently to pull him from the trance he had cried himself into. "I know this sucks. I know you love-" Arlo got eye level with him, following his gaze when Cael tried to look away. "I know you love him a lot," he said again. "There's nothing we can do about his mom or your feelings right now."

I swallowed tightly as Cael flexed in my arms. I understood all too well how he was feeling. Every emotion swirling around inside of his pretty little head. Hurt, guilt, shame. It was endless and suffocating. I waited as Arlo did what he did best, using logic to twist Cael from the impossible knot he had turned himself into. It was different from any approach I would ever use, and I hated it when he did it to me, but it worked. Every damn time. "But, what we can do—" Arlo held his face in his hand, squeezing tightly as he got close. "If we can go out there and ensure that Dean is okay, we can do that for him. Right now. We can set aside all those shitty feelings, we can satiate the guilt just for two hours, and you can hold him up when he needs you."

"It won't make this right," Cael huffed. "You didn't hear what his mom said to him, Ar," the words were strangled and whiny as he fought to control his tears.

"No," Arlo agreed. "It won't make it right, but at least try."

"Come on," I pushed up from underneath him, using all my body weight to help Arlo, who hoisted him from the other side. "He can't play the first inning, not like this."

"He has to," Arlo chewed on his lip and squared his shoulders. The Arlo everyone else knew was forced to the front. His mean scowl and intense stare seemed to burn through me as he gazed at me.

"I've done it before," Cael's voice was slurred, but he shook Arlo off and scooped his hat from the floor with a swing of his long arm.

"Sorry, Peach," he looked back at me with a tensed jaw, tears still brimming in his big blue eyes. His apology wasn't for wasting my time or having a freakout. His short-toned apology was for breaking a promise, cheating on himself, and shuffling the expectations of who he wanted to be on me because it was easier if I put him on the pedestal he had just toppled from.

Arlo faced away from me. Every muscle in his body was taut with rage, and as the door clicked shut, he turned back. "Give them to me," he held his hand to me. "Ella." He said when I didn't.

I hadn't even realized I had scooped the baggy from the floor, the plastic tucked into my closed fist. I looked down at my hand, the pills seemingly burning a hole through my skin. An itch that I had long forgotten about suddenly needing to be scratched.

BAD HONEY

Just one, I thought. One would make every bad memory slip away. I could forget about Ethan and my parents, just for today. Today, of all days, is the worst. The universe had seen my pain, called my bluff, and handed me a solution.

"*Baby*," his voice broke through every dark, fuzzy thought that clawed at my vision and threatened to swallow me whole. "Taking those won't make today hurt less."

My gaze remained fixated on the tiny yellow pills. He couldn't be sure of that. But I knew they would because, just like all the nightmares and bad memories, my body remembered how it felt to fly. How numb it could become with only one little pill.

Arlo reached out again, not for the bag but to roll his fingers around the ring on my thumb. The ring for Ethan, the ring that Cael had so thoughtfully gifted me. "Don't do it for yourself," Arlo cupped my chin, "set aside those feelings and do it for your brother. Just today, do it for him."

"Don't use your bullshit on me, Arlo King," I huffed.

"Two hours, two steps at a time, whatever you need to get through today. Set aside the feelings, and when the game is over, I will take you home, wrap you up in bed, and you can forget about it for as long as you need."

I looked up at him finally, tears brimming my eyes.

"We do it together," he slinked one finger through my pinky and pressed it to his chest. His other hand looped around my neck, bringing me close to him as his lips found the corner of the scar where it met my cheek and softly kissed it.

It didn't matter he had figured out that today was the anniversary, but I was grateful that he hadn't asked or prodded. He just put it together and showed up. He placed another quick kiss on my temple, scoping up my med bag before gripping my hand and wandering back into the tunnel where the team still waited. Arlo hid my hand behind his back, and for a second, I thought he would pull away, but instead, he pushed my palm to the wall.

The vibrations were like a weighted blanket around my shoulders.

"Here," he rested my bag on my shoulder. "Two steps at a time," he reminded me with two fingers to his chest.

I had been meaning to ask why he always said two steps instead of one, but at that moment, I realized. It was because he wasn't letting me walk alone. It was his step, in time with mine.

I mirrored the gesture back to him. "Two steps at a time."

MIELE

Cael barely survived the game, his focus on everything but the ball as he struck out late in the seventh. The game had been in limbo until Dean crushed a home run on loaded bases and won them the game. His anger was obvious as he stomped around the dugout and didn't wait for the MVP of the night to be announced before he disappeared to shower. Cael seemed defeated, but he had come down from his high and was chugging water when Mrs. Tucker approached him in the press tunnel.

"Not here," Arlo barked loudly enough for Silas and me to turn toward him as he guided Cael and her into a closed-door room away from the journalists and cameras.

"That was a good game today," I congratulated Coach tightly. Every silent word was a dagger to his chest. *Your son needs you.* I collected my things from the locker room. I'd brought my bike to class that morning, so I went into the fading light and unlocked it from the rack before disappearing up the hill to the Nest alone.

I couldn't be there anymore, between the lights and cheering. It all felt too close to home like I was back in another football stadium with Ethan on the field. My parents watched from the stands and the entire campus chanting his name.

My chest got so tight watching Arlo on the mound that I thought it might shatter into a thousand pieces that I'd never put back together again. It was too much today, and all I wanted to do was disappear into my sheets.

I showered quickly, taking advantage of the quiet house before slipping into clean sweats and my sweatshirt. The faded Cal State logo stared at me as I pulled back the covers on my bed and sighed. My phone buzzed madly on the table beside my pillow, Zoey, Arlo, and Cael all texting and calling at once. *Cael would have a stash.*

I let my head fall between my shoulders as I tried to steady my thoughts. His room was so close, just one set of stairs.

I rubbed my finger over the ring on my thumb.

No.

I didn't need drugs. I never had.

Feel it. You earned that pain.

Very few times, my father had turned his attention off his work, off Ethan. But the one time he had was the day I ruined my fastpitch career. I remembered it so clearly that it'd haunted me like some sort of boogeyman. He hadn't comforted me or told me that it would be alright. The words he said to me in the back of the ambulance as he scolded me for continuing to play were, *you earned that pain*. And in a sick turn of events, it had been one of the only things that ever worked to turn the tide on my addictive thoughts.

With a strangled sob, I slipped the hood over my head, swiped my headphones off the table, and wandered the ten steps to Arlo's room. I thought about crawling into his bed, weighing the options of how it might make me feel, but then the suffocating thoughts of human touch bombarded me, and I backed away.

He'd be home eventually. They all would.

I laughed to myself, settling on the next best solution. Turned the knob and wandered in to tug the blanket that smelled so much like Arlo off his bed before turning tail around the house and wandering out into the backyard toward the hammock. Somehow, it had become the most permanent fixture in my life, cozy and warm. It wrapped around me so perfectly that I couldn't help myself even when the air was hot and sticky or cold and rainy. It was where I wanted to be. It was where I felt the most at home.

But even there, huddled in what was expected to be safety, I felt the memories creep in, and before long, the tears started to violently pour from me. My chest cracked open so easily to the guilt, shame, and grief. My fingers twitched beneath the blanket, my mind trying to convince me to go out and find what I needed to make it better. I

BAD HONEY

laid it against my chest, pulling the ring into my palm and rolling it between my fingers as I curled my legs up and tried to get comfortable enough that my mind would forget about the drugs. About the urges, I so badly wanted to give in.

"Are you sure, El?" Ethan mirrored the goofy look on my face as I scooped the keys from the bowl at the front door. Drugs coursing through my bloodstream as I nod at him.

"Your car is in the shop, moms is a piece of shit, and I'm not letting you drive to a fundraiser being held in your honor," I shrugged. It had been so easy to hide the bottles, the addiction, the drugs. No one cared if it didn't have Ethan's name attached to it.

We walked toward my car, my heels digging into the soft gravel. Our parents trailed behind, dressed in fancy clothes, voices lowered as they talked business. There were more pills in my purse, and by the way things were going, I was going to need them.

"I put on this pretty dress. We aren't missing this. Besides, Connor will be there," I fixed my hair in the reflection of the car window and swiped my hand beneath my eyes, avoiding my makeup but worried about my blown-out irises.

"You drive him nuts," Ethan interrupted my panic as he opened the driver's door for me, shaking his head in disapproval. "Just let him take you out. It's all he talks about. The guys are about ready to lock him in a closet just to have one quiet practice without having to hear about how pretty you are."

"I am stunning," I winked.

The tingling sensation in my fingers seemed to rush through over the steering wheel, and I rubbed them over and back a few times to quell it before starting the engine. I turned on music, hoping it would let me settle how fast my heart was racing. I nearly floated above my seat. I couldn't feel my body or organize the thoughts that swam around behind my eyes.

"You alright?" Ethan tapped my shoulder as my focus came back to the car, my mind slamming violently back into my body. "You glassed over there for a second."

"Is that Queen?" I ignored him and turned the radio up louder.

I caught his scowl out of the corner of my eye as I pulled onto the highway in the pouring rain. "El, the nineteen is faster," Ethan nodded, but I just shrugged him off, continuing onto the highway.

"Estella," my mother warned from behind, "just listen to your brother for once."

Ethan this, Ethan that.

It was only Estella when they were directing criticism, anger, and disdain.

My temperature rose, and I could feel my blood coursing beneath my skin as the rain started to beat down on the car's hood. We weren't taking the nineteen, we were driving my car, I was in charge, I was driving. We were doing this my way.

I forced Ethan back into his good mood, singing at the top of my lungs and dragging him into song with me. He tossed his head back with a bright smile and belted the lyrics over the sound of the rain and music. I could see my parents scowling in the back seat from our antics.

"Hey!" I yelled, turning the music up louder, "Don't you see the karaoke happening!"

My dad looked up at me through his glasses, brows pinched together in disapproval.

"Watch the road, Estella."

"Watch the road, Estella."

"Watch the road, Estella."

You earned that pain, Estella.

Long after the sunset in the sky and the sticky air turned chilly, I felt Arlo scoop me up from the hammock, hauling me up the steps and walking me inside. I let myself fall against his chest without a fight. My eyes were dry and sore from crying myself to sleep, and my limbs felt like someone had pumped lead into them. He laid me down in his bed, closed his door, and stripped of his clothes. He tugged on a pair of pajama pants as I lay there watching him move around his room in the shadows, sliding over when he climbed into bed with me.

He pushed the hair away from my face before wrapping me in the blanket. "You're so cold," he mumbled, trying to get me warm. "Why the hell were you out there?"

"It was quiet," I whispered.

BAD HONEY

"You scared me," he chewed on his lip as the thoughts stirred behind his cautious eyes. "You were just gone, no one could get a hold of you, and you weren't in your room or in here—"

I kissed him to get him to stop talking. I hadn't meant to scare him, but the world had felt too big to handle, and escaping was the best option. "I almost searched Cael's room."

His brows knitted together as he pushed his forehead to mine. "But?"

"I didn't."

"I'm proud of you," he said, brushing his nose against mine.

Something was breaking down between us, a wall perhaps that I had built of steel and concrete to keep the feelings of wanting and safety at bay. To lock myself within walls of my own creation with the guilt and pain I thought I deserved to feel.

But the moment Arlo King knocked on those sturdy walls with his soft— *I'm proud of you*, I felt them crumble like I had made them out of paper cards. He had been so patient with me, and even though our lives had changed so drastically over the last six months, it had felt like Arlo had been there all along, just waiting.

He had never forced or pressed anything. He had let me decide about his brother, the team, and myself. Facilitating an opportunity to find myself again before finding him. Love wasn't the word right for it. That felt too rushed and sloppy for us.

Arlo tugged me a little closer, his hands wrapping under the blankets against the small of my back as he buried his face into my neck, and I wrapped my arms around his back. Breathing each other in was therapeutic.

I wasn't sure how to express the intense emotions swirling around in my chest, unsure if they were real or just distractions against the negative ones fighting for space and attention.

"Arlo," I whispered against his skin and inhaled the leathery smell of the *fastback* mixed with his sweat and cologne. Cinnamon and sandalwood. ❏

"We can just sleep, Ella," he rubbed a careful line up my spine with his hand.

But then the doubt crept in like it always did.

"I really like you," I said. "But I—"

"Sorry, Blondie," he cut me off with a nervous shake to his usually strong voice. "You aren't allowed to break up with me. You made a pinky promise."

A small smile formed on my lips, "just listen," I urged him. "I'm scared."

"Of what?" He asked, and I expected him to pull away, to put space between us, but his hands continued to draw languid shapes into my skin as his breath warmed my neck and shoulders.

"Of this."

Of us.

When he finally did unlink himself from my body, he rolled over onto his back and tucked his hands beneath his head, staring at me in the moonlight. He was waiting for me to say more, to explain myself, but the words seemed to catch in my throat like cotton balls. I memorized the soft lines on his face as a distraction from the devastating look in his eyes.

"So much has happened to me over the last year. I've been spun around, torn apart, and put back together in a hundred different ways, but this scares me. Arlo, what if I let you down?"

His eyes flickered up from my lips to my gaze and hardened.

"I'm scared that Nick was right, that you were attracted by the urge to fix all the broken things within me," I said. The real fear was that he was just interested in me because I was simply a well-equipped distraction from his troubles.

"I don't wanna fix anything," Arlo said without hesitation, "All those broken little pieces make up who you are. I'd be foolish to think I could undo all the hurt you've suffered the last few years. I'm just grateful I was allowed to love what incredibly beautiful heart that suffering formed."

"And if I let you down?"

"You won't. I have waited my entire life to love someone like you, Ella. Every little moment stitched together led to now, to you."

"Love can still hurt you, Arlo," I urged.

"I don't want to live a life that isn't painful," he licked his bottom lip. "Without the experience of pain, everything else seems muted and boring. Hurt, anger, disappointment," he paused, "heartbreak." He moved over on the bed and laid his hand across my jaw, his fingers knitting into the hair behind my ear. "Ella, I don't give a shit what anyone says," he whispered. "Six months, six days, six hours, it doesn't matter," a soft, throaty laugh tumbled from him, "hell, I don't want to go six seconds without loving every piece of you."

Tears burned at my eyes, threatening to ruin yet another sweet moment.

I wanted to tell him that I loved him, and I think a part of me did without even saying the words because he stared at me, not saying a thing, but I could see all the thoughts swirling around behind his dark eyes. It had been so easy to love Arlo King despite what everyone thought about him. He was easy to love, which had been the problem the entire time. I'd spent the last three months trying to find a reason not to love him. Searching for a reason to keep him at arm's length so badly, not even realizing he'd been a part of me since the day he gave me that stupid ring. He had seen me that day for who I was and who I am and didn't care.

"You are the counterweight of the bad moments in my life," I said instead.

He remained quiet. His muscles were tight, and his breathing re-formed.

"Say something."

"Patience is a virtue," he smiled at me.

He laughed at my angry face, wrapping me up and covering my body with his. "Blondie," he kissed the corner of my mouth. His brown eyes raked across my face, taking his time to admire them in the soft light. I brushed the pad of my thumb across the sharp angles of his cheekbones and smiled, sinking into the bed as I finally found a moment of peace.

"I love every scar," he kissed, where it met untainted skin at the corner of my eye.

My eyelashes fluttered in time, with my heart beating against his warm skin.

"Even the ones I can't see," his lips tingle against my chest, kissing the mangled scar that ran over the top of my heart.

I cupped his face in my hands, pulled him back to me, and kissed him as slow as my urges would allow me before my hands began to wander. I raked them gently down his back to the hem of his pants, pushing the satiny fabric over the curve of his ass as he ground down between my legs.

The kiss was careful, deliberate, and comforting. I don't know what came over me, but the release was instant and unstoppable in the form of tears that streamed down my face, soaking our cheeks and leaving a salty taste between our lips.

"Just sleep tonight," he inhaled as his nose brushed against my face, and he wrapped me back in his arms. "Today's been long enough."

I fell asleep shortly after, free of nightmares as my guilt subsided, and Arlo shoved his way into my heart to fill in all the hollow spaces the grief had left behind.

MIELE

The four-hour drive to a campus outside New York feels like the longest time I've spent in a car since the accident. Winning the following games was the only option. The World Series Finals were just out of their reach, and for the first time in three years, they could see it becoming a reality. I brought all my school work with us, with the last of my exams approaching fast. If I wanted to graduate from Harbor with a degree and a hope for a future, I needed to study.

Three weeks had passed since our conversation, and Arlo seemed drawn to me like a magnet. He was always two steps behind me, always there, always waiting.

I understood his worry. The anniversary of the accident set me back hard. I spent nearly two days in his bed, comatose to the world, before Cael finally dragged me from it, kicking and screaming. Brushing out the knots in my hair had been the most painful part. Staring at my reflection made me violently aware of why they teamed up to pull me from my depression cave. I collected myself and started meetings again, accompanying Cael not only to make sure he was going but also for my willpower and recovery.

Work kept my mind off things, but every day was a reminder that I had made it a whole year of grief and guilt, and I was still standing tall, or at least as tall as I could stand in the face of trauma.

"Where's your head at Blondie?" Arlo dug around in the backseat, looking for the bag of snacks I had packed. I wanted to snap at him, to tell him that he couldn't fix it, so he shouldn't dig, but that response was cruel. He was only trying to help.

I slapped a hand against his bicep. "Move."

He gave up without a fight and turned his body back in his seat. I grabbed the bag and pulled out one of the chocolate chip muffins for him, knowing that was exactly what his stomach was searching for. "Here," I unwrapped it, intending to hand it to him, but he pouted when he realized I wasn't going to feed it to him.

"You're such a princess," I tucked my feet up under my ass on the seat and started picking off small pieces for him."How much further do we have?"

"Hour or so," he said. His fingers found a piece of blond hair that fell against my back and curled into it mindlessly.

"Remind me why we left so late?" I asked him.

"Quiet roads," I giggled softly as his lips wrapped around my fingers. "And now we can sleep in tomorrow."

"You sleep in?" I rolled my eyes, "When hell freezes over, Arlo King."

"You make it hard to get out of bed, Ella Miele." My name rolled off his tongue like it had always belonged there, and I melted at the sound, sinking deeper into the leather of the fastback. What I wouldn't give for another week of lazy sex and depression sleep.

"Ow!" I yipped as his teeth nibbled at my fingertips, "don't bite."

His eyebrow raised in challenge, his lips curling into a playful smile as his eyes flickered back and forth to the road. "What?" I laughed, popping a bit of the overly sweet muffin between my lips. □

"Your smile," he shrugged, "it's been missing."

I hadn't expected his soft admission, but it seemed to settle in and warm all the leftover cold spots still hiding within me. Without a response, I fed him the last of the muffin and checked the bag for any vegetables that might satisfy me.

"Arlo, there are four chocolate bars in here!" I pushed around the sweets in the duffle bag with a low groan, "and gummy bears. Who were you packing for Cael?"

I looked up from the bag to find him laughing.

"I had a sweet tooth," he said.

"This is overkill," I whined.

"I could be satiated other ways," his hand tickled against my thigh.

BAD HONEY

"You need to eat something other than chocolate chips and me," I rolled my eyes, but heat licked at my thighs when his hand squeezed gently at the mention of his other favorite snack.

"Says the girl who eats two bags of snap peas in one sitting," he laughed. "There's plenty of nutritional value in that, and exercise."

"There is barely exercise in eating a girl out," I said.

"I'll remember that next time you're asking for more, Blondie." He flirted with a smirk.

My toes curled in my sneakers, we couldn't get to the hotel fast enough.

"Look," he nodded, the car rattling beneath us as he slowed and pulled down a darkening side road toward a dimly lit stand. The sign that hung around the front table promoted fresh fruit and vegetables, but it didn't look like anyone was even around as Arlo cut the engine and climbed from the car without me. He opened the door for me as I tied up my shoes and stepped out on the grassy ditch. Taking my hand, he led us down toward the small gravel padding, his head swaying as he looked around for anyone.

"Hello?"

A small old woman peeped out from behind the long trailer beside the stand, her gray hair curled and tucked into a loose bun. She gave us a warm smile and wiped her hands on her strawberry-patterned apron.

"Just in time. I was about to put everything away!"

She gave me a bag and told me to pick whatever I wanted. My fingers brushed over the stand but were instantly drawn to the selection of vegetables to the left side. Radishes, carrots, and fresh peas piled high in little crates.

"Do you want anything?" I asked him, looking over to find him watching with wonder in his dark brown eyes and a soft smile as he shook his head.

I collected some strawberries for him anyway, knowing he would complain later that he hadn't gotten something, and handed the bag to the woman.

"No, no," she waved me off with her delicate fingers, "it's too late to exchange money."

"Can I help?" He asked, noticing she was loading heavy crates onto the trailer.

She looked around at the crates, and I smiled at her. Arlo would bully the old lady into submission if she didn't let him. As expected, when she didn't respond, he sank and began lifting the crates two at a time, placing them down where she pointed deep within the trailer.

"He's a lovely man," she winked at me as she ducked uncomfortably below the stand to grab something.

It was easy to forget how sweet he could be when screaming orders at the baseball team, scowling, or fighting with the umps after ball calls. But she was right. Arlo King was a sweet man. Too sweet for his own good, and I woke up every day terrified that I might taint that, take away the sweetness he so sparingly shared with others.

"He really is," I smiled.

"I missed that look," she whispered, "I miss turning around in the kitchen covered in flour to find my husband with it on his face."

"What look is that?" I asked as Arlo grabbed two more and disappeared into the giant tin container.

"Love," she laughed under her breath.

I exhaled a little, the word like a cotton ball in my throat.

"Don't worry," she whispered, leaving over the table, "your secret is safe with me."

When he was finished helping, she spoke to him quietly by the trailer with a warm smile. He nodded, listening intently to whatever she was saying to him, his complete attention on a stranger. He could make everyone feel respected. She pointed out to her right and gave him a firm slap on the arm before both started laughing hard.

"You ready to go?" He asked, digging out the keys from his jeans.

"Yeah," I smiled, tossing him a fresh strawberry, "that was really nice of you."

"The least I could do after she fed my girl," he caught it and kissed my temple, and the warmth spread down through my toes as he popped the fruit in between his lips.

"Your girl?" I followed close behind him.

BAD HONEY

"You like that?" He dug out something from the trunk. His smile radiated in the light of the moon and the stars reflecting at me in his eyes.

"Maybe," I shrugged him off.

"Your voice gets all high when your heart starts beating fast," he rounded the car to where I stood with the fruit waiting for him. "Cheeks get all red," he kissed a soft line across my ear. "Eyelids heavy," he nibbled at my ear.

"Okay, you win," I gripped his jaw and squeezed, "I *really* like it when you call me that."

"I know, baby," fully aware that my tone had dropped and the air had grown tight, I aimed to cut it with a kiss, but he stopped me. "Follow me," he winked and linked our hands together.

"You're just going to leave the car there?" I asked as he walked us further down the road.

"It'll be fine," he laughed. He shifted the bundle he'd grabbed from the trunk in his arms and continued to lead me through the darkness. "I was told this place was quiet." The grass grew taller the further we walked, and eventually, we couldn't see the fruit stand or the highway over it.

"In here," he ducked into the grass, pushing through it, and stopped. "Perfect."

"Arlo, what are you doing?"

"I was warned not to waste warm weather and a clear sky, Blondie."

That old lady was a bundle of secrets.

He waved out the bundle, laying a blanket on the ground. Heat filled my chest like that day in the library, and I couldn't help but smile at him as I set down the fruit and closed the gap between us.

I knelt on the blanket, kicking off my shoes and rolling onto my back to look at the stars. Arlo dipped down against me, hips meeting hips as he helped me from the shirt I was wearing. The moon licked at his glowy skin as he nipped at my exposed neck. I was only wearing my sports bra underneath, and it did nothing to cover my pebbling nipples as the breeze washed through the tall grass.

"Help me," I asked, wiggling free of the fabric.

Heat licked at my core as he took a nipple into his mouth. I raked my fingers through his hair, and my body arched into his touch, desperate for friction. Arlo did that thing I loved, tongue swirling and flicking. Pulling back to let the air tickle at my sensitive nipple at the other breast. I laid back into the blanket, letting him work my pants down past my hips and then off to be discarded haphazardly.

"Don't lose them," I giggled. "Your turn."

"Not yet," he shook his head and ran his hands up my thighs. He couldn't resist the urge to dip his chin between my legs and lap up what dampness had already started to pool there. The smell of fresh grass and summer air wafted over us, making me feel weightless as he slid two fingers into my core and pumped gently at the sensitive spot within.

It took moments for me to fall apart in his hands, so when I tugged at his shirt, needing and wanting more, he was eager to provide. I dragged the hem of his shirt over the curve of his strong shoulders, leaving him to pull his jeans down on his own before he returned to me.

Arlo sucked in a tight breath as he pressed against my cunt, rocking inside with one powerful thrust. I was past my point of return, nerves shot, and hands raking down his back. I nipped at his neck and shoulders and dug my nails into his ass as he lifted my leg and angled deeper.

My mouth dropped open in a silent moan of encouragement as he watched me with lust-blown pupils. Both needy for more, Arlo's body didn't take long to seize up against me. His thrusts becoming sloppy, and our breathing ragged. The grass swayed above us in the breeze, and I was lost to the world for an entire moment. There is nothing but me and him together. Our bodies and our moans tangled with the stars.

"Don't stop," I grabbed his face, kissing him hard as he started to tremble in my grasp. Within moments, the cord that was pulled tight snapped, pleasure cascading down through my toes and into the blanket and ground beneath me. "Fuck Arlo," I moaned as my body ached into his touch and his hands wrapped around my back to pull me closer.

He pulled out, rolling to my side, and kissed a sweaty, sloppy line of kisses across my arm to my neck as his hand tickled across my bare

BAD HONEY

stomach. He nuzzled his nose and lips against my neck as I stared at the stars and wondered what I did to deserve such sweetness from him.

KING

"That was disgusting," Van slapped me over the shoulder, "Coach lit up like a Christmas tree when you threw that last pitch." It was a hard-fought game, but it wasn't over. They needed two more wins to secure their trip to the World Series.

"Get your hand off me, Mitchell," I groaned, looking down at his fingers curled into my muscle. "Unless you want to lose it?"

"Hey," he pulled away, "I'm just congratulating you. That game broke three school records, man."

"He's right," Cael stumbled from the locker room shower, scrubbing at the base of his neck with a towel. "You've never played better."

Cael winced when Todd's arm brushed against him as he sauntered past a few guys celebrating our win.

There was a strip of bruises along his ribs that had been hidden from me until that moment, and a steady thrum of rage built up from my toes into the back of my neck and made my ears warm.

"Who gave you those?" I grabbed the towel from his hand when he ignored me and tugged tightly on it around his neck so he'd look at me. "Answer me."

"I fell down the stairs at Delta the other night, relax." He rolled his eyes at me. I had been so focused on keeping Ella straight that the other cub had strayed. He tried to pull away from me, and I tightened my grip on the towel. "It's the truth, princess. Let go of me."

There was a tone to his voice that he rarely used. It was tight and dry. Void of any typical Cael inflections. The happy, neurotic atmosphere he usually carried so tightly to his chest and behind his blue eyes seemed gray and strangled.

"How?" I asked under my breath as Jensen slipped past us toward his locker.

"I'm clumsy," he shrugged, tugging away hard enough to free himself that time, and grabbed a pair of jeans from his locker, shrugging them on and turning away from me.

"It's bullshit, Cael, and if I find out—"

"What, Arlo?" He turned back to me with a smile that screamed *push me, I dare you.* "If you find out, what? You'll bench me? Weeks out from the finals?"

"I'm not fucking around," I stepped into his space, and the room went silent. pushed onto his feet, but Van stopped him from getting between us. "If you're using, you aren't playing. You're no good to me, strung out and sore."

"No good to you?" Cael laughed, shaking his head. Little water droplets trickled down his face and neck, "take inventory, boys. We're just objects to be used by the great Arlo King on his rise to the top."

I hadn't predicted a famous Cael blow-up would be in the cards for tonight's celebrations, but at least there was a fight in his eyes now that had been missing before.

"A couple wins, a few perfectly pitched games, and you turn into your brother."

Venom dripped from him.

"You're like a cornered alley cat," I spat, "the hair on your back is all ruffled."

"You aren't my keeper, Arlo," he snapped. "You're just another fucking college kid grasping at straws as you watch your career come to an end. Back off."

"You're an idiot."

"At least I'm not blind. I know what life has in store for me. I'm not going to spend what little of it that's left pretending I'm anything more than a fucking tweaked out, drugged-up *idiot*." He hung his arms out at the side and mocked a bow.

"You spend so much time in your own head with your standards for everyone else that you don't see how fucking unbearable you've become," Cael growled. I heard Dean clear his throat from beside us, everyone choosing a side in silence. "Quit pretending you care about me, us, and *her* to satiate your guilt."

The urge to wring him out by his skinny little neck was strong, but instead, I just laughed.

It was the drugs.

It was the stress.

It was the exhaustion.

It wasn't *him*.

"That's fine, Cael," I wet my bottom lip, "act out, throw a tantrum, show them exactly who you are, but remember when you are at rock bottom and begging for help, I'll be the one you call. They like you when you're hopped on cocaine, drunk off your ass, tongue down their throats, but not a single one of them will be there to pick you up out of your puke or bail you out of jail. You're nothing more than a party boy addict to them. *A good time, boy.*"

A feral vibration came from his throat. He was taller than me when standing straight up, but it didn't matter. He was still the same scared and sad little boy I had spent the last four years protecting from the monsters under his bed. He would break and bend, maybe not here in front of the team, but eventually, his guilt would swallow him whole and bring him to his knees.

"Let's go fucking party," his whole face changed in an instant as he leapt up on the bench behind him and threw his hands in the air. The team exploded with him, and the air in the room flushed of all the tense, hardened feelings. "I'll text you the address if you decide you wanna be a part of this team."

He swung his fingers in a large arch to the floor, scooping up his duffle bag and throwing a heavy pair of sunglasses over his eyes. He left the locker room, not bothering to button up the pale blue dress shirt he had worn, his arms slung over his teammates.

"He's fucking losing it," Dean said in barely a whisper.

"He needs to go to rehab," Van responded, and I turned on both.

"Neither of you speak a fucking word of that argument to Coach," I warned, "or Ella."

Van's face tightened, "she's going to figure it out sooner than later, and if she asks, I won't lie to her, King. Enough people do that to—"

"I'm not asking you to lie," I stopped him. I knew how delicate Ella was about her family, especially lately. If she knew how bad Cael was, she would follow him off the cliff to fix what she thought she was the root of. "Just avoid her until we get home," I said.

"Are you alright?" It was the outfielder's next inquiry.

"He's called me worse," I groaned.

"That was—" Van choked up, "bad."

"And what about tonight?" Dean asked, shucking a tight shirt over his massive shoulders. "He's going to implode."

"Cael doesn't implode," I corrected, my eyes still on the door, my thoughts a thousand miles away. "Call me tonight for anything."

"You aren't coming?" Dean's brows pinched together, but Van's face told me everything I needed. He understood why.

"Cody will only go harder to prove a point if Arlo shows up," Van explained, "you should know better."

"This is my fault," Dean said, "I told him we can't see each other anymore. It's too hard."

Guilt flickered across Dean's face, guilt he didn't even deserve to be feeling. This wasn't on them. I let him slip. It was my fault he was acting like this. "I told him he was too complicated, he can never make up his mind." Dean's hands ball into fists at his sides, the last confession the worst of all. "Too hard to love."

The words came out strangled, and he brushed off Van, pushing away from the lockers toward the hall. "Tucker," I barked before he left.

As angry as I was at him for doing this to Cael again, I couldn't blame him. It was a web they had weaved together.

He stopped his hand on the door and looked back at me. "For anything," I reminded him, tapping two fingers on my chest. I watched him inhale as deeply as he could without crying and returned the gesture. "Go, keep an eye on him."

"I want you to go back to the hotel. Bring me Cael's duffle."

"I can just scoop out whatever is in there..." Van shucked into his shirt, buttoning it haphazardly as he slid into a pair of sneakers.

"No, if he finds out you went through it, then he'll shut you out, and unfortunately for you, I need you to be his best friend right now."

Van nodded in agreement, "I know what you're thinking." He said, throwing his bag over his shoulder, "it's not your fault either."

"Valiant effort, Mitchell."

"Arlo," he swallowed tightly and used both his hands to push his shaggy brown hair off his forehead. "Taking care of Ella, taking care of yourself," he pushed his tongue against the inside of his mouth, "it didn't mean you weren't taking care of him. There's a lot happening, and he's crumbling from the pressure, not neglect."

"It doesn't feel like that," I sighed.

"Yeah, well, for once, just listen to me; I know I say a lot of stupid shit, but you all seem to forget what I'm at Harbor for."

Psychology.

I turned to him, and he flashed a tight smile at me, "I don't say shit to hear my own voice, as pretty as it may be, maybe just this once, listen to me? Go back to the hotel, take care of your girl, and let me handle Cael tonight."

"That's the problem, isn't it?" I exhaled. "Someone always has to handle him."

"Let's just get through regionals with our heads on our shoulders."

"Easier said than done, Mitchell," the laughter that bubbled up was sad.

"Baby," I pushed open the hotel door to hear the soft sound of music and all her binders on the pressed sheets. She hadn't noticed me yet as I set my duffle down and leaned against the wall, admiring her scrunched-up study face and messy blonde hair. She was wearing my sweater. The only time she ever took it off anymore was to *"return it for refreshing my smell,"* or at least that's what she told me the first time she tossed it back at me.

BAD HONEY

Something in her notes forced her to pout and swing her bare leg up and under her on the bed, leaning over to inspect better the soft curves of her hips and ass rounded out from beneath the heavy sweater.

I swallowed tightly, trying to behave myself as she tugged her bottom lip between her teeth and groaned in frustration as she scribbled something out and rewrote it. Just when I thought it wasn't possible to love her anymore, I managed to slip deeper into her gravitational pull.

All the stress of Cael's blow-up seemed to simmer beneath the warm and fuzzy feelings that Ella produced. I should have felt guilty about it, how easy it was to shove him to the back of my mind while he was hurting so much, but it was safe here, trapped in a little bubble with her. Nothing could bother us, not Cael or my brother. Not even the nightmares of my father could breach the little bubble that the two of us had formed.

It was a sanctuary.

She was my home.

My heart fluttered in my chest, leaving me short of breath as she peered up at me through a dangling curl and her soft, fluttery lashes with a bright smile on her face.

"Hey Cap," she giggled, "nice game today!" She sat up on her knees and braced herself on her thighs with her head tilted to the side. "A birdy told me there was more than one school record broken!"

I had seen her thirty minutes before in the dugout, but it felt like an eternity as I kicked off my shoes and stripped from the dirty t-shirt. Tossing it to the side without a care, she swiped her books from the bed and prepared for the incoming tackle.

"You're in a fantastic mood!" She giggled between kisses and tickles. I was not in a good mood, not even close, but one deep inhale of her shampoo and one more stolen kiss from her pouty lips seemed to mute those destructive emotions. I needed a way to work out the frustration that knotted my muscles and clouded my judgment.

"It would be better if there wasn't so much fabric between us," I nibbled on her jaw as my fingers played with the sweater's hem. Quickly stealing a kiss from her lips and taking a moment to appreciate the lightning bolt scar where it twisted and met the corner of her eye.

She smiled against my touch around her stomach not needing any convincing she tugged it up and over her head.

Short of breath, I tilted my head to the side, a goofy smirk forming on my lips at the sight of her braless in her gym shorts. "Oh yea," I hauled her up and into my lap, wrapping her legs around me and pulling her down against my throbbing cock, "fantastic mood," I mumbled into her skin, taking a nipple between my lips.

"Arlo," Ella shoved my arm to wake me, "your phone is going off."

I rolled over and felt around on the side table before the screen lit up again, and Van's name flashed across the screen. *Fuck.*

"Hey," I shove the phone to my ear and sit up in bed, trying to blink the sleep from my eyes.

"He's fucking lost it," Van yelled over the music, "you gotta get down here. He's—" There was a disconnection, a chorus of screaming, and a few shuffled swear words before Van came back to the phone. "Just get over here and hurry."

Van hung up the phone before I could ask any more questions. The hotel room was void of light except for the red numbers on the clock that told me it was nearly three a.m. I rolled from the bed, feeling around for my duffle bag, and shucked on a pair of sweats and my sweater. Ella turned on the lamp beside her, stumbling, with her knees tucked around her bare chest and one of her eyes still closed.

"Who was that?" She asked, tucking her messy hair behind her ears. I walked toward her, wrapping my hands around her perfect face, and kissed her sleepy lips.

"Van," I shook my head and looked around for my hat.

"What's going on?" She felt around in the bed until she found her shorts and padded from bed, reaching for her shirt and throwing it over her shoulders.

"Nothing, go back to bed," I swallowed tightly.

BAD HONEY

"Arlo," she snapped as I tipped to the side trying to get my sneaker on while still half asleep.

"Cael's out of control. I need to go get him."

"I'm coming," she grabbed her sweater, throwing it around her shoulders without pause. "There's no point in arguing," she warned when I opened my mouth to argue, "if you don't bring me, I'll go wake up."

"Fine," I growled, "shoes," I tossed her sneakers at her and flung the hotel door open for her. She followed behind me as fast as her legs would carry her, only stopping when I opened the car door and waited for her to slide inside.

Van didn't answer a single text I'd sent on the way down the elevator and by the looks of it. He wasn't answering Ella's either. She chucked her phone in the back seat with a huff and tugged her hair into a ponytail as she worked to slow her breathing.

"What the hell is going on?" She snapped at me eventually, her fingers nervously rolling around the ring on her neck.

I knew there was no getting around it.

"Cael had a meltdown after the game, but he seemed fine." *Yeah, that's it, idiot, lie to her.* I rolled my hands over the steering wheel and turned onto the sorority row. "Van was looking after him but—"

"He's still slipping," Ella drew a shaky breath.

"This isn't your fault," words that had been passed around far too much lately. But they were true. It wasn't her fault, and it wasn't her responsibility. "I knew he was on edge, and I let him go to the party, so I'm going to bring Cael home."

"Alright," she nodded, her jaw clenched so tightly I could see the muscles in her neck working as we pulled up to the massive house party. Drunk students and players poured from the house, circling what looked like an enormous fight.

"Fuck," I cut the engine, hopping from the car as fast as I could, and ran toward the crowd.

"Stay!" I threw one look at Ella, who was hot on my tail, stopping her in her tracks. "Try to get Dean on the phone or find him. He's here somewhere!" I yelled as I moved toward the circle.

"Get the fuck out of my way!" I barked, grabbing kids by the collar and shoving them out of my way to get to the front, only to find Cael perched atop a Pirate player, his hand pulling back to throw another sloppy punch.

Before he could, the player kneed him between the legs and threw him off into the grass with a loud yelp of pain from Cael. He scrambled to his feet, angled on all fours, and rammed the guy through the middle, throwing him backward into the hard fenced-in porch of the house. The boarding on the side rattled from the impact as Cael pounded his hand relentlessly into the kid over and over again. Fists flew, and not one person decided it had been enough until I stepped forward, fighting through the guys and trying to keep the fight going.

"Hey, Buddy!" One yelled. I ducked before his swing could connect with my face and struck him in the stomach with my right fist.

Van appeared from my left, his face bruised and bleeding, "these guys are fucking animals," he screamed, dodging a set of arms and pulling the attacking player down to the dirt. He laid a boot into his stomach and turned with me in time toward where Cael had been pinned down.

At the same time, we hauled the player beating the shit out of Cael up by his shirt and threw him across the lawn into a group of onlookers without giving a shit who he hit. Van swore, seeing Cael's fucked up face.

The idiot was laughing, blood dripping from his mouth, and his left eye bruised and swollen shut.

"Oh god," I heard her before I saw her, Ella sliding through the gaps of the crowd with her big brown eyes filled with tears and worry.

"Get off me!" She yelped.

Before I could tell her to go back to the car, she was caught by the ponytail and yanked backward by one of the other players.

Rage, as I had never felt before, filled every muscle in my body as I pushed straight and moved toward the guy with his hand wrapped tightly around her hair and arm around her waist. He pulled her back through the crowd, screaming at people to get out of his way as he tripped over and sent both of them flying into the dirt.

BAD HONEY

Ella kicked out hard, her sneaker connecting with his stomach as she shoved off him. He tried to grab her ankle, and in defense, she laid the other foot into his face with a sickening crunch.

I picked her up from the ground, grabbing her face, but she tried to frantically push me away, "Hey!" I said loudly enough for her to hear the tone in my voice and realize, "It's me, Blondie. Stop," I ordered and felt her body relax into my touch. "Go to the car, wait for Van."

She stared past me at the ground where the guy was groaning and pushing himself up from the dirt, "go, now." I said again, kissing her forehead and spinning her in the right direction.

"Do you know who that was?" I asked the second she was out of earshot. I towered over him, recognizing him as the third baseman from the game earlier today.

He shook his head, "do you know who I am?" I asked, and he nodded. "Good," I stared at him, my arm shot out, grabbing him by the throat before he could fight back. He clawed at my hands as I dragged him backward toward the stairs of the house and pinned him against them.

"Give me your hand," I snapped as he fought for air.

He shook his head no, still trying to escape my grip.

"Give me your hand," I said again, slower this time, as I tapped my foot on the staircase where I wanted him to put it. This time, I tightened my nails into his throat, restricting his airflow further. A few people had crowded around us, but it didn't matter. He had touched Ella. He had hurt her, "your actions have consequences," I said as he placed the trembling hand out from his body. "Don't ever touch my girl."

The sound of his fingers breaking tangled with his screams of pain as I let off his windpipe.

"Arlo!" Van called out through the broken, hushed crowd, "Let's go!" He had Cael hoisted beneath him, struggling to hold his weight as he hobbled across the lawn.

I took stock of the cell phones that recorded the fight, swearing under my breath. *There goes our privacy.* I cocked my head to the side as I looped around the other side of Cael. He was in rough shape, but he was breathing and conscious as we got back out to the road.

Van helped me lean him against the rental he had driven to the party before running off to find the others.

"What the fuck is wrong with you?" I clenched my fists at my side, my breathing uneven and my heart racing as my body came down from the adrenaline.

"You wanna hit me too?" He laughed, blood bubbled up, and he wiped it away with his arm clumsily.

"No," I flexed my hands and released the tension. "You've been hit enough tonight."

His eyes flickered up to me, so bright blue against the bruises that formed around them. The left was barely able to open, and the cut on his eyebrow already looked swollen shut with dried blood. He had gotten in more than just that last fight.

"Why?" I asked.

"It was better than hitting you, hitting my dad—" he sniffled, spitting out a hunk of blood to the tarmac. "Less guilt in the morning behind that."

"More pain," I shook my head in disapproval.

"I like the pain. It makes me feel alive." He sighed. "I shouldn't have said that to you today, you know," he poked me in the chest, clearly still a little high. All his movements felt choppy and lagged in their execution. "I'm not a good person, Arlo."

I opened my mouth to argue, and he stopped me.

"You don't get an opinion," he huffed.

"Everything I touch turns rotten." His face scrunched up in agony.

I inhaled sharply, feeling that pain deep in my chest.

"It all started with Momma. She was fine before I showed up, and then slowly, over time, I stole all her light, and now I'm doing it to you!" He backed up, standing in the middle of the road on uneasy feet. He keeled over, hands on his thighs, and cried. His whole body was wracked with sobs so violently that I stepped forward, concerned he wasn't breathing anymore.

"Fuck off," he shot up and pointed at me. "You know what she said to me the day she died? Her frail little hand was so tiny and cold in mine, then she looked at me for the first time in weeks. Like really looked at me, Ar," he motioned to his eyes and then to mine.

BAD HONEY

"And she said, *you take care of him*."

"Cael, you can't blame yourself for the state your dad is in," I tried, and he hushed me again.

"Not him," he waved me off, laughing and repeating it a few times as he rubbed his face painfully and looked to the stars above us. When he turned back to me, tears were pooling in his eyes, violently blue and full of agony. "She meant you."

That was stupid.

"You're high. You aren't thinking straight."

"She said that you came into our lives needing us just as much as we needed you!"

"Cael." I reached out to him. We hadn't fought over this particular strain of his sadness in a long time.

"I let her down, Arlo," he whispered, his voice breaking down, and the sound broke my heart. "You've been taking care of me, and I should have been taking care of you, but instead, I just made it rotten like I always do."

"You didn't let her down," I said, trying to hold it together.

"I turned it rotten, and if I don't stop, I'm going to turn her rotten too," he pointed over my shoulder to where Ella stood with tears in her eyes. I hadn't even heard her come up behind us. "I'm sorry, Peachy," his voice cracked again. "I gotta get out of here," he walked in a circle, patting down his shirt until he found his keys.

"Hell no," I said, but Cael angled away from me with the keys in his hand. "You aren't driving. You're not thinking straight."

"I can do whatever I want," he shrugged his shoulders at me. "I'm leaving, so you stay here or get in the car. I don't care. But I'm going with or without you."

I looked at Ella, her chest heaving.

"Arlo, don't." She mouthed at me.

I looked back at Cael, rolling the keys around his bloody knuckles.

"I have to," I said back to her.

"Do not get in that car," she stepped forward, cheeks flushed and the collar of her sweater soaked from crying.

"I don't have a choice," I walked toward her, but her head tilted to the side, and her eyes narrowed in my direction.

"You have a choice, and you're making the wrong one."
"I trust him," I said, "and he needs me."
"Your trust is fickle," she cried.

I could see the pain on her face. I *need you*, she wanted to say it, but her eyes flickered to Cael and then back to me silently, painfully.

"I know how this story ends, Arlo," she said, inhaling as deeply as she could before she tore down the collar of her sweater to expose the scar against her chest and tapped it twice with her two fingers. "I can't lose you," she whispered, "either of you."

I heard the car door slam behind me, and I backed away, jogging to the other side, trying to ignore the horrible nagging that clawed at my chest as I glimpsed once more at her. Cael peeled out of the parking lot, narrowly missing the car in front of us. I turned back to see her standing in the middle of the street.

There was no stopping what was to come.

MIELE

"What the hell?" Van came up behind me with Dean and Jensen in tow, short of breath and barely standing on two feet.

Arlo wasn't Ethan. I repeated the words over and over in my head.

"How fucked up was Cael?" I turned on Van, anger seething through, worry tangling in my tense muscles as I checked to make sure I still had the keys to the Mustang. "Answer me!"

I screamed at the three of them, all completely silent.

Arlo wasn't Ethan.

Van and Dean wouldn't break as easily, logically. I knew that, especially if Arlo had ordered them otherwise. He would have because that's just who he was, protecting us from each other by micromanaging our knowledge.

Arlo would end up just like Ethan if I didn't find them.

The moment I turned on Jensen, he snapped like a twig, "he took two pills before the party even started and has been in the bathroom all night with Todd and Dougie."

"Watch the road, Estella."

The thoughts of my dad seemed to creep in violently, his warning. Everything tangled together.

"El, help me!"

The voice of Ethan crept into the back of my mind while Van ran his mouth about something else in the foreground of my nightmare.

"atch the road, Estella!"

The last thing he had ever said to me.

"Watch the road, Estella."

You earned this pain.

"What?" Van's head cocked to the side.

I hadn't realized I said it out loud. Van's worried brown eyes stared at me for a long moment as he attempted to figure out what was happening in my head, but I had already moved past it.

"Round up the team. Get them back to the hotel."

Jensen groaned but was silenced by Van with a hard cuff to the back of the head. "What are you going to do?" He asked.

"Find Cael and Arlo."

His eyes flickered from me to the keys dangling in my hand, "I'm coming with you."

I shook my head, "I need you to get the rest of the guys back to the hotel."

"Ella," he sighed.

"You're outnumbered at a house party, get the team... and," I ran my finger through my hair, massaging my sore scalp, "fuck, call Silas."

"Ella!" Van called out to me as I took off toward the Mustang, "Stop!"

He yelled again. His legs were longer than mine, and he could slide in front of me.

"Wait," he put both hands on my shoulders, "take a breath, tell me what happened."

So I did. I told Van how Arlo King had looked me in the eye and still managed to rip my heart out. "I wanna kill them both, but I can't if Cael kills them first," I whispered, trying to hold onto what little strength I had left.

Van wet his bottom lip, "okay."

"You're processing the information too slowly for my emotions, Van. I can't be here now. Get out of my way and do as you're told."

Van huffed a frustrated breath, stepped to the side, and let me open the driver's side door. "Be careful, please, El," he ran his tongue along his teeth. There was a different sense of panic to his following words, "Keep your eyes on the road, okay?"

Understandable as it was, I didn't have time to ease that worry, so I nodded and climbed inside without another word.

I swallowed his statement like it was a ball of nails.

BAD HONEY

I was bleeding internally and trying to keep it together.

As the car door shut, all the emotions I was hanging onto seemed to cascade from me without anything to hold them back. The tears seemed to pour out of me in violent screams to the rhythm of my hands beating against the steering wheel.

It took nearly ten minutes, but eventually, I calmed down enough to grab my phone from the back seat and unlocked it as the rest of the tears dripped down my cheeks to the screen.

"Fuck, okay," my hands were shaking so hard the phone rocked back and forth between my fingers as I opened the find my phone app. Cael and I had linked our accounts in case of emergencies, and all I could do was hope that he was too high and flustered to remember that conversation.

"Ha!" I hollered when his ping started flashing on my screen. I dumped my phone into the passenger seat with the screen upright to follow the streets.

My heart was hammering in my chest as I wrapped my trembling hand around the stick and started the engine. It'd been a completely different exercise of my emotions and willpower when Arlo sat in the car with me. I hadn't driven alone in a very long time, and the fear gripped me tightly, threatening to drag me back down into that dark hole of grief. It was an animal clawing and nipping at me. It wanted to tear me apart.

But there wasn't time for that. Arlo had ripped my heart out and had taken it with him on a joy ride with a high Cael Cody as the driver. I inhaled deeply and threw the car into first. It was bumpy initially, but I followed the steps using the echo of Arlo's voice as a guideline.

I looked down to check for any upcoming turns, and the car swerved gently with the motion.

Watch the road, Estella.

Arlo staggered across my mind, my chest tightening at the thought of losing him the way I lost Ethan. I hadn't paused to think about how much I needed him, just how much I might have loved him until he walked away from me like that. Arlo wasn't just some guy. He was mine, and every ounce of trust between us seemed to snap when he got in that car. I was so angry with them, so scared for him... that I didn't know which was which anymore and decided to let the anger win out.

It was easier to be angry with him than terrified that he may not survive this.

He had let his guilt decide for him, even after telling me time and time again that I shouldn't let my guilt rule the choices I made. It was tricky and turned everything upside down. And look where our guilt had led us.

Each time I shifted into a new gear, I took a deep breath, choking on the air I desperately needed as my mind swam in opposite directions. Ethan, Arlo, my parents, Cael. One by one, like a chant, they screamed at me.

Watch the road!
Watch the road!
Watch the road!

I screamed into the void, cracking a line through the suffocating thick fog that wrapped around my mind without remorse. I checked my phone to ensure I was still on the right track to find that his ping had stopped. I turned the corner as fast as the car moved toward the location but saw empty roads and trees. Panic set in, seeing the dark treads that seemingly ripped into the pavement ahead of me, the street lights above creating an eerie flashing light across the road. I pulled the Mustang to the side of the road, turned the engine off, and climbed out.

The smell of gas and burnt rubber hit my nose like a wave as I stepped out onto the empty road. I could hear the sound of a sputtering engine, and just like that, I was shoved backward in time to a nightmare I couldn't seem to forget.

Ethan stared at me, trying to stay something, but I could never make it out. The sound of my own rambling and screaming drowned him out. The copper tang of blood was the next foul smell to hit my nose, and my heart rose to a rate I had never thought possible.

"Arlo!" I started screaming, the name coming out of my mouth over and over again as I began to search the darkness for them. "Arlo? Cael!"

BAD HONEY

"Ella?" He hollered back, and the sob that left me was clear and loud. I moved along the road until the smoke filled my nose, and the sight of the smashed car became clear.

I could hear the shuffling from the ditch below, and as my eyes adjusted to the darkness, I could see that the car Cael was driving was smashed up against a massive trunk, metal crumbled like a sardine can around the bark. Arlo's form stumbled up from the ditch, his feet digging into the mangled grassy hill as he worked to remove the car door.

It flew free with a loud groan, and Arlo slammed hard against the ground. The whimper that left my lips was involuntary, and I knew he heard it because he looked over his shoulder at me with sore, dark eyes. A thick line of blood seeped down his face, curling under the sharp angle of his tense jaw. The cut looked deep, and when he scowled at me, the skin split more, and blood seeped into his sight.

"I'm okay," he said, looking at my face and seeing the worry. His shoulders completely caved in over Cael as he hauled him out of the car with two arms under him.

"Help me," he begged, digging his feet into the soil and climbing from the ditch. "He's knocked out."

We managed to get him up and lay him in the grass, "Cael?" I ran my hands around his throat and the back of his head, checking for any bleeding before checking the rest of his body for injuries.

I turned on Arlo, giving him a once over before pushing my hands flat against his chest and shoving him back hard, "Fuck you!" I screamed every ounce of anger from my body.

"Hey!" He barked in pain, scrambling to his feet, his face scrunched up in agony.

"Get him in the Mustang," I said, ignoring the glaring hole that was ripped in the space between us. Trust shattered, a relationship torn open like an unstitched wound.

"El," he reached out his fingertips, brushing my bicep.

"He needs to go to the hospital, Arlo," I spat. "And so do you."

"Did you?" His brows kissed in confusion, and he looked at his car over my shoulder. A smile formed on his lips, pride leaking through his bruised, handsome features. "That's my girl."

"No!" I pressed my lips into a thin line and pushed up from the ground. The rocks dug into the palms of my hands. "Don't," the stinging sensation reminded me how angry I was at him. One simple line wasn't enough to wipe my memory of the fact that he completely disregarded my pleas.

"Help me," I shook my head at him.

"What the hell was I supposed to do, Blondie?" He got to his feet, rubbing his hands on his pants and hauling Cael up into his arms with an exhausted grunt.

"You could have listened."

I opened the passenger door, keeping my eyes trained ahead of me and off Arlo. I could feel how badly he wanted me to look at him, and I couldn't bear it. I was so angry. The only thing my heart wanted to do was forgive him, but my mind was a steel trap of nightmares reminding me that I was just traveling in the same vicious circle. Eventually, it would end the same for Arlo as it did for Ethan.

It would end with Cael carrying around the guilt of killing his best friend and my heart broken for the second time in less than a year.

It had barely just been put back together.

"You could have fought harder," I slammed the door and shoved the keys into his hand. "I told you what would happen."

"If I hadn't gone with him, he would be out here alone," Arlo argued, his cheeks soaked and his lip busted.

"Take him to the hospital, get your face looked at." I closed my eyes and pushed past him.

"Where are you going?" He scrambled to grab my arm, but I slipped free of his grasp, finally turning to look at him.

"I can't—"

I swallowed the urge to cry as his face softened with sadness and realization.

"I can't get in that car with you, Arlo," I said, trying to convince myself that this was the right decision.

His brows pushed together, and his throat bobbed harshly as his tongue flickered out over his bottom lip, trying to formulate a response. I could see him fighting with his emotions. He wasn't sure if he should yell or try convincing me otherwise.

BAD HONEY

"You need to go," I chewed on my lip, "he needs a doctor."

I leaned through the fastback window, tucking the ring out of my sweater and hanging it over the rearview mirror.

A heartbreaking whimper filled the silence.

"Hurry up," I said to him, straightening out and stepping off the side of the road. "He needs you."

That was all it took. Arlo nodded, his jaw so tight it looked painful as he shoved aside his overwhelming feelings and moved around to the car's driver's side. The engine roared to life, and without another look, he took off down the road, leaving me standing there with nothing but the chill biting at my cheeks to remind me that I was alive.

MIELE

"You okay?" Van stood in my doorway back at the Nest. Hovering because he wasn't sure what else to do.

It'd been three days.

The Hornets lost two games but managed to sneak out the third win without Arlo and Cael. Both were injured, and Arlo was suspended for a week over the video that surfaced of him breaking the player's hand. Silas said the lawyers would have him off and free of charges within the week, and he hadn't lied. Before I stepped foot back in the Nest, the charges had been dropped.

"Will you call—" I started and stopped.

"She's already on the way over."

I needed someone who understood the delicate emotions I was going through and would handle me with the care that I so desperately needed but couldn't bear to ask for. The airplane ride home was tense. Gossip swirled around what'd happened, and no one there seemed to wanna fess up to the truth. Arlo must have driven himself and Cael back to Rhode Island because neither was on the plane as it took off from New York.

Van had glued himself to my side, from the airport to the Nest, his hand tucked into mine, his nose in his phone, keeping Zoey updated. He was just as worried as I was for Cael and Arlo. I wasn't sure if it was sadness or rage. Sometimes, it felt like both and neither. I just wanted to scream and cry and scream some more, but none of that felt like it would help, even if I did. So, instead, I just turned it off. Going numb felt like the only answer.

"Van," I threw my bag onto the floor, "am I an idiot?"

BAD HONEY

"You'll have to wait until Zo gets here to get honesty," he joked softly, "I don't think I have it in me to be mean after everything this weekend."

I looked over my shoulder at him. "You and Zo are my oldest friends. If you can't be honest with me, who can?"

"That's why we play good cop, bad cop." He shrugged in his oversized hoodie.

"Can you be a bad cop for a second?"

"Don't get the courage," he rubbed a hand over his chest.

I sighed, the motion making me think of Arlo, and I nearly cried again.

"I'm better at being a good cop anyways." He opened his arms and allowed me to curl into his chest for a tight, lingering hug that eased all the knots from my sore muscles. "You aren't a dumbass, El," he said, tightening his grip. "You were protecting yourself. That counts for something."

"Even if it hurt Arlo?"

"Arlo's a big boy," he inhaled deeply.

I scoffed.

"I'm proud of you." He whispered against my hair.

I pulled away, turning out of sight to wipe the tears out of my eyes while I stared out the back window to find Cael tucked into the hammock with a hat pulled down over his eyes and his arm in a sling.

"I'm going to go get us some food," he said, "are you going to be alright? Zo should be here soon."

I turned to look at all six four of him cowering in my doorframe haphazardly and nodded, "I'll be fine."

Eventually.

He slapped his massive hand against the frame by his thigh and spun out of sight, leaving me alone for the first time in a week. I turned my attention back to the yard, watching Cael sleeping, and tried to work through the crowded, tender emotions surrounding my thoughts. I'd done the one stupid thing that an addict should avoid. Latch on to someone who wasn't sober. I had attached myself to Cael because he saw me for who I was, but he was still so sick, and sick people can't help sick people. The infection can only fester.

I'm rotten. He had said it out loud, but it was something that I had called myself so many times over the last five years of my life. Every time my mom picked me up off the floor, every time Ethan caught me stealing money or popping pills that belonged to him.

The word rotten was fitting for someone so selfish for so little gain.

All to feel numb momentarily. It was a coward's way out of handling everything that human existence was supposed to provide. Words had never been mine, but I had heard over and over. *You're a coward.* But Cael Cody was anything but rotten. He was a light, a force of wind, a hurricane of emotion that he felt so vividly without remorse, all to conceal the sadness he felt from losing his mother. Cael was the least rotten person I had ever met. Like he knew my eyes were on him, the brim of his hat tipped up, and his eyes peered toward my window.

The heat from his gaze licked at the guilt in my chest. Stinging and clawing at me like the guilt was alive until I backed away from the window, kicking off my shoes, pulling off my sweater, and chucking everything into a ball. I closed the door and found myself yet again curled up in my bed under the cover of my blankets.

It was safer there.

The Nest was busy, people coming and going. The door seemed to be revolving. Eventually, Zoey's tiny knock sounded, and before I could even welcome her in, she was shoeless and curled up across from me beneath the comforter.

"What happened?" She asked in a soft tone.

Van would have told her they told each other everything.

She took my shaky hands between hers and tucked them against her chest as I told her everything that had happened that night, not leaving a single detail out.

"You gave him the ring back?" She asked. "Again?"

"Third time's the charm, I guess," I laughed as the tears poured from me. It was all I could do.

"I talked to Silas on the way in," she said, tucking a piece of her dark hair behind her ear. "Cael dislocated his shoulder, broke three fingers, and ruptured some blood vessels in his eye, but he'll be okay."

"There's no way he plays in the finals like that," I noted. "Did you see—"

"Arlo's pouting in the garage. Silas said he hadn't left since they got back. He's pretty banged up. Has he come to see you at all?"

I shook my head no. I was glad, too. I wasn't sure I was ready to talk to him. My stomach turned over, even thinking about the shape he was in. The last time I'd seen him, there was so much blood.

The words from the cabin seemed to roll through my thoughts like a train running in a circle. *Promise me you won't ever stop because I don't think I'll survive the fallout.*

Ironically enough, he seemed just fine. It was me reeling from it.

Mulling over a decision made in anger to protect myself from the inevitable.

"Cael is going to rehab, El," Zoey said like she hadn't wanted to be the one to tell me. "He'll be gone for a couple of weeks, but it was his decision."

"Good," I nodded.

"Are you going to be okay?" She asked next.

"Eventually, I think," I chewed on my lip. "I never thought I would have a family again, Zoe, and for a second, I thought maybe the universe was through with my punishment. That I was finally free of the guilt and the shame that I brought down on myself, but when—"

I stopped to catch my breath. "When Arlo got in that car with Cael, it was like someone had pressed rewind on the tape. My heart is broken," I said, the tears flowing again, "but I can't watch Arlo sacrifice himself to save Cael. It'll kill me."

Every time I closed my eyes, I saw the look on Arlo's face when I told him I wasn't going with him. I couldn't get in the car with him. Fear had crippled me so many times before, but it hadn't been fear that night that prevented me from getting in the car with him. It had been a higher understanding of what getting in the car meant to him and what it would mean for me.

It wasn't that I was afraid of being second to Cael. It had never been a competition. It was that no matter how hard Arlo tried to save us both, one of us would always end up slipping. I was protecting him from stretching himself too thin to keep us both alive. He didn't owe us that, at least not me.

I would give him up a thousand times to save Cael, to save the friendship they had.

Hearing what Cael had said about his mother embedded a new, specific kind of guilt into my heart. They only had each other, and I had walked in between them with my own problems that Arlo shouldn't have had to deal with.

"I was a burden he never asked for," I said out loud. "So I removed myself from the equation so he could care for what mattered."

"Babe," Zoey pouted, placing her hands around my face. "You aren't a burden," she pulled our foreheads together with a soft look. "But you are kind of a dumbass."

"I knew it!" I whined and tucked my head into her chest. "Your boyfriend is a six-foot-four coward."

"You're going to be okay," she promised, chuckling lightly as the situation eased. "I'll make sure of it."

"I'm going to move out of the Nest," I said tightly. I couldn't be here any longer, not with Arlo and Cael lurking around every corner. It didn't matter that neither of them had tried to talk to me since returning. It was only a matter of time before they did.

"Are you sure?" Zoey asked me with a concerned look on her face.

"I can't be around them. It's too volatile, and if I can't shuck free of the feelings, I'll find other ways to quiet the guilt and sadness, Zoe."

"I missed my roommate," she forced a smile and pulled me in close for a hug.

Summer semester was coming to a close, and Professor Tucker seemed to enjoy piling on the work before finals. Dean groaned beside me as his father's assistant emailed another project.

BAD HONEY

"If this computer beeps like that one more time, I might smash it," he said, looking over at me with an annoyed look. His blue eyes had started to get the light back to them, but there was still sadness lingering there that I knew personally. He had lost someone, too.

"How are you?" I asked as I scribbled down more notes from yesterday's class. My wrist was throbbing from all the work I had been putting in. Between class and the medical job, paperwork seemed to pile.

"Fine," he answered too quickly.

"One-word answers aren't going to cut it," I responded, setting down my pen. "I'm sad, too."

"You have a reason to be," he said, not looking up from his laptop.

"Not sure I do."

"For a long time, I thought the presence of guilt meant the absence of sadness, or better yet, the reason to be sad. But it's not. You can feel both. You're allowed." I said to him.

He shrugged, "I guess."

"Cael doesn't know what he wants right now, and you just have to let him figure that out. It's solely up to you whether or not that means you work your way back to one another." I leaned forward on the table and pushed the screen to his laptop so he would look at me. "Don't blame yourself for Cael's mistakes. You'll run yourself into the ground. He might be a little haphazard sometimes, but he's still an adult. You can't expect yourself to be responsible for him."

"Arlo does," he said when he finally looked at me.

"Arlo's standards of how you should or shouldn't take care of someone are wildly skewed. You should know that." I missed him so much that every bone in my body ached just for one look from those dark brown eyes.

It was fine until I was alone in my bed at night. That's when the memories crept in. They ate at my heart and settled against my chest, leaving me unable to sleep without seeing Arlo. I could feel his hands on my skin, which burned in need of more. The only remedy was staying awake. I had read more than I ever had in the past weeks just to do so.

"True," he nodded, "have you spoken to him?"

"No." It was my turn to divert my gaze in a feeble attempt to hide my sadness from Dean. At that point, I wasn't even sure it was something I wanted. I had run through the conversation a thousand times, and Arlo's reaction to me walking away was always the same.

"Do you have the notes from Friday?" He asked, changing the subject.

I rifled through my bag for them, coming up with the notes and the sinking feeling of heartbreak as my hand made contact with Arlo's stupid sweater buried in the bottom of the bag. I closed my eyes, handed the notes to Dean, and let the feeling pass before returning to work on my assignment.

KING

"That was fucking stupid," Nick shoved me up against the wall of the dugout, my hand throbbing at my side after punching Harrison, the first basemen of the Lorettes, in the face. "We have three games left. We have to win! And we can't do that with your selfish ass on the bench!"

"Let go of me, Nick," I pushed him back.

I was falling apart without Cael at my back and Ella by my side.

"Quit acting like a prick and play the game!" He slammed me against the wall hard enough to make Coach turn from his position on the stairs, fire raging behind his green eyes.

"Nicholas," he snapped. "There are eyes everywhere, and you are acting like a liability right now." His eyes narrowed, and his tone dropped an octave. "You wanna keep acting like spoiled brats? Get out of my dugout, but I won't have you assaulting players with cameras on you."

The media storm coming back from New York had been a new monster. Everyone knew about Ella and me, the fight at the Pirates' frat house, and Cael. Sex, drugs, fights, all with my name at the center of the rumors. The worst was how they treated Ella. After her public stint with Nick, all the photos from the fundraisers circulated with questions about how she got the job on the Hornet's medical team. I couldn't scrub some of the horrible remarks made about her from my mind, and it made me furious.

I fought back against Nick, grabbing him by the collar in return.

"He needs the living shit kicked out of him!" Nick spoke out of turn and instantly realized his mistake, but he wouldn't go down without a fight. His fingers tightened around my jersey, and he raised his hand to hit me, but Coach caught it and pushed him off of me.

"Get off my fucking field!" Coach barked. "Your family can be fucked up on your own time. Here and now, you play by my rules. If you can't, I'll find a new pitching coach."

"Coach!" Nick tried to argue. His face was red and blotchy from screaming.

Coach just stared at him, raising his eyebrows and waiting for Nick to figure out how serious he was about it. "Go, now."

When the door finally closed, and before any players could catch their breath, Coach turned to me, "If you keep up the way you're going, you will destroy everything you've worked so hard for."

"Learn how to control your staff, *Coach*." I rolled my shoulders back.

"Go to the Nest and figure out your shit Arlo before you find yourself without a girlfriend or a team." He cocked his head to the side, knowing the shot would land and I probably deserved it.

I threw my glove to the bench with a thump, knowing full well that all the news would be about the blowup within a few hours, but it didn't matter anymore. I ignored them all on the way out of the tunnel. I climbed into the Mustang only to be face to face with my mother's stupid ring, hanging from the mirror, mocking my inability to be a decent human being the way she raised me.

I slammed my sore hands against the wheel before peeling out of the parking lot back up to the Nest, where I could be alone with my thoughts, but I just found myself staring at her empty room, bed, and hammock. Every spot she perched with her nose in a book felt barren, so I retreated to the garage, but even that was tainted by her absence.

I stared at the stupid blue bike like she would come home if I stared at it long enough. Vanilla filled my nose, and if I closed my eyes and rubbed my fingers together, I could feel her hair between them or her cheek pressed to my stomach as she drifted to sleep. I felt like a fool with my heart barely beating in my chest, tears pricking at my eyes, and my mouth dry. Barely a year had gone by. I had fallen too hard. Broken heart and broken mind, I still knew that if she called right now, I would run to her without hesitation.

BAD HONEY

She was my home. Now, I was left out in the cold.

"What are you doing out here?"

I opened my eyes, not bothering to turn to look who was there. I knew Silas hovered in the doorway, "dinner was ready an hour ago. Dean and Jensen made burgers."

I hadn't even noticed the sun retreating behind the sky.

"I'm not hungry."

I hadn't been hungry in two weeks.

Van helped her move out the week before. She had picked the day Cael went to rehab to sneak away, but I had been the one to take him. I hadn't gone to practice that day, and I pulled up as Van was piling her boxes into the back of his truck.

I almost snapped after deciding to give Ella some space and wait for her to tell me she needed me. Seeing her packing all her belongings and leaving me, leaving the Nest. It had broken a wall inside me that I didn't even know existed. A thin wall that prevented me from becoming my father, and it no longer existed. I didn't care. Every conscious thought was consumed by the image of her.

"*Ella doesn't want to talk to you, man,*" Van put his hand out, *blocking my entrance to the front of the Nest.*

"*Mitchell get the fuck out of my way,*" I snarled, *chest puffed up to make up for the height he had on me.*

"*I can't, King,*" he shook his head, "*it's her decision. Honor that.*"

"You don't get to tell me what to honor. Let me see Ella. At least ask her why she's sneaking out without saying goodbye. This is going to kill Cael."

"Cael or you?" He asked.

"Let me see her." *I shoved him backward, and the fists started to fly. His hand connected with my bottom lip and knocked me back down through the gravel, but I wasn't going to go down that easy. Throwing my own to his gut and then across his jaw, he stumbled backward but took the chance to lower his center of gravity. Charging me before I could steady myself, he wrapped me around the middle and chucked me in the dirt. Scrambling to get the upper hand, he ended up grappling with me until the guys pulled up from afternoon practice and tore us apart from one another.*

I chewed at the scab on my bottom lip from that day.

"You can't just stare at that bike all day."

"Silas, can you shut the fuck up?" I turned to look at him.

He had wandered further inside, hat pulled down over his messy, sweaty hair, the fabric of his tank top molded to his chest and leaving his arms exposed. He had come in from a workout to find me absent from dinner and was nosey about why.

"Princess is snappy today," Silas rolled his eyes and leaned against one of the metal shelves surrounding the garage walls. "You gotta figure your shit out. The last round of finals starts tomorrow, and the team needs you."

"Has she spoken to you?" I cocked my head to the side. Angry as ever without a proper outlet. Everyone was a target.

"This isn't about Ella," he shut me down.

"So she *has*," the sound ripped from me was savage. "She won't fucking talk to me, she won't look at me, she wasn't at the game today. Did you fire her?"

"No," Silas admitted. "She's doing therapy work. She requested to sit back from games for a while. I respected that."

There was venom at the end of his sentence. His words followed up with a silent, 'You need to respect that.' He licked his bottom lip and shook his head at me. "What did you expect after Tuesday's game, Arlo?"

"That game was a wash," I snapped.

"You went out on the mound and pitched three innings of meatballs. You barely won that game because you were too busy staring at her. If Nick hadn't subbed you out and sent you home—"

"I can't fucking think about baseball when she's right there! I can't think about anything but her! I can't eat, I can't sleep. She became everything. There's no setting her to the side. There's no focus because nothing else matters." I swiped the top of the tool bench and sent tools flying everywhere. "She didn't even give me a chance, Silas! I don't know what I did wrong, so I can't fix it."

"She doesn't want you to fix it!" He yelled back, pushing off the shelf to walk toward me. "Cael comes home tomorrow," he lowered his voice. "What matters is getting his head back into the game. You need him at your back, and he needs the team. So listen to me and fucking listen well, Arlo," Silas grabbed my collar and tugged at me. The only person in the world capable of manhandling me without repercussions.

"You're going to focus on Cael, you're going to pull your fucking head out of your ass, and you're going to do what you promised that team you were going to do at the beginning of the season. Before your brother, before Ella, before Cael."

Go out and prove something to yourself. We are going to the World Series Finals this year, and we won't stop fighting until we get there.

Two steps at a time.

That was a lot harder to do when I was walking alone.

"You told them that you were going to fight, so start fucking fighting. You're the heart of the Hornets. They need you."

"They need to grow the fuck up and stop relying on me to do everything for them." I rolled my eyes.

"That's your monster, Arlo!" Silas barked, "You created that problem. You don't get to leave them out in the cold just because you can't fucking get your shit together."

"Maybe that's exactly where we all need to be! We aren't going to win this championship with them acting like children," I argued.

"You're a fucking child!" Silas shoved me from behind. "Grow up, Arlo, you had your heart broken *so-fucking-what,*" he spat. "You're acting like your father. One little inconvenience in his life, and he's drinking himself stupid, sitting in a moldy chair complaining about old games on a TV from 1992."

"Get out, Silas," I growled.

"Or what?" He stepped into my space. "You gonna hit me too? Is that what you do now? You punch your way through your friends to feel better? You act more and more like Arthur every day."

I didn't have to tell him to leave at that time. He looked me over, disgusted with what he saw, and left. My foot found the bike, kicking it hard as I sunk to the ground against the fastback, reeling in the anger that flooded my chest like a rising tide.

KING

The grass was starting to overgrow on the front lawn again, so when I pulled up to my dad's, instead of going inside, I walked around to the back, pulling out the lawn mower and stripping from my sweater until I was in nothing but my sweatpants. It took me nearly two hours to get it down, but at least it looked like someone was living in the house. I walked through the back door, threw my belongings on the table, and got water from the tap.

"Who asked you to do that?" Dad hovered in the doorway toward the living room with a dark expression.

"No one. The city will fine you if you let it get too long."

"Why are you here?" He asked instead of saying thank you.

"Came to see Mom," I said, setting the glass on the dinghy counter. That was the truth until I had caught sight of the disrepair of the front lawn. I was too exhausted to even make my way out into the field to the tree to say hello to her.

He huffed, walking away. It set me off like never before.

"Fuck you," I spat, the venomous taunt exploded from me before I could stop it.

"What did you say to me, boy?" He turned back, his eyes dark under the cover of the doorframe.

"I said," I pushed off the counter, "fuck you."

All of the rage that had been contained seemed to spill from me like he had taken a knife to my throat. I was bleeding red all over the dirty kitchen tile.

"You blame all of us for your problems," I waved my hands in the air, brows pushed together, and my jaw clenched so tightly my teeth ached. "We didn't kill mom!" I slammed my hand against his chest, shoving him backward.

"You did that!" I yelled, and fuck, it felt good to direct it at him. "You killed mom and have spent the last thirteen years taking it out on us! Do you know why Luc and Sawyer don't come around?"

His fist balled at his side, but he didn't answer me.

"It's because they can't stand to fucking look at you. They can't stand what you did to mom or her home." Everything I have ever wanted to say to him comes spilling out of me. "You turned Nick inside out until he couldn't even recognize himself in the mirror anymore. Mom tried to love you, she tried, but she did that for us, and you killed her because you couldn't fucking stand that she loved us more than you."

Not a word came from him. He was stunned, staring at me with wide, glossy eyes.

"You were never a dad, you're just a spiteful abusive prick, and you will die alone in this fucking house."

His laughter settled against my tired muscles like a sticky, uncomfortable film. He looked around at the piles of boxes and piles of dust before his dead eyes landed back on me, his lips pressed into a thin line before he said, "I'm not alone. You always crawl back because there's only one person in this family more spiteful than me, and that's you."

It was like the air had been knocked from my lungs. "Go back to the Nest, Arlo," my father spat. "Continue to pretend that's where you belong. I may die in this house, but I will do it with the satisfaction of knowing you will, too."

I scooped up my sweater from the table and went to the back door.

The fastback roared to life without persuasion.

The drive to the rehab facility seemed longer than it should have been, stewing in my own emotions as I wrestled with who was right in the situation. My father was an asshole, but his point had been concise and stabbed clean through me the way he had intended it to. I pulled up to the curb, my thoughts a million miles away, admiring how Ella's hair looked in the sunset of my mind. I would give anything to be back on that dock with her. Unburdened and blissfully happy.

The building looked like a prison dolled up with some flowers and pale orange paint. It was large and rectangular. And even the orderlies who wandered outside on their smoke breaks looked like they hated being there.

"How are you feeling?" I leaned against the fastback as he sauntered out of the rehab center in a baggy sweatshirt and jeans. It had only been two weeks, but he looked like he had lost fifty pounds, and his pretty smile seemed hollow. His arm was still tangled up in the sling, and the cuts on his face were dark red scabs that looked bothered, but he was healing.

"Like I've just been locked up with a bunch of fucking drug addicts." He took a deep breath of fresh air and pushed his sunglasses down the bridge of his nose. "You look like shit," he laughed so hard it rattled his scrawny frame.

"Get in the car, Kitten, so I can find a bridge to toss you over."

"I could use the swim," he whined, climbing into the passenger seat and throwing his phone on the dashboard. "I smell like pudding and bleach."

He giggled like a little kid when he realized what was in the bag at his feet, "is that Hilly's?" He tore the bag open to get at the fries.

I didn't ask him any questions about rehab. would grill him enough on the topic, and making the kid do it twice seemed pointless. He shoved his face full of warm, salty potatoes and leaned back against the seat with a heavy sigh.

"I haven't had real food in two weeks." His phone buzzed on the dash, and Ella's name flashed across the screen. His hand darted out, but his movements were sluggish, and I beat him there, catching a glimpse of the pretty photo he used for her contact. It was blurry, but her hair was messy, and she smiled wide, tucked into the hammock with her hand in front of her, trying to stop him from taking the photo.

The nasty side of me, the monster I kept tucked away from Cael, wanted to throw it out the window. To smash what was left of their communication into pieces out of jealousy, I buckled down and threw the phone into his lap without another word.

BAD HONEY

I was pissed that she was still talking to him. He had forced this turn of events. He had backed me into a corner by playing the guilt card, knowing that I wouldn't be able to leave him afterward. I wanted to forgive him and blame the drugs and the addiction, but everything became so much more complicated with the arrival of Ella. But the animal that I coined resentment growled in my chest. I'd be no better than his father if I lashed out at him now for that.

My hands flexed around the steering wheel, a searing rage blanketed every other emotion I was feeling, and I needed out of this car before I started in on him. I was trying, with every fiber of my being, not to remind him how fucking stupid he was at that moment. My heart was pounding in my chest so fast I was just waiting for it to leap out of my chest, hoping that maybe if it had, the pain would end and I could die, left alone with those sunset-kissed memories of Ella.

We were five minutes from the Nest when his phone rang again.

Cael silenced it as I spun into the driveway and threw the car into neutral.

"Go ahead, answer it," I spat, cutting the engine and turning to him.

"Arlo," Cael shook his head and shoved the phone into his pocket.

"Answer her," I said again.

"Say what you need to say, Arlo," he unbuckled his seatbelt and removed his sunglasses to reveal his heavy, exhausted eyes. "Quit doing whatever," he waved his hand around in a sloppy circle, "this is."

"Why the hell is she calling you?"

His tongue brushed over the scab on his top lip before he spoke, "Because I needed her."

His honesty made me violent.

"Ar," he swallowed, opening his mouth to say something else but closing it just as quickly.

I inhaled, but the air burned its way down into my lungs.

"This shit show is your fault," I pointed to the ground like it meant something more, but it was simply just a way to force the anger into the dirt beneath the fastback. "You put us here, you almost killed us, and yet."

She's calling you.

"Not because—" he stopped. We both knew it wasn't in a romantic way.

That made it worse in some sick and twisted way. Ella, needing Cael on a level that was simply platonic, ripped my heart from my chest. She didn't trust me.

"Arlo, I'm well aware of my mistake and the decisions that led to this, and apologizing isn't make you less angry with me. We both know that." In his rehab jargon, as if it was supposed to make us both feel better. "Ella understands the part of me that can't help but make those decisions. She understands who I am when I'm high."

"I didn't do anything fucking wrong, and she won't talk to me."

He stared at me. With that wall gone, all I saw was a liability.

"I don't care what you need anymore. I am done. We're days away from the finals, we don't need this shit Cael. Turn off your phone and get your head in the game. No more drugs, no more sex, your entire fucking life is baseball as of now."

"Arlo, I can't play," he cocked his head to the side. "I have to have surgery on my shoulder. Didn't Silas tell you?"

"No," I ground my teeth together.

Everything was slipping out from beneath me, and the tighter my grip on the things I cared about most, the more they slipped away. Cael's phone vibrated against the leather seat, and I couldn't take it anymore; my hand snapped out before I could stop it, and I punched him hard enough in the face for his head to slam against the window.

The door opened behind him, and Silas helped him out. He stumbled in a disorientated pattern across the driveway, falling to his knees before sliding up to sit on the broad steps of the Nest.

"What the hell is wrong with you?" Silas barked as I climbed from the car and slammed the door shut so tightly that the car whined from the impact. "You okay?" He pointed a hand out to Cael, who nodded and wiped the blood that poured from his nose with the sleeve of his sweater.

"This is about her again?" Silas narrowed his eyes at me, "Real rich giving the *'baseball is all you know'* speech when you can't even follow it!"

BAD HONEY

He stepped forward, and my hands balled into fists, "you gonna hit me, big guy?" He scoffed, "That's cute. You sucker punched a cripple going through withdrawal."

He waited a moment, watching my every move, "If you hit me, you better hope it puts me on the ground."

"I've won my share of our fights, Silas. Sit down."

"Arlo, your heads all fucked up! You aren't thinking straight. You're turning on the people that are trying to help! Do you think losing her is bad? Wait until there's no one left." He snarled at me. I had never seen Silas so angry. "You wanna fucking pick on someone? You pick on me. Cael's letting you kick him around cause he feels bad. Van won't fucking stand up to you cause you're his Captain. But you got nothing on me, princess, and I swear I will lay you out if you don't get yourself together right fucking now."

He nodded his head and stared at the ground for a moment.

"You're Arlo-fucking-King," Silas looked up at me, closed the gap between us, and grabbed the collar of my shirt roughly.

"I'm exactly what he made me into," I whispered as I wrestled with him, my hand wrapping around his. "I pushed everyone away just like he does, beat the love out of them. That's who I am. I'm what he wants me to be."

I pushed back on his chest, but he didn't budge, "do you know what I remember about your mom, Arlo?" He whispered so only we could hear, "She sat in those stands, the same chair her entire life. Section one hundred, row ten, seat eleven. Your number. And she did it covered in bruises. She never hid them, was never shy about who gave them to her, and do you even understand why?"

Bile flooded my throat because I remembered all too well.

"She didn't hide them because, to her, they were trophies. She wore them like a badge of honor for protecting her sons. You wanna act like Arthur and pretend that anger is all you have, but it's not true. You aren't your father. The minute you walked into the Nest, you left him behind. It's why he resents you so much."

Tears pricked at my eyes, staring into his stone gray ones, so deep and concerned. His hand slapped against my face, holding it there so I couldn't look away from him, "you have always been *her* in here," he pushed his other hand against my heart. "I know it fucking hurts, I know it feels unfair."

"It is unfair."

"I know what Momma meant," Cael groaned, as he clumsily pushed his lanky body from the steps. "You take care of him," he laughed, wiggling his nose and checking for more blood. "It's not broken," he mumbled, "I don't think." He came and stood close to our huddle, shoulders eclipsing ours, "I thought it meant taking care of you the way you take care of us, all scary and shit."

Silas sighed, letting a pathetic, exhausted laugh fall from him. "Elegant."

"But she never took care of you like that." Cael licked his lip, "She was all tough love mom to us, giving it to us straight hard but—"

"That's right," Silas clicked his tongue in agreement, "I don't think Lorraine ever raised her voice when it came to you, no matter how stupid you were. Remember when you and Jensen fist-fought in the downstairs bathroom."

"You didn't even get in trouble for breaking that mirror." Cael rolled his eyes, "and she gave Jensen three weeks of dinner duty."

"Or when you smashed up your dad's car in the parking lot?" Silas added.

"She helped you pay to replace the windows and bandaged up your hands so Dad didn't find out."

"She was just being nice," I managed to choke out.

"Momma used to take your side over mine," he huffed, and Silas kicked his boot out against Cael's foot to tell him to shut up.

I thought about all the times that Lorraine had been there for me after my mom died and how I never realized that she had used a different hand than all the other boys in the Nest. Too busy being angry at the world to notice my mom had sent me a replacement who knew precisely what I needed.

"She knew what you needed," Silas said aloud like he was reading my mind, "and I'm sorry we forgot how to do that for you." He wrapped his hand around my neck and pulled our foreheads together. "You don't have to be the brave one all the time, Arlo. Let us pick up the slack. You had your heart broken. Give it some time."

BAD HONEY

The anger dissipated along with the guilt that I wasn't doing enough for everyone. Silas could feel it, and he loosened the hold on my neck in response.

"I—" I turned my head to look at Cael, inhaling a fresh breath before saying, "I'm sorry."

"You really need to work on your apologies. That sounded painful," Cael laughed, but the smile he gave me was soft and genuine.

"It was," I groaned and grabbed him, pulling him into the hug. "I shouldn't have hit you. I just don't—" the sob caught in my throat. "She's under my skin, and I know," I licked my lip, catching my breath. "I know she doesn't want to talk to or see me, but I just want to explain myself."

"I might have a plan," Cael knocks his fingers against his chest. "Just give me some time and help us win the championship."

MIELE

It was my first time in the dugout in nearly three weeks.

It's not that I didn't want to be there. It was that being there was to have my heart broken over and over again every time Arlo stepped onto the field. He looked miserable. Without Cael at his back, he was a man lost in a storm.

He had let the facial hair grow out of control, and his hair had grown so long it stuck wildly out of the base of his hat. Arlo looked over at the dugout where I stood against the bench behind a wall of spare players, trying to remain as hidden as possible. His dark brown eyes were decorated with heavy purple bags, but the bruises from the accident appeared to be healed.

I wanted to evaporate into the brick and cease to exist as the crowd boomed above us. I pressed both hands flat to the wall and let it echo through my muscles to my heart, quieting all my nerves.

Silas had asked me to be here because it was the last game before the championship if they managed to win tonight. They would go to the finals. He needed an extra set of hands and ears, but I missed the safety of the therapy room. It was easier to breathe behind those walls where Arlo's intense stare couldn't find me.

"Breathe, Peachy," Cael said from beside me.

Unable to play with his arm and scheduled for surgery, he would be by my side for longer than either of us wanted. It took all of twenty-four hours of him being in rehab for me to call to make sure he was okay. Eventually, the doctors put me on the visitation list.

BAD HONEY

He barely looked at me that day. His big blue eyes were red and glassy as he stared out the window and picked paint chips off the sill absentmindedly. We never spoke about what happened. Everything was still too fresh, and I couldn't bring myself to do that to him. He already blamed himself for what had gone down, and it didn't help to rehash it when he was so vulnerable. He was working so hard to get better, to stay clean. I was too scared of him relapsing to tell him that I had moved out of the Nest, so when he finally got out of rehab, I waited for his phone call. Instead, he showed up at the dorm room door with a bag of junk food, a broken nose, and an apology.

"I'm sorry, El," *he whispered, sweater pulled over his chin. His hurt shoulder was folded up inside, and he looked so small, slumped down between all the pillows on my bed.* "Don't blame him, okay? He was just—"

"Being Arlo?" *I hovered beside him on my knees and finished the sentence for him as I inspected his nose,* "He punched you in the face."

"That was nothing, I deserved it."

"I don't think that matters, Cael," *I sat back and looked down into my lap.* "I saw him that day," *I said,* "Ethan, everything was so tangled, and all I could think was that the longer and tighter I held onto him..."

"He's not Ethan," *Cael looked up at me and grabbed my hand. His thumb brushed over the ring he gifted me for my birthday.* "How come you didn't take this off?"

"Because it's special, and you gave it to me." *I shrugged, looking down at the carefully etched letter 'e.'*

"So why this," *he pointed to the vacant spot on my chest where Arlo's ring had hung for nearly nine months.*

"Because that was special to him," *I swallowed tightly.* "What happens the day I slip up? The moment I give back into the drugs, and Arlo tries to save me?"

"You're stronger than me. You always have been. You know that won't happen."

"What if it does?" *I asked him.* "I lost Ethan and—" *I stopped.*

"And I almost took Arlo from you." *He choked out softly, angling his face away from me.*

"He's fine, you're fine." I brushed my hand across his face, "I'm not mad at Arlo," I whispered. "I'm terrified for him. He's so hell-bent on protecting those around him that he forgets himself."

"You're never going to change that about him," Cael said, "he's been that way for as long as I've known him."

"I don't want to change who he is. I just wish he would let us protect him sometimes."

"Will you talk to him?" He asked, wiggling his nose painfully until he was told to stop.

"Will it help?" I shrugged, "I don't even know what to say. Every single one of my feelings can be explained away with Arlo's logic, and I hate it. But I'm not sleeping, either...I can't close my eyes without seeing Ethan and Arlo in his place."

Cael slid closer, wrapping his legs around me and pulling me into a hug. He tucked himself against my stomach, and I cradled his head. "How do I balance loving Arlo without suffocating on the idea that his path is paved for tragedy by my side?"

"Do you believe that?" He angled his chin to me, and I hummed, hugging him a little tighter. "That no matter what you do, your story is written, and there's nothing you can do to change it? If you have no hope, then there's no hope for me."

"Is that a Star Wars quote?" I teased with a hint of confusion.

"You still haven't watched them? Peach, you're killing me." He fell back against the bed. "Just talk to him."

"This is giving me deja vu," I sighed.

"You're afraid that he'll convince you of some other narrative than what you have in your mind, and maybe that's a good thing. You aren't that same person from a year ago," he said.

"You didn't know me then," I looked away from him.

"But I know you now," He argued. "And the Ella I know deserves love."

"I can feel him staring at me," I whispered, lining my shoulder up with Cael and leaning into him.

"He's alright, just—" Cael seemed anxious. "Surprised you're here. Give him a moment."

"You mean Silas didn't warn him?" I sighed.

"We have a no "E" word rule in the locker room as of last week." He laughed.

"Why?"

"Arlo charged first base with malicious intent, then fought with Nick... Do you open the school papers?" He said, and I shook my head. "Dad kicked Arlo and Nick out of the dugout and sent them home."

"What?" I scoffed, "That's ridiculous."

"You underestimate how deep your claws went," Cael shrugged, wincing at the movement when the ache trickled down into his arm, "and how much Arlo liked that pain. He's been chasing that high around like a lost, rabid dog. He's fought nearly everyone on the team since returning from New York, even Coach."

"He fought Coach?" My mouth fell open.

Silas turned to look at me and shook his head, "Just some choice words were thrown around, no fists."

"Unfortunately," Cael stifled his laugh.

Coach had failed to climb the mountain that prevented him from being a good dad and hadn't visited him the entire time he was in rehab. Cael's only visitors came from Silas and me.

The Ump called two clean strikes in the second last inning, but Logan was back up to bat. His left eye sported a dark bruise.

"Arlo?" I asked Cael.

"Deserved," he dropped his tone, "Logan opened his mouth about you and Arlo snapped."

"About me?" I chewed on my lip, I really had fucked everything up for him. "Is there anyone he hasn't fought?"

"Tucker," both of them answered at the same time.

Before I arrived at Harbor, Arlo would have had a normal season, gone on to get a sponsorship, and maybe even had a decent career. Now, he was a loose cannon, a liability in the eyes of any scout watching. No one would be able to trust him to control his temper if he couldn't make it through a single inning without a blow-up.

"Read a newspaper, for the love of god," Silas rubbed the bridge of his nose. "Hold this, I need to grab some things for my kit from the office."

He handed me his bag, and I set it on the bench beside mine before returning to catch Arlo's last pitch. Logan had a hateful smirk on his face, but his back leg was shaky, he was nervous, and the entire game was riding on him, bringing in second and third. They needed those runs to catch up to the Hornets and stay in the game.

Logan's mouth opened, saying something that no one could hear over the sound of the stadium, but Arlo's stance grew tighter, his fingers flicking over the ball. I forced through spare players to the dugout fence, climbing up on the ledge and looking over it.

You can do this.

His eyes darted to me, and his chest rose and fell in time with my heartbeat. When he looked at me, every scream, clap, and order from the dugout seemed to fade away. His dark eyes were so sad and far away. His jaw clenched as he inhaled again and turned away from me, the sounds of the stadium erupting the minute our connection broke.

Arlo's body arched back, following the line of his arm like an invisible string ran from his fingers to his toes. Logan dug his heel into the dirt, and Arlo pushed all his anger into one last breath before throwing the ball as hard as he could.

Strike three.

The crowd seemed to thrum with excitement as they funneled off the field. The last inning would be challenging, but the Hornets were ahead, and the adrenaline was high. I pushed back against the wall as they flooded the dugout, Cael and Van eclipsing me on either side tightly as Arlo passed by.

It felt wrong, pinning them all against each other for the sake of my feelings, but I wasn't ready to break his heart or mine. I had made up my mind, and it wouldn't be easy to say out loud, but I couldn't let Arlo continue to risk his career and his life to look after another junkie. I wouldn't do that to him. I wouldn't ask him to take on that burden.

I had to say goodbye.

Dean was the first to bat. His attitude, still on edge, proved helpful in stressful situations. He didn't bat an eye as he crushed the first ball thrown to him into the left-out field over both players' heads, aiming to catch the ball and get the easy out.

BAD HONEY

Dust kicked up at third before the ball returned to the infield, and I was still surprised at how fast the six-three first baseman moved. Van was next, his luck not as sturdy as Dean's before him. He struck out hard and stomped back to the dugout in a huff. Zoey's voice could be heard over the crowd as she heckled him playfully, trying to bring his mood back.

"She never quits," I laughed, rubbing a hand over his head as he slumped down and chucked his hat roughly across the dugout.

"It's annoying," he huffed, letting his head fall against the wall. "I fucking love her for it."

"Atta boy," I praised.

The air seemed to rush from me as Arlo rolled out his shoulders and took the box, Logan's taunting smile falling when he saw him.

"I would have paid to see him get laid out," I whispered to Van.

"I'll send you the video Zoey took." He said without skipping a beat.

Arlo missed the first pitch. The ball hit the glove with a loud clap, and the cheers died down, granting him a hushed silence as he readjusted his back foot. His hands rolled over the narrow end of the bat, seemingly so still, until he inhaled and exhaled. The ball connected with the bat with an explosive crack and a hardliner blew straight past Logan's head, throwing up the hair on his neck with the gust of wind it created before bouncing into the outfield.

Dean pushed home quickly, leaving Arlo to struggle as he slid roughly into second.

A yelp of pain filled the air along with the dust he kicked up as he rolled over and hit the bag with an echoing slap. I tensed, waiting for the dust to clear to see his body seize up in pain and his head thrown back over his shoulders.

Coach was the first to move. Everyone else stood frozen with worry as the Ump went from third to where Arlo rolled around in the dirt. The second baseman put his hands in the air and backed away slowly as Coach's hand pushed him away.

"Somethings wrong," Cael jolted beside me, "get your bag!"

"Where's Silas?" I asked, throwing the strap over my head and jogging out to the stairs of the dugout.

"Just go, I'll get him!" Cael barked, swinging open the door and taking off down the hallway.

One foot in front of the other, two steps at a time. His voice rang clear through my mind as I stepped out onto the field. "Move your ass, Miele!" Coach hollered over the hushed worries of the crowd.

Everyone was on their feet, watching and waiting. My heart was beating a million miles an hour inside of my chest. The only sound louder was the vicious sound of camera shutters going off.

I could read the headlines now: *Hornet Harlot comes to the rescue of violent captain Arlo King*.

My hands trembled as I pushed the Ump aside and dropped to my knees.

Arlo's eyes were wet with painful tears as he cradled his thigh in his hand. His lips were pressed into a tight line, and he looked away from me the moment I sat down. *Fair.*

"Can you move this?" I asked, wrapping my hands around his ankle.

His response came in the form of a tight nod.

"You have to talk to me—" he growled before I finished the sentence.

"Fine," I sneered, "can you reach your feet? We need to get you to a bed."

He nodded again. Van and Dean appeared behind us and wrapped themselves around Arlo, lifting him from the ground in clumsy footsteps and deep groans. They slowly hobbled him off the field, Arlo keeping the weight off his left knee and his eyes off me. The crowd and the other team erupted into supportive cheering, all except for Logan, who watched as Arlo was taken across the infield toward the dugout. I trailed behind Coach and the Ump, who were whispering, trying to keep up with their fast footsteps.

"Coward," he snapped, loud enough for me to hear as we passed. "You play just like your drunk dad!"

I turned, adjusting the bag on my shoulder before walking four long steps and slamming my fist into Logan's face. Knocking the cocky grin permanently from it and sending his head flicking back so forcefully that he stumbled off the pitcher's mound.

BAD HONEY

"Now you have the matching set." I rolled my eyes as the players ran to his defense, and the Ump screamed me off the field. "I'm going!" I yelled back, my hand throbbing at my side, at least three of the five knuckles broken and maybe a finger or two, but it had been worth it just to see their faces when I stepped down into the dugout.

"That's our girl!" Jensen called out first, causing them all to holler and clap.

I turned, expecting to see Coach with a scowl on his face. He leaned up against the open door, hands clapping together.

"You heard what he said."

"I did," Coach huffed, and the corner of his mouth curled a touch.

"Is that a smile?" I asked in passing, but he just shook his head.

"Nice to see the hook you taught Mitchell in use. Now go," he nodded toward the medical bay.

MIELE

"Where is he?" I walked up to the doors to find Cael and Van outside, whispering to one another.

"What the hell did you do to your hand?" Van stepped forward around Cael, who looked over his shoulder at the medical door.

"Punched the Lorrettes' pitcher." I walked by him.

Van looked at Cael and then back at me. "Excuse me?"

"It's fine. You have an inning to play!" I ordered, sending him back to the dugout as I walked toward the doors, but Cael shot his good arm out to stop me from entering. "What?"

"Go easy on him," he said tightly before opening the door for me, "he's in the side room." I kept my bag on my shoulder, moving to the small secluded room. It was where we kept Cael when he was coming down from drugs or someone needed to sleep. I expected Silas to be inside, but Arlo laid alone on the bed.

"This needed to happen, Peach," Cael said before shutting the door behind me and clicking the lock shut from the outside.

I turned and tried the doorknob, but it wouldn't budge.

"Cael Cody, you let me out of here right now!" I yelled but was met with silence.

The minute I got out of this room, I would kill him.

"Did he just *Parent Trap* us?" I pressed my head against the door and tried to breathe.

"He had help," Arlo said tightly from behind me. When I turned, he stood on both legs just fine, his dark eyes watching me carefully as I realized what they had done. "I needed to talk to you."

"And Silas? Is that why he asked for help?" I groaned, turning around to face him as he nodded. "So you're okay?" I asked, my lip trembling as I fought not to cry at the sight of him uninjured.

"Yeah," he wiggled his leg to prove no pain was there. "Hey," he stepped forward when he saw the look in my eye. I pushed myself back against the wall.

He inhaled and nodded to my hand, "You're hurt."

"I'm fine." It was throbbing, and I could feel the swelling build between the bones.

"Ella, I know when you're in pain, can I at least look at it?" He swallowed tightly and put his hand out to me. "What did you do?" His brows kissed together, and his eyes darkened as I rested my palm against his.

I sucked in the air through my teeth as we made contact. Nearly three weeks went by without seeing him or smelling him, and now I was trapped in a tiny room without escape. My head was dizzy with anxiety and emotion as he lifted our hands together closer to his face.

"Ba—" he stopped himself, pressing his lips together in a line to keep from saying the word. His eyes flickered up to meet mine through his thick lashes, "your hand is broken. What the hell did you do?"

When the adrenaline wore off, I would be in a world of hurt, but until then, it was just a dull, consistent throb that radiated up through my wrist into my forearm muscles.

"I punched Logan," I sighed, knowing Arlo would lose his mind, but instead, laughter filled the tiny room, and when I looked up at him, there was a massive smile on his face. "You're laughing?"

"You punched the captain of the Lorrettes? Just now?"

"I thought you were hurt, and he was being an ass!" I threw my hands in the air and let the bag drop.

"You were standing up for me?" His voice dropped an octave and became deliciously whiny as he let go of my hand and stepped forward.

I put my hand out to stop him even though every muscle and fiber begged me to let him close. My heart screamed in agony to keep him at arm's length, but I had to protect him from what darkness still clouded my judgments.

"Ella," he sighed, staring down at my fingers. They were nearly brushing against his chest, inches from it, and I could see how badly he wanted to touch them as his hands slowly flexed at either side. "You promised."

"That was before," I scrunch my face, keeping my arm out to stop him from getting closer. "When it was easy."

"Nothing was ever easy," Arlo swallowed, inhaling deeply, and his chest brushed against my fingertips, causing me to hold my breath. "I didn't mean to break your trust, but I know I did," his head and shoulder moved in an angled line, dipping low so he could catch my eyeline and raise it back to his. "But I need to know why you think this is your fault because it's written all over your face, and Cael's not going to let us out of this room until you do."

"*He's right!*" Cael yelled through the door, and both of us groaned.

"Get the fuck out of here, Cody!" Arlo barked, and feet shuffling echoed from the other side. "Talk to me, Ella." He whispered.

I huffed because it was the only way of communicating the frustration that hummed through me, being forced to face him before I was ready and against my will. But he waited, not saying a word. He was quiet and patient, just like always, as I searched the depths of my fear for courage. Arlo, if anything, deserved an explanation.

"When you climbed into the car with Cael, who was on your mind?" I asked.

"Cael," he shrugged like it was the most obvious answer.

"When your brother attacked me on my birthday, who was on your mind?"

"You," his jaw tensed.

"And at the pool party with that asshole?" He tried to step closer, but I pushed him back. Hurt flickered in his eyes. "The problem isn't that you love me, Arlo. It's how you love me."

"That's insane," he whined, as if the words hurt leaving him.

"You are always putting yourself second," I responded calmly, "and when the two people you are trying so hard to protect manage to tear you limb from limb, who puts you back together?"

I swallowed the cotton in my throat when he couldn't answer me, "Cael is volatile, and I am a mess, but *I'm alive*. You scared the shit out of me getting in that car with him because you didn't stop to think of the consequences of what might happen to *you*."

He stared at me so intently that it caused the heat to rise on the back of my neck, and I didn't even notice that his hand had come up to brush against my fingertips.

"Cael talked about how he was rotten," my tongue pushed against the inside of my mouth to keep me from biting down on my lip. "I won't be the one to destroy what heart you have left, Arlo. I can't."

I closed my eyes as his fingers slipped between mine, and the image of Ethan flashed across my memory violently and loudly. His big brown eyes were just reflections of my own as the light went out in them, and in the blink of an eye, he was gone, and Arlo was trapped there, strangled by his seatbelt, me unable to do anything but watch as life slowly drained from his body.

"So you're angry with me because I take care of you and Cael too well?" He sounded so hurt and confused.

"I'm not attacking your character. I'm questioning your lack of self-preservation. Cael will need you more than ever to get through what comes next. If he wants to stay sober, he's going to need you consistently and constantly. It's going to be exhausting, and some days it's going to feel like you made a mistake loving him, but you'll do it anyway because he's your little brother," hurt flickered across his features, but understanding flooded in. "And I know that if you had the choice, you wouldn't pick. You would just run yourself into the ground for the both of us."

"So you're removing my choice?" Arlo whispered. "How is that fair?"

"It's not," I said, "but it's the only way I can protect you."

"No," he licked his lip and shook his head. "No."

I could feel the tears coming, but there wasn't any other way. He wasn't thinking clearly, and he wouldn't. Not when his judgment was so clouded.

"You have no idea," his tone still so quiet as he spoke, "the last three weeks, I felt like all my thoughts were a screw loose like everyone around me had never seemed so dull. I have been closing my eyes and praying for a daydream just so I can—" he paused, fingers wrapping around a lock of my long blonde hair, "see you, feel you again. You can't make that choice for me. I won't let you."

"You're my missing piece, Ella. I'll be damned if I let you just walk away from me because you're scared." He sounded so sure of his words. "You've survived hell! You had everything taken from you, and this is what you are scared of?" He clenched his jaw. "Me? Love?" He groaned, "What did I do that made you so afraid of being with me?"

He opened his mouth to say more, but I yelled, "What if you leave?"

"I'm not going to leave Ella," he fought back. "The world will have to throw a lot more in my direction if it wants to separate us."

"Don't say that!" I shook my head, "don't tempt fate."

He stopped then, heavy breathing slowing and his eyes softening, "Ella, I'm sorry that I got in the car." He whispered, closing the gap, "I know I scared you, but I'm never going to leave you again, not for anyone."

"I want to believe that!" I argued. "But you are so consumed you don't see how bad this can be!"

"Did you stop to think that it's good for the both of us?" He smiled at me, "You aren't as messy as you want people to think, and maybe the protection goes both directions in ways neither of us understand."

"You can't be sure of that. It's unknown and can be ripped away so easily." I swallowed tightly, thinking of the light dying in Ethan's eyes. It had been like a light switch. It was there one second, all the love and loyalty, flipped off and turned dark, never to be seen or felt again.

"It's not unknown. Do you want to know the minute, down to the second I knew, Ella?"

That I loved you.

He didn't finish his sentence, but I could hear it, clear as day, as it rolled through his thoughts.

"*I can beat these assholes with my eyes closed.*" He smiled so wide I thought he had captured the sun.

"You heard that?" Amusement tickled at the corners of my mouth.

"From the moment I saw you step into the kitchen, I haven't taken my eyes off you." He stepped closer, wrapping his hands around my face and tilting my chin upward. "Ella, *baby*." His bottom lip ghosts mine, and I could feel my entire body give into him without hesitation.

"You are the counterweight to all the bad moments in my life, too, and whether or not you walk away from me right now, I will follow behind you for the rest of your life because if there is one thing you can not take from me," his breath fanned against my skin. "It's my right to choose."

Every defense I had against him crumbled.

"And?" I tugged at the collar of his uniform, unable to resist myself any longer. "What do you choose?" My heart was racing, and my skin was hot. I knew there was no convincing him otherwise, and even though the fear was tangible, I might somehow destroy what he was so convinced of.

"I choose to love you," he brushed his nose against mine and kissed me, our bodies melting together the way they were meant to and had begged for the last few weeks apart.

His hands tangled into my hair and tugged me as close as I could get as his tongue slipped into my mouth, and my hands untucked the bottom of his jersey from his pants. I needed skin, and as soon as my hands found it, a strangled whimper left my lips and had Arlo smiling against my mouth. "I missed you too, Blondie," he pulled back only to say before nibbling at my bottom lip and letting our eyes connect.

"I'm sorry I shut you out," I whispered.

"I'm sorry I let you," he responded.

"I didn't make it easy," I kissed him quickly.

"There's no fun in easy, baby," he nuzzled his forehead against mine.

"You punched Van," I sighed.

"Keeps his ego in check." He dragged his teeth over my bottom lip.

"You should probably apologize for that," I giggled when he groaned in protest.

"Did you really hit Logan?" He asked in a fit of lazy laughter.

I nodded against his mouth, stealing another round of hot, needy kisses from him, wincing only as the memories of my broken knuckles resurfaced. Arlo let go of my face but didn't break the kiss as he pounded his fist against the door behind my head.

"Cael," Arlo pulled away for a split second to yell before returning for another quick kiss, "I know you didn't leave, shithead. Let us out."

"*Did you stop fighting?*" He asked through the door, and I couldn't help but laugh.

"Yes." We answered at the same time.

"Now open the door so I can get ice for this tough guy," Arlo kissed the sore knuckles on my hand, finally backing away from me so we could both catch our breath.

KING

"We won, in case you two idiots were wondering," Coach hovered in the doorway as Silas looked over Ella's hand. "And you broke Logan's nose," he pointed his judgmental *dad* eyes on her.

"What did he say anyway?" Cael asked, his long legs dangling down off the counter he had perched on to watch.

"It doesn't matter," she said, still focused on what Silas was doing.

She hated the hovering, but neither of us could help it. She had spent weeks not letting anyone take care of her. Zoey busted through the medical doors, Mitchell and Tucker on her tail, pushing past all of us with a scowl on her face. Van looked like he had just been chewed out as he walked past Coach, sweaty and flushed, before settling down against the counter next to Cael.

"Why did you do that!" She scolded, "You've got two exams left to graduate. How the hell are you going to write them?"

"With a broken hand, I suppose."

"This is your fault!" She pinched my arm and sneered at me. "Idiot!"

Cael laughed loudly, but the sound was silenced when Zoey turned her scowl on him. "Sour patch," he mocked her with a grin.

"Don't *Sour patch* me!" She pointed at him, "You're all terrible influences!"

"Hey, she taught me that hook!" Mitchell laughed, "She's the bad influence!"

"It was a really nice punch," she gripped the side of Ella's face. "Are you?" She looked between Ella and me.

"I'm okay," Ella whispered, "promise."

My chest felt lighter, and another laugh left me. Seeing Cael sober and happy, Ella by my side again. My family was home, and everything was right again. Coach cleared his throat from across the room, "are you all finished?"

"Yes, Coach," I grunted.

Silas seemed happy with the wrap he put on Ella and turned to where Coach stood in the doorframe. Dean, Van, and Cael all stood with their shoulders pinned back in a line like he was the leader of a regiment and waited for him to lose his mind on us.

"There are three games left to win," he swallowed tightly, looking at the ground, pieces of his sandy brown hair falling out of place as he walked into the room. "We ignore the press, we ignore the fans, we fix broken ties, and we sweep them to take the Finals. Do you understand me?" Coach looked up at me, dark evergreen flooding his usually mossy eyes.

"Yes, Coach," we all barked, including Ella and Zoey.

"Practice, five a.m. Do not be late." Coach ordered, and we all echoed in time. "Novak, I need to speak with you, please." He called to Zoey.

"I love you," she quickly kissed Ella on the cheek, "No more punching men, please?" She asked.

"Only if they really deserve it?" Ella teased.

Zoey looked around the room at all of us and raised her eyebrow at Ella, "I'll get you a set of boxing gloves for Christmas." They both laughed and when Zoey was satisfied that Ella was comfortable, she scurried from the room to find Coach.

"Did you see this?" Van chucked his phone at me. On it was a sloppy edit of Ella throwing a disgusting-looking punch straight to Logan's nose.

I blew out a stream of hot air that turned into a low whistle and looked over at her, "my baby has a nasty right hook."

Van winked at her, taking his phone back. "She gonna be okay, Doc?"

"Yeah," Silas pursed his lips together, which meant he was worried about something. "It will be sore for a while, but it's set and won't need surgery."

BAD HONEY

"Are you sure?" I asked him, pressing my chest to her shoulder.

Silas scowled at me. "Are you questioning my medical expertise, King?"

"Yes," I smiled, "maybe we need a second opinion." The air in the room felt light for the first time in nearly a month.

Cael leaned against the counter with his head pressed against Dean's shoulder and laughed with his whole body.

"I'm not above kicking your ass again," Silas warned.

"Alright, that's enough," Ella shook her head, "there's been enough fighting, and you'll mess up his money maker," she grabbed my chin with her good hand and shook it between her fingers as I scoffed at her.

Silas laughed, "I want you to get some x-rays done tomorrow to be sure."

"Alright," she gave him a phony salute, "were you in on the parent trapping?" She asked him.

"I'm almost offended you thought Cael came up with that plan on his own," Silas groaned and shook his head in disbelief. "But Ella," his brows came together in a stern line. "If you ever break his heart again, there will be no coming back from that."

"Promise," she slapped two fingers to her chest. His eyes dropped to them, and returned the promise. "Can I take him home now? There's something I've been meaning to do for a couple of weeks."

I tensed beside her, seeing the mischievous grin on her face.

"Home?"

"Home." She confirmed with her tongue pressed to her teeth.

When I finished my shower, I found Ella in Coach's office discussing her suspension. She wasn't allowed in the dugout for the remainder of the games because of the apparent assault on Logan, but Coach seemed more upset about it than her. Calling it unfair and ridiculous for a first-time offense.

"I'll be with Zoe," she scrunched her nose up at me as I collected her jacket and helped her into it. "It was worth it."

I kissed a line across her scar, holding her head between my hands. I just wanted to stare at her for a second, count all the freckles that danced across the bridge of her nose and the streaks of gold in her big brown eyes. I exhaled slowly as she smiled up at me, my sunshine incarnate, my girl. "Stay here. I'll bring the car around," I left her standing at the front entrance, jogging out into the pouring rain.

"Hey, number eleven," She called to me, stepping out from under the awning, her blonde hair soaking wet and sticking to her pretty face. "I forgot to mention something earlier," she said with a smile. "I love you too."

"Say it again," my heart fluttered as I dropped my duffle against the tarmac and stepped back toward her. The rain poured down my face and neck in sheets as I closed the gap between us more urgently than ever.

"I love you, Arlo King!"

"Blondie," I stalked toward her and scooped her up in my arms, her legs wrapping around my waist as I kissed her in the rain under the light of the moon. I carried her, unwilling to part for a second. I needed her closer.

As we moved toward the car, I realized there was only one thing missing from the moment. I set her down, opened the door for her, and let her out of the rain before snatching up my duffle and running to my side.

"Don't ever," I said as I closed the door behind myself and reached around, pulling the necklace off the rearview mirror, "take this off again. *Please.*"

I dropped it over her head and wrapped my hand around the ring to pull her toward me, "I'm really sick of giving it back to you."

"You didn't throw my bike out, did you?" She pouts at me.

"I always knew you were coming back, Blondie," I kissed her, taking her lips between mine with my hand still wrapped around the necklace so she couldn't pull away.

"For such an angry man, you rely greatly on blind faith."

"It wasn't blind faith," I smiled at her.

"If you say—"

"It was true love," I cut her off with another kiss.

"You have been reading way too many romance novels."

"Oh, come on," I laughed, "that was a good one."

"Cael is going to double over when I tell him that one," she teased.

BAD HONEY

"You wouldn't dare," I finally let her go and started the fastback.

"You should have seen his face when I repeated back, *'Kissing you is like pitching the perfect inning,'*" she mocked my voice.

I growled and hammered down on the clutch, shifting the car and pushing it up the hill faster. "Please stop telling Cael what I say to you in the privacy of our room."

"Our room?" She turned in her seat with a smile on her face.

"Our room."

MIELE

Arlo wasted no time pulling me from the car in the pouring rain, not even bothering with the garage as he scooped me up against his waist and stomped up the steps to the Nest. My hands tugged at the hem of his shirt, pulling it over his torso as he kicked open his door and set me on my feet.

"Take it off," I grumbled.

Nodding, Arlo did what he was told, pulling his hands away to shuck the shirt over his shoulders. My hands found his chest, running my fingers over his muscles and tracing all the curves around his shoulders and neck. He worked quickly to help me out of my shirt, his hands returning to cup my face and throat as he kissed me again.

With my hands against his chest, I could feel how fast his heart was beating. Nervously, I moved away from him and hooked my healthy fingers into the band of his shorts to pull him toward the bed. Arlo positioned his knees on either side of my hips, and the view was spectacular.

His tawny skin glowed in the dim lighting, all of the tight muscles in his chest working together as he flicked the button of my jeans free. Arlo rolled them down over my hips and disposed of them without a second thought, kissing small, delicate circles on my hips before returning to his position above me. His tongue darted out over his bottom lip as he adjusted himself in his shorts, the fabric stretching over his growing bulge.

He lowered himself to my mouth and kissed me slowly before moving his lips and hands lower. Tracing a line down my neck and over my chest to the swell of my breast in my bra. Arlo hummed as his fingers brushed against the fabric, his teeth pinching at the soft skin as he disposed of it.

"I haven't stopped thinking about you," he grumbled, "not for a second."

Warmth spread through my stomach.

"The way you feel beneath me," his hand roved over my stomach, "every tiny sound you make for me," he sucked a nipple between his teeth and dragged a whiney moan from my throat.

Arlo let out a tiny sigh, his breath leaving his trembling body as his hands continued lower. "I have been dreaming about you," he groaned, "waking up hard without you in my bed was torture."

Raking my fingers through his hair as he kissed across the scar on my chest, down my stomach to my hips, I whispered, "Beg for it." I lifted my leg and pressed my toes against his chest, pushing him back off the bed.

His eyes flickered at me, glimmering in the darkness as he stood tall over me, lust hazy in his dark eyes. "Baby," he started, and even as my body tensed from the sound, it wasn't enough. I wanted him to grovel.

"On your knees, Cap." I ran a hand over my breast, across my stomach.

With a slight, tense nod, he sat back, pushing his shorts down over his thick thighs. He pulled from the shorts entirely and kicked them away to the floor before he sank slowly to his knees before me.

"Now beg," I warned him.

"I need you," he started, his chest rising slowly in the soft light that poured in from the windows. He looked like an angel. Taut muscles like ridges of carved stone, his shoulders tense and biceps flexed as he worked to control himself. "Ella, please let me touch you," his voice dropped when I didn't respond, but my hand dipped between my thighs.

"Baby," he whined, inching forward closer to the bed. "I will mark your body with every apology I owe you until all you can do is sleep for a week. Just let me help, please. God, Ella, I can't take this."

I peered at him, watching his throat bob as I slipped a finger inside of myself, "you should *feel* how much I missed you."

That was enough to break him, "I am begging you, *baby*," he moaned and leaned forward on the bed to grip the sheets, "I will beg on my knees for the rest of our lives, Ella Miele. Now let me fuck you."

"Show me how much you missed me, Arlo King."

There was no hesitation when he stood from his knees. His kisses turned hot, firmly planted against my neck. He moved his hand against my chest, between my breasts, tangling into the necklace resting there. He grazed my skin until his hand was wrapped against my throat, his thumb cupping my jaw, and his lips teased the skin behind my ear.

"I love you," he breathed out, "I love every goddamn inch," his kisses turned urgent.

"I know," I responded as I arched my back and pressed our hips together. I could tell how desperately he needed this to be soft, but I needed him too badly to wait. My body ached with every tender touch of his lips, and if I didn't get more soon, I was going to explode.

Hooking my leg around the outside of Arlo's, I grabbed his shoulders and flipped him over on the bed so I was perched on his hips from above. "I love you too," I finally responded, and a shiver ran through his body beneath me. I rolled my hips against him, grinding down as deeply as I could to express my urgency.

His hold on my hips was tight as he pretended to have control, but his fingers dug deeper, and his breath became shakier the more I rocked against the fabric of his boxers. Reaching between us, I snapped their elastic, "Take them off."

"Ask nicely, Blondie." He purred as his hands followed the curve of my hips to my stomach and then back to my ass, where his fingers dug deep enough to leave delicious bruises.

"*Please,*" I pushed into his hold, and a deep growl vibrated from him.

I lifted to my knees so he could shimmy from them, and the second they were gone, I could feel the impressive length of his cock slap against my thigh. Bracing my hands on his chest, I ground down once more against him. The skin-on-skin contact as his head brushed against me was enough to drag a few choice moans from my lips.

Arlo's choked moan echoed in the room as I slid down over his length. "God," I breathed out, sitting back and taking him all the way to the shaft. "I will never get tired of that," I braced myself against his thighs, arching my back and letting my hair fall over my shoulders as I took him all.

"You take me so well," his hand brushed against my stomach, traveling up until his fingers were pinching my sensitive nipple. "Move," he dug his fingers into my ass and pulled my hips toward him. "You act tough," he teased, squeezing my nipple harder, "but your weeping cunt tells me just how much you missed me, Blondie."

I clenched around him in response, my entire body betraying my words as he arched his hips upward, forcing me to move. I cried out as his fingers moved in a simple, delicate line to my clit, his thumb dipping between us with his other fingers firmly splayed against my sweaty skin as he worked in slow, deliberate circles.

"Arlo," I gasped, mouth hanging open as the pressure mounted.

"Say it again," he ordered, his fingers relentless as his cock hit every spot inside of me over and over again.

"Arlo," his name was a whine that time as my thighs trembled around him.

He stares at me with heavy lids and his pouty bottom lip red from kissing, "Again."

I repeated his name over and over again as my body grew so tightly wound that the slightest movement from him had me whimpering for more. His hands wrapped around me, flipping me onto the bed with ease as he rocked into me hard.

"Hold on," he licked his bottom lip as I did what I was told, and I extended my hands to the wall above my head.

My muscles tightened as he slammed into me, true unbridled pleasure uncoiling and sending tiny shockwaves through my body. Every time Arlo pulled back, my body missed the feeling of being full and clenched from the absence until it returned tenfold.

"God," the word left my lips as a growl.

"Wrong name," he dragged himself fully free of me and waited, pumping himself in his hand and laughing proudly at the pout on my face.

"Arlo King," I propped up on my elbows, "if you don't fuck me right now." I emphasized every word to him, "You will never get to again."

"Look who's begging now," he cocked his head to the side. "Is that a threat?"

"It's a promise."

He slammed back into me with a cocky grin on his face, not giving me any time to brace myself against the wall I slid on the bed. He grabbed my ass and pulled me across the sheets down against him roughly.

Arlo let out a delicious moan. His head fell back between his shoulders as he began to snap his hips faster and harder. Even holding myself in place, the force of his brutal thrusts rocked me back and forth on the bed.

"I'm not going to last much longer," I moaned as his fingers found my clit again.

"You don't have to," he hushed me, wrapping his arm around my back. He pulled our bodies together and angled himself deeper still as I nuzzled my face into his neck. He smelled like cinnamon and sweat.

I fell back in his grip as everything released inside me at once. His forearm strained, and his hand found my ass again, bouncing me against him until he came undone alongside me.

"Don't stop," I begged.

He stifled a breathy laugh and pumped harder inside of me as my entire body flexed taut around him, and the orgasm washed through me down to my toes. My nails dug into his shoulders, and his fingers tightened around me until neither of us could breathe, and Arlo's eyes were screwed shut tightly.

I rocked into him, rolling my hips against his as he shook beneath me. Thunder rumbled outside as the rain persisted, and Arlo took his time driving into me and spilling so full that he leaked down around himself and onto his thighs.

I kissed him hard, gripping the baby hairs around his neck and tugging him roughly against me. His hands wrapped around my waist, and without removing himself from me, he lifted me off the bed.

"What are you doing?" I asked, lips finding his sweat-licked throat.

BAD HONEY

"I need another shower," he mumbled against the onslaught of kisses, teeth, and tongue tangled together so he couldn't get out any other words.

GAME ONE

"You'll drive me to my exam tomorrow morning?" I asked, who was fidgeting with her jersey.

"Of course, we should probably study tonight." She shrugged.

"I'm ready, just—" I paused.

"Ready to graduate but not ready to move on?" She finished for me.

"I don't know what to do after this. Harbor was supposed to be temporary." I shook my head.

Zoey laughed over air horns, screaming, "You know what you want." I followed her eyeline to Arlo on the field. "You just need to be brave enough to ask for it."

"Everything is riding on today," I said, swallowing the consuming feelings of love and anxiety.

The walk from campus to the stadium was long and full of honking horns, but once we had shoved our books from finals into my office and made our way up into the sun of the open stadium, the sun flushed away all the worry, and I felt alive. Anxious for the guys, but alive.

"It's best of five," she looked up through her sunglasses, her chocolate brown pigtails swinging in the wind. "they got this. I've never seen them play so tightly."

"Without Cael backing up Arlo, it will be a long series." I sighed, fidgeting with the ring around my neck.

"Dougie can do it. He proved that last match at short. People just need to stop comparing him and Cody. They aren't the same player."

BAD HONEY

I stared down at the ring, and every emotion seemed to hit me at once.

"Am I an absolute idiot?" I asked, completely changing the subject, but Zoey didn't miss a beat.

"No," she laughed. "Arlo King is the love of your life. Nice jersey."

I looked down at the dark blue Hornet's jersey, Arlo's number painted on the back, and just like that, all of the doubts and fears washed away.

They won the game, six runs to four.

GAME TWO

Game two was long, with three extra innings that seemed to drag on until Jensen found a pocket and dropped the ball between the outfielders to bring in Dean from second base. Winning them the game two to one.

"Don't be nervous," Arlo kissed me quickly as I buttoned up the last few beige buttons on his dress shirt in the locker room. "They're going to love you."

"I can barely handle one King sibling."

"You're very capable," he brushed his nose against my neck and kissed a line down my exposed collarbone. "I should know."

"You're going to give me a hickey," I giggled, pushing him off. "Stop, your brothers will think I'm a harlot!"

He backed away with a dramatic pout on his lips. I would never get used to how handsome he was. With his dark swoopy hair pushed back off his face, and his sun-kissed skin that seemed to glow. He tilted his head to the side, watching me with his dark brown eyes, and a smirk formed.

"How much do you like that shirt?" He asked, playing with the fabric around my stomach.

"A lot," I rolled my eyes.

"Shame," he licked his bottom lip, "I have ideas for it later."

"Are you two finished?" Cael leaned with his hat pulled down over his head in the doorway. "Sawyer is grilling me with questions about my recovery, and if he asks me one more time how I'm feeling, I'm going to hit him, Princess."

"Alright, Kitten," Arlo laughed, "take a beat. We're coming."

BAD HONEY

He kissed my cheek and sauntered toward Cael, knocking him on the shoulder as I rechecked my reflection. The wind in the stadium had pushed my soft curls around, making them too messy to keep down, so I pulled them back into a ponytail that exposed the scar on my chest and highlighted the one on my face. I swallowed the bile that rose in my throat, digging down deep for that confidence that I knew existed below the shame and anxiety.

"You look beautiful," Arlo said from beside Cael.

Both of them smiled at me. Cael's big and goofy, Arlo's still so serious and tight.

"Come on, Peachy, I'm starving." He whined, wiggling around in his lavender oversized shirt and wide-legged bleached jeans. He threw his arm around me as I got closer and tucked me into his side.

"Say it with me, Lucas is our favorite King brother."

"Debatable," I looked over my shoulder to where Arlo walked just behind us.

Arlo would always be my favorite.

MIELE

"Can I talk to you?" Nick grabbed Arlo by the strap of his duffle bag, crinkling the fine press to his new blue suit. It tapered at his waist and made him look so broad in the shoulders. The collar of the white dress shirt beneath barely buttoned around his neck and accentuated his jawline.

I couldn't wait to get him out of it.

"I don't have anything to say to you," he held onto my hand with a suffocating grip, and I could feel the stress that cascaded through his muscles with every step away from Nick.

"Arlo!" He barked.

"What, Nick, what could you want that's more important than today's game? We are this close," he raised his hand in Nick's face, "to having a championship title again."

"Dad's coming," his gaze softened as he looked at me. "I wanted—" Nick paused, scratching his neck nervously, "I wanted to apologize."

"Apologies mean nothing without action, Nick, and I'm sorry if I don't have faith in your words." Arlo waved him off, our arms growing taut as I followed slowly. "What?" Arlo looked over his shoulder at me with a tense jaw when he realized I had stopped.

"Just hear him out," I whispered loud enough for only him to hear, and all of the tense, sharp lines of his expression shifted from frustration to confusion.

"For what?" he said, not turning around to look at Nick.

"I should have never let Dad get between us." He said.

Arlo's shoulders deflated.

"Making you feel small made me feel invincible, and I shouldn't have taken advantage of that. I should have protected you. My perspective of the situation was screwed up, and Dad whispering in my ear never helped. I'm trying, and if words aren't enough, I'll keep trying."

When he finally turned around to meet Nick's eyes, a strangled silence fell between the brothers. I squeezed Arlo's bicep as the camera shutters echoed through the parking lot, alerting us that we had been found.

"And?" Arlo said, but I missed whatever passed between them.

"I'm sorry, Ella," Nick said, "for hurting you. I'm not that person. I just needed a minute to get back." I didn't say anything in response as Arlo squeezed my hand tightly, his fingers flexing around my palm uncomfortably. Neither moved for another long minute, but Arlo nodded, tapping his fingers to his chest. Nick mirrored the movement, and they both inhaled sharply. *A truce*, at least for the time being.

"What the hell are you guys doing? Get into the stadium," Van barked, swinging his truck into the parking lot and pointing to the army of journalists that hovered around, growing closer with every second.

He helped Zoey, navy blue ribbon braided in her dark hair, from the truck as Dean and Jensen dropped from the back seat, looking as handsome as ever.

"Has anyone seen Cael today?" Van asked as they circled Arlo and I.

Dean's eyes were dark as he pointed toward the main entrance where Cael seemed to be arguing with Coach. They were standing a foot apart, but his body was rigid as Coach ran his hands through his hair. Whatever they were talking about seemed heavy.

"Come on, boys," Nick ordered in his big boy voice, causing Van to flinch beside him. "We have a game to win."

They all looked to Arlo for confirmation, which came as an exasperated huff. "You heard him." He nodded, and they tightened the circle around Zoey and me. "Stay close."

Before Arlo veered toward the locker room, I grabbed him by the arm and pulled him into an empty side office. He laughed and locked the door behind him. "Not sure Coach would approve of sexual activities in his office before game three."

"This isn't his office," I shrugged it off, "and get your head out of the gutter."

"It's hard when you look like that," he stalked toward me, hands around my hips, and lifted me to the empty desk before slotting himself between my legs. "And smell so good," he groaned against my skin as he peppered my neck with kisses.

"Okay, lover boy," I laughed as his hands roved over my thighs and around the curves of my ass on the table. "I have something important to give you."

He whined, "I have everything of importance in the palm of my hands," he squeezed my ass in protest.

"You're ridiculous. Pay attention." I pushed his arms away playfully, "Hands to yourself," I chirped, and he groaned but removed them and stood with them behind his back like he was in trouble.

I admired him for a moment longer. His sturdy shoulders were pinned back, and his thick neck flexed with restraint as my eyes raked over him. Soft, glowing skin and dark almond eyes that traced my features curiously like he was always trying to learn something new about my face.

He was beautiful, and no matter how long I stared, I never got sick of how he looked back. Love was weird and messy. It was hard at the best of times, but Arlo made it worth it. He made living worth it.

"Here," I dug out a small box from my back pocket and handed it to him.

"What's this?" He asked, not taking it from me.

"Just open it," I laughed and pushed it toward him.

Inside the box was a golden chain. Hanging around it was a simple gold ring that matched the one that hung around my neck. The only difference was the tiny 'e' etched into the band, much like the ring I wore on my thumb.

Arlo looked from the ring, brows scrunched and his smile bright, "is this for me?"

"No, I bought it for my other boyfriend," I groaned as he set the box on the desk and lifted the chain over his head.

"We match now," he flicked the ring against my chest with a smile.

"No matter the outcome today, whether or not you win, I'm proud of you this season. You've put in so much work to get here." I took his hand in mine, staring down at the bruises that maimed the other side. Even in subtle, agonizing pain, he pushed through. I linked our pinky's together and kissed his palm gently. "You got this, Cap."

"Inspiring speech, Blondie." The corners of his mouth dropped into a serious line before he kissed my hand back, "Thank you for being here with me."

"Wouldn't wanna be anywhere else."

"I love you, Ella," he said so softly the words barely registered before he kissed me again.

"I love you too," I let him steal as many as he needed before a knock on the door interrupted us, and Silas poked his head in.

"I need to wrap those before the pregame. Come on."

Arlo pulled back, tucking the ring beneath his unbuttoned dress shirt, but returned for another stolen kiss from my lips. "I love you!" He said again, flicking his finger beneath my chin.

I settled down in my seat next to Zoey, Lucas, and Sawyer on the other side. Mirror images of each other, there was no mistaking them as King siblings. Lucas, the eldest, was tall with short dark hair and the same brown eyes all of them had. Aside from the numbers on their backs, he wore a King jersey that looked well worn in and matched Sawyer's. Eight and Nine. Sawyer looked uncomfortable in his seat as he checked his phone and whispered something to Lucas.

"What's wrong?" I asked, too nosey for my own good.

"Arthur is here." Sawyer huffed, brushing his long dark hair under his ball cap, and settled in his seat, not bothering to look back in the stands at Arthur's typical place in the stadium.

Put your hands together for your Harbor Hornet starting Pitcher and Captain, Arrrrrrrrrrlo King!"

He should have been a bundle of nerves, but he was like a man possessed. From the minute he stepped out on the field with his hands raised above his head, he wore a large, bright smile. He radiated pure energy. Everyone could feel it as they rose and cheered for their Captain. He looked up to the stands, the sun beaming down on him and making him glow. For a brief moment, I thought he was looking for Arthur, but his eyes drifted to where we stood, cheering and hollering for him, and landed on me.

Instead of two fingers, he raised his hand, looping his pinky through the ring around his neck, and pressed it to his heart with a soft, proud smile. I fished mine out and tucked my pinky into it, raising it to my chest in response, "good luck," I whispered, and even though he couldn't hear me, he tipped the brim of his hat in my direction and turned to stand in line for the national anthem.

The guys were sweat-drenched by the fourth inning, with the sun beating down on the afternoon game. The game was at a standstill. Not a single run had been let in. It wasn't the end of the world if they lost this game, but something in my heart told me that Arlo wasn't ready to go for another round. He wanted the championship, and he wanted it today. He may not have looked to Arthur for support, but he had a point to prove, and it wouldn't get done with another game.

"He's still there," Lucas said after Arlo missed his first pitch in the fourth inning.

He wouldn't be for much longer.

So much was riding on this game.

"I'm going to go get a drink," I announced, pushing from my seat.

"Do you want me to come?" Zoey asked, leaning back in hers, but I just shook my head no. She was worried about the media getting a hold of me, but with so much commotion going on with the game, the halls of the Concord were empty as I stepped out of the sun and into the concrete hallway.

As expected, I found Arthur King wandering toward the exit.

"Where are you going?" I asked him as he appeared in the hallway, a tunnel down from me. His old shoulders were broad like his sons but shaky from his old age as he turned to look at me.

"Miss. Miele," his jaw was tight when he turned, and again, there wasn't an ounce of his son in his eyes. It made me wonder what their mother was like. "I'm leaving."

"Why?" I asked, stepping toward him without fear in my body.

"Because it's not worth my time if it's not perfect."

"What happened to you in life that made you so cruel?" I cocked my head to the side, "Not the failed career or dead wife," I took my time to fire the shots clear and true. "Before that, something horrible must have happened to you to treat your sons with such disrespect."

"It's tough love," he responded without hesitation, but his hands were trembling in his pockets. "It pushes them to be better."

"It's not love." I shook my head.

"What does a girl without a family know about love?"

He had done his research since our introductions, but I had family and was given a second chance to have another.

"More than a man with a family he didn't know how to love."

"If you think for a moment that Arlo is capable of love, you're wrong. He has always been an angry little boy without an outlet. He is my son, and I think I know better than some orphaned drug addict how to love him."

His words meant nothing to me. It wasn't something I hadn't been called in the past and would be called in the future. I was comfortable with who I was and secure because of the family I had gained with Arlo and the Nest.

"You act like you're better than them because you made it into the majors, but all they ever wanted was a father. You're a substandard, abusive drunk, and despite your best efforts to turn their hearts rotten, every single one of your sons is magnificent, even the ones I'm still getting to know. It shows their strength and courage that they've survived your ruin."

"How dare you!" Arthur stepped forward, the air leaving my lungs as his hand came up to strike me, but I didn't flinch.

"Oh, Arthur, settle down," I said, inches from his face. "*We're just having a laugh.*"

His expression shifted, a rat caught in a trap before he huffed in my face, spreading his hot, whiskey-laden breath across my cheeks.

"You belong with them." He whispered, backing down and storming out of the tunnel.

He meant for the words to get under my skin, but I was proud to belong to them. I was a Hornet and proud of it.

"How about that drink?" Lucas stood behind me with his arms crossed.

"I'd like that." I followed him to the line, and neither of us spoke. Small talk was hard, and he had just witnessed me taking a chunk out of his father.

"Was that your first time meeting him?" He asked, carrying the two drinks he brought back to our seats.

"Unfortunately, no," I sighed, stepping out into the sun and excitement. "We met on a family weekend at the Shore cabin."

"He went up there?" Lucas looked over his shoulder at me, and I nodded. "Arlo must have had Nick in knots for him to involve Dad."

"I think they're okay now," I added about Nick and Arlo. Lucas shrugged, descending the stairs.

"Nick and Arlo have their ups and downs but always figure it out. I'm not proud that I left them to deal with Dad, but you have to understand getting out was the survival tactic of a twenty-three-year-old, not who I am now." He stopped short of our aisle.

"I understand. You don't have to justify your actions to me." I gave him a tight smile. It would take a minute to figure out my emotions when it came to Lucas leaving his youngest siblings to Arthur's abuse, but I'm sure his reasons were sound.

"Sit down!" An old man barked from the seats to our right, and we scurried across the aisle to take our places. "You're good for him," was the last thing Lucas said to me before settling into this seat.

A year ago, I wasn't good for anyone, not even myself. Lucas would never know what the comment meant, but a sense of pride filled me, warming all the dark corners and lighting them up like fireworks in the night sky.

MIELE

Everyone collectively held their breath.

Two extra innings that had stressfully gone back and forth left the Hornets at four runs with the Vikings at three. They needed a run to tie it and push it to a third extra inning, and Arlo needed to pitch the perfect inning to shut them down. The players were exhausted, and you could tell that exposure to the sun was starting to get to them. It had to be the hottest day of the year so far. I was sweating buckets in my seat and wearing Arlo's jersey and shorts. My legs stuck to the hard plastic, and every time I strove to get comfortable, the skin pulled and slid against it.

Arlo stood on the mound, and even from a distance, I could see how tight every muscle in his body was. Thick, corded, dehydrated veins ran down his neck and arms in ropes as he inhaled once and threw the ball as hard as he could.

Strike.

I couldn't sit in that seat anymore. I was going to be sick to my stomach. I rose, waiting for his back to be turned, and wandered out to the concourse, down through the staff door, swiping my card from my back pocket.

"It's about time, Peachy," Cael waited at the dugout door, that devilish grin I loved so much spread across his face. "You should have broken the rules in the fifth inning. Here," he chucked a staff jacket at me, "stay out of sight."

The energy in the dugout engulfed me like a blanket. Silas took my hand, helping me down over the ledge and into the uneven sand my body knew so well. I hauled myself up against the fence and squished between the players in the dugout.

Home.

It took Arlo less than a second to find me. His eyes trailed from the empty seat in the stands to where I stood in the dugout with a nervous smile. The first time I watched him do this was burned into the back of my mind. The smooth curve of his back arched as all his muscles worked together in tandem to throw the perfect pitch. The corners of his mouth curved slightly as the ball smoked past the bat and into Jensen's glove.

Strike two.

One more, and the Hornets would be national champions for the first time in three years.

Cael pushed onto his toes behind me, head resting on my shoulder with everyone waiting and watching. I expected Arlo to look terrified, but he wasn't. There was confidence, exhaustion, and pride but no fear in his eyes. He shuffled back, watching as Jensen signaled and pulled the ball from his glove.

I heard the pitch, but everything after was noise as everyone in the stadium erupted, the canons lit off, and the confetti started to fall from the sky.

Strike three.

Cael was screaming something as he ran out to meet his teammates. Arlo was scooped from his feet and raised into the air clumsily by his friends and his family.

"Ella," Silas called from the stairs of the dugout. Sweat coated the collar of his shirt, and his beard was in shambles around his big, proud smile, "what are you doing?"

Appreciating.

"Giving them a second," I said in response, and he turned over his shoulder to look at them all jumping up and down, arms wrapped around each other, chanting something over and over again as music and cheers pumped into the stadium.

"You earned the right to celebrate just as much as they did," he said, brows scrunched up as he flipped his hat backward.

"We both know they did this. It had nothing to do with me."

BAD HONEY

I took my eyes off Arlo for ten seconds, and he disappeared. I chewed my lip and looked around for him without luck.

"It had everything to do with you!" Silas argued, but I was too focused on getting my eyes back on Arlo to care.

The huddle separated, the celebrations breaking off into small sections of rambunctious excitement, and as the hug Arlo had Coach in broke apart, his head turned to me. My heart fluttered, breaking into a thousand tiny butterflies as his eyes found mine and his lips curled into the softest smile he could form.

I nodded at him, no words passing between us as he was caught up by Van, who was proclaiming his love for baseball and booze at the top of his lungs. The tears I cried were happy, but I wiped them away with my hand and forced myself to breathe in the moment.

Arlo sauntered through the crowd toward me, still hanging over the dugout fence and watching him. Confetti floated down around him in feathery patterns, sticking to his forearms and chest. His jersey was half unbuttoned, and his hat turned backward over his sweat-drenched black hair, but he had never looked so happy, and it made my heart full to know he had everything he had ever wanted. He deserved it all.

"Hey, have you seen my girlfriend around?" He teased, hands wrapping around the navy cushioned railing. The trap muscles in his shoulders tensed, and his forearms stretched as he looked back, pretending to search.

"No, it's a little chaotic right now. Maybe I can help. What does she look like?" I trailed my eyes lazily down his throat, where the sweat pooled in the sharp, muscular lines of his collarbone and chest.

"Big brown doe eyes, soft blonde hair, prettiest smile in the world, smells like heaven." He paused to look me over, eyes tracing the curves of my body. "Very agreeable, rule follower, never gets in trouble. Certainly not sassy or outspoken. Answers affectionately to the name Blondie." He leaned in closer, showing off that crooked, playful smile.

"Sorry, I haven't seen her." I ghosted my lips over his. "Although, if you close your eyes and call me *baby*, I'm sure I can help you forget about her."

"I could never. She's all I think about," he whispered, and it sucked all the air from my lungs.

I had waited long enough. I tangled my fingers into the hair at his nape and pulled Arlo tightly against me as I brought our lips together. He nearly toppled over the barrier. His hands wrapped into my hair, palms pressed to my jaw as he kissed me back until we were both left breathless.

"You stink," I scrunched my nose and pulled away from him slightly. He hung over the banister, his hips rocking as he put his hands back and pushed down from it.

"Eleven innings in the sun will do that to a man," he laughed, chucking off his hat and running his fingers through his sweaty, damp hair as he looked over his shoulder at the team still running circles around each other.

"Go celebrate," I whispered.

"Don't go anywhere, Blondie." He pointed at me.

"Wouldn't think of it, Cap."

I chatted with his brothers and Zoey as the team took photos and did press conferences. I wandered through the empty concourse and down into the medical wing as the guys showered, and slowly, the numbers dwindled. They were all making their way to a party at Delta, Cael promising to behave if he was allowed to join. Zoey had left with him and Van, agreeing to keep an eye on him when she saw how nervous I had become.

A party was a temptation for Cael, but I trusted him, and to prove it, I had let him go without a fuss. I found Silas in a clean shirt, organizing medical supplies from his bag into the cupboards.

"Ask me then, Mr. August," I leaned against the door frame. It was time to take what I wanted.

Silas laughed softly, and the sound echoed through the empty room.

"That calendar is the bane of my existence. I told them I didn't want to be in it, but they insisted." He didn't look up from his bag. "*Harbor's most eligible bachelor.* You know Cael bought a box of those and wrote my phone number in them before handing them out in the courtyard."

"And you still don't have a wife?" I teased. "You might wanna work on that."

"Glad to have you back, Miele." He huffed.

"I nailed my finals. I'm a grown-up now, and I need some real-world experience. So, ask me."

"You've been spending too much time with Arlo," he groaned, setting down the pack of bandages against the bed and looking up at me. "Ella, it would be an honor if you joined the Hornet's team full-time. Strictly as a recovery therapist, no more dugouts for you." He shook his head, "I can't have you punching people."

"He earned that," I stood by my actions with confidence. "I would love a job."

"He sure did, and it's yours, no questions."

"You don't have to talk to Coach about it?"

"It was his idea," Silas nodded, "I wasn't sure if you'd want to stay or if disappearing was your plan once school finished. He had faith that you would stick around."

"Why?" I asked.

"Because Cael told him so, and despite their differences, Ryan holds his son's opinions in high regard." He had vouched for me. "You start Monday," he shrugged. "This isn't going to be easy. Now that we're a winning team, there's more pressure to hold that title."

I nodded. I understood his concerns. "I'm going to go find Arlo," I smiled and patted the door frame.

"Give my regards to Mr. January," he smirked.

I wandered down the hall to the locker room expecting to find more than just Arlo sitting, still in his ball pants with his hand against the locker and his eyes closed.

"Hey, handsome," I cooed, kicking off my shoes and padding across the carpet in the center of the room to curl up next to him. He opened one eye to look at me and extended his arm so I could tuck into this side. "You didn't shower?"

"I'm too exhausted." He rolled his head over so it was resting on mine. "I heard you went toe-to-toe with Arthur King today." He nudged me with a soft laugh. "You gotta stop doing that."

"No," I responded.

"He's not worth it," Arlo shook his head and buried his face into my hair.

"You are." I shrugged. I would fight a thousand Arthurs for him, a thousand more Logans. Every single one of the people didn't understand who Arlo was and what he stood for. "We protect each other, remember. Two steps at a time."

"Alright, tough guy," he laughed. "It impressed the hell out of Luc. I don't think I've ever seen him crack a smile."

"It was a relief to know your brothers are human. I was starting to get worried after dealing with you and Nick."

"What's that supposed to mean?" Arlo squeezed my side with his fingers and groaned from the pain he had forgotten about.

I pulled back, taking his hand in mine while laughing that both of us were bruised and broken but still so happy. "It means you two have more drama than a telenovela."

"They're going to need surgery," he tugged his hand away from mine and flexed the fingers sorely out in front of him. Throughout the season, the tendons in his fingers had become so overworked that the only fix was surgery. We both knew it, and Silas had cemented the idea. It wasn't a suggestion. It was an order. He had to have surgery.

"All that work," he sighed.

"Surgery isn't the end of your career," I noted.

"Scouts will look at that as trouble. I was pushing my luck with my age as it is. This is a death sentence."

"That's not up to the scouts. It's up to you." I pushed out of his arm, checking the locker room for anyone else. I wandered back to the doors and locked them, tugging on them to ensure they were closed.

"Trouble," he laughed with an exhausted breath.

"Let's get you in the shower before you ponder any more extreme life decisions."

"I have a couple to discuss, but they can wait," he said as I dropped to my knees to help him out of his cleats. He tried to work at the buttons of his shirt, but his face twisted in pain, and I shooed him away.

"Just let me do it," I smiled at him, running my hands over his calves and thighs. I flicked the metal clasp of his pants and helped him shimmy free of them before slotting myself between his knees and working on his buttons.

BAD HONEY

I kissed a soft line down his chest as I went, lower and lower, until the last one popped free, and he shucked the sweaty, sandy fabric from his strong shoulders. His muscles were still so tense from all the exercise, and I couldn't help but admire him in the light of the locker room.

Running my fingers against his stomach and along the band of his boxers, he took slow, deliberate breaths that turned shallow as I wrapped around his ribcage and back up over his taut chest to where the ring hung between his pecs.

I left him there, wandering toward the locker room showers. I heard him push from his seat to follow as I disappeared behind the tiled wall and into the showers. I waited until he was back in sight as I unbuttoned my shorts and pushed them down over my hips, bending at the waist to show off the tight black lace thong I wore beneath as a reward. I unbuttoned the jersey he had given me, one button at a time, until it hung loose against my stomach.

The water pouring from the head was cold initially, causing me to hiss as it soaked through my matching bra beneath the jersey. I ran my hands through my hair, turning to find him leaning against the wall, staring at me.

"The restraint is fascinating," I commented.

"I was just waiting to see what you'd do next," he cocked his head to the side. "You were doing so good on your own."

Mischief grew on his face in the form of a smile, and I could see how hard he was through his boxers as I trailed my hand down between my legs. The fabric was soaked through and easily pushed aside by my fingers. His eyes drifted down over my body like the water in long roving strokes as his chest rose and fell in shallow breaths, trying to control himself.

I leaned back against the cool tiles and braced myself with a hand to the wall as I worked my fingers through my folds. The urge to order him to touch me thrummed through me, but two could play the game he started. I let the water roll down over me, closing my eyes as I slid two fingers inside of myself, and a loud moan fell from my lips.

His hands were on me within seconds. The clasp of my bra snapped as his mouth wrapped around my pebbled nipples, and his hand braced against my lower back beneath the soaked fabric of his baseball jersey. His boxers had been discarded in the shuffle, and his erection pressed to my thigh as he rocked up against me.

Pressed up against the wall, he kissed me, teeth and tongues clashing together like we hadn't touched each other in months. Heat flooded my body and sent my senses into overdrive, every touch and tickle from his fingertips igniting a primal need for more.

"Never take that off," he warned, teeth grazing my bottom lip as his fingers tugged at the wet jersey. "You look fucking amazing in it." Arlo pulled away to draw a line with his lips down my chest, over the swell of my breasts, and across my stomach as his hands raked down my sides and he dropped to his knees.

"And it drives me nuts to know everyone is jealous you're mine." His words made my stomach flutter and chest get warm as his teeth nibbled at the fabric of my underwear, dragging it over my hips and sliding it down. He carefully helped me step from them, ghosting his tongue over my most sensitive parts as he stood again and pushed his erection against my dripping core.

The water muffled the sounds that dripped from me as he pushed two fingers deep inside and lazily circled my clit with his thumb.

"Arlo," I whined, unashamed of how badly I needed him inside of me.

Steam billowed up from the floor in pillowy circles as he removed his fingers and aligned himself to my entrance, equally as eager to be inside. It was surprising every time how much I stretched as he eased within, remaining still for a moment to cherish the sweet feeling of coming together.

"You take me so well," he said, pressing hot kisses along my neck as his hands dug into the meat of my ass and lifted me into his hold.

"High praises," I giggled, face hidden in the crook of his neck while I held onto him, the feeling of fullness overwhelming my senses. "Quit wasting time and fuck me. We have some celebrating to do."

"Baby, this is celebrating." He growled.

The sound of water muddled with the heavy pants and gasps as Arlo picked up his pace and thrust roughly inside of me. I clenched around him, wrapping one of my legs around his waist as the orgasm coiled deep in my belly. My resolve to drag it out crumbled the moment his thumb returned to rub my clit in fast circles. I dragged my nails down his back, tugging a throaty moan from his lips as his hips worked relentlessly to pull us both to the edge. Up and over the edge, both of us tightened drastically against each other as our climaxes exploded, and my eyes rolled back into my head, completely out of control.

Arlo's hips continued to rock slowly as he came to a finish with his lips against my wet skin. "That was better than winning," he laughed and brushed a finger against the soaked hem of the jersey.

"Good showing, Mr. January," I said, trying not to laugh too hard when he looked up at me with a grin. Dark strands of his hair fell against his forehead, and the fluorescent lighting of the shower room made his eyes glimmer. I kissed the corners of his mouth, giggling as his fingers dug into my thighs.

"I'm burning that calendar when I find out where you put it," he rolled his eyes and kissed me again.

KING

"ARLO!" The whole party cheered as we walked through the front door, hand in hand. We had to stop at home to get a change of clothes, and it ended with Ella bent over the hood of the fastback.

The image of her ass bouncing against my dick still seared into my brain as she slipped into the black t-shirt she was wearing, and then again when she bent over to dig through her bag for her jeans and even then when she padded beside me, fingers tightly tucked into mine.

I couldn't wait to get her home. I was ready to stay in our room for a month to compensate for lost time.

"Where the hell have you two been?" Zoey scoffed, already tipsy in Van's arms, as he leaned down to wrap around her tiny frame.

"Fucking in the Hornet's locker room," Ella said, and Zoey raised an eyebrow at her.

"How come we haven't-" Zoey turned to Van with disappointment, and he just gave both Ella and me a dirty look.

She laughed, and everyone laughed with her, but I just scowled with the shake of my head. I tugged her through to the kitchen, throwing her up by her hips to the counter, and leaned between her legs. She ran a hand over my shoulder and down my chest, resting it on the soft fabric of my black T-shirt.

"What, no throne tonight?" Jensen teased as he made his way by, pointing to the ugly leather chair in the corner where I usually sat to avoid every booze bag at the party. It was where I sat the first time I looked at Ella. "Tonight of all nights!" He threw a beer in my direction, and I popped it open on the counter before handing it over my shoulder to Ella behind me.

"Throne looks a little different now," Ella giggled into my ear as her arms wrapped around my neck.

"The view is better too," I kissed the inside of her wrist gently, "where is—"

"Right here, Dad," Cael paraded into the kitchen, arm still in a sling, a smile on his stupid boyish face. "And sober to boot."

He moved past the crowd, angling himself in so he was positioned beside us and the fridge, leaning down against the counter with his good elbow. "Hey, Peachy," he smiled up at her through thick lashes, "do you wanna dance?" he asked, and Ella instantly shook her head no.

Cael clicked his tongue against his teeth, "boo."

Ella nudged him with her sneaker, but he didn't budge. They were playing a game I didn't understand. Months later, I still hated being outside of their jokes.

"You wanna get drunk and make out in a closet?" He asked her, and I couldn't stop the snarl that left my throat.

"Easy princess, it was a joke." Cael wiggled his nose at me, and I flicked it with my hand.

"How about a game of beer pong?" Ella suggested, her legs squeezing around me, "Loser pays for pizza."

"We play doubles in this house," I said, leaning my head back against her.

"You better find a teammate then," Ella leaned in close and dragged a soft upside-down kiss from my lips before pushing me away from her and sliding off the counter.

"So quickly her loyalty shifts!" Cael's laughter boomed as she circled to where Zoey stood.

"Kitten was my partner anyways," I threw my arm around his shoulders with a smile, "it's you that needs a partner, Blondie."

"I have one," she smiled, wiggling her nose at Zoey beside her. "You guys are so screwed."

"What, no guise of being bad this time?"

"To be fair, I was just trying to impress you," Ella quipped, "I think it worked. Time to toss the niceties aside."

"You won't win twice. Cael's sober this time. You're the one playing with the handicap, baby."

Zoey stumbled as Van let go of her and leaned against the counter, "I've won in worse conditions. And you're in a sling."

"Alright, you're on. Losers buy pizza." I leaned forward to meet her stare.

Everyone cheered and flooded into the backyard, where the table was already propped up, and Van was carrying a case of beer in our direction. It didn't take long for everything to get set up before we stood across from each other just like that first night, only this time, I would get to go home a winner no matter what.

It also didn't take long to realize that Cael and I had entered another trap. Zoey missed her first shot with her eyes crossed and a giggle forming on her lips. Ella didn't miss, her eyes locked on mine. It seemed silly, almost foolish, but my chest was filled with a warmth that engulfed every worry I'd ever had. Ella Miele was the only person I ever wanted to stare at again. I wanted to wake up to her and go to bed with her. I wanted to share every thought and dream. My fingers itched to touch her, not even six feet from me, and I missed her.

I didn't even blink when the ball hit the beer and spilled out onto the table.

"You better pay attention to what's important, Cap," she cooed at me.

"Oh, I am," I fished the ball from the cup and tossed the beer back. "Don't you worry about me."

Her cheeks turned a soft pink in response as I accidentally chucked the ball from the table. Cael's shot soared clean and true, hitting the furthest left cup. "Turns out I'm better sober!" He cheered as Zoey pounded back her cup.

Zoey didn't miss a single shot after her first one, "looks like I'm better sober, too," she smirked. I wasn't sure if it was luck or sheer talent, but she couldn't be stopped. "I warned you," she flashed her teeth at me. "We were taught by the best."

BAD HONEY

Ella smiled from behind her with a shrug of her tiny, perfect shoulders. "Ethan was a really good big brother." She rolled the ring around on her finger, and where I usually saw the sadness in her eyes, there was happiness and remembrance. "He was an even better teacher."

"Beer pong, right hooks. Life skills, really," Cael teased with a shrug.

"I don't know why we agree to these games," I shook my head with a smile.

"Hey, did you hear!" Dean bulldozed down from the back steps onto the lawn, shoving his massive frame through the crowd toward us. "They're sending some hotshot reporter to interview us for a television segment!"

"They wanna interview us?" Cael laughed wildly.

"Something about wanting to document our fight back to the top?" Dean hung himself over Van, slumped in a lawn chair, watching the game.

"Maybe they'll send Lisa Jackson," Cael cooed, "god, she's the prettiest damn girl I've ever seen in my life."

"There's no way a woman that smart ever looks at you and thinks, that's the man I want to be with." Van laughed.

"Shut up, Mitchell. Just because you tricked *Sour Patch* into thinking that you're a catch doesn't mean the rest of us are brainwashed by your mullet and horrible mustache," Cael kicked the leg of the lawn chair and sent it buckling under the weight of Van.

"Hey, Blondie," I whispered across the table, staying out of the bickering contest that had erupted.

She looked over at me with a smile, my sunshine incarnate.

"Yes?" She mouthed quietly.

"You wanna dance, get drunk, and make out in a closet?" I winked at her.

When she nodded, her smile grew, and so did the temperature in my body.

"How come that works for him?" Cael scoffed, catching wind of the interaction.

"Love makes you do stupid things," she responded as I circled the table toward her and scooped her into my arms. She wrapped her legs around me and over my shoulder, she said to a disappointed and confused Cael. "One day, you'll understand."

EPILOGUE

MIELE
AUGUST LONG WEEKEND

The sun was so warm coming out of August that I swore I was sweating through my tank top as I tied my sneakers in the dugout. Cael was still recovering from his surgery two weeks before, and Arlo's was fast approaching, but we thought it might be nice to take a break and get out of the city. It turned out that most of the team was following behind. It was nice to have everyone back together before most of them disappeared for the real world or were separated for the few winter months when no one would be playing ball.

He pouted to my left because he wasn't allowed to play still and had shown up to the field in his workout gear.

"You can play bat catcher, and you can't swing a bat," I warned, standing up from the bench.

"That's not fair, Peach," he whined.

"Buck up, Misery, you don't get an opinion." He rolled his eyes at his newly titled nickname.

Arlo stifled a laugh from where he was leaning against the metal pole of the awning, shirtless in his gym shorts. I ran my hand against his taut stomach muscles.

"Be nice. He's sad," I said to him in passing as I went out to warm up my arm.

"You heard her. Doctor's orders." Arlo mumbled in the least sympathetic way as Cael began to bargain with him. Some things never change.

Zoey handed me a hat, and I settled it over my braided hair, turning over my shoulder to look at the boys in the dugout.

"How's he doing?" She asked about Cael.

"Sober, sore, sad." I sighed.

"But sober," she added optimistically. "Triple threat."

"He's doing well," I nodded. "It's going to be a long recovery without pain meds. Most nights, he barely sleeps, and when he does, I don't because he cries in his sleep."

"Cael's going to be okay, Ella," Zoey smiled at me, "He's recovering in the ideal environment, and he has you to look after him."

"I learned from the best," I squeezed her fingers at my side. "I love you, Zo," I said quietly, and she said it without pause.

"You know, in four years, I've never had to play baseball until now." She scowled at me and rolled up the hem of her knee-high socks.

"You're going to sweat to death in those," I laughed.

"But I'll look so cute," she popped her hip in her tiny jean shorts and polo top before shucking her hand into a glove and running to the field to Van. Who slapped her ass and promptly pointed her in the direction of where she needed to be.

Arlo was first to bat because he couldn't help himself, stepping out into the box with a smirk, a ring dangling from the necklace I gifted him, and a hat turned backward. He was handsome as ever, bathed in sunlight and smiling like a kid in his natural environment.

He had gotten a few calls from major teams across the country asking about his hands, taking meetings, and inquiring about his future, but he hadn't settled for any of them. He had given up hope that he would be drafted, but the door to his career hadn't been wholly slammed shut. Coach offered him a position with the team staff if he wanted, and a few other college teams across the counter had similar ideas.

"You gonna daydream all day?" He called out, swinging the bat lazily at his side.

I didn't grant him a response before throwing him a softball pitch that was nothing but a meatball, forgoing the windmill throws just for the day. He caught the pitch easily against his bat and kicked out to the left field above Zoey's head. He rounded first quickly, "You let me have that!" He pointed to me with a grin on his face.

"Everyone needs a win, Arlo," I called back, watching as Van tried to make up the distance Zoey had fallen short on.

"Don't you ever go easy on me, baby!" He hopped over second, Dean juking to the left in a sad attempt to slow him down.

"Next time!" I laughed as the ball soared over my head and crashed into the fence just behind Cael's face, who wasn't being helpful, as he dropped to his knees laughing.

"You are zero help as a bat catcher!" I yelled, causing some of the other guys to lose their shit, laughing, "Someone stop him!"

I ran to cut off third as Cael chucked the ball with his bad arm, but the ball went over my head and passed Dougie's glove. Arlo stumbled coming home from laughing so hard and tumbled around in a circle before slamming into the cage with a loud thump.

"I'm not falling for that again, Arlo King!" I called him from the mound when he didn't get up.

He cradled his knee in his hands, his face scrunched in a ball.

"I don't know, Peach... that looks bad!" Cael said, starting to walk toward his crunched-up position. Worry began eating at my conscience when Cael kneeled beside him with wide eyes. "El—"

Instantly, I was moving, the concern in Cael's voice pumping through me as I slid on my knees to look him over. He looked up at me, dirty fingers curled and palm to the sky to reveal a dainty diamond ring in the center.

"That was awfully dramatic, Blondie."

"Arlo," his name came out in a whimper as I tried not to cry, but the moment his palm touched my cheek, the tears started and didn't stop. "What the hell?"

"You needed your own, one that wasn't attached to your grief," he touched the ring that hung around my neck, "or mine. One just for you."

"That's silly, I love this one." I rubbed it between my thumb, "and—"

"And nothing, when I gave you that ring back, it was a promise that I wasn't ever going to stop loving you. You're it. This is our family," he said, looking at Cael and back at me. "You're my family."

He smiled and gripped my chin with his fingers. Cael hovered, impatiently rocking on the balls of his feet, and all of the other guys had started to huddle around.

"Just say yes."

"To what? You haven't even properly asked." I teased, my brows coming together in a furrowed line, tears streaming down my face. "You drive me insane."

"Marry me, Ella, so I can spend the rest of my life driving you insane."

I looked down at the ring, my heart beating so fast that I thought it might jump from my chest if I didn't hold it in. I turned my left hand over, letting Arlo place the ring on my left finger, but before he could kiss me like he had been so desperate to do, I linked my pinky into the ring around his neck and pulled it against my heart. It tugged him closer, and I rested my head against his forehead, staring between us.

"Promise me."

"The world."

"Nothing so trivial," I laughed.

Arlo King would give me anything if I asked him. That had always been him. It would always be us. But staring at him, the wind pushing around the sweaty strands of his dark hair, covered in sand, and surrounded by all our friends, I knew I had everything I could ever want. I just needed him.

"Promise me you won't ever stop loving me," he smiled before I could finish and returned the gesture. Linking his pinky through the ring hanging around my neck, pulling it tightly to his chest, "because I don't think I'll survive the fallout."

Arlo kissed me then, harder and more profound than ever. His fingers tangled around my neck, pulling me against him without hesitation or restraint. I pulled back from him, cupping his face with my hand and finally letting go of the breath I was holding.

"I love you," I whispered.

BAD HONEY

"Mom and Dad are getting married!" Cael screamed from the top of his lungs, tackling Arlo with both arms and tumbling him into the sand. "Fuck!" He hissed in pain but started laughing at the same time. He grabbed Arlo by the face and kissed him before scrambling to his feet and taking off. "Worth it!" He screamed over his shoulder.

"Cael Cody, I'm going to fucking kill you," Arlo jumped to his feet and chased after him muttering a thousand different threats as he went.

I rolled onto my back and looked up at the cloudy sky. The sun peeking through created a long beam of light that touched the horizon.

"Thank you," I whispered to the clouds, "for sending me them."

The breeze blew over the ball diamond in response, like Ethan had said, a quiet, *you're welcome.* Then the sun disappeared behind the clouds, my tears disappearing into the sand.

I had found my home, or better yet, home had found me.

EXCLUSIVE CHAPTER

A first look into Honey Pot, book 2 in the Hornet's Nest Series
2017

"Cael, don't," I warned, putting my hand up to stop him from coming any closer. He stalked me, his white t-shirt sticking to his biceps and abs, covered in mud and leaves from the creek, with the devil's smile on his face. "I swear to god, if you touch me, I will kill you!"

I screeched, stumbling backward as he chased me up the embankment away from the rushing river of the creek that ran between our properties. My feet slipped in the wet dirt beneath my toes. I slid down before I could get to the top and crashed into Cael. His legs flew out from beneath him as he collided with me and wrapped his arms around me to protect me as we rolled to the base of the hill and back into the creek.

"Cael!" I gasped as I broke from the surface. My whole body curled up from the frigid temperatures, and I barely made it back to the shore before my toes and fingers began to feel stiff and numb from the water.

"That wasn't even my fault!" He helped me out of the water, and we rolled onto the backs, sopping wet and breathing heavily.

His head lolled to the side, and the sun bathed his tanned skin in the warm light that peaked through the covering of trees above us. His hair was so light from the summer sun that it was practically bleached blonde, and I had the insane urge to brush the streaks of mud that clung to it around his forehead and ears.

BAD HONEY

We lay there like that in the grass with only the sound of heavy breathing and the wind pushing through the trees to fill the silence.

"Mama said you're leaving early." I used all the courage to say the words that had settled heavily between us in silence for the last three weeks of August spent together.

"The job in Rhode Island at the university needs him up there before the season starts," Cael inhaled sharply, "I don't wanna go, but," he trailed off into silence.

"You don't have much of a choice," I shrugged. I wound a piece of long dark hair around my finger, trying to avoid the devastating look that swam around in the glassy blue color of Cael's eyes.

II could count the flecks of green that stared back at me, heartbroken and already so tragically lonely. Cael and I had never been apart. Not in an entire seventeen years. We had been born three hours apart, in the same hospital. Our mother's best friends, our houses on the same land in backwater Texas an two hours outside of Austin, our hearts beating to the same rhythm.

Cael was a part of me, and in the most bittersweet way, I was a part of Cael.

"What's going to happen?" I asked him, terrified of the answer.

Distance and time didn't apply to us. It never had.

"We'll talk daily on the phone," he said, rolling over onto his stomach and inching closer to me. "We can email, and I'll even send stupid letters."

At this distance, I could count every freckle on his face and trace them until I found all my favorite constellations. The most noticeable was the cluster that decorated his left cheekbone. Sharp and smooth, I was tempted to reach out and touch it. Curious to the point of being in agony over whether or not Cael felt the same about me.

If he loved me like I loved him.

"Clem," my name rolled from his lips. "Did you hear me?"

I knew that the pain was written all over my face. It wasn't something I would be able to hide much longer, if at all anymore, and Cael had always been able to read me like an open book.

"Letters," I said softly, dropping my stare and focusing on the tie around my dress. "I want letters."

"Every day," he promised, brushing his finger beneath my chin and raising my gaze to meet his. "Momma will get sick of buying stamps. I'll send so many."

"We were supposed to leave together," I whispered so softly it's barely recognizable over the breeze. Letters wouldn't be enough. The sadness I felt couldn't be satiated by words on paper. Cael would go off and charm every pretty girl in Rhode Island. He would fall in love, find himself, and never think of me again. The thought of slowly fading out of his existence was terrifying and heartbreaking, but he didn't seem to care.

"Now I'll be alone." The words left my throat, choked and clumsy, as I felt a tear slip down my cheek.

"You won't be alone, Clem. You got other friends. I'm just one lame guy," Cael suggested, trying to bring my mood up. "You'll be okay."

"I don't have any other friends, Cael," I said as I sat upright in the grass. His grip on my chin suddenly felt too hot, and I needed some space. He moved with me, sitting up, the fabric of his dirty white shirt tugged against his skin and crumbled around his hips.

"You have other friends. Everyone loves *you*! I'm just the chubby girl you take pity on because we grew up together. They don't see me as a friend. They see me as your little sister, and so do you!"

I swallowed so tightly it hurt my throat.

"I'm just your shadow."

Cael flinched like I had slapped him.

I did everything in my power to hold the wave of tears at bay as they pricked the corners of my eyes and formed a lump in my throat. He would never love me the way I loved him. I pushed from the grass when he didn't say a word, his blue eyes glossy from fighting his emotions. He simply watched me walk away. I stomped through the path, taking out all my anger and agony on the trees and moss around me.

"Hey, lovebug," my mom cooed from the porch as I straightened myself out and wiped away the tears. "What's wrong? You're all covered in mud, baby."

My mom stood from the garden and wiped her hands on her overalls, making to stop me before I entered the house through the back door, but I just brushed past her, avoiding her gaze.

BAD HONEY

"Nothing, Momma, I just tripped." I couldn't look at her. My mom would see through the facade and lies, furthering the breakdown that edged closer. "I'm going to go shower. Tell Cael I went to the library. If he comes looking, I don't wanna talk to him."

As the back door swung shut, I heard Mom call out for more explanation, but I kept walking up through the house to my loft where the world couldn't hurt me, and Cael couldn't come.

I clicked the door closed once I was inside, making sure the latch was tight, and no one could bother me before climbing into bed in my muddy dress and muffling my sobs with the soft, clean fabric of my pillow.

I cried myself to sleep, my shoulders sore and head pounding, every part of my body in pain over losing my best friend. The reality that he was leaving had finally sunk in, but the truth that the distance would change everything about us had hit me like a freight train.

When I woke, the sun had gone down, and my pillow was damp from the tears I cried, making my face sticky and clammy. I groaned, pushing from my bed and stripping from my dress, leaving it in a puddle on the floor near the foot of my bed. I wandered to my bathroom, still painted sky blue from my sixth birthday, when my dad let me pick whatever color I wanted. I ran warm water, briefly staring at my pale, freckled face and stringy dark hair in the mirror.

The girl that no one could love.

Cael Cody's shadow.

The water seemed to ease the tension from my shoulders but only made my headache worse and, after a while, made me dizzy enough to sink to the floor of the tub and put my head between my knees. I had been so stupid to think that Cael would ever see me as anything but a friend.

I distinctly remember the moment I saw Cael as something more, the exact day to the hour the sun cast differently on my image of him. He had stepped down from his porch, baby blue button-down undone at the top to show the gold necklaces he had stacked up on top of each other before the party. His hair was longer than usual, and chunks of dirty blonde had fallen against his forehead. He smiled at me that day, and I felt my chest open up and swallow the feeling of being loved by him whole.

I climbed from the shower, trying to focus on anything, but my mind kept slipping back to his face. It was a year ago, somewhere between being kids and turning into teenagers, I had forgotten how to be his friend and started to become a lovesick puppy. I just hadn't realized it until that moment.

I rummaged through my drawers for shorts and a tank top, changing into them and drying my hair before chucking the towel back into the washroom. Quickly, I changed the dirty sheets on my bed, kicking the muddy ones into a pile and crawling back into my fresh-smelling bed. I pulled my journal from the dresser beside me. The top was carved apart and painted on with tiny little doodles that I couldn't get out of my head.

I kicked around under my sheets until my feet hit the tiny knit bag full of pens, and I dragged it up to myself, picking out my favorite black one before throwing the bag somewhere into the void of my messy room. I could hear my parents in the house below, dancing in the kitchen to Tim McGraw like they always did.

I sighed. I had been taught that love is forever. It's like cement. Once you're in it, there's no getting out. I craved it, longed for it, and it seemed to always pass me by in the form of watching Cael pull girls into his lap or flirt with the cheerleaders during lunch hour in the cafeteria. I had a list as long as my leg of the girls Cael had loved that weren't me.

Time seemed to creep by, and as the sun set in the sky, a soft knock came from my door, scaring me into hiding my journal beneath my pillow. I padded across my ugly, thrifted floor rug and turned on the small, dingy lamp on my desk beside the door before popping the latch and opening it.

"Mrs. Matthews said you didn't eat," Cael stood before me, his eyes cast to the ground like he was in trouble holding out a plate of my favorite fries. "I went and got them from Duke's."

"Why?" I asked like I didn't know the answer, my door still half closed like it might protect me or even stop me from letting Cael come in.

BAD HONEY

"Because I made you sad, Clem, and I didn't mean to," he looked up at me through his thick lashes, and I could see that he had been crying too.

"You didn't make me sad, Cael," I bit. "I made myself sad, wishing for something I couldn't have."

"What do you want? I'll go get it for you," he said without hesitation, and I felt my heart shatter like a piece of china inside my chest.

"What I want, you can't just go get," I said, strained and twangy.

"Just tell me what it is, Clem, I won't leave until I know. Your momma and daddy went to a movie, you're all alone in this big house, and I sat outside for two hours until they let me in. And Mr. Matthews threatened me with a gun before they left, so you better tell me what you want before he comes back and shoots me."

"Stop!" I yelled louder than I ever had before, and Cael's head cocked to the side in surprise. "I can't tell you."

I said each word with purpose and intent so he understood that it wasn't something he could buy from a store, wasn't something he could fix with his pretty smile and perfect jokes.

"You can tell me anything, Clementine," he said, pushing his foot against the door, "and you're gonna tell me right now what's making you so sad."

"What if saying it out loud makes you sad?" I asked, backing away as he made his way into my room.

His flowery blue eyes scanned his surroundings, and for a second, I had forgotten that this was the first time he had ever been here. My daddy was strict about boys being in my room. Even knowing Cael from diapers didn't give him special privileges.

"I'm already sad Clem, I have to leave you."

If my heart wasn't already cracking in two, Keith Urban started to play over the radio in the kitchen below, and the lyrics to Making Memories of Us cascaded up into the loft.

His soft voice made me want to cry, "Don't do that."

"What?" he asked. He set the plate of food on the dresser as he explored further into my room. "Tell you the truth," he shrugged, his jaw flexing as he looked around and avoided my stare. "Come into your room?" He asked with a soft smile, "It smells like lavender in here."

"Cael!" I said, my emotions bursting, "Don't force me to tell you."

"We don't keep secrets from each other," he played with the threaded friendship bracelet on his wrist that I gave him the summer prior. It was sun-bleached and frayed, but he never took it off.

"This isn't a secret," I replied, walking back until my heels pressed tightly against my side table.

"Then tell me," he begged now, a sound I had heard from him so often that I thought myself immune. But his eyes seemed bluer, his voice pleading, and all resolve in my body cracked under the weight of the sound.

"I want you," I whispered, tears rolling down my face. "My first kiss, my first time," I swallowed the cotton ball in my throat. "I wanted you—"

When I looked up, he closed the space between us, and his hands were tangled into my damp hair without hesitation. His fingers pressed into the back of my neck as he collided with my mouth, his lips tracing the shape of my own. Breathlessly, he pushed into me, begging silently to come closer, but I was paralyzed, my hands gripping the table, my toes curling into the carpet.

I stared in surprise for a long moment at the freckles on his nose before finally closing my eyes and sinking weightlessly into the soft feeling of his mouth. My hands came up around his waist and gripped tightly into his shirt, my fingers tugging at the fabric. He pulled back, and a slow whimper dripped from my lips, following his path as he peppered more delicate kisses along the corners of my mouth and up my jaw to my ear.

"Your daddy's definitely gonna shoot me now, Clem," he chuckled, nibbling at my ear lobe.

"Wait," I said, pushing him back. My head was dizzy from his kiss, and my heart was beating faster than I had ever felt it move, "are you only doing this because I'm sad, Cael, because--"

"Clementine Mary Matthews, please be quiet for once in your life," he hushed me with another long kiss that felt like flying.

He gripped the back of my neck as his hand raked down my side and cupped my thigh, lifting my leg until he was wrapped around his waist and rolled his hips against mine. I could feel every inch of him through my pajama shorts, and suddenly, everything felt too real and too warm.

"Hey," Cael tugged back without me even opening my mouth and moving his hands to cup my face as he looked at me. "What's wrong? Was the kiss that bad?"

He laughed, and I felt the shift in my anxiety from the sound, "no, no," I shook my head in his hands. "Of course not."

"It's too fast," he said, rolling his tongue over his bottom lip. "I'm sorry."

He took a whole step back, and before I could even think about what I was doing, I followed him, linking our fingers together in the soft light that peered from my bedroom lamp. "I'm not..." I stopped, looking away from him, trying to collect myself when he hooked a finger around my chin and pulled me back. "Experienced like the other girls."

Cael's pouty lips curled at the corners, "Clem," he laughed, his nose scrunching up and his eyes catching the moonlight, "do you think I slept with all those girls?"

"Well, you—" I started and then realized how horrible I sounded, "I just thought--"

"I'm never opposed to a little heavy petting, but Plum, I've never slept with any of them." His finger slipped absentmindedly between the strap of my tank top and skin as he talked, his eyes drifting down to my shoulders and collarbones.

"That seems like a secret, Cael," I said, not trying to start a fight, just wanting to shift the embarrassment away from my jealousy.

"You never asked."

I gave him a sharp look that only made him laugh, but he roped his fingers through my hair again, moving slower. This time, he kissed my bottom lip, tugging it into his mouth. My hand tangled into the collar of his shirt, brushing against the buttons and pulling him closer as he took his time kissing me.

"How come you never told me you wanted to kiss me?" Cael asked, his breath hot on my neck.

"You never asked," I smiled against his mouth as his tongue slid between my lips and tangled with my own, sending all my senses haywire. I felt his fingers play at the hem of my shirt, tickling a line across my stomach to my hips before he wrapped them tight and tugged me closer.

"I'm asking now." He said in such a sober tone that all the thoughts in my head went fuzzy, and all I could focus on was how nice it felt to have his hands all over me and his lips on my mind. "Clem, don't make me beg," Cael whined against me as his hands moved further under my shirt, tickling my ribs slowly as he worked his way up.

"I think you should," I giggled, skirting away from his touch to steady my pounding hard. I pushed back and sat down on my bed, staring up at him with stars in my vision and butterflies in my chest. I had forgotten how tall he had grown over the summer, towering over me with built-in waves of slim muscles from farm work and horse riding.

I watched him roll the blue button over his shoulders, dropping it to the floor and showing his toned muscles beneath. I had been around him more naked than he was now a thousand times, but the sight of him made my breath catch in my throat. He flicked the heavy metal latch of his belt buckle and slipped the leather from its loops, the sound echoing through my room. Without a second to breathe, he shucked from the jeans and stood in front of me in nothing but a pair of loose boxers, his white tank, and the golden pendant necklace I had given him for his birthday. I dug my fingers into the sheets beside me to balance myself as he dropped to his knees before me.

"Clementine," he stepped forward on his knees, slipping from his undershirt and chucking it into the pile of his clothes. "Mary," he crawled forward a little more until his fingers were within reach to brush a line up my calf. "Matthews," he whispered, and his breath hitched, causing his stomach to flex as his fingers roved over my thighs and dug into the meaty outer muscles.

"Yes, Cael Cody?" I answered with tight, sticky words that I barely got out.

"If you'll let me," he kissed the inside of my knee before positioning himself between us carefully, his hands daring to rake up under my shorts to my upper thighs. "I will spend whatever time we have left kissing every inch of your skin until the feeling of my lips is burned so brightly into your memory that you never kiss another boy again without thinking about me."

I had never been talked to like that, and I had certainly never heard Cael speak to anyone like that, so I must have turned the color of a ripe tomato because Cael just smirked at me.

"Is that a yes, Plum?" He asked, kissing my thigh, "You have to say it out loud for me."

"Yes," for such a tiny word, I managed to stumble over it as I said it, but Cael didn't seem to mind as his fingers found the band of my shorts and began to pull them down over my thighs.

I felt warm, but I loved the way his eyes traced over all my bare skin as he exposed it slowly. He set the pajamas next to me, and as I went to remove my tank top, he stopped me, "just wait," he said, "I want to do it."

I felt giddy at his authority; I had never seen him so serious. The light-hearted, playful boy I had grown up with had receded behind the walls of a grown man. I dared to touch him again and realized I could, lifting my hand to brush it through his dirty blonde hair. I momentarily raked them back through the soft locks and tangled them there when I realized he was staring up at me in awe.

"What?" I huffed lightly.

"You're beautiful," he said so quietly that if the wind had wanted to steal the sound, it could have.

There was no stopping him once he had declared what was on his mind. I had seen that look in his eyes a few times before. It was determination and want, and Cael never stopped until he had what wasn't his. The problem was that I had been his from the beginning, and I was worried he might get bored without the chase.

"Why'd you get sad?" He pushed up onto his knees, brushed his nose against my jaw, and kissed a soft, wet line down my neck to the swell of my breasts in my tank top.

"No reason," I whispered, wrapping my hand around his neck and leaning back onto the bed. Cael followed my touch, crawling over me until his legs framed my thighs. With so little fabric between us now, I could feel the hardened length of him against my thigh. A fire burned in the pit of my stomach like I had never experienced before as he pressed a hand between us and brushed against the damp fabric of my underwear.

He looked up at me, blue eyes shining in the moonlight, and smiled, "If you need to stop, want to stop," he paused and kissed me, tugging my bottom lip between his teeth as gently as he could. "We stop, no questions."

"I thought you said you had never done this before," I pressed my hands against his chest. It was so warm beneath my palms that I nearly got distracted from my worry.

"Clem, this is still second base," he kissed me, and I could feel his boyish smile on my mouth. "Do you want to stop?" He asked me.

I shook my head no and stole another long, much-awaited kiss from his lips. He smelled like fresh grass and the fruity cologne that he swore he hated but wore because he loved his momma, and it was a gift from her. I loved that smell. It reminded me of home and safety and of Cael and all the things I had been lucky enough to love about him over the years. It was a smell that I would hold on to after he was taken from me. Soon, it would be the only thing I had left of him. It was bittersweet to be consumed by it only to know how quickly that moment would end.

He held his promise and kissed me until he could no longer, smiling against my skin like he savored the taste of it. For the longest time, I had felt awkward in my skin, like it was too tight and worn in for someone who had only lived for seventeen years. But Cael Cody proved every thought that swirled around my head wrong with every kiss of his lips, every pinch of his fingers around my thighs and tummy. He honored me for who I was, not who the world told me I should be.

"I'm going to take this off," he informed me, "you look so pretty in the moonlight, and I want to remember all of it." He smirked, rolling the hem of my tank top up until he needed me to lift my arms. But he didn't throw my shirt away. He wrapped the fabric carefully around my crossed wrists and left them above my head.

"Cael," I huffed, wiggling a little as he did so. My mouth was so close to his chest that every time he shifted, his skin brushed against my lips, eventually tempting me to kiss him there over and over until he directed his attention back to my face. "I can't move my hands now," I said.

"Good," he said, "I don't want you covering up," he chuckled and kissed a hot line down my collarbone to my breast.

My hips lifted from the bed as his tongue licked a slow circle around my nipple. My body lit up in clusters of fireworks that only seemed to spread as he continued to work his tongue over all my most sensitive spots. His fingers hooked into the sheer fabric of my underwear and tugged them down over my thighs, sinking his head between them and kissing a pattern against my skin.

I wiggled against the ticklish feelings, "do something," I whined impatiently, "anything."

He didn't respond with words as his tongue brushed against my thigh. "Cael Cody, if you take any longer to make me feel good, I'll let Daddy shoot you just for good measure."

That produced a laugh from him, but it was short-lived and drowned in the sound of a sharp gasp that dripped from me as he licked a trail through me. The fire in my belly seemed to rage as his fingers dug into my thigh, and he worked his tongue deeper. The bit of stubble he had managed to grow rubbed against my skin and tickled me as he moved in light circles. I wanted to touch him, but he had tied my hands to the rungs above my head, so instead, I raised my hips to meet his face and curled my free leg up against his shoulder.

My back arched against the feeling of his fingers slipping into me. I was too tight and unready for the sensation. It burned at first but slowly faded to a dull heat as he moved them in and out of me.

"Cael," I said, pressing my leg against his shoulder tighter in an attempt to control the cord that wound as tightly as it ever had within me. If he didn't stop soon, it would snap before we even had sex. "I'm not going to last to third base if you don't quit," I warned.

"Oh baby," his breath was warm and tickled against my sensitive clit as he spoke between nibbles and licks, "I don't want you to last," he said, "I want you to come for me now and then again when I finally get inside of you."

"Cael Cody!" I gasped at how dirty he was talking to me, "I thought you were a gentleman."

"You never thought that," he laughed wildly, his blue eyes glimmering up at me like he had stars trapped behind them. "Besides, I am being a gentleman," he kissed my clit, "ladies first."

His hands started to move faster, his tongue working in time, and he began to rub soft circles with his thumb against all the sensitive spots. I couldn't form a thought to argue with him. Stars exploded across my vision, and heat rose through my neck and consumed everything around me. The world seemed to be hazy except for Cael, who was in perfect focus as he kissed his way up my stomach to my breasts.

Cael's thumb brushed over my nipple, followed by his tongue and a trail of soft kisses back to my mouth. I leaned into the taste, chasing the high that my body was coming down from as he pushed my legs apart with his knee.

"There she is," Cael whispered as my eyes finally focused on him. His chain hung between us and slowly brushed against my hot skin.

"Again," I pushed up to him, nipping his bottom lip, making him laugh excitedly as his hands came up to frame my face.

"Patience Plum," he kissed my nose gently and then worked carefully to untie my hands, kissing and licking the few spots that had imprints from my tank top. "It was too tight," his pretty smile turned down at the corner.

"It was perfect," I insisted, kissing the corners and, finally free of my bindings, able to touch him the way I wanted to. I pushed him back, ready for a sense of control, and flipped him onto my mattress with a giggle as his hands raked up my back. "Thank you," I said, peering down at his dumb, pretty face and big idiot grin.

"Anything for you, Clem," he said, the words hanging between us. "Now kiss me before your daddy comes home 'cause I ain't looking to find the end of a shotgun between my legs tonight."

"Shut it," I kissed him a little longer that time, savoring every tiny twitch of his hands and legs as I pressed down against him, still separated by his boxers. His hands kneaded my ass and helped me find a rhythm as we made out until our lips were sore and we couldn't breathe any longer.

BAD HONEY

"What do you need," Cael asked as he buried his mouth into the curve of my neck. "Tell me so I can give it to you," he begged, "please Plum."

"You," I huffed, dragging my hips along him until I felt him catch on my ass with a long groan, "I just need you."

"That I can manage," he smiled against my skin as he wiggled free of his boxers. I felt him bounce free against my ass, and I practically whimpered as he raked and handed me over in preparation. He hesitated just for a moment, the wet tip of his cock pressed at my entrance, "if it hurts, tell me," he kissed my jaw, "we'll go slow."

I nodded and buried my face against his neck to brace for it, and he was right. As he pressed deeper, stretching me around him, it burned for a moment, just like it had with his fingers, but over time, it faded, and all I could feel was the pulse of us moving together.

"That's my girl," he raked his hands over my hair, tangling into it and gripping the nape of my neck as he rocked deeper. I pressed my hand up around his back, curling my fingertips into his shoulders, and kissed my way across his neck as he pumped and brought us closer together than we would ever be.

"You okay, baby?" He asked quietly when I paused, but the cord was rewinding, and my breath was caught sticky in my throat. "Clem, you gotta talk to me. I don't wanna hurt you," he whispered to me.

"Don't stop," I choked out as he pushed all the way in, bumping every sensitive spot within me. "Cael, I'm not gonna make it," I could feel myself spiraling. Before I could beg further, he picked up his speed, and all the pain turned to an intense wave of pleasure that seemed to crash down over me.

His breathing became labored, and his grip around my body tightened as he pushed us both closer to the edge. "Almost there," he kissed my sweaty temple, rocking into me as the cord snapped. He pulled from me, quickly shifting away as he finished, his warmth spreading over my stomach as he did so. "Sorry," he whimpered breathlessly, sounding embarrassed.

"Don't," I said, brushing his sweaty hair away from his forehead. I pushed from the bed on weak knees and padded to the bathroom to clean up. I stared at myself in the mirror, and even though nothing was different about my thick thighs, belly, or swollen breasts, I felt different. I felt alive, like every inch of my skin was sparkling, and for the first time, I felt seen.

I returned and handed him a clean cloth, tugging my shorts on and climbing into bed beside him. I felt him wrap me up in his arms, and his lips found home against my neck as he buried himself into me again. "I'm sorry if you're sore," he apologized, looking up at me.

"I'm not," I lied.

"That feels like a secret," he narrowed his eyes on me and kissed the corner of my mouth.

I was a little, but it wasn't anything that would ruin all the good things about that night. "I am, a little, but you were gentle and perfect," I kissed him, pressing our foreheads together when I pulled away, "and I will never kiss another boy without thinking about you."

He stared at me with those sad, indigo eyes and whispered, "I wish you would have told me how you felt. Sooner, I guess. I've gone my entire pitiful seventeen years knowing one thing." He brushed a piece of hair from my face and ran his thumb across my bottom lip.

"I could die a thousand times over loving you, Clementine Matthews, and it wouldn't hurt for a second."

I wanted to say it, to tell him that it was true, but I was afraid to let the sadness creep back in. I tried to tell him how much I loved him, but I couldn't without crying, so instead, I curled into his arms and closed my eyes. Giving us a few spare moments to be Cael and Clementine one last time.

THE HORNETS WILL RETURN IN 2025

Acknowledgements

Bad Honey is very special to me and I hope that it finds its way into the hearts of others the way it has mine.

Writing a book is damn hard, being an indie author is equally so. I wouldn't be here writing if it weren't for all of the amazing support systems I have surrounding me every day.

My husband is relentless in his kindness toward this journey. His kind words, time spent reading unedited work and hours subjected to me ranting about everything that goes into publishing from writing to editing and back to social media. He's a hero. I couldn't do this without him. Behind him is every single friend new and old that pushes me to be as good as I can be, reminding me that reviews are simply subjective and I can only get better as I go along. This journey isn't easy but with every book I get better, the stories get better. So thank you for always sticking by my side even when I'm not at my best. To my support system that doesn't know these exist, I promise one day I'll be brave enough to show you my books. Until then, thank you for keeping me sane, and steady through hours of writing and editing. For watching movies with me, for playing games with me, for listening to me rant. You're there through it all. *My Holy Trinity, my Freakshow, my Golden Girls, my little fucks.* My little found family. Thank you. I love you. You are the light in the dark. Vinny, my twinkle toes, my Jess. This year has been insane, we've grown as writers and as friends. Thank you for always being my cheerleader, my teacher, my editor, my friend and therapist. Rory, who spent hours working on the cover for Bad Honey and nailed it. I love you so much. My beta readers, Twinkle toes, Jess, Rory, Thea, Jessica, Bec, Chrissie, Alice, Gia, every single one

BAD HONEY

of you made Bad Honey the best it could be and I'll never be able to repay that kindness. Jessica for letting me use her formatting software and for letting me run her ear off as I tried to figure everything out for this release.

To my momma and dad, for always believing in me.

Most of all, to my Bubbe and my Hank, for encouraging me to follow my dreams and for *walking two steps at a time with me my entire life*.

Also By Aubrey Taylor

You Left us in Georgia
Our Time in Japan: A You Left us in Georgia Novella

At The Hour Of Our Death

The Hornets Nest Series
Bad Honey (Book One)
Honey Pot (Book Two)
Coming 2025

www.ingramcontent.com/pod-product-compliance
Lightning Source LLC
Chambersburg PA
CBHW031054080526
44587CB00011B/681